FOUR FARMS:
Life in Lake Andrew Township, 1864-1964

By
Carolyn Mankell Sowinski

Copyright © 2019 by Carolyn Mankell Sowinski
All rights reserved.

ISBN: 9798567108185
LCCN: 2019911808

Kindle Direct Publishing
Books can be ordered at amazon.com

For more information:
carolyn.sowinski@gmail.com

Image on the front cover is the silo at the Mankell farm.

Image on the back cover is the gravel road which connects the four farms, with the view that looks to the east from the Mankell farm. Trees from each of the four farms are visible in the photograph.

Cover design by Naomi Sveholm: naomi.sveholm@gmail.com

DEDICATION

*This book is dedicated to the immigrants
who settled in Lake Andrew Township
and started a new chapter
in the landscape of Kandiyohi County.
They traveled across the Atlantic Ocean,
left family behind,
experienced a life-changing journey,
and transformed this area of the county
for the many generations who followed.*

THANKS

This book would not have been possible without the help and knowledge of friends, family, former neighbors, descendants of the families on the four farms, and fellow local history enthusiasts. This list is too long to share each person's name, but please know that I am most grateful for your documents, recollections, insights, ideas, clarifications, images, and family genealogies. Of special note is my sister Susan (Mankell) Muellner who edited my text for clarity and corrections for this project and previous projects. Thanks to my daughter, Lynae Mankell Sowinski, who was my proofreader. She also added more comments and questions which helped me clarify my story-telling. My thanks also extend to Naomi Sveholm, my layout editor. This is our fourth project together.

Two people who helped with this project died in 2019: Jane Hauser Pejsa (Mankell family) and Myron Hauge (Norway Lake Lakers). This book is better because they shared parts of their lives for this book.

Carolyn Mankell Sowinski
Summer 2019

carolyn.sowinski@gmail.com

TABLE OF CONTENTS

Introduction   9

Chapter 1: Locale   13
Includes: Monongalia County, government structure, township descriptions and Public Land Survey System

Chapter 2: 1864-1869   19
Includes: first immigrant settlers, School Districts 16 and 25

Chapter 3: 1870-1879   37
Includes: Nannestad Lutheran Church, Lake Florida Lutheran Church, creation of Lake Andrew Township, blizzards, and grasshoppers

Chapter 4: 1880-1889   71
Includes: Arctander & Lake Andrew Mutual Fire Insurance Company, baseball

Chapter 5: 1890-1899   83
Includes: Norway Lake Creamery, Norway Lake Band, Norway Lake Choir

Chapter 6: 1900-1909   109
Includes: Jericho, blacksmith Swen Swenson, Lake Andrew & Dovre Telephone Company, automobiles, School District 25, politics and government

Chapter 7: 1910-1919   137
Includes: School District 25, Lake Andrew & Dovre Horse Company, Highway 5 improvement; Norway Lake Band, World War I, Influenza Pandemic

Chapter 8: 1920-1929   175
Includes: School District 25, Lake Florida Mission Church

Chapter 9: 1930-1939   189
Includes: drought, Norway Lake Lakers baseball, electricity

Chapter 10: 1940-1949 — 207
Includes: memories and friendships, confirmation on December 7, 1941, World War II, Nannestad church building

Chapter 11: 1950-1959 — 223
Includes: closure of Lake Florida Mission Church; faith, family, and duty

Chapter 12: 1960-1964 — 253
Includes: closure of School District 25, memories from former students, riding a school bus

Appendix 1 — 273
1939 map of Rural Electric Association transmission lines for Kandiyohi County

Appendix 2 — 274
School bus route, mid to late 1960s

Appendix 3 — 275
Chart of farm owners and renters

Bibliography — 277
Index — 283
About the Author — 290

INTRODUCTION

This is a book about the families of four farms along one mile of gravel road in a Scandinavian farming community in Lake Andrew Township, Kandiyohi County, Minnesota.

———————

"Want to walk home?" If the weather was good, my siblings and I would ask each other this question at about 3:30 each weekday afternoon as the school bus approached Peterson's Corner (today, the corner of County Highway 5 and 165th Street NW). To avoid a long circuitous bus ride, we often stepped off the bus with the Peterson kids and then walked west a mile to our home, arriving about 15 minutes before the bus would arrive from the west. (See a map of the bus route in Appendix 2.) This last mile home was a gravel road.

As we walked this final mile we first passed by three other farms, locally known as the Peterson farm, the Haglund farm, and the Railson farm, before we came to our Mankell farm. We marked certain milestones along our journey. We enjoyed looking at Eldora Peterson's flowers. We always walked quickly by the Haglund farm because of a tethered dog who barked at us and strained to get loose. We knew we would soon be home when we reached the approach to the field road on the little hill and the fence line of our farm. Our walk was shortened if a neighbor driving in our direction gave us a ride home.

This gravel road was often dusty in the summer, muddy in the spring, and snow-packed in the winter. It was the last mile home after a 5-mile trip to Sibley State Park, a 9-mile trip to New London, or a 15-mile trip to Willmar. At Christmas time, as we crested the last of two hills on the gravel road, with snow all around and darkness coming early, we saw a 10-foot star, all lit, leaning against the arbor vitae tree by the Mankell farm's stately, white Victorian-style farmhouse where four generations had been born, lived, and died. I lived on this farm from my birth in 1958 until I graduated from college in 1980, as a member of the farm's 5th generation, though we lived in a smaller house on the property which my dad built for the family.

CHAPTERS

This book, divided into 12 chapters, explores the lives of the families living on these four farms along this one mile of gravel road, starting in 1864, the year the first of four Scandinavian immigrant families arrived. Chapter 1 provides key details of the setting of the book: the prairie frontier that greeted these immigrants at the end of their travels which had begun in Norway or Sweden. Subsequent chapters each cover a decade. The last year covered in this book is 1964, chosen because this year was a key community milestone. The children of the four farms, and of Lake Andrew Township, now attended school in New London after the country schools closed in 1963.

While this book captures the lives of the families on these four farms, this mile was one of many such miles of immigrant settlers and their descendants whose lives interwove with other families in the area, so this becomes a story about a vibrant Scandinavian farming community in west central Minnesota. During this span of 100 years, the families of these four farms and their neighbors encountered hardships, worked to better their lives, cared for their spiritual growth and educational needs, experienced the joy and sadness of life, and found themselves impacted by inventions and events outside the Township. This list includes the following:

Natural disasters: blizzards, droughts, and grasshoppers
Life passages: births, marriages, and deaths
Farm economics: renters and farm laborers, co-operatives, and businesses which served the farmers
Society's institutions: the development of two congregations and rural one-room schools;
International events: wars and an influenza pandemic
Technology: telephones, automobiles, and electricity
National politics and local township government
Social activities: picnics, music, and baseball

Each chapter covers one decade of the lives of the families, and generally is organized as follows:

Diagram

A Diagram noting the ownership of the farms. (Diagrams in the book are not drawn to scale.)
Three were 160-acre homesteads. The fourth farm, initially 80 acres, was not an official homestead because the property was not secured through the 1862 Homestead Act. Over time some of the farms grew or decreased in acreage. The diagrams also include years of ownership, as best as I can determine when examining the Kandiyohi County Recorder Office information, as it sometimes took a few years to acquire ownership from extended family following probate. When examining these lists notating transfers of ownership, I looked at no financial transaction records.

Farm Summaries

Farm Summaries will provide highlights of activities and life passages at each of the farms. Residents of Lake Andrew Township often refer to a local farm by the surname of the owners. This book will reference farms in the same way. The names of the farms will change when the ownership changed. Appendix 3 is a decade-by-decade chart of farm owners and renters. The farms will be presented in the order as I walked from Peterson's Corner to the Mankell farm many decades ago:

Stenseth/Christenson/Peterson
To complicate the story telling, John Syvert Christenson owned two farms and small lot. He first bought the Stenseth farm along the mile in Section 17 following his marriage to Carrie Stenseth. A few years later, while he still owned the Section 17 farm, he purchased the Solberg farm in Section 8, on the southeastern shores of Norway Lake. For clarity in this book the farms will be called the Christenson farm and the Solberg farm. He also purchased a 7-acre lot between Norway and Middle lakes. The family called this property "Hollywood".

Brattlund/Reierson/Haglund
When ownership of the farm transitioned from one family to the next, the local community began to recognize the farm with the name of the new owner.

Norman/Railson
The Norman farm stayed in the family for four generations, and was called the "Norman farm" for many decades, even when William and Johanna (Norman) Larson owned it. William owned two farms concurrently which were one mile apart. The local community distinguished the two farms by calling his Section 17 farm the "Norman farm" and his Section 21 farm the "Larson farm." In the 1920s when Edwin and Edith (Larson) Railson owned the Section 17 farm, it then became known as the Railson farm.

Mankell
The Mankell farm has had continuous ownership by the Mankell family for several generations, so it has been consistently known as the Mankell farm.

Community Events and Activities
Community Events and Activities will highlight key milestones which affected the four farms.

SPELLING
Accurate spellings of people's names is another item worth noting. The Americanized spellings may be different from the spelling used in the home countries. Also, consistent spelling of a name wasn't as much of an issue 100+ years ago. For consistency in this book, Nils/Nels Stenseth and Nils/Nels Brattlund will both have the first name "Nils", unless quoting a newspaper item. Other preferred spellings include Marie not Maria, Mankell not Mankel, Christenson not Christensen, Reierson not Rierson.

OTHER RESOURCES
There is some overlap with previous texts I have written:
my website (mankell.org)
A 2016 book about the Mankell family, *Niederasphe to Norway Lake: Mankell Family, Minnesota, and Immigration*. (available from the author)
The 1873 blizzard documented in *Four Farms* is featured in my 2017 book, *Almost Saved, But Lost: The January 1873 Blizzard in Kandiyohi County*. (available at amazon.com)

CHAPTER 1:
LOCALE

Local geography and governmental history are key backdrops to this story. West-central Minnesota was on the edge of the frontier when settlers arrived in the mid-1800s. By the 1860s Minnesota had just attained statehood (in 1858) and the United States was embroiled in the Civil War.

THE LOCATION[1]

BEFORE THE SETTLERS ARRIVED

For centuries the Eastern Tribe of the Dakota Native Americans had lived, hunted, fished, and fought in what would become central and southern lands of the new State of Minnesota. The Chippewa were in the northern part. Between these two large Native American peoples was a "no man's land" where neither group settled. These lands, which included lakes later known as Lake Andrew, Green Lake, and Norway Lake, comprised the hunting and fishing grounds for both groups and were fought over at times. As the territory of Minnesota was settled and then became a state in 1858, these First Tribes found their lands and ways of life encroached upon and threatened. In the State and Federal governments' endeavors to make the new lands "safe" for the growing number of settlers, the Dakota fled because of broken treaties of 1851 and 1858, relocating to newly established federal reservations along the Minnesota River, or fought back.

EARLIEST SETTLERS

The earliest settlers in northwestern Monongalia County (which would later become part of Kandiyohi County) were part of the Norway Lake Settlement—primarily Norwegian immigrants—who had pre-emption claims under the Pre-emption Act of 1841. This act allowed settlers to buy, at a minimal price, public land they had developed. During Minnesota's Dakota War, which began in August 1862, some of these settlers were killed by the Dakota. Fearing for their safety, and as ordered by the military, immigrant families fled east, many to the St. Cloud area. The August 1862 Dakota War was one of the bloodiest of the Indian Wars fought on U. S. soil. In less than one month 500-800 men, women and children had been killed across the southern and central parts of the state. On December 26, 1862, the federal government held a mass execution of 38 Dakota in Mankato, Minnesota, which stands as the largest single-day execution in American history.

SETTLEMENT RESUMES

With the removal of the Dakota, the early settlers who had fled due to the 1862 war in Monongalia County and other area counties soon returned. More land became available to new and returning settlers because of the 1862 Homestead Act. The lands in Minnesota were part of the westward expansion of a country not yet 100 years old.

Beginning in 1864, farmers returned to the Norway Lake area once it was determined to be safe—and with a new military fort on the west side of Norway Lake. In addition to returning settlers, new farmers arrived, having applied for land via the 1862 Homestead Act or in other ways, including purchases from the railroad companies which had acquired many acres of land in Minnesota. The settlers in the four

---

[1] *Illustrated History of Kandiyohi County*; Urdahl, *Uprising: a Novel*; Wikipedia.org; Minnesota Department of Transportation, 1927 map.

farms were part of this post-1862 migration and settlement. Herman Wilhelm Mankell (H. W.) was the first settler to arrive on what would develop into this one mile stretch of four farms.

There was no gravel road when the first settlers arrived at the four farms. They forged their own paths or followed long established Indian trails. A path traveled by Dakota Chief Little Crow and the native tribes for decades or even longer was commonly called the Little Crow Trail, currently identified as County Highway 5. The trail came north from the lakes by Willmar, then turned west by the four farms, to the north side of Lake Mary, and then north to the western side of Norway Lake.

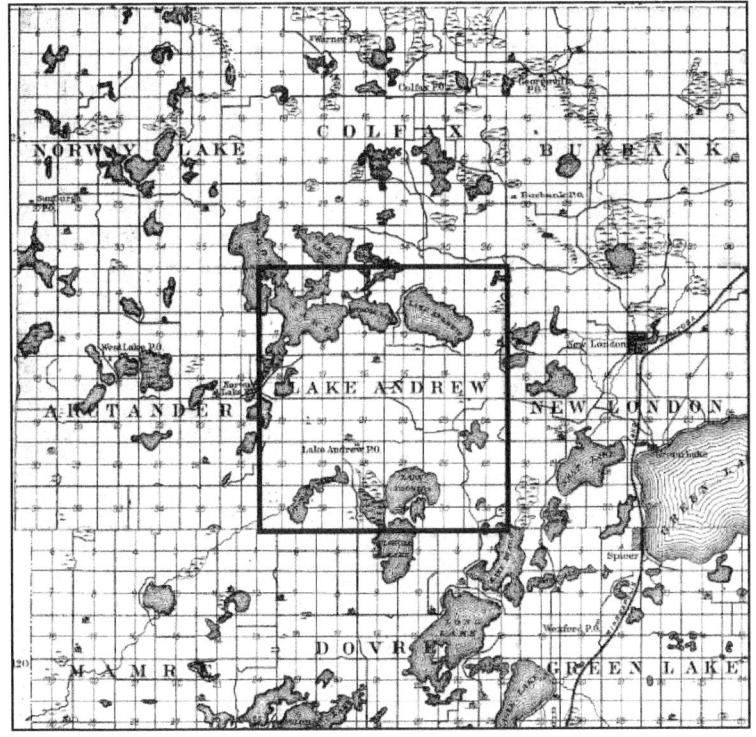

This 1886 map shows the townships in the northwestern part of Kandiyohi County. Lake Andrew Township is highlighted.

People and locations in the surrounding townships also became part of the four farms story.

GOVERNMENTAL STRUCTURE CHANGES

When the first settlers arrived in the 1860s, this "four farms mile" was part of Norway Lake Township in Monongalia County. New London was the county seat. Within ten years, the governmental structure of the area changed in order to accommodate the expanding population:

- In 1870 Monongalia County merged with Kandiyohi County to the south and the larger entity retained the name Kandiyohi County. Willmar was the county seat.

- Over a span of about a dozen years, the large Norway Lake Township which had been a part of Monongalia County, was split into five smaller townships as part of the newly merged Kandiyohi County. Lake Andrew Township was "pulled out" of Norway Lake Township in 1872. Shown right is a diagram of these townships, along with the organization year and surveyed description. Each township is six miles by six miles.

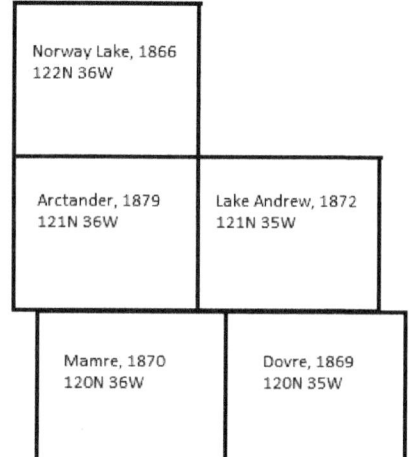

Five townships which had been part of Norway Lake Township in Monongalia County.

Beginning in 1872, the area which includes the four farms would officially be known as Lake Andrew Township, Kandiyohi County, Minnesota.

TOWNSHIP DESCRIPTIONS: PUBLIC LAND SURVEY SYSTEM[2]

The farms, churches, and schools in this book are often identified using township legal descriptions, township names, and section numbers. Here is information about the PLSS to help the readers better understand this type of land division.

Each surveyed township consists of 36 square miles, sections into 36 one-mile squares, with each section divided into quadrants: NW ¼, NE ¼, SE ¼, and SW ¼. Each of those quarters can be further subdivided. Each township had a town hall and one or more local country schools located within its borders. In Kandiyohi County each township had a name, such as Lake Andrew Township and Arctander Township.

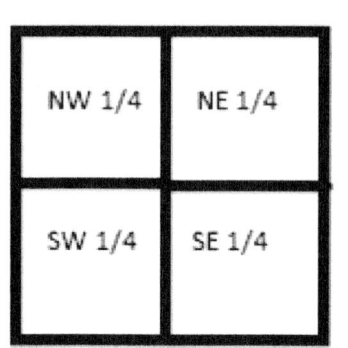

---

2   Information taken from author's book: *Almost Saved, But Lost: The January 1873 Blizzard in Kandiyohi County, Minnesota.*

THE FOUR FARMS

The four farms highlighted in this story are located 100 miles west of Minneapolis, 15 miles north of Willmar, and 9 miles west of New London. One mile of gravel road connects the four farms and today has the street address of 165th Avenue NW, New London, Minnesota, and intersects with County Highway 5 which runs north from Willmar for more than 20 miles. Two farms lie in Section 17 and two lie in Section 20, with the road and electric poles separating these two township sections and the farms. Over the decades and centuries people have driven, biked, walked, steered wagons or ridden horses to traverse this one mile and other roads in the township and county. Here is an 1874 map of Lake Andrew Township (and the eastern portion of Arctander Township) with additional locations marked that enter the four farms story.

The four farms are on the southern half of Section 17 and the northern half of Section 20. Farm families from other sections in the township enter the story, too. The eastern edge of Arctander Township borders the western edge of Lake Andrew. Notated on the map or added to the map are the following places relevant to events in the book:

- Nannestad Lutheran Church, Arctander, Section 14 (southeast corner)
- East Norway Lake Lutheran Church and the community of Jericho, at the eastern border of Sections 13 and 24 in Arctander Township
- First Lutheran Church of Norway Lake, Section 7
- Lake Florida Mission Church, Section 21
- Lake Florida, southeast of the church which bears the same name
- Lake Mary, northwest corner of Section 19
- An early location of School District 25, Section 20
- Norway Lake in the northwestern part of the township
- Lake Andrew (the lake, not the township) in the northeastern part of the township
- Highway 5 which runs south to Willmar and north to Norway Lake and Colfax Township

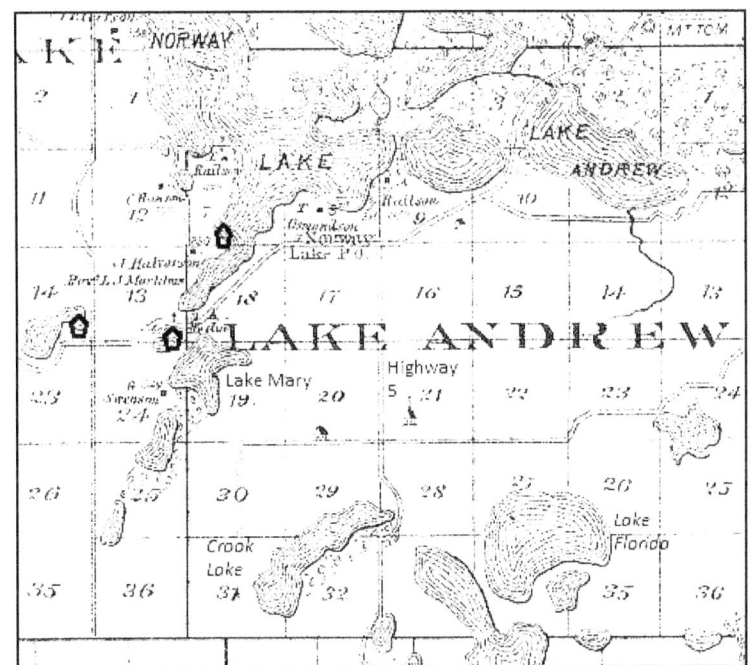

Lake Andrew Township in 1874.

In this area of the county, there are a few geographic and structural references which bear the same name, thus adding confusion to the narrative about the four farms. The following descriptions will add some clarification.

- "Norway Lake" refers to several locations:
    - A sprawling lake in the northwestern part of Lake Andrew Township, southeastern Norway Lake Township, and southwestern Colfax Township. A portion of the lake is known as West Norway Lake.
    - Norway Lake Township, in the northwest corner of Kandiyohi County.
    - The early settlement of primarily Norwegian immigrants with territory covering much of the northwestern part of the original Monongalia County.
    - A crossroads community or hamlet on the eastern edge of Arctander Township, where it meets Lake Andrew Township. From the 1870s to the 1930s, the local Post Office was at Norway Lake. Local families have called this location "Jericho" for more than 120 years. This name change may have been to help relieve some of the confusion when talking about "Norway Lake". In this book, "Jericho" will be used when referencing this crossroads community, the location of East Norway Lake Church and cemetery.
    - Two churches: "East Norway Lake Lutheran Church" and "First Lutheran Church of Norway Lake". (Another church "West Norway Lake Lutheran Church" no longer exists, though the cemetery remains.)
- "Lake Andrew" refers to Lake Andrew Township, and to a lake in the northeastern part of the township. The lake is the location of Sibley State Park, which celebrates its 100th anniversary in 2019, at the time of this book's publication.
- "Lake Florida" refers to a lake in the southern part of the township and to a church which had several names over its 85 years of existence: "Lake Florida Swedish Lutheran Church," "Lake Florida Mission Church," "Lake Florida Mission Covenant Church" or "Lake Florida Covenant Church". Local families also referred to this church as the "Swedish Mission Church".
- Nannestad refers to Nannestad parish in Akershus, Norway and the Nannestad Lutheran Church in Arctander Township in Kandiyohi County. Many of the families who began this church were from the Nannestad Parish in Norway. The church was also referenced as "Haugean Lutheran" or "Hauge's Lutheran" which identified the type of Lutheran theology these immigrants brought to their new congregation.
- "Township" refers to a six-mile by six-mile local government entity, such as "Lake Andrew Township". However 100 years ago, "the town of Lake Andrew" was additional terminology.

CHAPTER 2:
1864-1869

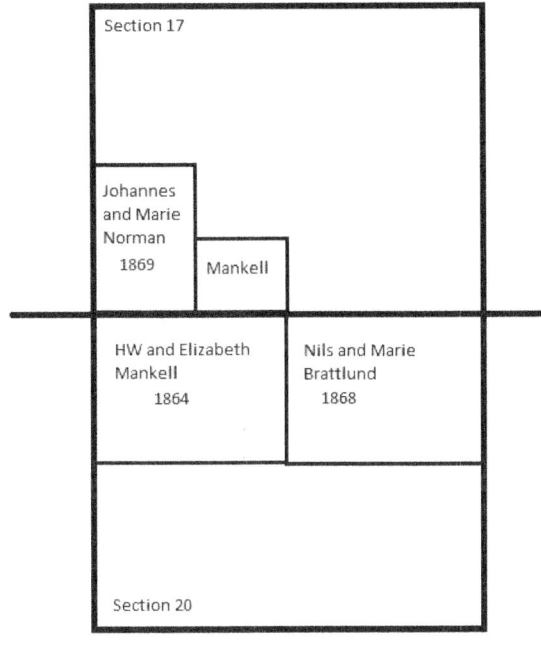

The first settlers along one mile in Norway Lake Township in Monongalia County, later known as Lake Andrew Township in Kandiyohi County, late 1860s.

HIGHLIGHTS

- Three of the four farms are settled by Swedish immigrants
- School Districts 16 and 25 are established to serve community children

IMMIGRANT SETTLERS ARRIVE

The first white settlers at the four farms arrived as follows:

1. **Herman Wilhelm and Elizabeth (Olsdotter) Mankell**, Swedish immigrants. He arrived in Lake Andrew Township, 1864; she and their children, 1866.
2. **Nils and Anna (Alvig) Brattlund**, Swedish immigrants, 1868
3. **Johannes and Marie (Johansdotter) Norman**, Swedish immigrants, 1869
4. **Nils and Karen (Larsdatter) Stenseth**, Norwegian immigrants, 1870

MANKELL HOMESTEAD ESTABLISHED[1]

Herman Wilhelm (H.W.) Mankell (1835-1889) arrived on his new homestead in July, 1864. H. W. and Elizabeth (1832-1914) emigrated from Sweden. H. W. was born on February 20, 1835, in Stockholm, the son of Wilhelm and Margareta (Igelström) Mankell. The family later moved to Vadstena and then Gothenburg on the west coast of Sweden in 1849. While a bachelor, H. W. left Gothenburg in July 1854 on the *SS Cynosure* for the United States. After arriving in New York City, he lived briefly in Rockford, Illinois. He returned to Sweden to wed Elizabeth Olofsdotter in Kållered, Göteborg Och Bohus, on July 12, 1857. Elizabeth was born on June 29, 1832, in Kållered. Her parents, Olof Bengtsson and Johanna Olofsdotter, and grandparents were from the Kållered area and lived on the Heljered Sörgården farm.

One month after the wedding ceremony the couple boarded the sailing ship *SS Humboldt* in Hamburg, Germany, and arrived on September 14 in New York City. They continued their journey to Goodhue County in Minnesota Territory, briefly to Red Wing and Vasa, a small community founded by Swedish immigrants. By 1860 H.W., Elizabeth, and children lived in Northfield, Rice County, where H. W. was a cabinet maker. Four years later H. W. and Elizabeth and children prepared for another journey, one that would take them to central Minnesota.

On July 13, 1864, Swedish immigrant H. W. Mankell applied for his homestead at the St. Cloud Land Office and paid the $14.00 processing fee. One week later he arrived on his newly acquired 160 acre homestead, the NW ¼ of Section 20 of what was then the large Norway Lake Township in Monongalia County. His wife, Elizabeth, and four children remained in Northfield, Minnesota, for a few months and then moved to St. Cloud where their fifth child was born. H. W. prepared the family's new homestead for their 1866 arrival. Per the Homestead Act of 1862, H.W., like all homesteaders, had requirements to complete before he could file final paperwork at the Land Office. H. W. needed to improve the land, live continuously on the land, build a solid house (no sod houses), and become an American citizen. Here is his July 13, 1864, application statement at the St. Cloud Land Office:

---

1 Also spelled Mankel. For more information about the immigration journey of HW and Elizabeth, read *Niederasphe to Norway Lake: Mankell Family, Minnesota and Immigration*. Sources include Hamburg Passenger Lists, 1850-1934; New York Passenger Lists, 1820-1957; Kållered Parish records; U.S. Federal Census, Minnesota State Census; Mankell Family Collection; newspapers. National Archives and Records Administration, Record Group 49: Bureau of Land Management, General Land Office Records, St. Cloud MN Land Office, Document No. 691. (accessed glorecords.blm.gov)

CH 2: 1864-1869

> *I, Herman W. Mankel of Monongalia Co Minn having filed my application, No. 638, for an entry under the provisions of the act of Congress, approved May 20, 1862, entitled "An act to secure homesteads to actual settlers on the public domain", do solemnly swear, that I am a married man over the age of twenty one years & have declared my intentions to become a citizen of the United States that I have never borne arms against the government, or given aid and comfort to its enemies; that said Application No. 638 is made for my exclusive benefit; and that said entry is made for the purpose of actual settlement and cultivation, and not directly or indirectly for the use or benefit of any other person or persons whomsoever. Neither have I ever abandoned an entry…made under this Act.*

When H. W. arrived alone in Section 20 in 1864, he had few neighbors. His closest neighbor was Alfred Clark who arrived from Rice County in May 1864, two months before H. W. Mankell. Clark lived in Section 18, less than ¼ mile to the north and west from Mankell's new farm. Both men were from Northfield Township in Rice County. Both men arrived at about the same time to the same area of Monongalia County. Both men applied for homesteads and prepared for the arrivals of their families. It's highly probable that these men knew each other in Rice County and decided to have neighboring farms in Lake Andrew Township.

ALFRED CLARK FARM[2]

Alfred Clark applied for his homestead on May 28, 1864, also at the St. Cloud Minnesota Land Office. According to his land patent files, Clark arrived at his homestead on the same day of his application. Soon he marked his property and started to build a house—preparing the way for his wife, Martha, and their two sons, Charles and Augustus. While Alfred made initial settlement, his family waited in Northfield Township, Rice County for this area of Monongalia County to be safe from the Dakota Indians. One year later, the wait was over. Alfred's family would arrive in July 1865. Clark's October 12, 1865, Affidavit document tells part of his story and notes repercussions from the Dakota War:

> [Clark] *has erected a dwelling house on said land. It is built of logs and is 16 by 16 feet in size, one and ½ stories high, double roof, two floors, two windows, one door and is a comfortable house to live in.*
>
> *Applicant moved into said house with his family about the 26th day of July 1865 and has resided there to the present time* [12 October 1865]. *At the time he made said homestead entry all of that section of County was considered to be unsafe to live in thereby, no protection from the incursions of hostile Indians and all those who had lived there for years previous had abandoned their homes for that reason and dared not return till military posts were established there in the summer of 1865.*
>
> *Beside the house upon said tract he has good stables erected and* [a] *good well dug and hay cut and stacked thereon. Military protection not being established till so late he could not get his house built in time or put in a crop this season. Has lived constantly with his entire family therein since he moved them there in July as aforesaid. Was there*

---

2 National Archives and Records Administration, Record Group 49: Bureau of Land Management, General Land Office Records, St. Cloud MN Land Office, Script Warrant No. 38684. Ancestry.com (Federal Census data, 1860; Minnesota State Census, 1865)

working upon his house some time before moving his family there as aforesaid and now makes this homestead.

One year after he arrived, Clark decided not to complete his homestead process. Rather, he secured his 160 acres with a Bounty Land Warrant which he purchased from George W. Armstrong who had served in the Massachusetts Militia during the War of 1812, (a sergeant in Captain Pages Company).[3]

Clark and his family remained on the farm for a very short time, having left in about 1867—for reasons lost to history. No buildings remain on this 160-acre farm site. Less than ten years later these 160 acres would be purchased by one of the families in this story.

OTHER NEIGHBORS[4]

When H. W. Mankell arrived, his nearest neighbors (other than Clark) were Norwegians—to the north and west—and included:

- Thomas and Bergit (Svensdatter Borgen) Osmundson settled on their homestead (spring 1859) 1.5 miles north on the southern shore of Norway Lake. (Section 8)
- Johannes Halvorson and his first wife Olena (arrived 1859) settled on their homestead in Section 18, a mile north of Mankell.
- Sven Gunderson Borgen with his wife, Marit (Syvertsdatter), daughter Ragnild (later Mrs. Christopher Engen) and son Gunder Swenson, arrived in 1860, and lived one mile west at their homestead between Lake Mary and Swenson Lake, Section 24 of Arctander Township. They came to the county about a year after daughter Bergit Osmundson and her husband Thomas. One generation later, Minnie Swenson, the granddaughter of Sven Borgen, would marry Oscar Mankell, the son of H. W. and Elizabeth.

H. W. MANKELL'S FAMILY ARRIVED, 1866[5]

H. W. Mankell, as with most farmers and homesteaders in the expanding country, built his farm from nothing—using tools, probably a wagon, horses or oxen. Before his family would arrive, he needed to build a house and dig a well. The closest source of water was Lake Mary, one mile to the west. This

---

3   Ibid. It is not clear why Clark did not complete his homestead, though it probably has to do with his citizenship, based on a letter in his homestead file requesting said documentation. In his initial application he stated that he was a naturalized citizen, but there was no documentation. It's possible he wasn't a citizen and rather than admit to this incorrect information he decided to obtain his land by purchasing the Bounty Land Warrant from a person who served in the US military, for a purchase price not indicated. At this time in US history, soldiers received a certificate or warrant which they could redeem for farm land, or sell to someone else who wanted farm land. The warrant was not for specific land site, rather the soldier (or the person who purchased the warrant) would select land at the time he redeemed the warrant.
4   These families had originally settled on pre-emption claims prior to the 1862 Dakota War. They evacuated and returned to their farms. Sowinski, *Niederasphe to Norway Lake: Mankell Family, Minnesota and Immigration*; mankell.org.
5   National Archives and Records Administration, Record Group 49: Bureau of Land Management, General Land Office Records, St. Cloud MN Land Office, Document No. 691. (accessed glorecords.blm.gov); Kandiyohi County Recorder's Office; Sowinski, *Niederasphe to Norway Lake*.

spring fed lake was the water source for Sven Borgen and his family who settled on the south side of the lake. Mankell also needed to "break" the virgin soil and prepare it for planting. He acquired cows for milk, from which the family would make butter. Elizabeth and the children lived in St. Cloud for about two years and arrived at the homestead after the 1866 birth of Hulda in St. Cloud.

His homestead documents attest to the work H. W. and Elizabeth accomplished between 1864 and 1871, to build a house and other buildings:

> *That the said Herman W. Mankel entered upon and made settlement on said land on or about the 20th day of July 1864, and has built a frame house thereon 16x16 feet in size with all 16x16 feet in size with two doors, 4 windows, two floors, and two rooms and good shingled roof. Has also a good frame granary 16x24 ft in size—one ½ story high and has good stable about 150 ft in length. He has lived in the said house and made it his exclusive home from the 20th day of July, 1964, to the present time, except such time as he was kept from home by the Sioux Indians[6] then hostile and roaming through the county and that he has since said settlement ploughed, fenced, and cultivated about 82 acres of said land, and has made the following improvements thereon, to wit: Has fenced the entire quarter section with post and rail fence, and has two acres planted with forest trees.*

The house was not the traditional log house that many early settlers built as a first home on their new farms. Rather, H. W. built a frame house. His skills as a carpenter came in handy when cutting and sawing trees and then measuring and fitting the lumber into this sturdy home. Not mentioned in the description to the Federal Land Office, are the cottonwood and other trees H. W. and Elizabeth planted on the wind-swept building site to help protect them from cold winds during the winter months and provide shade in summer's heat. Four of these cottonwood trees marked the four corners of the building site, with one tree to the west of the farm house, the second to the east, the third near the barn and stables, and the fourth by the granary. More than 150 years later, one tree of the four remains standing, west of the site of the original homestead house.

Soon after applying for his 160 acre homestead, H. W. purchased an additional 40 acres, located just to the north in Section 17. He purchased this land from the St. Paul and Pacific Railroad (later known as St. Paul, Minneapolis & Manitoba Railway Company, then the Great Northern Railway). Later the road (the "gravel mile") which connects the four farms was built, dividing the two properties. Elizabeth and H. W. purchased other property from the U.S. government in the following years. These were cash sales not homesteads.

- A few acres in Section 3, between Middle Lake and Lake Andrew, which provided the family with timber for buildings and firewood.
- Lot 4 (30 acres) in Section 5 on the northern shore of Norway Lake. Elizabeth purchased this lot from the federal government in 1865. She sold the lot in 1866.

---

6   Also known as Dakota People or Dakota Tribe. Sioux Indians terminology was used by white settlers and government for the Dakota Tribe. Today the terminology for these Native Americans is "Dakota".

- Lot 6 (about 30 acres) of Section 5 on the northern shore of Norway Lake. This property was divided and sold from 1869-1872. In 1869 Johannes Norman purchased 19 acres. This property remained in the Norman family for several decades.
- A lot in Section 32 of Douglas County northwest of Kandiyohi County.

Life on the prairie was not easy. The winters were cold and the winds blew. Thus their two acres of trees were an important wind break. The summer months were hot and filled with flies and mosquitoes. In a December 1868 letter to his sisters Hermina and Augusta, who lived in Sweden, H. W. wrote about financial difficulties on the newly established homestead. He refers to Thilda (Mathilda), who was the sister of his wife Elizabeth (Betty). In this portion of the letter H. W. writes on behalf of his wife who could not write—noting her desire for Thilda to come to America. (Mathilda immigrated to Minnesota in 1870.)

> *I am sorry that you will not get my letter before Christmas. I had just decided to write when I received your letter, with your concern over Thilda's not making the journey here. It seems not to be our lot to see anyone of our families here, at least not when we need them most. If Thilda wants to come here, I will help her with the travel costs even though money is scarce. My income is not nearly enough for the requirements of the household in addition to the cost of starting a farm in what until recently was wilderness. I hope in a few years to have a larger income and fewer expenses...Greet everybody at Heljered from Betty and me. If only Betty could write herself, she would be so happy to tell you about all sorts of things that she does not want to ask me to write.*

Here are the children of Elizabeth and H. W. Mankell: four oldest born in Northfield; one in St. Cloud; four youngest at the homestead. Their lives and those of some descendants will be highlighted in later chapters.

1. **Jenny** (1858-1948) married Andrew Gordhamer, 1876
2. **Mary** (1860-1887) married Johnny Young, 1881
3. **Anna** (1862-1914) married Nels Quam, 1879
4. **Amanda** (1864-1947) married Julius Landquist, 1882
5. **Hulda** (1866-1931) married Hans Melgaard, 1893
6. **Oscar** (1868-1936) married Minnie Swenson, 1895
7. **Sophia** (1871-1894) married John Quam, 1893
8. **Otto H.** (1872-1939)
9. **Esther** (1874-1915) married Gustave Erixon, 1899

Drawing of the original church building of the Norway Lake Settlement.
(*Keeping the Faith*, p. 16)

Hulda and Oscar were baptized on December 4, 1868, at the newly built Lutheran church of the Norway Lake Settlement, probably by Pastor J. C. Moses. He served the congregations at the Norway Lake and Crow River settlements in 1868 and 1869.

NEW SWEDISH NEIGHBORS

H. W. and Elizabeth Mankell were some of the first Swedish immigrants in this area of the township. By the end of the decade H. W. and Elizabeth had new Swedish neighbors whose farms bordered the Mankell homestead:

- Nils and Marie Brattlund to the east, in Section 20
- Johannes and Marie Norman to the north, in Section 17

NILS & MARIE BRATTLUND FAMILY[7]

Nils Hindriksson Brattlund (1819-1900) and his family settled on their homestead on August 11, 1868. Nils was born in Brattfors Parish, Värmland County, Sweden. On December 26, 1840 he married Maria Christina Olsdotter (1817-1905) from Elfsbacka/Älvsbacka Parish, Värmland. The family lived in several Värmland parishes before their emigration.

- 1841-1843, Fernebo/Färnebo Parish, Bosjö Bruk farm
- 1843-1854, Lungsund Parish, Bjurbäcks Bruk farm
- 1854-emigration, Lungsund Parish, Sladbråten farm

Nils and Maria Brattlund had nine children; all were born and lived in Värmland County, Sweden. However, Nils fathered an illegitimate child, Nils Johan, with a woman named Maria Jonsdotter (born 1816 in Brattfors Parish) before his marriage. Here is a list of the Brattlund children:

Nils Brattlund and Maria Jonsdotter who did not marry, one child:
    Nils Johan Nilsson (1 November, 1840-unknown) was born illegitimate in Elfsbacka Parish and this is noted in his birth record with the word "*oägta*". Household census records indicate that Nils Johan lived with his mother Maria Casja Jonsdotter and 3 half-siblings at the Stenåsen farm in Elfsbacka Parish until he was about nine years old. In 1849 Nils Johan went to live with his maternal step-grandparents, Olof Andersson (1788-1856) and Maria Jansdotter (1790-1855), at Mångstorp, Elfsbacka Parish. These were the parents of Nils Brattlund's wife Maria Stina Olsdotter. After his step-grandmother's death in 1855, Nils Johan and grandfather Olof moved to the Stenåsen farm. Olof died in 1856 and Nils Johan then worked as a farmhand at several farms in the Elfsbacka and Brattfors parishes until 1862. He then moved to Nedre Ullerud Parish in Värmland.

    Nils Johan married Anna Cathrina Olsdoter on February 19, 1865 and had two children. Daughter Anna Sofia died at about age one. Son Carl Johan was born in 1866. The family lived at Norra Mohn farm in Nedre Ullerud. By 1875 Nils Johan was in Aust-Agder, Norway: first in Tvedestrand, then Holt, and in 1900, Vestre Moland. He fathered at least two more children: Hulda Maria Nilsen Bratlund, born in 1876 and Nils Alfred Bratlund, born in 1885.

---

7 Swedish church records (riksarkivet.se), Norwegian census: 1875 and 1900, Norwegian church records; familysearch.org. *Illustrated History of Kandiyohi County*, p. 281; *Willmar Tribune*, September 13, 1905, April 2, 1919; Marie's obituary confirms that the family left Sweden and lived near Moline Illinois [Rock Island] for about two years, then moved to Lake Andrew Township; National Archives and Records Administration, Record Group 49: Bureau of Land Management, General Land Office Records, St. Cloud MN Land Office, Document No. 3123.

Immigrant settlers Nils Brattlund and Maria Stina Olsdotter married on December 26, 1840 in Värmland. They had nine children, all born in Värmland:

1. **Maria Cajsa** (February 16, 1842-May 13, 1910) was born on the Fernebo/Färnebo Parish at the Bosjö Bruk farm. On September 11, 1862 she married Johan Bäckström (in the U.S., named John Beckstrom) in Kroppa Parish, where he was born. From 1862-1864, the family lived in Nyed Parish. In 1864 until emigration, the family lived at the Lesjöfors farm in Rämmen Parish. Maria Cajsa and John Beckstrom are buried in Oaklund Cemetery, Burt County, Nebraska.

2. **Kristina** (October 5, 1844-unknown) was born at the Bjurbäcks Bruk farm in Lungsund Parish. On March 23, 1867 she married Olof Hullsson (born 1839) from Fryksände Parish, Varmland. The family lived at the Lesjöfors farm in the Rämmen Parish.

3. **Olof Henrick** (March 11, 1847-unknown) was born at the Bjurbäcks Bruk farm in Lungsund Parish. He emigrated from Sweden in 1867. There is no record found regarding where he lived.

4. **Carl** (January 7, 1850-August 18, 1850) was born and died at the Bjurbäcks Bruk farm in Lungsund Parish.

5. **Karolina/Caroline** (a twin, June 27, 1851-March 31, 1919) was born at the Bjurbäcks Bruk farm in Lungsund Parish. Her obituary states she was born July 28, 1851. On November 3, 1882 she married Christian C. Selvig (1862-1922) a businessman from Willmar Minnesota who was born in Drammen, Norway. Christian and his parents were neighbors of the Brattlund family, to the east in Section 21 of Lake Andrew Township in the early 1870s.

6. **Lovisa** (a twin, June 27, 1851-November 3, 1857) was born at the Bjurbäcks Bruk farm in Lungsund Parish. She died at the age of 6 when the family was at the Sladbråten farm.

7. **Sofia/Sophia** (January 31, 1854-February 12, 1914) was born at the Bjurbäcks Bruk farm in Lungsund Parish. On January 31, 1877, she married Albert E. Rice, then a State Senator for the State of Minnesota. An immigrant from Vinje Parish, Telemark, Norway A. E. Rice (born Halvor E. Rismyr), was a prominent businessman, banker and politician from Willmar. They are buried in Fairview Cemetery, Willmar, Minnesota.

8. **Johanna (1)** (October 7, 1856-1857) born and died at the Sladbråten farm in Lungsund Parish. She died from scarlet fever.

9. **Johanna (2)** (August 30, 1858-February 28, 1923) born at the Sladbråten farm in Lungsund Parish. She was the second daughter to have the name "Johanna." On October 24, 1874, she married Swedish immigrant and farmer John Olson (1847-1922) in Kandiyohi County, Minnesota. They couple stayed in Kandiyohi County for four years, moved to Clinton in Big Stone County Minnesota, and returned to the Willmar, Minnesota, area in 1901. Johanna and John had eight children, including Adolph, Lillian, Robert, Myrtle, and Cecilia. Johanna and John are buried at the Tripolis Cemetery, Kandiyohi County, Minnesota.

Emigration

Members of the family emigrated at four different times from Lungsund Parish, Värmland County, Sweden.

- May 1866: Nils Brattlund and daughter Sofia/Sophia. Homestead documents notate their arrival in the U.S. as May 19, 1866. They lived in Rock Island, Illinois, for two years.
- April 18, 1867: son Olof Henrick Brattlund. He may have returned to Sweden a few years later.
- October 1, 1867: daughter Maria Cajsa, her husband Johan Bäckström (later John Beckstrom) and children.
- April 30, 1868: Nils' wife Maria Stina (Olsdotter) Brattlund and daughters Johanna, Karolina/Caroline joined the rest of the family in the U.S.
- Daughter Kristina and her husband Olof Hullson remained in Sweden.

In 1868 the re-united family moved to Monongalia County.

The Brattlund Homestead

On August 11, 1868, at the St. Cloud, Minnesota, Land Office, "Nelson Brattlund" applied for a 160-acre homestead, (121N 35 W, Section 20, NE ¼). The family settled on their new home on the same day and soon began improving the land. Requirements to have a homestead included building a house, improving the land, and becoming a U.S. citizen. Information about Brattlund's completion of the homestead requirements will be in the 1870s chapter.

In addition to his 160 acres, Nils Brattlund purchased Lot 4 (about 10 acres) in Section 34 on the south side of Lake Florida in 1865. This wood land lot was previously owned by Alfred and Martha Clark. The Clarks had several more lots (total of 112 acres) along the southern shore of the lake and Lot 2 in Section 12 on the eastern shore of Lake Andrew. Alfred and Martha Clark bought and sold these lots in 1865. In 1885, Brattlund sold this Section 34 lot to Marie Norman, his neighbor. Later this lot was owned by daughter Sophia (Brattlund) Rice and her son Cushman Rice.

NORMAN FARM[8]

Johannes and Marie Norman and their four children arrived in Kandiyohi County in the summer of 1869, and settled on 80 acres (Section 17, W ½ of the SW ¼) in Lake Andrew Township.[9] They purchased their property in 1869 from the St. Paul and Pacific Railroad, which owned much of the land in Section 17 and sold acreage to the settlers.

---

8 Swedish Church records; Norman Family Collection; ancestry.com; Kandiyohi County Recorder; emigration journey quote from Corrine Johnson, written in 1993 (from Christy Hicks)

9 Marie Norman's obituary incorrectly states that the family arrived in the spring of 1870. However, the Norman farm was part of the 1870 federal agricultural census, which tracked cultivated acreage, livestock, grain and supplies. To have a more developed farm, and based on immigration information from Johanna Norman, the year 1870 is incorrect. The farm was not officially a homestead because Norman did not obtain the land directly from the Bureau of Land Management, via the Homestead Act.

Johannes Andreasson Nerman ("Norman" in the U.S.) was born on November 19, 1827, in the Gudhem Parish, Skaraborg County, (now Västra Götaland) Sweden. The sixth child of Anders Pehrsson and Cajsa Andersdotter, the family lived at the Hällestorp farm at the time of his birth. Two years later the family moved to Segerstad Parish, also in Skaraborg. When Johannes was eight years old, his father Andreas died; when he was 14, his mother died.

Maria Johansdotter was born on January 13, 1823 at the Bjärågård farm in Segerstad Parish, Skaraborg. Her parents were Johannes Nilsson and Maria Jonsdotter. Mother Maria died two years after her daughter's birth. Widower Johannes Nilsson and his children soon moved to Backgård farm in Segerstad Parish.

Johannes Nerman and Maria Johansdotter married on June 2, 1854, in Segerstad Parish and soon moved to the Arvid Jonsgården farm in Håkantorp Parish, Skaraborg where their four children were born.

1. **Clara Matilda** (Tilda, 1856-1894) married Swedish immigrant Peter H. Dahlstrom in Kandiyohi County, on January 21, 1892. They were members of Lake Florida Mission Church until her death.

2. **John Andrew** (Anders Johan, 1858-1913) married Christine Sampson (1872-1952) on July 2, 1892. The family lived in Hayes Township, Swift County Minnesota where their first child was born. The family briefly lived at the Norman farm and returned to Swift County.

3. **Johanna Christina** (1863-1947) married William Larson, an immigrant who lived about a mile east of the Norman farm. Johanna and William would later own the Norman farm.

4. **Gustav Albert** (1867-1893) is buried in the Lake Florida Mission Church cemetery.

Johannes Andreasson Nerman (1827-1884), his wife Maria Johansdotter (1823-1906), and their four children left their farm Arvid Jonsgården in Håkantorp Parish, Skaraborg (Västra Götaland) Sweden in April 1869. Their multi-stage travels mirrored that of many Swedish families during this time of emigration. Because no ships left directly from Sweden to the U.S., Swedish emigrants needed to first travel to England, Norway, or Germany to make the next connection in their journeys. The Norman family first traveled to the Swedish port at Gothenburg where they took passage to Hull, England, on the *SS Plato*, which left on May 7, 1869. Once in Hull on England's east coast, they boarded a train for Liverpool on England's west coast. From this port they booked passage on the steamship *SS City of Antwerp*, arriving in New York City on May 25, 1869.

A descendant of Johannes and Marie wrote these thoughts and questions about her ancestors' journey. Similar questions have probably been asked by many emigrants, from Sweden or any other country, whether in 1869 or in the 21st century:

> *Johannes Nerman and his wife Maria Johansdotter decided to emigrate to American in 1869. No one knows what prompted that decision—whether the drought in several prior years with poor harvests; or the encouragement of ship and railway companies to promote business and the 'promise of America'; or the religious revival spreading throughout Sweden and Norway whereby the state church was prohibiting 'freedom of religion' other than in the state owned church; or possibly the letters sent by Swedish immigrants*

in New Sweden, Delaware and other settlements in Iowa and Wisconsin had enticed the Nermans to leave Sweden and the small farms to homestead for up to 160 acres of 'free' land in the unsettled West of USA. None of their parents were living by this time...

Can't one imagine traveling with these young children, tired, hungry, uncomfortable in new dress-up shoes, woolen socks, suits, hats, coats, dresses etc? One could also ask—Was baby Gustaf Albert toilet trained? Could he talk? The parents were in their early forties. What were their anxieties? Their expectations? Would they miss their homeland which they would never see again? Would they find peace and satisfaction in the new land? Was America really so much better a place to work and live than their Sweden? Would any of their family or friends come to Minnesota also?

After settling on the farm, the Norman family built a log house, made from trees at Norway Lake. He probably harvested trees from the wooded lot in Section 5, which he had purchased from Elizabeth Mankell in 1869. The family hauled the logs during the winter, so it isn't clear if the family built their home in late 1869 or early 1870. This log house remained on the farm for many years, even after the newer farmhouse was built in 1890.

FARM STATISTICS[10]

The 1870 federal census for Monongalia County, Minnesota, (later Kandiyohi County) includes agricultural records (acreage, value, livestock, crops, wool, butter, potatoes and more) which provide a glimpse of farm life, c1869-1870. Statistics about the three farms include the following:

Mankell homestead of 160 acres in Section 20, plus 40 acres in Section 17:[11]
- 30 acres of improved land; 40 acres of woodland; and 130 acres of unimproved land
- value of the farm: $1000; machinery and farm implements: $350
- 2 horses, 3 milk cows, 2 oxen, 2 head of other cattle, 2 pigs; value of livestock: $350
- 170 bushels of spring wheat, 25 bushels of oats, 20 bushels of barley
- 9 pounds of wool, 50 bushels of Irish potatoes
- 150 pounds of butter, 15 tons of hay
- value of slaughtered animals: $10

Brattlund homestead of 160 acres in Section 20, plus 10 acres in Section 34:[12]
- 13 acres of improved land; 10 acres of woodland; 147 acres, unimproved
- value of farm: $800; value of machinery and farm implements: $25
- no horses or mules, 2 milk cows, 2 oxen, no sheep or pigs; value of livestock: $200

---

10 US Federal Agricultural Census for 1870, Monongalia County. Due to the poor quality of the census ledger image, Norman's acreage is unclear, but based on ownership, the number should read 75 acres of unimproved land.
11 There was no mention of his other lots near Norway and Middle lakes.
12 These 10 acres, used for timber, were on the south side of Lake Florida, Section 34.

- 60 bushels of spring wheat, with no other grain
- 15 bushels of Irish potatoes
- 25 pounds of butter; 9 tons of hay
- value of slaughtered animals: $10

Norman farm of 80 acres in Section 17:
- 5 acres of improved land; 75 acres of unimproved land
- value of farm: $300
- no horses or mules, 2 milk cows, 2 oxen, no pigs or sheep; value of livestock: $200
- 40 pounds of wool, 100 pounds of Irish potatoes
- 100 pounds of butter, 30 tons of hay
- value of slaughtered animals: $30

SCHOOL DISTRICTS 25 & 16

The late 1860s proved an active time for these immigrant farmers to pursue community responsibilities. They soon would answer the call to establish schools for the township. When the first immigrants arrived in this portion of the Monongalia County, there were no established schools for a growing population of children. At this time the State of Minnesota was a young 10 years of age (established 1858). Many local families, including Brattlund and Mankell, were instrumental in developing the School District 25 which was vital to the longevity of this farming community. The Norman and (later) Stenseth families who lived in Section 17 were initially districted to District 16 and later District 25. These schools would serve area children for almost 100 years.

DISTRICT 25[13]

County School District 25 began in 1868. Several area farmers and immigrants (H. W. Mankell, Ole Dahl, Amund Syverson, Erik Erikson, Lars Hedin, and Iver Gulveson Stene) petitioned the County Commissioners of Monongalia County for an organized school district in this portion of what was then the large Norway Lake Township.

> *The undersigned, a majority of the legal voters of the territory to be affected thereby, do hereby petition your honorable body to organize a new school district to be comprised of the following described territory, to wit: In the town of Norway Lake, sections 19, 20, 21, 28, 29, 30, 31, 32, 33, in township 121, range, 35, or the southwest quarter of the above named township containing nine (9) square miles. Dated at Norway Lake this 26th day of February, 1868.*[14]

---

13 Sowinski, Carolyn, *Niederasphe to Norway Lake: Mankell Family, Minnesota and Immigration*, written in 2016; *Willmar Tribune*, November 17, 1945; 19 Jan 1916; 6 April 1910. *The Illustrated History of Kandiyohi County*, 1905;

14 At the time, this area was part of Norway Lake Township in Monongalia County which merged with Kandiyohi County in 1870. Lake Andrew Township was created out of Norway Lake Township in 1872

CH 2: 1864-1869

The petition was granted and the notice to organize was sent to H. W. Mankell on May 2, 1868. For the first months in 1868, 17 school children met at the Mankell homestead, in a dug out east of the farmhouse.

The Amund Syverson farm (SW ¼ of Section 30) was the next short-term location for these school children. The Syverson family emigrated from Gudbrandsdalen, Norway in 1854 and arrived in Lake Andrew Township in 1866. Per her obituary, Sophia Brattlund, the daughter of Nils and Maria Brattlund, was the teacher at this Syverson location.[15] A year later the district grew to include a portion of Section 22 and all of Sections 27 and 34. In 1869, the school was moved to its first wooden structure—a log building located at the Ole Slattum farm, about one mile south of the Mankell homestead, and about one half mile west of the intersection of County Roads 29 and 5. The district used this 16x20 foot log building, built by the local families, until 1881.

In September, 1869, H. W. Mankell, clerk for the Township, registered the enrollment of 38 children in District 25. This list includes three Brattlund daughters and four Mankell daughters.[16] Sophia was listed as a student at the same time that she began teaching students in the area.

Theodore Bjornstad, 6	Otto Hedin, 6	Axel F. Nordin, 20
Sophia Brattlund, 15	Adrian Hemming, 8	Christian Olson, 8
Caroline Brattlund, 18	Leonard Hemming, 6	Beatha Olson, 11
Johanna Brattlund, 10	Ben Iverson, 13	Arnt Reese, 8
Olai Christofferson, 6	Peter Iverson, 7	Gabriel Stene, 13
August Christofferson, 6	Lena Iverson, 11	Ole Stene, 11
Karin Christofferson, 10	**Jennie Mankell, 11**	Frederick Stene, 9
Axel Erickson, 10	**Mary Mankell, 9**	Henry Stene, 7
Johanna Erickson, 7	**Anna Johanna Mankell, 7**	Julia Syverson, 11
Erick Hedin, 6	**Amanda Mankell, 5**	Martin Syverson, 10
Johanna Hedin, 20	Inger Maria, 5	Inger Syverson, 9
Emma Hedin, 9	Lars Nelson, 16	Carl E. Warholm, 15
Josephine Hedin, 6	Ingeborg Nelson 4	

The following excerpts are from a letter H. W. Mankell wrote in December 1868 to his sisters Augusta and Hermina Mankell who lived in Sweden. He described the education of his children and the beginning of District 25.

> *The children have had only three months schooling during the last two years, so you can surely understand their limited learning. With much trouble and inconvenience on my part, I was able to start a District School here last summer. It lasted three months. I had dug a cellar to be used as a shop for doing carpentry, which I seldom find time for. Thus we*

---

15 Sophia also taught at District 16 and District 12 in Colfax Township before she married and moved to Willmar.
16 Classmates of note: The Iverson children survived the Dakota War of 1862 in which their father Johannes Iverson was killed. The daughter of August Christofferson [aka Christopherson] would marry into the Mankell family in the 1920s. Gabriel Stene would write more than 200 articles for local newspapers in which he highlighted stories about immigrant settlers and events in Lake Andrew Township.

fixed it up for a schoolroom. There were seventeen children. The English school teacher was an eighteen-year-old girl [Elenore Cartis]. She lived with us during the time and was a companion and of great help to Betty. We will have school next summer, perhaps in the same place, as there is very little prospect of getting a schoolhouse built before then.

Gabriel Stene wrote an article[17] for the *Willmar Weekly Tribune* where he reminisced about school life in 1868-1869, describing early pioneer life, the development of the school, and the adventure of obtaining school supplies. At the age of 12, Gabriel was one of the first children to attend the new District 25 School.

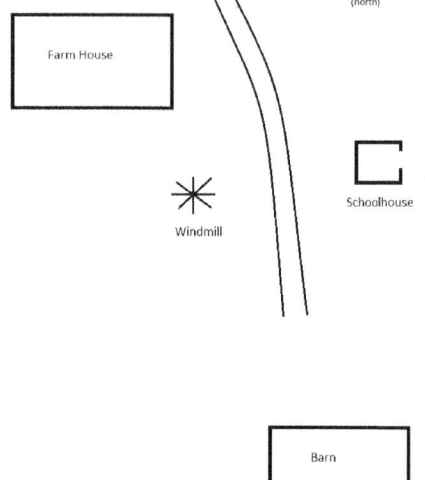

Approximate location of the first District 25 schoolhouse, 1868. The building was the carpentry shop at the farm of H. W. and Elizabeth Mankell in Section 20.

School District No. 25 of Kandiyohi County, originally Monongalia County, was one of the old pioneer landmarks. It was organized in the spring of 1868. At that time this country was a wilderness. There was not a single road laid out in a section line. The roads ran curving and winding about wherever it was found expedient, partly along buffalo and Indian trails. There was no school or schoolhouse but a large bunch of children of school age.

About four rods [20 yards] west [sic: east] of Mankell's residence may be located the spot which shows the place where Pioneer Mankell had a dugout in the hillside—clay floor, clay walls, rails, hay and sod for roof. There was a door to the east and a little window by the door. This dugout was used for a carpenter shop, and here Mr. Mankell had his tools stored away. He was a carpenter by trade. He volunteered to move out and surrender his dugout for school purposes. Miss Rose Burdick opened the first term of school in District No. 25, in said dugout and it continued there until the log schoolhouse, 16 x 20 feet, then under construction three-quarters of a mile west of where the present schoolhouse now stands—could be completed. Logs for this building were donated free by owners of timber and work was done free of charge by citizens of the district. Take a look at the present modern schoolhouses and note the contrast.

One day when standing up in the spelling class and having been given a word to spell, I was overtaken with feelings which I could not understand—a fainting spell. I grabbed hold of Carl Syverson by one hand and Mary Mankell by the other, but went headfirst to the floor. Pioneer Mankell was called and responded. When I had recuperated (they had me out on the ground and applied cold water to my head) Mr. Mankell, who was a man of sound judgment, said: "This hovel is not fit for school purposes. It is too close [small].

---

[17] *Willmar Weekly Tribune*, July 10, 1927. In an earlier version, published in the September 7, 1925 issue of the newspaper, Stene wrote that Sophia Brattlund was the teacher who needed the supplies. Elenore Cartis was the teacher for the first three months, summer 1868, when the school was on the Mankell farm. Rose Burdick followed next, 1868-1872. Sophia Brattlund also taught for District 25, 1869-1870 (possibly between Burdick's years) and taught at the home of the Skoglund family.

CH 2: 1864-1869

We must either stop school or secure better quarters." We were then transferred to the log cabin of Amund Syverson, where he lived with his family. Here we were accommodated and made the best of the situation as we could.

Finally the little log schoolhouse was completed—rude log walls, home-made door, home-made desks and table made by Pioneer Mankell and unplaned rough boards for the floor. One fine Monday morning the key was turned over to Miss Burdick, who dedicated the building by the initiation of an enrollment of 42 pupils. These were the happiest bunch of school children west of Minnehaha Falls—Minneapolis was not heard of in those days. The first week slipped by. It was hard to study in a schoolbook, with two or three pupils hanging over one book! The teacher had made out an order for necessary supplies which was approved by the board. This was on Friday night. The question arose, "Where is the supply to be found and how to get them?" The teacher said: "They are to be found a Sam Adams' Store at New London." But everybody was using ox-motors [ox-pulled wagons] in those days. I was only 12 years old but volunteered to travel on foot and get them. I started off bright and early Saturday morning. At New London I found only six slates and some slate pencils. Scratch books and pencils were not in use then as now. Every child had to be supplied with a slate and slate pencil.

Examples of slate pencils and a slate book. Often the slate pencils had decorative paper at one end and were used to write on the slate books or boards. The slate books were typically erased with soft fabric.

Next morning being Sunday three young men at the age of about twenty years, Axel F. Nordin, Simon Syverson and Gunder Swenson, met at the schoolhouse for the purpose of organizing a Sunday School. The school supply question then came up and I gave my report. I told them that Sam Adams had said that such supplies could not be had nearer than St. Cloud or possibly Paynesville. I said that I had promised to get them and would redeem my promise if I had to go to Paynesville.

Peter Nordin, a homesteader on the now Carl Danielson place, spoke up and said: "I just returned from the new Foot Lake station last night. I saw school books at the store there. Feel sure that they may be had there." "Where is Foot Lake Station?" "South of Foot Lake on the new railroad being built out from St. Paul." I asked "Where is the road leading to it?" He said: "There is no road direct. No bridge across Shakopee Creek south of Crook Lake. But there are two ways of getting there. One is by Nest Lake, Eagle Lake and south. The other is west to the soldiers' patrol road, crossing the creek at Gunder Pederson's place on the Government log bridge."

At four o'clock Monday morning I made for the soldiers' patrol road westward in Arctander. This I followed to Lake Mamre, where that road ran east towards Eagle Lake. There I had to take a faint trail running south towards the new track going west of Solomon Lake and east of what is now Pennock, then east five or six miles to the railroad builders' camp.

> *Had a great time crossing the outlet stream near where the cemeteries are now located. There was no bridge. The trail led me to this grove where our Memorial Pioneer log cabin is now located, then through a wheat field in what is now First Ward of Willmar. I found a little store north of the track. South of the track there was nothing but mules, horses, ploys, scrapers, and busy railroad builders.*
>
> *What I was looking for I succeeded in finding at the little store. I had two dry slices of bread in my pocket which I devoured with the aid of water from a pail, my first lunch in the now city of Willmar. Then shouldering my luggage, I started back...I struck the patrol road where Solomon Lake church now stands. Here I met a homesteader who said that a bridge was just completed across Shakopee Creek near Crook Lake grove... He took me to the top of the Dovre hills where I saw the whole Norway Lake panorama...*
>
> *I had walked from 4:00 in the morning till midnight and had covered 40 miles to get those supplies for the new School District 25. This is my old home school district where I spent my pioneering childhood and boyhood days, where I first learned to read, write and spell.*

The November 1945 obituary for Gabriel Stene included information about the schools where he was a student. Here is the description of the third location, south of the Mankell homestead, which was the location of the first schoolhouse:

> *In 1869 a log schoolhouse was built. It stood on what is known as the old Ole M. Slettum [sic Slattum] place about a half mile west of the present school of Dist. 25...Among his teachers were the late Sophia L (Brattlund) Rice, prominent in Willmar, and the late Carl A Syverson.*

Here are the teachers for the first 13 years, with names connected to the four farms in bold:

Elenore Cartis, 1868, Summer
Sophia Brattlund, 1869-1870
Rose Burdick, 1868-1872
John Matson, 1873
Olaf Aschim, 1874
Sophia Swanson, 1875
Anna Egge, 1876
Maria Railson, 1877
C.A. Syverson, 1878
Thorwald Nilson, 1879
Jennie Henderson, 1880
Jane Johnson, 1881

Sophia Brattlund, c1880.
(image courtesy of the Kandiyohi County Historical Society)

DISTRICT 16[18]

The Board of Commissioners, Monongalia County, established School District 16 in September 1868 when they granted a petition from several area farmers. Classes began in 1869 or 1870. The first school house was 14 X 16 feet and made of logs and was located two miles north of District 25. Because this school district initially included Section 17, the Norman children attended District 16 in the 1870s; the Stenseth children, the 1880s. By about 1900 these two farms on the southern edge of Section 17 would be re-districted to District 25, thus allowing neighboring children of the four farms to all attend the same school. Martin Reierson and John Syvert Christenson, who enter the four farms in later decades, attended District 16 in the 1880s. Martin's father, Bjorn Reierson, was one of the farmers who petitioned for the establishment of the school in 1868.

Here is a list of teachers at District 16, 1870-1902, with names connected to the four farms in bold:

Ellen Blakely, 1870-1871
Sophia L. Brattlund, 1872-1873
Mary Blakely, 1874
C. S. Ham, 1875
C. A. Birch, 1876
Winnie Hudson, 1877-1878
George Markhus, 1879
Malinda Christie, 1880-1881
Rachel Knutson, 1882
Laura Christie, 1883
Etta Geer, 1884
Cornelia E Hudson, 1885

Laura Christie, 1886
Carrie E Daugherty, 1887
Carrie Stenseth, 1887
Emma D Smith 1888
Lillian S Reikvam, 1888
Belle Ward, 1889
Maggie E Burns, 1889
J. J. Jenson 1890, 1892
Alice Hennings, 1890
Anna Railson, 1891
Belle E Burr, 1892
S. Agnes Lawler, 1893

Julia Halvorson, 1893, 1894
Nels J. Swanson, 1894
Carrie Christenson [nee Stenseth], 1895
Oline Shipstead, 1895-1897
Jose Lindberg, 1897
Ellen Shipstead, 1898-1899
Christine Erickson, 1900
Julie Sonstegord, 1900
Julie Ramstad, 1901
V. Maud Howard, 1901-1902

The decade of the 1860s closed with three of the four farms settled and children attending school. The 1870s would see more changes in this small neighborhood of farms, including the arrival of Norwegian neighbors as well as the establishment of two churches and the local township government. The families would face difficulties due to natural disasters.

---

[18] *Illustrated History of Kandiyohi County*, p 278.

CHAPTER 3:
1870-1879

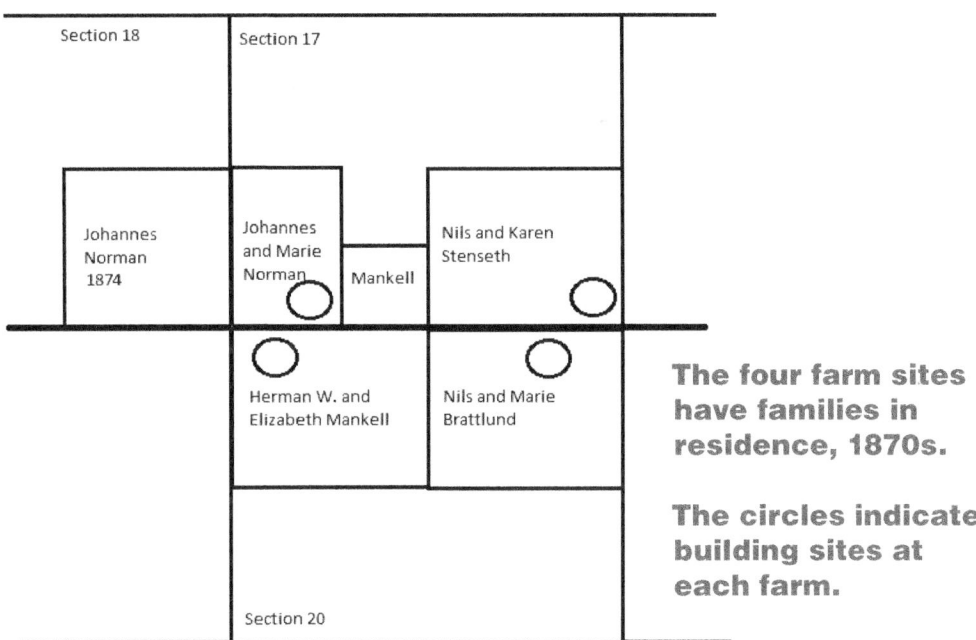

The four farm sites have families in residence, 1870s.

The circles indicate building sites at each farm.

HIGHLIGHTS

- The fourth immigrant family arrives on the mile
- Families are involved with founding two Lutheran churches: one Swedish, one Norwegian
- Lake Andrew Township is created
- Natural Disasters: blizzards and grasshoppers

NEW NEIGHBORS ARRIVE— STENSETH FAMILY[1]

New neighbors, Nils Stenseth, his wife Karen, and children arrived in in Lake Andrew Township in June, 1870. The family was from the Stenset farm in Nannestad Parish, Akershus, northeast of Oslo, Norway. Nils and Karen married on April 19, 1855 in Nannestad Parish. The family left for the United States in 1867, living for about two years in Fillmore County before taking a homestead in Lake Andrew Township, Section 17, SE ¼.

Nils Nilsen Stenseth (1828-1882) and Karen Larsdatter (1825-1909) had five children. The oldest four were born in Nannestad, Norway; the youngest, born in Fillmore County.

1. **Maren Sophia** (1856-1919) was deaf and attended the Minnesota Institute for Deaf and Dumb, graduating in 1876. She was the last surviving member of her family and is buried near her parents' graves at the Nannestad Cemetery, Arctander Township.
2. **Lina**, born 1859 and died before 1902.[2]
3. **Sorine**, born 1862 and died before 1902.
4. **Nicolas** (1864-1902, aka Nicolai N.) moved to Minneapolis, about 1894, where he worked as a street car conductor. He married Hilda G. Hanson (1876-1902) on June 24, 1896, in Hennepin County, Minnesota. In 1900 he and his family moved to Mamre Township where he and Hilda soon died from complications of tuberculosis. Nicolai and Hilda are buried at the Nannestad Cemetery in Arctander Township.
5. **Carrie Dorothy** (1868-1904, aka Karen) born in Fillmore County; married John Syvert Christenson in 1894. Both are buried at the Nannestad Cemetery.

While he eventually applied for a homestead in 1875, Stenseth initially took the role of squatter on the farm upon the family's arrival on June 25, 1870 when he began to build a home. For a few months, while Nils built the house, the Stenseth family lived with the Iver Gulveson Stene family on the eastern shore of Lake Mary, two miles west. The Stene and Stenseth families had several commonalities:

- Norwegian immigrants
- Both families had lived in Fillmore County, though not at the same time
- Members of the Haugean Lutheran piety movement, which was part of the heritage of many Norwegian immigrants

Five years later, on December 30, 1875, Stenseth went to the St. Cloud Land Office, submitted a Declaration Statement about improvements to his land from 1870-1875, and applied for his 160-acre homestead in Section 17, SE ¼, Lake Andrew Township (121N 35W) in Kandiyohi County. He paid a $14.00

---

1 Ancestry.com; moms.mn.gov; *Willmar Tribune*. Norway Parish records; findagrave.com. *Willmar Tribune*, April 23, 1919. Homestead documents: National Archives and Records Administration, Record Group 49. Bureau of Land Management. Final Certificate No. 4855.
2 Possibly married John Nordby, 6 March 1884, Kandiyohi County

processing fee and also completed forms stating his intent to become a U.S. citizen—a requirement to receive a homestead. He received his citizenship on October 12, 1880. By derivation, Stenseth's wife Karen and their children received their citizenship.

In his 1875 Declaration Statement, Stenseth described the house and other buildings which he had built.

> One log house 16x17 feet square, shingle roof, 2 doors, 2 floors, 2 windows, a cellar and the house is a good and comfortable house to live in and that I have lived in the said house from June 1870 and also that I have got a log stable and other out buildings and 120 acres fenced.[3]

Neighbor Herman W. Mankell was the witness to Stenseth's December 30, 1875, statement about his farm improvements prior to Stenseth's application for a homestead. In 1881 Nils Stenseth returned to the St. Cloud Land Office to file his Final Proof, pay the final paperwork fee ($4.00), and then wait to receive the Land Patent a few months later. Two men from the four farms were his 1881 witnesses: Johannes Norman and Nils Brattlund. Other neighbors who acted as witnesses were Hans Christenson, whose son John Syvert would later marry Carrie Stenseth, and Christian Larson (aka Christian Sjogodt) who lived directly east in Section 16.

TWO HOMESTEADS & CITIZENSHIP

While Stenseth began the process of obtaining his homestead, two of his neighbors were completing their paperwork, securing ownership of their own 160 acres. In the 1870s Nils Brattlund and H. W. Mankell filed their final paperwork at the St. Cloud Land Office, to receive their Land Patents to their homesteads.

Herman W. Mankell

On June 3, 1871, H. W. Mankell returned to the St. Cloud Land Office to file the paperwork necessary to obtain final ownership of his 160 acres, the NW ¼ of Section 20, 121N 35 W. The first document was the Proof Statement from witnesses. His witnesses were S.G. Walberg and B.K. Bond.[4]

> We S.G. Walberg and B.K. Blond do solemnly Swear that we have known Herman W. Mankel for seven years last past; that he is the head of a family consisting of wife and seven children and is a naturalized citizen of the United States; that he is an inhabitant of the NW ¼ of section No. 20 in township No. 121 of Range No. 35 and that no other person resided upon the said land entitled to the right of Homestead or Pre-emption.

H. W. Mankell, c1880.

---

3   The log house was located directly west of the current farmhouse and was later used as a granary and shed. From other family information, Stenseth may have moved into the house in December 1870.
4   Swen G. Walberg was a Swedish immigrant who had a homestead in Section 22 of New London Township. He later moved to Becker County, Minnesota.

> *That the said Herman W. Mankel entered upon and made settlement on said land on or about the 20th day of July 1864, and has built a frame house thereon 16 x 16 feet in size with all 16 x 16 feet in size with two doors, 4 windows, two floors, and two rooms and good shingled roof. Has also a good frame granary 16 x 24 ft. in size—one ½ story high and has good stable about 150 ft. in length. He has lived in the said house and made it his exclusive home from the 20th day of July, 1964, to the present time, except such time as he was kept from home by the Sioux Indians then hostile and roaming through the county and that he has since said settlement ploughed, fenced, and cultivated about 82 acres of said land, and has made the following improvements thereon, to wit: Has fenced the entire quarter section with post and rail fence, and has two acres planted with forest trees. S.G .Walberg B.K. Blond.*
>
> *I, T. McClure, Receiver, do hereby certify that the above affidavit was taken and subscribed before me this 3rd day of June, 1871. T. McClure, Receiver.*
>
> *We certify that S. G. Walberg and B. K. Blond whose names are subscribed to the foregoing affidavit, are persons of respectability.*

H. W. became an American citizen on August 29, 1870. By derivation his wife Elizabeth and his children also received citizenship. He took his oath in the Seventh Judicial District in Stearns County and provided a sworn statement to the Land Office.

> *Be it remembered, That on the 29th day of August in the year of our Lord one thousand eight hundred and seventy Herman W Mankel appeared in the District Court, said Court being a Court of Record, having common law jurisdiction, and a Clerk and Seal—and applied to the said Court to be admitted to become A Citizen of the United States of America, pursuant to the provisions of the several Acts of the Congress of the United States of America, for that purpose made and provided; and the said applicant having thereupon produced to the Courts such evidence, and taken such oaths as are by the said acts required.*
>
> *Thereupon, it was ordered by the said Court, that the said applicant be admitted and he was accordingly admitted by the said Court to be A Citizen of the United States of America.*
>
> *In testimony whereof, the Seal of the said Court is here unto affixed, this the twenty ninth day of August one thousand eight hundred and seventy in the Ninety fifth year of our Independence. G. S Mattoon, Clerk*

Herman W. Mankell paid his final $4.00 fee. The Land Patent was issued on June 10, 1872, signed by President Ulysses S. Grant.

In addition to the farm (160 acre homestead plus 40 acres directly north) Mankell purchased property from the St. Paul and Pacific Railroad in Willmar: lots 8 and 9 of Block 25 which currently lie between Pacific and Benson avenues and 2nd and 3rd streets. For a few years in the 1880s the family lived in Willmar and H. W. had a carpentry business. This may have been the location of his business.

Nils Brattlund

Brattlund's Land Patent was issued October 15, 1875, by President U.S. Grant. To receive this final deed to his land Brattlund filed the same types of documents, with witness statements, and paid final paperwork fees, just as Mankell had done three years earlier. Brattlund, with witnesses Olof Larson and Lars Nilsson, went to the St. Cloud Land Office on June 15, 1875 to file the documents.[5]

Requirements to have a homestead included building a house, improving the land, and becoming a U.S. citizen. Their log home was described in homestead documents as

> *15 x 30 feet and has a shingled roof, 3 doors, 7 windows, 2 floors and a cellar and has lived in the said house and made it his exclusive home from the 11th day of August, 1868 to the present time, and that he has, since said settlement, plowed, fenced, and cultivated about 23 acres of said land, and has made the following improvements thereon: a log stable 15 x 50 feet square, hay roof, 80 acres fenced and a well.*[6]

Nils became an American citizen on October 26, 1874 at the 4th Judicial District in Kandiyohi County. His wife Marie received her citizenship by derivation. Their adult children would not have received citizenship by derivation from their father. Nils paid his final paperwork fee of $4.00 on June 15, 1875. The following fall, on October 15, he received his Land Patent for 160 acres, the NE ¼ of Section 20, 121N 35W.

NORMAN FARM[7]

In 1874 Johannes Norman expanded his farm with the purchase of 160 acres in Section 18. The first owner of this quarter section in Section 18 was Alfred Clark, who arrived in 1864.

The Norman farm was now 240 contiguous acres in two sections of Lake Andrew Township.

LIFE EVENTS: Births, Marriages, Deaths

This was a momentous decade for family events on the mile: three births and four weddings.

Births[8]

The Brattlund, Norman, and Stenseth children were born before the families arrived on the mile. The first babies and young children at these four farms were in the Mankell family. While the oldest four Mankell children were born in Northfield and one in St. Cloud, the four youngest children were born

---

5 Lars Nilsson and Olof Larson were both Swedish immigrants and both lived in Section 26. The families also used the surname Rodlund. *Illustrated History of Kandiyohi County*, p. 285.
6 National Archives and Records Administration, Record Group 49: Bureau of Land Management, General Land Office Records, St. Cloud Minnesota Land Office, Document No. 3123.
7 Kandiyohi County Recorder.
8 *Niederasphe to Norway Lake*

on the Mankell homestead—with one born in 1868 and the three youngest in the 1870s. There is no record of which women in the area acted as midwives, but one can be certain that neighboring women who had given birth years or decades earlier were available to help Elizabeth when she birthed these four children at the farm:

1. **Oscar** (1868-1936) married Minnie Swenson, 1895
2. **Sophia** (1871-1894) married John Quam, 1893
3. **Otto H.** (1872-1939)
4. **Esther** (1874-1915) married Gustave Erixon, 1899

Elizabeth Mankell, c1890.

Weddings

In the 1870s, the Mankell and Brattlund families shared the joys of having four of their daughters marry. While there is no written record noting in detail who attended these weddings, it is highly probable that neighbors, including the families highlighted in this book, attended and celebrated these joyous occasions.

Johanna Brattlund & John Olson[9]

The first of the four brides was Johanna Brattlund (1858-1923). On October 24, 1874, she married Swedish immigrant and farmer John Olson (1847-1922) in Kandiyohi County, Minnesota. According to his obituary John was born in Urshult Parish, Kronoberg, Sweden, the son of Olof and Anna Haroldsson. It is probable that they married at the Lake Florida Mission Church where Johanna's parents were founding members. The couple remained members of this congregation for four years, until they moved to Clinton in Big Stone County Minnesota, returning to the Willmar, Minnesota, area in 1901. Johanna and John had eight children:

1. **Sophia Caroline**, born 1877 when the family lived in Lake Andrew Township, and died before 1922.
2. **Adolph H.** (1879-1963), married Agnes Vickstrom (1885-1957). Both are buried at Lakewood Cemetery, Minneapolis, MN.
3. **Melvin**, born about 1885 and died before 1922.
4. **Lillian M.**, born about 1890 and died before 1922.
5. **Robert L.** (1891-1962) married Myrtle Halverson (1897-1990). Both are buried at Sunset Memorial Gardens, Minot, ND.
6. **Myrtle J.** (1895-1984) buried at Clover Leaf Cemetery, Willmar, MN.
7. **Cecilia S.** (1900-1951) married John Baptist Gagnon (1894-1983) who was a veteran of WWI. Both are buried at Fort Snelling National Cemetery in Minneapolis, MN.
8. **Son**, unidentified.

Johanna and John Olson are buried at the Tripolis Lutheran Church Cemetery, Kandiyohi, Kandiyohi County, Minnesota, a congregation founded by Swedish immigrants.

9   Ancestry.com; findagrave.com; Lake Florida Mission Church records; *Willmar Tribune* 22 March 1922; moms.mn.gov;

Jenny (Jennie) Mankell & Andrew Gordhamer[10]

On June 24, 1876, family, friends, and neighbors gathered at the Mankell homestead for the wedding of H. W. and Elizabeth's oldest child, Jenny (1958-1948), and Andrew Gordhamer (Hans Andreas, 1854-1934) of Arctander Township. Andrew was the son of Norwegian immigrants, Halgrim Jonson Gordhamer (1804-1869) and Mari Oldsdotter Ringerud (1812-1900). The family lived in Buskerud County and emigrated from Norway in April, 1856, first settled in Winneshiek County, Iowa, moved to Minnesota, and settled in Arctander Township (then part of larger Norway Lake Township in Monongalia County), being early settlers in the area. After Halgrim's death in 1869, widow Marie lived with her son John H. Gordhamer, Section 34 in Arctander Township, Kandiyohi County. Halgrim and Marie are buried at East Norway Lake Lutheran Church, Arctander Township.[11]

In his *Willmar Tribune* Pioneer Kid column, dated July 14, 1926, Gabriel Stene wrote about the couple's 50th wedding anniversary and reflected back on the activities—for young and old—at the wedding.

> ...the early settlers and neighbors of this vicinity from their respective crude new settlers' homes in their pioneer vehicles, mostly old wagons, were heading for the old pioneer home of Mr. and Mrs. H. W. Mankel [sic] in response to the invitation to the wedding of their oldest daughter, Jennie, about 18, to Andrew H. Gordhamer, a little past 20. Ceremony was performed by the pioneer ministry Rev. D. T. Booth of Willmar. It being June 24th, Midsummer Day, a Midsummer pole was planted in the front of the house and decorated with wild flowers from the bottom to top. A good old settlers' time was indulged in during the day and the pioneer kids enjoyed a good time towards evening in getting pioneer and Civil war veteran, now of New London, C. K. Lund[12], in the lead for merriment [and] singing (Ut ock gå på brandvagt), Drop the Handkerchief, etc. Being a fine evening, the enjoyment lasted the most part of the night.

Jenny and Andrew lived their married life on a farm in the community of Jericho [aka Norway Lake] on the hill west of Lake Mary, located in Section 24 of Arctander Township, and one mile west of the Mankell homestead. They had 12 children:

1. **Dena** (Andine) (1877-1950) married Severin O. Tjosvold (1872-1932), brother to Louis. Both are buried at Sunset Memorial Park Cemetery, Minneapolis, Minnesota.
2. **Mary Elizabeth** (1879-1951) married John Oliver Halvorson (1870-1932). Oliver was the son of Johannes Halvorson, an early settler of the northwest area of Kandiyohi County. Oliver was the first buttermaker at the Norway Lake Creamery and a postmaster for the community Mary and Oliver are buried at Bethel Cemetery, Park Rapids, Minnesota.

---

10 *Festskrift*, p 34; mankell.org; ancestry.com; *Niederasphe to Norway Lake*; Boyd, Gregory. *Family Maps of Kandiyohi County*, p. 95; moms.mn.gov;

11 Halgrim died before this congregation was built. He was probably buried at the cemetery of the original log church of the Norway Lake Settlement. His casket may have been moved after the log church congregation divided into West Norway Lake and East Norway Lake congregations or, later, when Marie died and was buried at East Norway Lake Church.

12 Carl K Lund (1842-1929) was a brother-in-law of Andrew, married to Johanna Gordhamer (1846-1928). During the Civil War he served as a private with the Iowa 12th Volunteer Infantry, Company G using the name Carl B Kittelson. He received a pension (#727,132) from the US government. Carl and Johanna lived on a farm, Section 27, Arctander Township.

3. **Johanna Wilhelmina** (1881-1941) married Louis A. Tjosvold (1868-1960), brother to Severin. Both are buried at Sunset Memorial Park Cemetery, Minneapolis, Minnesota.

4. **Anna Jeannette** (1885-1971) married Walter C. Hoglund/Hoaglund (1886-1959). She died in Texas and is buried at East Norway Lake Lutheran Church near the house where she was born. Walter is buried at Lakewood Cemetery, Minneapolis, Minnesota, near his second wife, Eleanor.

5. **Harry** (1883-1950) married Thea Quisberg (1884-1955) from Stearns County, Minnesota. Harry died in Young County, Texas. Both are buried at Sunset Memorial Park Cemetery, Minneapolis, Minnesota.

6. **Theoline** (Tella) (1885-1962) married Gilbert M. Anderson (1879-1965). They are buried at Hillcrest Cemetery in Granite Falls, Minnesota.

7. **Victor** (1889-1944) married Carrie Erickson (1891-1978). They are buried at Woodlawn Cemetery, Argyle in Marshall County, Minnesota.

8. **Arthur Walter** (1890-1920). He is buried at East Norway Lake Lutheran, Arctander Township, Kandiyohi County, close to his home.

9. **Austin** (1893-1969). He is buried at East Norway Lake Lutheran Church Cemetery, close to his home.

10. **Eddie** (1895-1976) married Astrid Steen (1896-1975). Both are buried at Riverside Cemetery, Fargo North Dakota.

11. **Axel** (1895-1981) married Clara (Byrdie) Aasen (1896-1995). Both are buried at East Norway Lake Lutheran Church cemetery.

12. **Joseph David** (1898-1976) married Christine Vold (1895-1992). Both are buried at Grace West Cemetery, Belgrade, Stearns County, Minnesota.

Jenny Mankell Gordhamer died on May 26, 1948. She was the eldest of nine Mankell siblings and the last one to pass away. Funeral services were held at East Norway Lake Lutheran Church, located near the Gordhamer home in Jericho.

Sophia Brattlund & Albert E Rice[13]

Sophia (1854-1914) was a school teacher, having studied at the State Normal School in Winona. In her first years of teaching she taught kids from Lake Andrew Township—children of her neighbors. For a few months (c1869-1870) she taught children of Swedish immigrants in the growing area of Lake Andrew Township at the home of John A. Skoglund on the north side of Lake Florida. During 1872 and 1873, she was the teacher at District 16, located about a mile north of her father's farm. Two of her pupils were Johanna (age about 9) and John Andrew Norman (age about 14), her neighbors to the west. In 1874, she left the rural area of the county and came to Willmar, the county seat. Three years later, on January 31, 1877, she married Albert E. Rice (1845-1921) a local businessman and State Senator at the time of their marriage. Lake Florida church records state that they were married at her home. For many years they lived on the north shore of Green Lake, near Spicer, Minnesota.

---

13 *Willmar Tribune*, 18 Feb 1914, 14 Sept 1921; ancestry.com, findagrave.com; Wikipedia.com; *Illustrated History of Kandiyohi County*; *Kandi Express*, June 2015, p 12-13.

Rice (born Halvor Aslaksen) was an immigrant from the Rismyr farm in the Vinje Parish, Telemark, Norway who left his homeland in April 1861. He served during the Civil War (Company K, 15th Wisconsin Volunteer Infantry). In about 1869, he came to Willmar, Minnesota, and was a local businessmen (Paulson & Rice, General Merchandise and Country Produce) founder of the Bank of Willmar and the *Willmar Republican* newspaper. Later in this chapter, in the section about the January 1873 blizzard, we find A.E. Rice serving as the liaison between those who sought financial relief and the Minnesota governor's office. In later years, A.E. Rice served in both the Minnesota State House and State Senate. A Republican, he served as Minnesota's Lieutenant Governor from 1887 to 1891.

Sophia and Albert had one child, son Captain Cushman A. Rice who served with the U.S. military in Honduras, Cuba, China, Philippines and in WWI. Rice Hospital in Willmar is named for the Rice family. Rice family members are buried in Fairview Cemetery, Willmar.

Anna Mankell & Nels Quam[14]

Anna Mankell (1862-1914) and Nels Quam (1859-1937) married in October 12, 1879 and lived in the Norway Lake area until 1895, when they moved to New London, Minnesota. Anna worked at a boarding house and later as the landlady of the Great Northern Hotel which she and Nels owned. Nels played a prominent role in both state and local politics. He served as a State Representative for Kandiyohi County in the Minnesota House, 1889-1890. He also served in various township offices, was a school board member, and was mayor of New London (1899-1904, 1906-1907, 1911-1912). He organized the Farmer's Insurance Company and was President of the Farmers Alliance.

Nels Quam's parents, Johannes and Anna Thompson Quam (Kvam) were born in Norway and married in 1852. They immigrated to the United States in 1854, arriving first in Quebec Canada and then traveled to Koshkonong, Wisconsin. In 1856 the family moved to Havanna, Steele County, Minnesota, where the family had a pre-emption claim. In about 1878 the family sold the farm and moved to Kandiyohi County—to Section 19, on the east side of Swenson Lake (southwest of the Mankell homestead), and owned additional land in Section 30. Johannes and Anna had eleven children, (several children died young). Two sons (Nels and John) married two Mankell sisters (Anna and Sophia).

Anna and Nels had six children; a daughter died in infancy. They also raised a niece, Sophie Quam, daughter of Sophia Mankell and John Quam (postmaster in Jericho) because Sophia had died in childbirth.

1. **Andrew Neptune** (1880-1936) was a business partner with his uncle Otto Mankell (brother of Anna) in New London. He is buried at Oak Hill Cemetery, New London, Minnesota.

2. **John William** (1881-1951) is buried at Fergus Falls, Minnesota, State Hospital Cemetery.

3. **Edward Lawrence** (1883-1974) married Pauline Thorvig (1885-1979) on November 24, 1909 in Kandiyohi County. Edward and Pauline are buried at Dawn Valley Memorial Park, Bloomington, Minnesota.

---

14 Moms.mn.gov; *Niederasphe to Norway Lake*; mankell.org, findagrave.com, *History of New London*. The Great Northern Hotel was located on the northwest corner of the main intersection in New London. It was torn down in 1955.

4. **Estella Amanda** (1885-1976) married Dr. Hans Johnson (1881-1952), a family physician who had his office in Kerkhoven, Minnesota, on June 6, 1907. Hans' father was Dr. Christian Johnson, a Danish immigrant, who had a medical practice in Willmar. Hans' mother was Christina Sorensen, also born in Denmark. Hans and Estella are buried at Hillside Cemetery, Kerkhoven, Minnesota

5. **Oscar Arnold** (1887-1969) was well known for crafting wooden duck decoys and duck calls. He married Elizabeth Brix (c1902-c1968) from New London and Lillian Knudtson Prestrude (1907-1978). Oscar and Lillian and Elizabeth are buried at Lakewood Cemetery in Minneapolis.

In 1912, with Anna's health failing from cancer, Nels and Anna sold the Great Northern Hotel. Anna died in 1914 and is buried at Oak Hill Cemetery, New London, MN. Nels later had a business creating cement products and also owned a general merchandise store until 1916 when he moved to Willmar. He married Vendla Ohberg on March 24, 1916, in Minneapolis and they moved there in 1921. Nels died in 1937, and is buried at Crystal Lake Cemetery in Minneapolis. Vendla is buried in the same cemetery.

TWO CONGREGATIONS FORMED

Religion, religious traditions, and spiritual health played powerful roles in the lives of these Swedish and Norwegian immigrant families. In 1870, the same year they arrived, the Stenseth family helped develop the Norwegian language Nannestad Lutheran congregation to the west. In the same year the Mankell and Brattlund families joined with other Swedish immigrant families and started the Swedish language Lake Florida Swedish Lutheran Church to the east, later known as the Lake Florida Mission Church and Lake Florida Covenant Church.

NANNESTAD LUTHERAN CHURCH[15]

Nannestad Lutheran Church.
(image courtesy of the Kandiyohi County Historical Society)

When the Stenseth family arrived in Lake Andrew Township from Fillmore County, the family first lived with fellow immigrants from Nannestad Norway and fellow Fillmore County residents: Iver and Inga Stene and their children. The Stene family first settled first in Wisconsin, then Fillmore (1862-1864) and Goodhue counties (1864-1866) in Minnesota, and moved to Kandiyohi County in 1867. The Stene family settled on the eastern shore of Lake Mary, in Section 19, and started to farm. Within three years they welcomed this other Norwegian family with connections to Fillmore County.

---

15 *Illustrated History of Kandiyohi County*; p.119, 216, 438. Stene, Gabriel, "From Sogn, Norway to Norway Lake, Minnesota" *Willmar Tribune*, April 13, 1927; *Centennial History of Kandiyohi County*, p. 148. *Willmar Tribune* 25 October 1922. Gjerde, S.S., *The Hauge Movement in America*; *The History of Renville County, Minnesota*, p. 1265; Wikipedia.org.

The Stenseth and Stene families did not live in Fillmore County at the same time, with the Stenseths arriving after the Stene family had left. However, Iver Stene was a preacher of the Haugean Lutheran tradition in Fillmore County, so it is probable that the Stenseth family learned about the preacher and Nannestad native, Iver Stene. Soon the Stenseths were in Lake Andrew Township, living with the Stene family.

According to the 1905 *Illustrated History of Kandiyohi County* Iver Stene was the first Haugean Lutheran in Kandiyohi County. In 1870 he established the first Haugean congregation, then called Urland, located at the Stene farm, Section 19 of Lake Andrew Township. This was also the location of the congregation's first cemetery. In 1876 the congregation was reorganized and renamed Nannestad Lutheran Church, because most of its members, including Nils and Karen Stenseth, were from the Nannestad area of Norway. Nils Stenseth was a trustee of the congregation's first organization and later, a secretary.

On March 27, 1877, the congregation legally incorporated with the name "Nannestads Congregation at Norway Lake, Kandiyohi County, Minn., of Hauge's Norwegian Evangelical Lutheran Synod." By 1879 the Nannestad congregation decided to build a church, with cemetery, in Section 14, Arctander Township, two miles northwest of the Stene farm. The building was 24 x 32 feet and 12 feet high.

Congregations in the Haugean Lutheran tradition were identified as "low church" which emphasized lay-leadership, revivals, and strong personal relationships with God. They de-emphasized formal worship settings. The Synod was named after a lay preacher in Norway: Hans Nielsen Hauge (1771-1824). This version of Lutheranism challenged the state church of Norway, and some followers experienced persecution. Hauge was imprisoned. When Norwegian emigrants traveled across the ocean and settled in Kandiyohi County, they brought their religious traditions and established congregations, including Nannestad Lutheran Church.

Here are the pastors who served Nannestad Lutheran Church. Several of them served concurrently at other Haugean Lutheran churches, including Bethany Lutheran Church of Long Lake (aka Betania) located in Section 10 of Dovre Township, Green Lake Lutheran located in Section 15 of Green Lake Township, Hof Lutheran in Sacred Heart in Renville County:

- Rev. Lars O. Rustad, 1870-1878. He served until his death on January 1, 1878 and is buried in the church cemetery with several members of his family.
- Rev. Johannes Halvorson, 1878-1880
- Rev. Karl C. Holter, 1880-1889
- Rev. Torstein J. Oppedahl, 1890-1892
- No pastor for two years
- Rev. B. Reitan, 1894-1898
- Rev. S. E. Hanson, 1899-1902
- Rev. I. A. Johanson, 1909-1912

Early pastors of the Haugean Lutheran Churches in the county.
(*Illustrated History of Kandiyohi County*, page 438)

The Nannestad congregation's first pastor was Rev. Lars O. Rustad, a Norwegian immigrant. He and his family lived in Section 19, on the southeast side of Lake Mary; their neighbors were the Iver Stene family. Here is a description of this pioneer pastor, of the Haugean Lutheran tradition, taken from the book *The Hauge Movement in America*.

> *Lars O. Rustad was a heart-stirring lay-preacher and soul-winner who came among us in 1869. He was then 51. He was born in the parish of Lom, Gudbrandsdalen, April 2, 1818. He moved with his parents to Tromso, in Northern Norway, while young. Up in this northern country he experienced a very earnest awakening and change of heart. "He first saw the light of God in all its clearness while he was turning the grindstone." This was in 1840.*
>
> *Then his soul-winning career began which was almost apostolic in its power, zeal and spirit among Norwegians, Finns and Laps. Later he came south again. No salary. His clothes were worn out. "When I look at my tarred pants (bekabuksa), I feel they are very shabby, but when I begin to speak, I forget it all," he said. During his last years in Norway he lived in Nannestad parish, near Oslo and traveled with the Gospel over wide stretches in eastern Norway.*
>
> *In 1869 this fiery soul-winner came over here. The Hauge-Elling people ordained him the next year. He labored among us only eight years—at Norway Lake, near Willmar, Minn. He served six congregations. His preaching was in spirit and power. He also sang the praises of God that touched the hearts. He had after-meetings with those who sought salvation. He won many souls. But his great powers soon wore out. January 1, 1878, the Lord called him home. He was married twice and had six children.*

The Hauge Movement in America also includes this testimony from Pastor Idan Melom then of Montevideo, Minnesota, about the first two pastors from Norway and of the Nannestad congregation: Revs. Rustad and Johannes Halvorson. Halvorson later lived in Sacred Heart and Lac Qui Parle, Minnesota.[16] In the story, Melom, the son of Johannes Halvorson, mentioned the Red Wing Seminary and families from Lake Andrew and Arctander townships: Slattum and Holter.

> *In about 1840 the Haugean revival was still going good in Norway. Laymen filled with the Spirit of God, and with an earnest zeal and longing for the salvation of souls, were making house-to-house visits in the country and in the villages. These laymen were very often hated and slandered by the organized church. They were called unchurchly. They were classed as trouble-makers. The pastor of the Jevnaker parish, Hadeland, northwest of Oslo, for instance, did all he could to oppose this so-called new religion and have it stopped. However, a man named Oppegaard, a well-to-do land-owner, opened up his spacious house for meetings by the despised lay-preachers, in spite of the protests from the minister.*
>
> *A revival broke out. Young and old were saved. Among the new converts was a young man, Johannes H. Slaatland (Brother Melom's father). One year later young Johannes*

---

16 This was not the Rev. Johannes Halvorson who served during the initial years (1886-1889) of the new First Lutheran Church congregation which was the minority group that split from the East Norway Lake Lutheran Church. He married Bertha Glesna in 1889. This was not Johannes Halvorson (wife Christense) from Lake Andrew Township, who owned a farm in Sections 8, 17, and 18.

CH 3: 1870-1879

joined a group of young men who traveled from place to place giving their testimonies of salvation in their simple way. On one of these journeys Johannes visited the parish of Lom in Gudbrandsdalen where he met a man of wonderful courage and spiritual vision, named Lars O. Rustad.

In 1872 these young men met again. They were not so young then. Rustad was 54, Halverson 42. They met in Renville County, Minn., this time. Rustad was to install Halvorson. (The Haugeans had just ordained him.) It certainly was a most happy meeting—to find each other again in such a way.

Rustad was telling his younger co-worker of his mission work in the new land. He had met hindrances similar to those in Norway, but at invitations of Christian friends he had held house-to-house meetings here and there at Franklin, Sacred Heart, Dawson, Willmar and as far north as the present city of Fergus Falls. Rustad lived at Norway Lake, near Willmar.

Rustad told his friend that to organize a church according to the Bible was not an easy matter to be done in a hurry. (The "old constitution," which was then practiced, required that all church members ought to be truly converted, at least earnestly seeking souls.)

Rustad rejoiced in the fact that souls had been saved and a church was in the making. The members were not many, but they were happy in the Lord. Among these new converts were Ole Slattum and wife, K. Hendrickson and wife, the Holter brothers and many others. The Holter brothers were converted through L. O. Rustad and later became leading ministers in the former Hauge Synod. The young men who were trained for the ministry in those days had a living experience of salvation. When the presidents of the Hauge Seminary at Red Wing, H. H. Bergsland, M.G. Hanson and .J. N. Kildahl (Kildahl was president one year, 1885-86), when they examined the young men who wanted to be trained for the ministry, it was not about the high-school diploma they asked; but the main thing was that they really had gone through a genuine conversion from darkness to light, from the power of Satan unto God.

Lars Rustad encountered much opposition in his house-to-house visit-work and stress on a living Christian experience, by the formalistic ministers who went around and organized churches of all kinds of unconverted people, just so they were baptized and confirmed. Under these circumstances brother Halvorson succeeded Rustad at Sacred Heart in 1878.

Intemperance and dancing were the outstanding sins of the day. People would swing on the dance-floor and be dead drunk on Saturday night. Next morning they would go to the Lord's Supper. Pastor Halverson could not tolerate this and denied the openly ungodly the sacrament. This worked two ways. Some saw their sins and came to a true repentance. Others got angry, left the church and were admitted to another Lutheran church, where they were not so particular.

The trials and humiliations of these early lay-pastors were many. They had very small salaries, and often large families. (O. H. Oace writes that Halvorson had only $50 a year in salary.) But they had offerings at each of the three festivals, on which they had to depend to quite an extent. At one Easter people had organized a plan not to respond and go around the altar when the offering was announced. This they got to work so adroitly that even the Christians, and perhaps others who would have taken part in the offering, sat like they were dumb-founded, so no one arose. In his closing words Pastor Halverson said: "I want everyone who belongs to God's people to hear what Jesus says: 'Be not *afraid' and 'Peace be unto you.' Then a young man who had recently been led to Christ through him got the courage to arise and go around the altar to deposit his offering. He was then followed by almost all the rest. 'Blessed are they that are persecuted for righteousness sake.'*

The old laymen's pastors were not so stylish. A woman from Chicago who had moved to Sacred Heart wrote back that the pastor wore a red handkerchief around his neck, but his words carried conviction. After all it was not the robe that made the man.

Having the reputation that he was a real laymen's pastor, Halverson was invited over to the neighborhood of Dawson, Minn., where there was a small group of converted souls. Pastor Utheim, who at that time was vice-president of the former Hauge Synod, encouraged the young converts to gather in the school-houses on Sunday afternoons. The group also invited other speakers and soon a spiritual awakening was in progress.

When Halverson retired from the ministry in 1892, he and his eight children moved over to near Dawson and bought a farm. He kept his home open for the old-fashioned meetings...

During his short stay on the farm, and here on earth after this, Halverson was busy for God. Sometimes going east, sometimes west, always encouraging the young Christians to use their talents. He died in the fall (November 11th) of 1892, aged 62.

(Pastor Halvorson's wife, Marie, nee Iverson, survived. His many children, of whom four became pastors—an unusual record—had the same living experience of salvation as their father. As so many Norwegians have two or three different names, so also Halvorson-Slaatland-Melum. Most of the children have adopted the name "Melom." –Ed.)

Rev. Karl Christofferson Holter (1851-1923) was the congregation's third pastor. Born in Nannestad Parish, Akershus, Norway, Karl immigrated with his siblings and parents, arriving in Quebec, May 1862. Holter was the son of Anne Christophersdatter and Kristoffer Olson Holter. The family soon was in Fillmore County in southeastern Minnesota. Karl's father Kristoffer died in Fillmore County. In 1867 widow Anne and her 10 children (ages from under one year to 20 years old) moved to Arctander Township. The Holter family's journey paralleled those of the Nils Stenseth, and Iver Stene families: Nannestad, Norway to Fillmore County, to Kandiyohi County and the Nannestad Lutheran Church. Their Haugen Lutheran traditions traveled with these families to the county and became the spiritual foundation of the Nannestad Lutheran Church.

Karl attended Augsburg Seminary, became the pastor at Nannestad in 1880, and married Anna Marie Anderson in 1881. They lived in Section 13, across the road from Nannestad Church located in Section 14, and had two daughters: Magdelene and Klara. With most of his siblings taking the name "Holter" from the farm where they lived in Norway, several of Karl's brothers farmed close by. Otto Holter and Martin Holter had farms in Section 14; brother Ole C. Olson, Section 14; Hans Holter, Section 23. Karl's uncle Lars Christopherson (aka Holter) and his family had a homestead in Section 26, having arrived in Arctander Township soon after his sister Anna and her children.

Karl was pastor of the Nannestad congregation from 1880 to 1889. The family then moved to Minneapolis and Karl soon founded the K. C. Holter Publishing Company. By the 1890s all the Holter and Olson siblings had left Arctander Township. Descendants of Lars Christopherson family have lived in Section 26 for several generations. Karl and Anne Holter are buried in Lakewood Cemetery in Minneapolis.

The congregation's fourth pastor was Rev. T. J. Oppedahl. Here is a description of the pastor in the book *The Hauge Movement in America*.

> *Oppedahl...was most brotherly and sympathetic. He could comfort the sorrowing. He knew how to win the confidence of people and reach their hearts, as very few have been able to do.*
>
> *By nature he was straight forward, outspoken and impulsive...His impulses were at times of a rash nature that would carry him on without so much reflection. But his personality had a peculiar magnetism in it. He drew people, that is, Christians and seeking souls and even worldly people. He drew them by love, tenderness and his very outspoken ways and unusual frankness...*
>
> *As to lay-activity, he was always in the front rank, always encouraging and inviting the laymen to be along. He had revivals in his churches at Spicer, Minn., his first charge, and at Sacred Heart where he served so long in two terms, and also at Dawson, Minn.*
>
> *Oppedahl...had gone to school in Chicago and Red Wing, but he was above all a self-made and God-made Bible student. He could perhaps not dig so deep in the Bible, but he could make such peculiarly striking applications to real life. He could take a string of Bible passages and somehow get under them—and apply them and make them fit the every-day conditions of life. He was especially against all sham and hypocrisy. He had a special aptitude to preach against dead faith and for a living experience.*
>
> *By degrees he became one of the most outstanding pastors in the former Hauge Synod. His record as a member on the Union Committee of the former Hauge Synod deserves some special consideration.*

The congregation closed in 1912 and sold the building to the Church of God congregation in Willmar. Many of the immigrants and their descendants of Nannestad Lutheran Church transferred membership to other area Lutheran congregations. In 1917 the Hauge Synod merged with the Norwegian Lutheran Church of America which later merged into the American Lutheran Church (ALC) and then merged into the Evangelical Lutheran Church in America (ELCA).

Lake Florida Swedish Lutheran Church[17]

The four farms bordered between two large settlements of immigrants who arrived in the late 1850s and 1860s. The Norway Lake Settlement, comprised of primarily Norwegian immigrants, was to the north and west in what was then Monongalia County. The primarily Swedish Nest Lake Settlement was about five miles due east. Both of these settlements developed congregations. (Another Swedish settlement, Eagle Lake, was 12 miles to the southeast.) These settlements, located and named for the

---

17 *Niedersaphe to Norway Lake*; *Illustrated History of Kandiyohi County*; *Willmar Daily Tribune*, 1929; *Anniversary Album, 1859-1944, Lebanon Lutheran Church, New London, Minnesota*, p. 7-15. Lake Florida church records.

lakes around which the farm families clustered, were part of several Scandinavian settlements which developed 50-100 miles west of St. Paul. Swedish and Norwegian pastors ministered to these families, rotating their scheduled visits to the new congregations on the prairie. (At times, a Swedish or Norwegian pastor would minister to those of the "opposite" nationality.) Notable pastors in these first years at the settlements included Rev. Bernt J. Muus, Rev. Andrew Jackson, Rev. Lars J. Markhus, Rev. Peter Carlson.[18] These periodic visits (sometimes once a month) were occasions to celebrate, sing, baptize, commune, listen to scripture, and worship together.

More and more immigrants arrived—from Norway and Sweden—and they settled on land newly available from the federal government, obtaining acreage via homesteads, bounty land warrants, or by purchase.

The first Swedish immigrants had arrived in former Monongalia County in 1857 and settled in the Nest Lake and Eagle Lake areas where congregations developed. These areas were several miles east and southeast of where the Lake Andrew Township Swedes would later settle. When Mankell, Brattlund and Norman families arrived seven to ten years later, they could worship with the Norwegians at Norway Lake or the Swedes at Nest Lake, or read from their Bibles and psalm books at home. Prior to 1870 the H. W. and Elizabeth Mankell family was part of the Lutheran congregation of the Norway Lake Settlement, about five miles to the northwest. Two of their children, Hulda (born 1866) and Oscar (born 1868) were baptized into this congregation on December 4, 1868. Daughter Sophia was born in 1871 and the family probably had her baptized in the newly organized Swedish congregation, though there is no extant written record of her baptism.

By 1870, these families decided to establish a church which would be about two miles from their farms and serve other Swedish families closer to Lake Florida in the southeast part of the Township. These families wanted to worship in their familiar Swedish language.

The congregation began in 1870 when several Swedish settlers gathered at the home of J. A. Skoglund on the north side of Lake Florida and formed "The Swedish Evangelical Lutheran Church of Lake Florida". Nils Brattlund served as the first chair of the new congregation. The St. Paul Pacific Railroad Company donated ten acres of land to the church on January 10, 1871, and the church was constructed during the summer of 1873. The original building was 20 feet X 30 feet, with walls 12 feet high. H. W. Mankell and John Lungstrom were the architects of the building, according to local historian Gabriel Stene. Mankell, who was a carpenter and one of the builders of the second church building of the Vasa Lutheran Church, east of Northfield in the early 1860s, was a logical choice. Here are other highlights of Lake Florida Lutheran Church's formative years:

- In early January 1874 the congregation adopted the Lutheran Augustana Constitution and was formally a member of the Swedish Lutheran Augustana Synod.

---

18 Bernt J. Muus went on to found St. Olaf College in Northfield MN; Andrew Jackson was instrumental in founding Gustavus Adolphus College in St. Peter MN.

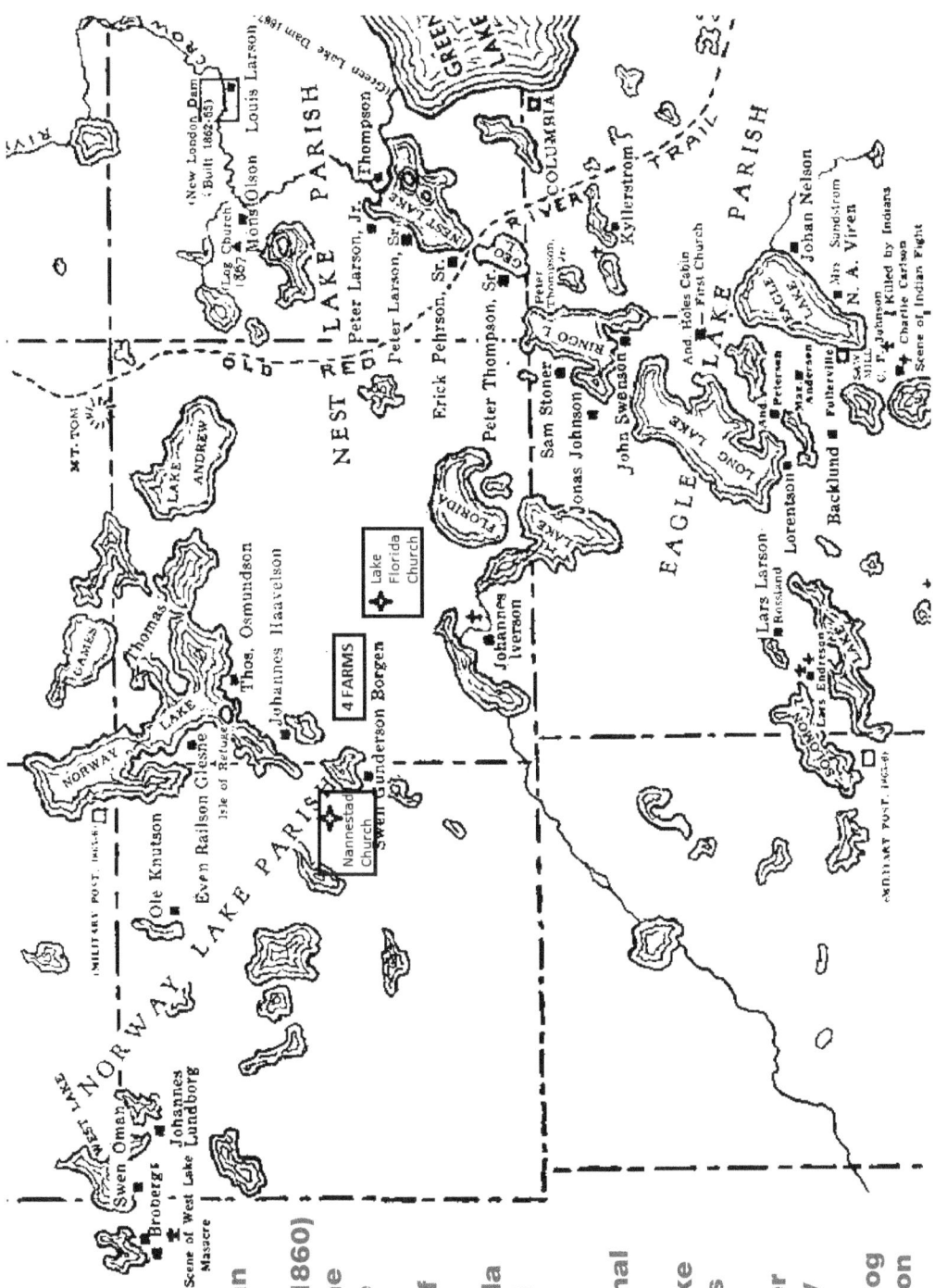

Early Norwegian and Swedish settlements (c1860) located near the four farms. The author added the locations of the four farms and Lake Florida and Nannestad churches, both established in 1870. The original Log Church of the Norway Lake Settlement was near the Ole Knutson marker west of Norway Lake. Today a replica of this log church stands on the site.[19]

---

19 *Anniversary Album, 1859-1944, Lebanon Lutheran Church*, New London, Minnesota, p. 9; *Willmar Tribune* 10 August 1945; *Illustrated History of Kandiyohi County*; Niederasphe to Norway Lake.

- By 1878 a schism occurred within this congregation revolving around the doctrine of redemption (which also affected other congregations in Minnesota). The division over the Waldenstrom doctrines resulted in the resignation of the pastor, Rev. Hedeen, and the church severed connections with the Augustana Synod and the Lutheran church.
- In 1879, the congregation transferred its membership to the Swedish Mission church when Rev. C. M. Youngquist arrived.
- The chimney was added in 1881.
- There were problems with the deed of the railroad's donated acreage, so the congregation ceded its land back to the railroad and then purchased a 3.5 acre tract from the railroad in 1885.

Lake Florida Swedish Lutheran Church, built in 1873.
(*Illustrated History of Kandiyohi County*, p. 278)

Pastors in the early years shared ministerial duties with the Nest Lake (to the east) and Mamreland (to the west) congregations. They worked a circuit for these congregations, ministering about one Sunday a month at each location. One of the more well-known pastors was Rev. Nels Frykman who served the congregations for 17 years (1890-1907). Described as a good preacher, deep thinker, and philosopher, he was also a poet and singer. He composed several Swedish hymns (both words and music); many have been translated into English. One of the most beloved Frykman hymns has been "I Have a Future All Sublime" (1883) which has been sung (one verse in Swedish) at the annual homecoming services and the funerals of many members and former members of this Swedish congregation.

Min framtidsdag är ljus och lång,
den räcker bortom tidens tvång,
där Gud och Lammet säll jag ser
och ingen nöd skall vara mer.

I have a future all sublime,
Beyond the realms of space and time,
Where my Redeemer I shall see,
And sorrow nevermore shall be.

Here is a list of the congregation's pastors—noting years of service, frequency of preaching, and other congregations where they served concurrently:

- Rev. Beckman, 1870 (once a month)
- Rev. P. Unden, 1871-1873 (every third Sunday)
- Rev Lagerstrom, 1873-1874 (every third Sunday)
- Rev. Erick Hedeen, 1874-1878 (every third Sunday)
- Rev. A. Sundberg, 1878
- Rev. C.M. Youngquist, 1879-1882, also served Salem congregation (once a month—with Revs. Grolander, Sundberg and Dahl visiting occasionally)
- Rev. A. G. Peterson and Rev. Sundberg, 1883-1889 (each preached once a month.)

- Rev. Sundberg, 1889
- Rev. Nels Frykman, 1890-1907, also served Salem, Lundby and Frank Lake congregations
- Rev. A.W. Franklin, 1908-1912, also served Salem and Lundby congregations
- Mr. Anton Ostling, 1912-1913, he conducted services but was not ordained.
- Rev. G. Moline, 1913-1916, also served the New London congregation
- Rev. Theo Paulson, 1916-1920, also served New London
- Rev. David Segerstrom, 1920-1923
- Rev. John Anderson, 1923-1932, also served New London, Litchfield and Bethany (south of Litchfield)
- Rev. Chester Dahlberg, 1932-1937, also served New London
- Myrtle Dahlberg, 1937, she preached from the pulpit but was not ordained[20]
- Rev. Theodore J. Paulson, 1937-1955, (second call at the congregation, served twice a month) served the congregation at its closing in 1955.

FORMATION OF LAKE ANDREW TOWNSHIP[21]

Minnesota became a state in 1858 having formerly been a part of the Wisconsin Territory and Iowa Territory (remnants of the Old Northwest Territory and the Louisiana Territory). Monongalia County was created from land previously part of Meeker and Stearns Counties. From 1858-1870, Monongalia County's county seat was New London. In 1870, Monongalia County merged with Kandiyohi County to the south. The new and larger county was known as Kandiyohi County, with Willmar as the county seat.

Two years after the merger, in early March 1872, a group of residents in the southeast area of the large Norway Lake Township petitioned the County government to split off a large part of Norway Lake Township and create a new independent township (121 North, 35 West). The petition was approved, creating "Stockholm Township," reflecting the heritage of many residents who wanted to honor part of their homeland while also creating a new local government entity. But the name "Stockholm" didn't last long, maybe because many Norwegian immigrants had signed the petition with the Swedes. By the end of March 1872, the name was changed to "Lake Andrew Township". (Chapter 1 has more information about other townships formed out of Norway Lake Township)

Fifty-one residents from the township signed the petition, with efforts led by Herman W. (H.W.) Mankell. The four men who settled on the four farms all signed the petition, noted in bold. Here is a partial list of men who signed, notating the Section number of their homestead or farm within 121N 35W and their country of birth (S-Sweden; N-Norway).

---

20 A sister of Rev. Chester Dahlberg, Esther married David Estwick. Esther and David are buried at the Spicer Cemetery.
21 *Centennial History of Kandiyohi County*, pp 28-35, 146, 153, 156, 184, 193, 197. *Illustrated History of Kandiyohi County*, p. 277, 281; Boyd book; plat maps; *Festskrift*

Section 2: Paul P. Nordin (S)
Section 3: Haavald Havoldson (N)
Section 5: Hulver Hulverson (N?)
Section 8: Thomas Osmundson (N)
Section 10: Erick Evenson (N)
Section 12: Erick Hallsten (S), John Nelson (S), John G. Nystrom (S)
Section 14: Mathias Lundberg, Elling A. Storust (N), Tollef Thorson (N)
Section 15: Bjorn Reierson (N)
Section 16: Andrew Halvorson (N), Christian Larson Sjogodt (N)
Section 17: **Johannes Norman** (S), **Nils Stenseth** (N)
Section 18: John Halvorson (N)
Section 19: Lars O. Rustad—Pastor of area Haugean Lutheran congregations (N), Iver G. Stene (N)
Section 20: **Nils Brattlund** (S), **Herman W. Mankell** (S), Christian Burnstad (N), Hendrick Larson (N)
Section 21: Bengt N. Blom (S), Peter E. Warholm (S)
Section 22: John Lungstrom (S), Reier Thorson (N), Thor Thorson (N)
Section 24: Andrew P. Almquist (S), Frank Anderson (S), John Bengtson (S), Fredrick Gustafson (S), Peter Anders Nordstedt (S)
Section 26: Andreas Bengtson, (S)
Section 28: Ole Dahl (S), Peter Erickson (N), Lars Hedin (S), Charles J. Odell (S)
Section 30: Hemming Hakanson (S), Arne Pederson Mostue (N), Peter Peterson Mostue (N), Amund Syverson (N)
Section 31: Simon A. Syverson (N)
Section 32: Peter A. Odell (S)
Section 33: Emil Sjodin (S)
Section 32: Nels Eliason (S)

Many of the men on the above list held official elected positions within the Lake Andrew Township government. They petitioned for the need and stepped forward to answer the need. The list of officials includes men from the four farms.

- **Chairmen**, serving two-year terms: H. W. Mankell, 1874; Nils Brattlund, 1876
- **Supervisors**: Nils Brattlund, 1872
- **Treasurers**: Nils Brattlund, 1874 for two terms
- **Assessors**: H. W. Mankell, 1872 and 1877; Nils Brattlund, 1873
- **Justices**: H. W. Mankell
- **Constables**: H. W. Mankell

During the decades to follow other men from the four farms would also serve as Township officials, including Oscar Mankell, Herman Mankell (son of Oscar), John Syvert Christenson, and Earl Peterson. [22]

---

22 A complete list of early township officials is available in the *Illustrated History of Kandiyohi County*, p, 277.

CH 3: 1870-1879 57

NATURAL DISASTERS:
Blizzards & Grasshoppers

BLIZZARDS

Farm families regularly respond and cope with weather conditions—too much rain, too little rain, summer heat and winter blizzards. In the early 1870s, the families in this book experienced two intense blizzards, with each lasting several days. People died; livestock froze to death; families were isolated for days or weeks. Here are stories of two blizzards—in February 1872 and January 1873.

FEBRUARY 1872

The blizzard which affected much of the Midwest, began in central Minnesota on Monday evening, February 12 and ended Thursday morning, February 15. At the time, newspapers stated that this storm was "unprecedentedly severe". At about 6:00 on Monday evening it began to rain and within an hour rain changed to snow. The rain and wet snow turned to ice several inches thick. Then the winds blew intensely from the north. The storm gained strength in wind, snow, and descending temperatures. The blizzard did not stop for three days. Businesses closed and remained closed. Trains were delayed, got stuck, or stopped. Livestock froze to death. People who were caught in the storm risked their lives. Some were severely injured; some died.

The farmers and their families, including 15-year-old Gabriel Stene, were snow-bound for three weeks. Fifty-four years later Stene wrote the following article explaining how the families dug themselves out of the ordeal to purchase necessary supplies. Working together, men from the Mankell, Norman, and Brattlund families, as well as other snowbound men, dug their way south to Willmar to procure groceries, mail, tobacco, matches, and hay for the horses. The journey from the Stene farm to Willmar was 16 miles. The crew consisted of nine men who had teams of horses, and four additional men who had shovels (three of the four-farm men are mentioned in bold below). Of the twelve identified men, nine were Swedish immigrants, Reese was a Norwegian immigrant, and Stene was the son of Norwegian immigrants.

> *Allow me to tell in part about the worst snow winter I ever experienced back in the early seventies and give names and places in detail. Snow was from 2 to 3 feet on the level and snow drifts from 5 to 7 feet deep. The winters of 1881 and 1887 came closest to it. Wind and snow were two good companions, being on the job night and day. What they could not fill up going one way they completed going back, snow running all the time like a huge stream of water.*

> *No barns in the country those days. Stables, hay stacks, wood piles and at many places even the houses were snowed under. Many had a great time to locate their wells which usually were simply a frame and a lid over it, some pulling out the water by a stick so devised for a pail. Others used a rope with a sinking weight on it. There apparently was more water in the ground at that time then now. From twelve to twenty foot canals had to be dug in snow every day between houses. No country stores then. Did not have either groceries or mail for three weeks. The situation became desperate.*

Those being used to filling in between their chewing apparatus, began to eat their pockets or anything tasting tobacco. Women threatened to strike if attention was not given to the kitchen department. The most serious matter was if matches run out. That would mean freezing to death. Kerosene lamps, not being much in use, were considered as explosive stuff. Home-made tallow candles were all the go. When they ran out, they filled a saucer with lard, made a wick out of rags, soaked it in the lard and lit one end extending over the edge. This gave a light sufficient to avoid collision in the room. Wading in snow and borrowing between neighbors might do for a while but not last. In the long run something had to be done.

I knew Sven Borgen had a pair of fine skis made out of ash. I had previously tried them. Playing mole and pocket gopher in the deepest snow drifts was fine sport. I conceived the idea of borrowing those skis and organizing a road gang to open up the road to Willmar. But that half mile walk to go there and get them was the toughest walk I ever had. The Swensons approved of the idea. I got the skis. Gunder Swenson, otherwise so accommodating and ready at any emergency hesitated to go himself, but rigged out a good man with a good team and necessary outfit sufficient for a trip to the North Pole. Thinking the matter over I did not wonder so much as he had just taken to himself a young wife of 17.

*Next move was to Hedin's at A.H. Gordhamer's place. Albert Hedin said he had a pair of high fliers who hardly would touch the ground enough to make a mark. But he would come out and try. Next I went to Pioneer **H. W. Mankel**. Pointing at Oscar, about 4, and said, "That's my only help. Am alone with chores." But the girls, Jennie, (now Mrs. A. H. Gordhamer,) and sister, Mary, urged upon him to go and said, "Don't worry for chores." So he enlisted. Next move was to **Johannes Norman**'s. He had what we called Ioway flyers, a team purchased by Reir Thorson and who sold them to Peter Odell who again traded them to Norman for his oxen. Norman said, "They are too high lifted and will not follow the ground." I said, Never mind. They will be glad to follow the ground by the time we get to Willmar. So he was on the job. The next move was to **Nels Bratland**'s an oldish man. Did not insist on him going, as he had all the chores to do. But the women folks did not give up. His wife and three daughters—the oldest Caroline, later the well-known, Mrs. C.C. Selvig, Sophia, the next oldest, later Mrs. Sophia L. Rice; Johanna, 15, the youngest, did not give a snap for anything else but the mail, so Mr. Brattland was to come along.*

The next man was Nicolas Blom, living in a little log cabin on the naked hill where now stands the fine home of Oscar Larson. Blom said, "I have no team of any kind, but I have a good shovel, good arms and a good will." I said, That is satisfactory. The next was Peter Warholm, also living in a log cabin on the naked prairie, which now is the finely equipped home of John Nelson. Lars Hedin was up against it. His team was adorned with horns. He could not mix. But would send a good man, which he did, a Mr. Skoglund. Ole E. Reese came there to borrow matches. Mrs. Hedin said, "Our supply is low but we must divide." Ole volunteered to take a shovel and go with us. J. Axel Hedin and Peter A. Odell were also drawn, bringing with them John Bergen, and extra shoveler. This completed the gang that was to meet next morning at the Ole Dahl's home, now the home of Mrs. O. B. Railson [east side of Crook Lake].

The next morning we were on the job, nine men and teams and four extra shovelers. We at times unhitched, drove the team thru and returned for the sleigh. One team could not stand it at the lead very long, so we had to change off. We selected the lake roads and fought through until we got to the summit, half-way between Lake Florida slough and Long Lake when we came to a halt. It was now clear to our minds, that we could not make Willmar and return the same day. Hard enough if we could make one way.

After some discussion the majority wanted to return and give it up as being too hard on horses. I said, it is a shame to be hard on the horses, but a bigger shame to give it up after we got such a good start. I shall insist on proceeding. Peter Odell, J. Axel Hedin and Peter Warholm, said "Same here." Gunder Swenson's hired man refused on the grounds he had no authority to stay away. Albert Hedin's and Norman's teams were all in, completely worthless. Mankell had a lame horse. Bratlund was excused for old age. Before leaving us they chipped in for lodging expenses. Now we were four men and teams and four extra shovelers to proceed. When we got to Erick Bergerson's on Long Lake, We sprung a draft on him. But he only gave us a good laugh and the same situation as Gunder Swenson. He had just taken to himself a young wife in her teens, which he picked up at the cozy home of Pioneer Syvert Olson at Eagle Lake. I said, You will be excused but let us see what your young wife is good for. We have some crumbs of bread in our pockets but they are frozen as hard as rocks. Would like some warm coffee. She was soon at work and asked how many we were. I said, Eight. And she proved herself equal to her job. We did not only get good coffee but a good dinner after which we proceeded across the chain of lakes, reaching Willmar a little before sunset.

Along on Pacific Avenue I was at the lead and got lodged in the slough pit in front of Pacific House, which was easily done as our horses were all in. Senator Rice then approached us swinging his cap and shouted, "Hold on boys, take it easy. You have been doing well, we will do the rest." Shovels were ordered from Costello's hardware on Pacific Avenue and A. N. Lewis, and a good man at the end of each shovel under the supervision of A. E. Rice. We were soon piloted to Dunn's livery barn, where we found plenty of room, but no hay. They said, "There is no hay in town." A. B. Robbins one of the best men who ever walked the streets of Willmar (believe he was station agent at the time) spoke up and said, "There is some hay upstairs in my barn. You are welcome to it." I asked, where is that barn? He said, "It's way out on the outskirts of the town. The very last house to the right going south on 3rd Street. It later became the A.E. Rice property, and was purchased from Robbins. Hay began moving by the armful. A young tailor, Louis Rodlun, was at the head. He had his shop on corner where Lundquist hardware is now. We were treated fine, President Grant with his cabinet could not have been treated any better, free lodging and free meals.

The merchants were glad to see the farmers, and the farmers were glad to see the merchants. It was proven that one could not very well get along without the other. We did the shopping in the evening and in the morning got all the mail for three weeks. Snow had been drifting all night and returning was just as bad as going, if not worse. We met three teams on Foot Lake—Syvert Olson, Nils Grue and Mr. Anderson. This was a lift to us. We reached Erick Bergerson's for another good dinner. Leaving there we met four teams—Ole Johnson, Lars Nelson, Hans A. Halvorson and Andreas Pikhaugen, who were also on the good road job. We reached home a little before sunset where we had grand opening and delivery of groceries and mail. This was one of the old style pioneer trips to Willmar which took us two days and hard labor.

JANUARY 1873

Residents of Minnesota remembered their suffering and isolation during the February 1872 blizzard. Another blizzard occurred about a year later, and again the farm families found themselves battling wind, blinding and disorienting snow, and severely cold temperatures. The storm, which arrived suddenly and with no warning, was described as a hurricane. People sought shelter; cattle froze to death; twelve people died in Kandiyohi County during the January 7-9, 1873, blizzard, though no one died from the group of immigrant families in Lake Andrew Township. [23]

Farmers across the Midwest, Minnesota, and Kandiyohi County and their families took advantage of the warmer temperatures on January 7, not knowing a severe storm was approaching. They brought grain to the mills, cut firewood in nearby forests, helped neighbors thresh grain, visited family or tended to other duties. Nils Stenseth let his cattle out of the stable to enjoy the warm day and then he decided to walk to visit another immigrant family from Nannestad Norway, Lars Christopherson [aka Christofferson] who settled on a homestead in 1869.[24] Stenseth's four and one half mile walk would have taken him west, past the three other farms in this story, the Stene farm and Lake Mary, then southwest, arriving at the Lars Christopherson homestead. Half way along his journey, Stenseth may have met another Norwegian immigrant, Gunder Swenson. Almost 28 years old, Gunder also took advantage of the warm winter's day to help a fellow neighbor, Even Railson with his threshing of grain. Nils and Gunder's paths probably crossed that winter morning near Lake Mary, with Gunder walking north, and Nils walking west.

Gunder joined another Norwegian, Halvor Hande, on their visit to Railson's farm about two miles north. At about 2:00 in the afternoon, when the storm began, Halvor and Gunder initially decided to go home (a frequently traveled, two-mile journey south), but travel this day proved impossible. The two men followed a rail fence to a nearby farm, taking shelter at Gunder's sister and brother-in-law's homestead (Ragnhild and Christopher Engen) in Arctander Township. Gunder's 18-year-old wife, Gemine, waited for the storm to pass at their homestead by Lake Mary with their two-month-old son, Swen, not knowing if her husband was alive or dead. Halvor's family waited for his safe return, too.[25]

Stenseth arrived at the Christopherson homestead while the weather was still warm on January 7. These men probably visited in their native Norwegian language, drank coffee, talked about their families, reflected on their immigration journeys from Nannestad, Norway, to Kandiyohi County, professed their faiths, and promoted the Lutheran churches in which they worshiped. Nils Stenseth was part of the growing Haugean Lutheran tradition, which was new to Kandiyohi County and represented at the Nannestad Lutheran Church, as described earlier in the chapter. While his sister Anne Olson Holter

---

[23] Learn more about the 12 victims and their families in Carolyn Sowinski's book, *Almost Saved But Lost: The January 1873 Blizzard in Kandiyohi County, Minnesota*.

[24] Aka Lars Kristofferson Holter, Christofferson, and later Christopherson—this author's great great grandfather. Learn more about Lars, his sister Anne, and their families in *Niederasphe to Norway Lake: Mankell Family, Minnesota and Immigration*, or mankell. org, written by this author.

[25] Gunder and Gemine Swenson were also this author's great-great-grandparents. Decades later their son Swen Swenson was the blacksmith in Jericho, with customers from across the area. Stene, "The Storm of 57 Years Ago." *Willmar Tribune*, January 13, 1926. Stene's recollections are partially incorrect. Gunder's experiences were in the January 1873 blizzard. The rest of the article relates to the February 1872 blizzard.

was part of the Haugean tradition like Stenseth, Lars Christopherson and his family were part of the Norwegian Lutheran Church of the Norway Lake Settlement, where he was the religious education teacher. This Norway Lake congregation of the Norwegian Synod followed a tradition more closely connected to the Lutheran Church of Norway.[26]

Stenseth's day with Lars and his family turned into three days when people from across the township and county took shelter from the storm. Here is the rest of the story, described by Kandiyohi County writer and local historian Gabriel Stene who was a neighbor and friend of these families. In 1926, Gabriel Stene wrote his recollection of what happened to the Stenseth and Brattlund families during those long three days during the blizzard of January, 1873.[27]

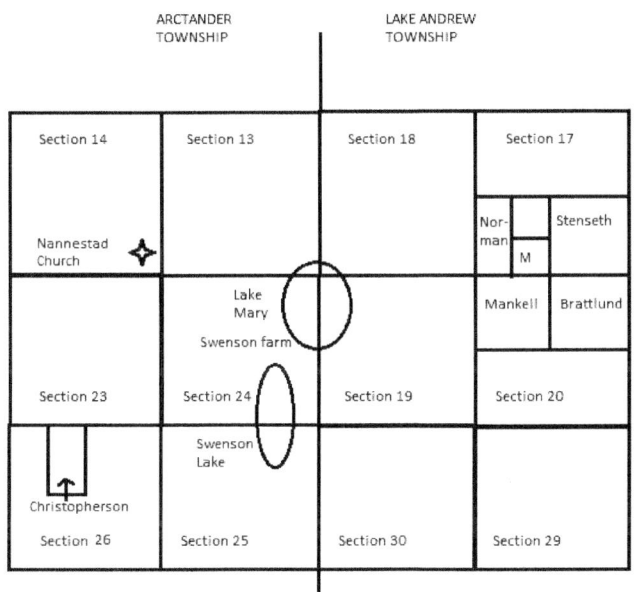

Nils Stenseth's journey in 1873, from his farm in Lake Andrew Township to the Christopherson farm in Arctander Township where he stayed for the duration of the blizzard. His exact route is not known.

Nels N. Stenseth, the pioneer settler of SE ¼, Sec. 17, known now as J.S. Christenson's corner, lived then in a log cabin. Turned out two oxen and three cows. Then leaving for a walk to Lars Christofferson's in Arctander, where he stayed three days and three nights, worrying for his home. A few days after the storm I went over there where we exchanged experiences (myself also in the storm.) Wife and five children were at home. She told me how she left the two smallest in the house. Taking the three oldest girls along to try with great difficulty to get cattle in. They did not receive any further attention or care till storm was over. How they all four hung together and finding the house was a mere luck. How they built fire. How the stove pipes turned red from hot blaze. How she threw salt in to the stove, closing up all drafts, which quenched the blaze. After that scare they did not dare to keep fire going as there was no damper in the stove pipe, and suffered greatly. To make fire they would run chances of burning to death. With no fire they took chances of freezing to death, to say nothing about hunger. They had pork and meat in an outdoor shed and could not venture getting it, and if they did they did not dare to keep fire up to prepare it. Then they were worrying for husband and father. They stayed mostly in bed.

She told me with tears running down her cheeks how Mr. and Mrs. Nels Brattlund, living just across the road, came to their aid early the fourth morning. They knew of their distress, that father was away but had not been able to aid them till then. They took them over to their

---

26 *Illustrated History of Kandiyohi County*, p. 119
27 *Willmar Tribune*, September 1, 1926.

home into a warm room and gave them a good breakfast. Nothing like good neighbors. Mr. and Mrs. Nels Brattlund, the good Samaritans, were the parents of Mrs. Sophia L. Rice and Mrs. C.C. Selvig, grandparents of Mayor Selvig of Willmar and Col. Cushman Rice.

Nils Stenseth took shelter at the Christopherson farm, four miles west. But did his wife, Karen, know that he was safe? Did she wonder if he was trying to find his way home in the storm because of his concern for his family's safety? The Swenson, Hande, and Stenseth men were separated from their families for the duration of the three-day storm. After the storm the men found their way home and families reunited. Other families were not as lucky.

Three miles west of the Lars Christopherson homestead, five people were trapped outside in the blizzard for the duration of the three-day storm. Three people survived and two people died. These Soland and Truelson families were returning home from the Village of Kerkhoven in Swift County to their neighboring homes in Norway Lake Township. These families were part of the Norway Lake Settlement. Surely Lars Christopherson knew them. He was the religious teacher—of both the congregation and the children. One of the victims was a 13-year-old boy, Helge Stengrimson who was a friend of Gabriel Stene.[28]

THE GRASSHOPPERS[29]

Three years after the deadly 1873 blizzard, the families of the four farms, along with families across the county, faced another series of crises: grasshoppers in 1876 and 1877. While the insects had been elsewhere in Minnesota since 1873, destroying wheat, oats, corn, and barley fields, Kandiyohi County suffered a few years later. Families faced extreme financial difficulties when they lost their grain and thus a food source and seed grain. Following these agricultural crises in Minnesota, with Kandiyohi County one of the most severely affected counties, people sought financial relief from the State of Minnesota and from private donations. (For a more detailed look at how Kandiyohi County was affected during 1875-1878 grasshopper plague, read *The Illustrated History of Kandiyohi County*, published in 1905, pages 50-56, or *The Centennial History of Kandiyohi County*, published in 1970, pages 42-48.)

The Swarms

The Rocky Mountain locusts, a form of grasshopper, were prominent in the western half of the U.S., in the mountains and the prairies, in the 1800s. As farming, with new fields of grain, expanded westward, so did the grasshoppers' territory. One description of a large swarm in 1875 described the Albert's Swarm as consisting of more than 12 trillion insects, weighing 27 tons, and covering 198,000 square miles, an area larger than the size of California. These insects ate crops but they have also been described as eating wool, wood, leather and even clothing. A swarm could last for years because of the eggs laid in the fields, which would mature the following spring, thus repeating the cycle.

---

28 Read more about the deaths of Margaret Soland and Helge Stengrimson, their family members who survived, and their journey on that fateful January day, in the book *Almost Saved, But Lost: The January 1873 Blizzard in Kandiyohi County, Minnesota*, written by this author, pages 49-61.
29 en.wikipedia.org/wiki/Rocky_Mountain_locust; Governor John S Pillsbury Papers (folders #372, 373, 386, 388, 394, 398).

CH 3: 1870-1879   63

Grasshoppers arrived in southwestern Minnesota in 1873 and started to spread east and north. By 1875 Kandiyohi County's farmers experienced high crop yield, but they were only one year away from having their turn to face hardship, crop loss and, sometimes, financial destitution. They knew that the grasshoppers were coming. The eggs laid in 1875 hatched in the spring/early summer of 1876 and started feasting on crops in other counties, and Kandiyohi. Damage occurred in 1876 and more intense destruction followed in 1877, when the insects traveled east and south. The farmers highlighted in this book did not escape this devastation to their crops and to their livelihood, and neither did their neighbors.

Farmers, businessmen, families and settlers tried to destroy these insects in a variety of ways: fire, coal tar, brooms and shovels, deep plowing, deep ditches, traps, poison, gunpowder and newly developed machines which would act like a vacuum cleaner—sucking up the insects—and even yelling. But the swarms were too large for these remedies to be effective. Farmers and states also focused time and energy by destroying insects at hatching time; all proved to be futile endeavors.

Minnesota locusts (grasshoppers) c1870s.
Photograph originally from Jacoby's Art Gallery.
(image courtesy of mnopedia.com/event/grasshopper-plagues-1873-1877. Shared by the Minnesota Historical Society and licensed by Creative Commons CC BY-SA 3.0)

'The Grasshoppers Are Coming'
Pastor Joel Njus wrote a detailed description of the grasshoppers' arrival, the destruction, the destitute farmers, the response, and the recovery. His essay is part of the book celebrating the history of First Lutheran Church of Norway Lake, whose early members lived through these events.[30]

> *It began in the year 1876, the year the nation was celebrating its first centennial. For the farmers at Norway Lake the spring and early summer were dry and the wheat fields suffered. Then on July 4th, they saw a cloud in the west. Could it be that rain was on the way? The cloud turned out to be swarms of grasshoppers. They were so thick they darkened the sky and covered the ground. The grasshoppers did most of the harvesting that year. The farmers managed to save enough for seed for the following year. The destruction was not complete but it was serious.*
>
> *The year 1877 was worse. The grasshoppers were present in the spring and devoured every green sprout as soon as it was out of the ground. Farmers used every means imaginable to destroy them, but without success. The grasshoppers were so numerous that some claim that one could not put a finger to the ground without hitting a grasshopper. The destruction of the crops was complete. The Skaalruds [Skaalerud] lived on the Andreas Railson farm at that time. Martin Skaalrud says that they got their water from the lake and when the wind was from the northwest, there was a bank of dead grasshoppers over a foot high along the shore. Sometime in the latter part of June, the grasshoppers*

---
[30] *Keeping the Faith....Sharing the Faith* pp 23-24

left. On a clear bright day with a northwest wind blowing, a roar filled the air and cloud of grasshoppers arose, dense enough to dim the sun as they took their flight presumably to the east. Sailors on the Great Lakes reported seeing vast numbers of insects floating in the water there and immigrants coming to the U.S. in the fall of 1877 claimed they saw great numbers of dead grasshoppers floating in the Atlantic Ocean.

1877 was a difficult year. In the Centennial History of Kandiyohi County *we find this poignant letter, dated July 8, 1877, from Uncle Gabriel of Irving [Township] that no doubt expressed the situation many others were facing.*

> "No money, no meat, no flour, no credit, no—not even potatoes. What is to be done for the poor? Where are the Good Samaritans? Autumn's blasts and famishing storms of winter will quickly come. Shall steps be taken to provide for the physical salvation of the poor and needy? We submit this question to a Christian people."

Help was on the way. At a meeting in September, 1877, a committee of five from Kandiyohi County was appointed to meet with Governor Pillsbury about obtaining seed grain from the government. Pastor L. J. Markhus [Pastor of East Norway Lake Lutheran] was a member of that committee representing the Norway Lake area. That such help was needed was recognized in an article appearing in the St. Paul Globe *that said,*

> "Of all the afflicted territory…which needs assistance in the line of food, clothing and seed wheat, none can take precedence over Kandiyohi and Swift counties. Their all has been taken for two years and suffering and destitution exists."

Congregations of the Norwegian Synod that had escaped the grasshopper plague responded with donations to help those in need. In the latter part of February, 1878, L. O. Thorpe [Lars Thorpe, Postmaster of Dovre Township] on behalf of the committee composed of himself, Rev. L. J. Markhus, and Rev. O. Estrem [Lutheran pastor in Atwater] went to the Twin Cities to buy cornmeal, potatoes and other food items for the grasshopper victims. An amount of $5,781.50 had been given them for this purpose. The food supplies, seed potatoes, and clothing gathered by this committee were distributed at the old Nordin Building in Willmar.

But it was not always easy for those who needed help to accept it. One farmer when told that he could receive some flour and meal from the county, said that it was very humiliating to ask for bread from the county. The answer given him went as follows, "You can ask for it without a blush, as you are not to blame for what happened."

In February of 1878 the legislature authorized to make available $30,000 or as much as was needed, to assure loan funds for farmers to purchase seed grain. The number of applications for such loans numbered 118 from Norway Lake Township and 46 from Lake Andrew Township. This shows how great the destruction of the crops had been. The only record that we find in the minutes of the congregation that refer directly to the grasshopper plague and its economic effect upon the congregation, is this item in the March, 1877, meeting of the congregation.

> "It was decided that the new hymn book should be purchased and put into use on December 25 as the hymn book of the congregation provided that God to some extent spares us from destruction by the grasshoppers."

CH 3: 1870-1879

The blizzard of 1873 lasted three days[31]. The grasshopper invasion and its effects lasted for three years. The grasshopper times constituted without a doubt the most discouraging period both for the farmers and the businessmen in the county's history.

1878 was a good year as far as crops were concerned and conditions soon returned to normal. But the memory of the grasshopper invasion remained for many years and even to this day as a reminder that farming is a risky business.

Gabriel Stene, who lived on the east side of Lake Mary and a half mile west of the Mankell homestead, wrote about his experiences when caught outside in 1876 as the grasshoppers descended upon him and his horses. At the end of his story, he writes about a boy, John Syvert Thori, who was adopted by Hans Christenson. John Syvert becomes a part of the four farms story when he becomes an adult.[32]

That afternoon was clear with bright sunshine, a day in June. Getting within four miles of my destination, I was puzzled. It all of a sudden looked to me like an eclipse of the sun. Soon grasshoppers began descending like thick snowflakes in a snowstorm. They were some full grown beasts, heavy and sharp as iron when they hit the face. Then they dug their feet in for a jump. I have been out in different kinds of storms, but that was the worst storm I ever experienced. Horses would not go against it. I had to turn with the wind. I had a good supply of handkerchiefs with me. I put one over the eyes of each horse and one over my own face, and then proceeded. The horses crushed grasshoppers at every step, and buggy wheel tires were smeared with crushed hoppers...

At Norway Lake, as at everywhere else, if harnesses were left outside they would eat them. If a coat, vest or a sack was left outside, they would eat the surface so completely you could pick it apart with your fingers. They soon had completed the harvest even to the grass. They laid a good supply of eggs. Then they all disappeared, flew away. In the following spring of 1877 the farmers in hope and good faith again put in their crops as usual. But the fields from spring on resembled an ant pile. The eggs were hatched and those greedy eaters, at first the length of an eighth of an inch, kept the fields black and bare so that at harvest time the fields were just as black as the spring work. No harvesting, no threshing. Difficult even to get hay. But that year the whole regiment as soon as they got wings, disappeared and flew off just like scaring a flock of black birds. No eggs were laid that year so we got rid of them for the future. Never bothered since. The third year, 1878, farmers had to get state aid to procure seed....

Like the old saying, when troubles come they don't always come singly, but sometimes double up. Paul Thori deeded his Granite falls farm to Even Railson [Lake Andrew Township] and mortgaged the [Thomas] Osmundson farm [south side of Norway Lake] for the balance. Thru these struggling years he lost both farms and not only that, but also his wife. I was one of the pall bearers and remember she left behind a 2 year-old boy by the name of John Syvert, who was adopted by a childless couple, Mr. and Mrs. Hans Christianson [Christenson].

---

31 Learn more about the blizzard: Sowinski, *Almost Saved, But Lost: The January 1873 Blizzard in Kandiyohi County, Minnesota*.
32 *Willmar Daily Tribune*, 5 May 1926.

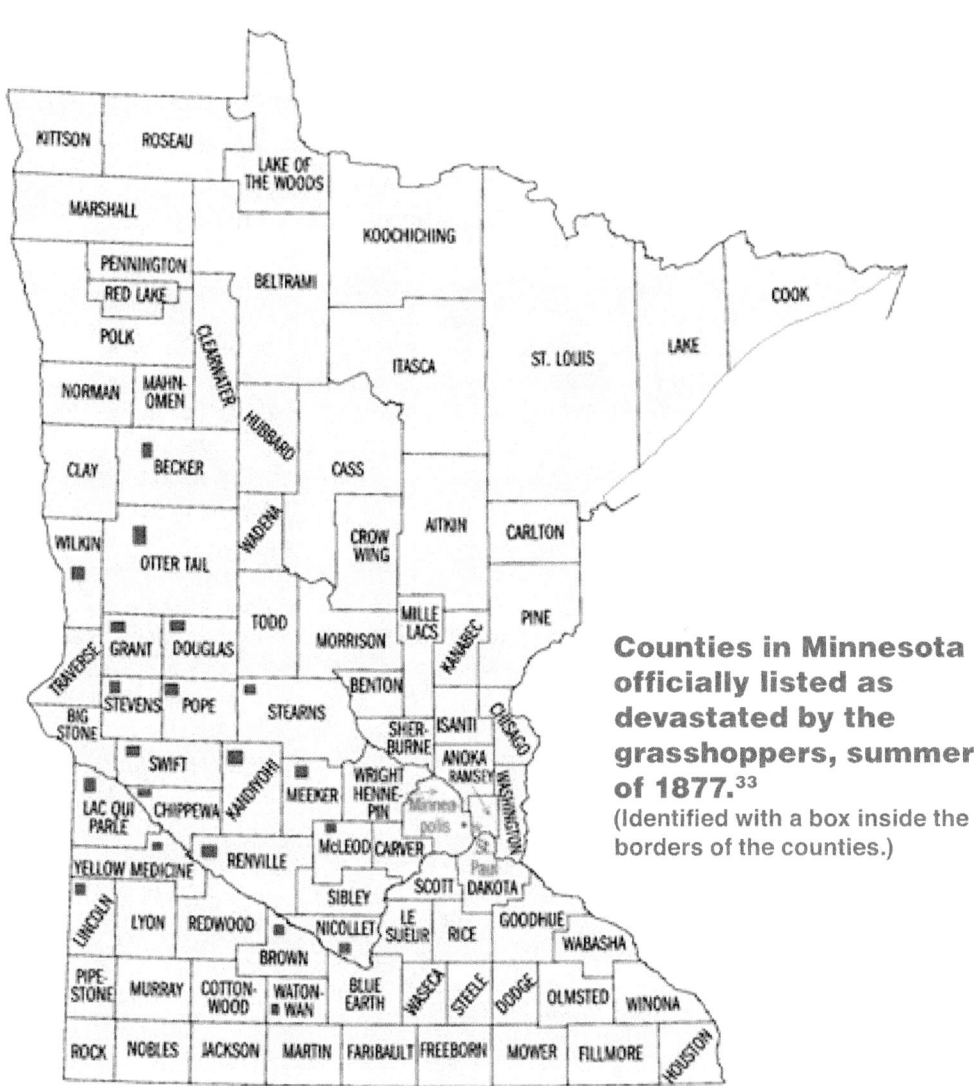

Counties in Minnesota officially listed as devastated by the grasshoppers, summer of 1877.[33]
(Identified with a box inside the borders of the counties.)

---

33 *St. Paul Daily Globe* 19 August 1878

Crop Losses[34]

In August, 1878, the *St. Paul Daily Globe* published crop statistics, noting the corn and wheat yields by county, for the 1877 growing season. Polk County in northwestern Minnesota, not affected by the infestation, had the highest yield for wheat with an average of 25.29 bushels per acre. (A typical yield for farmers in years of good harvest was about 14 bushels per acre for wheat; 25 bushels per acre for corn). Kandiyohi had the lowest in the state, at 1.12 bushels of wheat per acre—not enough grain for seed the following spring. Here is list of counties bordering Kandiyohi, noting 1877 crop yields, with bushels per acre, compared to Polk County's highest yields:

	WHEAT	CORN
Kandiyohi	1.12	3.16
Chippewa	3.01	5.05
Meeker	6.77	13.61
Pope	3.78	7.10
Renville	*no information provided*	
Stearns	2.95	8.71
Swift	5.86	9.45
Polk	25.29	25.53

'What Shall We Do?'[35]

Many farmers, who set aside their pride and independence due to their difficult economic circumstances, sought help. The primary mechanism for receiving help was the system of area Relief Committees comprised of men who were leaders in their area of the county. The Relief Committees raised and received private and church donations, paid for provisions from local mills, and then paid for the food and grain shipped by rail to the closest railroad stations, primarily in Atwater, Kandiyohi, Willmar and St John's (aka Pennock), and distributed food and grain to destitute families. Notices were in newspapers, informing readers of the need for donations. Individuals, churches and businesses made donations. Church members and congregations in the Norwegian Lutheran Synod provided a donation of more than $5,000.00. The Norway Lake area in the northwest part of the county had a committee, comprised of two ministers and a postmaster, as described in Pastor Njus' essay.

Response from the Governor's office[36]

The Governor's office provided relief efforts, in various forms, during the 1873-1877 devastations. With the leadership of Governors Horace Austin (served 1870-1874) and Cushman Davis (1874-1876), the State of Minnesota provided direct financial aid to the farmers. Dollar amounts to each applicant with crop losses were about $21.00. (About $500.00 in 2019, adjusted for inflation.) The State also encouraged charitable giving from the private sector, with those funds disbursed to the families. Direct aid ceased with the next Governor. Under the leadership of Governor John Pillsbury (1876-1882) the direct financial relief, due to destroyed crops, ended with an expectation that the farmers should rely on themselves

---

34 *St. Paul Daily Globe*, 19 Aug 1878, p. 5. USDA "Crop Production Historical Track Records", April 2016, p. 28, 206
35 *Keeping the Faith…Sharing the Faith*; *Illustrated History of Kandiyohi County*.
36 "Grasshopper Plagues, 1873-1877" in mnopedia.org; Governor Pillsbury collection. *Illustrated History of Kandiyohi County*.

and each other. The State's response focused on how to eradicate the grasshoppers on the local level and securing government funding so that farmers could apply for and pay for seed grain for planting.

One Farmer's Plea[37]

C. W. Hudson lived in Roseville Township, in the northeastern corner of the county. While not connected to the families in the four farms, his plea for help provides a glimpse as to what financial difficulties many farm families faced in the aftermath of the summer 1876 devastation and the financial help they sought. He wrote his letter, dated January 16, 1877, to Governor John S. Pillsbury.

> *Dear Sir,*
> *Seeing in the paper that you were helping those whom the grasshoppers have destroyed their crops, I thought I would write to you to see if you could help me. I am the man that clerked for Mr. Butler, the blacksmith, the man you gave the turkey to at Christmas. Hudson is my name. I left the Butlers employ last year and sought me a farm in Roseville, Kandiyohi County and moved on to with my family, and went in debt considerably, and I put in 50 acres thinking I should have a good crop but the grasshoppers came and destroyed them. We can live till another harvest, but it is <u>poor living</u>. I do not mind that if I could only get some wheat for seed for this year I have 40 acres ploughed ready for crop, but no seed to put in and I cannot get any without money. I have tried a good many, but they are afraid of the hoppers another year. I know there are a great many who need seed and provisions perhaps worse off than I am, but I have not a cent to my name and cannot get any. I did not raise any of this to speak of not enough to keep us till next harvest. We are living mostly on potatoes now and no groceries at all. There are nine of us in family and I tell you it goes hard. Now Gov. Pillsbury if you can send or help me ever so little it will help me ever so much. Our nearest [railroad] station is Atwater and would you please answer this and let me know if you can help me. I can get along if I could only get some seed wheat—if only a few acres. I would come to Minneapolis and see you but I have not the means to come. If I should come down to Minneapolis do you think you could do any of this for me amongst the mills if you cannot help me otherwise. I should like to hear from you if you would please answer this and greatly oblige.*
> *Your Respectfully*
> *CW Hudson*

Charles William Hudson, an immigrant from England, served in the Civil War with Company A of the 3rd Minnesota Infantry (1861-1865). He and his wife Nancy, and their family had lived in Minneapolis for many years, having moved from Massachusetts to Minnesota in about 1855. They arrived in Roseville Township in 1876, and farmed 80 acres—the southern half of the SW ¼ of Section 20. The family continued to live in the township until their deaths and are buried at Roseville Cemetery near Hawick, Minnesota. Did Hudson receive help from the governor? There is no record found.

---

37 Governor Pillsbury collection, Minnesota Historical Society, file 373; ancestry.com; National Archives, Record Group 15, Civil War Pension files; *Illustrated History of Kandiyohi County*.

Farmers in Lake Andrew Township[38]

In 1877, farm families found their food supplies diminishing, with sometimes only potatoes left to eat. By December 1877, relief goods were distributed to the chairs of the local relief committees. Farmers in Kandiyohi County, including several connected to the four farms, received goods and/or seed in late 1877 and in the spring of 1878—after the second round of adult grasshoppers had left. Herman W. Mankell received five sacks of cornmeal and one sack of bran (total value of $6.75). Nils Brattlund received oats. Two men, whose sons are a later part of the four farms story, also received food. Hans Christenson (Section 16), the adopted father of John Syvert Christenson, received unbolted cornmeal. Bjorn Reierson (Section 15), father of Martin Reierson, received corn, peas, and bolted cornmeal. Mankell's neighbor to the south, Ole Slattum, received unbolted meal; Gunder Swenson, neighbor to the southwest—oats and corn. Farmers in Kandiyohi County received a variety of food products and seed grain via the private and state programs. Food included bran, cornmeal (bolted and unbolted), pearl barley, rye flour, peas, beans, wheat shorts, and middling (the latter two were both protein by-products of wheat milling). Grain was primarily wheat and oats, with some corn.

1878 Applications by Township, Kandiyohi County[39]

The State of Minnesota passed a law allowing farmers to apply for seed grain via loans, approved on February 13, 1878. By early 1878, about 5,000 farmers appeared before local relief committees and applied for a total of 158,085 bushels. Kandiyohi and neighboring counties Stearns and Meeker were considered to have suffered the most, applying for 30,000, 15,000, and 12,000 bushels, respectively.

The sworn application:

> *County of , (name) , being duly sworn, says that he is a resident of the town of _____ in said county, that this application is made for the purpose of procuring a loan of bushels of wheat and bushels of oats, from the State, for seed grain, under the provisions of "An act to furnish and distribute seed grain to sufferers from grasshopper ravages." Approved February 13th A.D. 1878; that this applicant has plowed and will have plowed in time for seeding acres of land, which said land is described as follows, to wit . That he has not, and is unable to procure the necessary seed grain, or use the same for any other purpose, under the pains and penalties as provided in said act; that the crop in the year 1877 was destroyed by grasshoppers, or if only partially destroyed, that he raised bushels of and bushels of , if there was a deposit of grasshopper eggs, that he was deterred from sowing his ground in the year 1877, by reason thereof. That he is the owner of the following real and personal property, to wit and which are mortgaged as follows: On real property, $___; personal property, $___. Subscribed and sworn to before me this day of February A.D. 1878.*

---

38 Governor John S. Pillsbury Collection, files 386, 388, 394, 398. Gunder Swenson was the father of Minnie who married HW's son Oscar. Unbolted cornmeal is coarser than bolted cornmeal which is more finely ground.
39 Governor John S. Pillsbury Collection, file 398. *St. Paul Daily Globe*, 21 February 1878, 23 February 1878;

Each farmer made a second sworn statement regarding the terms and payment of the loan agreement:

> I hereby promise to pay to the said State the sum of dollars, the cost of said seed grain and agree that said sum shall be taxable against my real and personal property, the same to be levied by the County Auditor of said county, and the said tax to be collected by virtue of the laws of this State; and I hereby further agree that said sum so levied shall be a first lien upon my crop of grain, raised each year, until said tax is paid.

Here is a list of applications and seed grain received, divided by township. No information was provided for Arctander, East Lake Lillian, Holland, and Roseville townships.[40]

Township	Applications	Total Acres	Bushels Wheat	Bushels Oats
Burbank	43	1,608	1,482	330
Colfax	60	1,562	1,752	278
Dovre	72	3,041	3,341	874
Edwards	7	237	211	141
Fahlun	14	600	545	102
Gennessee	81	4,345	4,201	884
Green Lake	51	2,444	3,065	531
Harrison	56	3,690	3,332	895
Irving	45	1,587	1,687	481
Kandiyohi	71	3,426	3,604	918
Lake Andrew	**46**	**1,798**	**1,915**	**470**
Lake Elizabeth	23	1,460	888	192
Lake Lillian	1	25	40	—
Mamre	75	3,462	4,527	694
New London	25	979	1,068	262
Norway Lake	118	5,060	5,542	1,255
Roseland	23	1,357	1,505	516
St. John's	11	374	473	64
Whitefield	46	2,114	1,908	197
Willmar	47	2,171	2,224	605
TOTALS	**915**	**41,340**	**43,310**	**9,689**

The farm families in this story survived the natural disasters which befell the county and much of the state, but the next decade brought transitions at each of the farms. One man quit farming and moved; the other three farmers died. Did the physical struggles and emotional hardships of the 1870s affect their physical health and bring forth their deaths? Were they broken men?

---

40 Twenty-four additional applications were not included in these official records of the Governor's office. Those applicants either did not make sworn statements or used modified forms. However, the applications were accepted under certain conditions. It is possible that some of these applications were from the four townships not included in the chart.

CHAPTER 4:
1880-1889

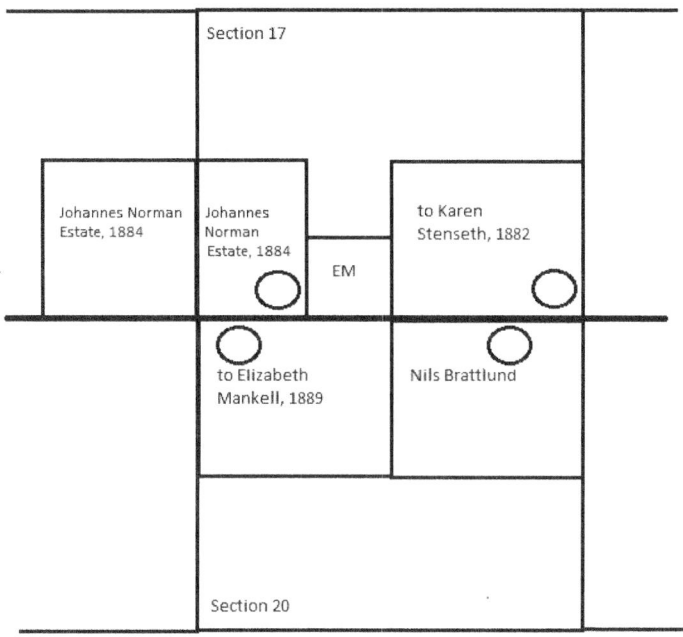

HIGHLIGHTS

- Farm Transitions: three of the immigrant men who settled the farms died with widows and their adult children assuming farm responsibility; the fourth family moved to Willmar
- The final homestead "on the mile" was approved
- Farm laborers worked and lived at three of the farms
- Business: a mutual insurance company was formed
- Baseball became a community activity

STENSETH HOMESTEAD[1]

Twice in early 1881 (January 20 and March 4) and six years after his initial application, Nils Stenseth returned to the St. Cloud Land Office, with his witnesses, to submit the final paperwork required to complete the homestead and complete the Final Affidavits to receive the deed to his 160 acre homestead in Section 17.

Stenseth's neighbors, Johannes Norman and Nils Brattlund, were his witnesses. They swore testimony on behalf of Stenseth, as H. W. Mankell had done in 1875 for his initial application. In addition, Hans Christenson (Nils' neighbor to the east and daughter Carrie's future father-in-law) was a witness.

Stenseth and his witnesses stated that Nils had accomplished the following:
- Established residency upon the land on December 1, 1870
- Resided on the land continuously to the time of their statements
- Built stables and a granary
- Broke farm land and cultivated 55 acres of wheat, oats, corn, and potatoes
- Partially fenced several acres
- Placed a value of the improvements at $500.00
- Completed his house in December, 1870
- Obtained a certificate of naturalization

He became a United States citizen on October 12, 1880. By derivation, his wife Karen also became a citizen. After Stenseth paid the final fee of $4.00, his land patent was issued on April 20, 1882, with the patent signed by President Chester A. Arthur.

Stenseth Family Death

Sadly, Nils never saw the paperwork from the President. On February 10, 1882, Nils Stenseth died—two months prior to receiving this most important deed and recognition of his ownership of his 160-acre homestead. Following Nils' death, widow Karen and his children kept the farm and saw his dream of owning 160 acres come true. Nils was buried at the Nannestad church cemetery about three miles west of his farm. Over the years other family members would also be buried at this small cemetery in Arctander Township.

There is no record of hired help living at the Stenseth farm after Nils' 1882 death. Widow Karen relied on their son Nicholas (aka Nicolai, 1864-1902) to take over the farm duties for several years, until about 1895.

---

[1] National Archives, Record Group 49: Bureau of Land Management, Certificate 4855. *Illustrated History of Kandiyohi County*, p. 282

CH 4: 1880-1889

BRATTLUND HOMESTEAD[2]

The Brattlund farm had at least two men who worked for them and stayed at the farm in the 1880s. Swedish immigrant Wilhelm Larson (aka William/Willie 1857-1911) worked at the farm in 1880, having left Skaraborg Sweden in May 1879 and traveled alone to the United States. His parents Lars Johan and Katherine Larson would soon follow their son to Lake Andrew Township. William became a part of this story with his 1890 marriage to Johanna Norman.

"A. Venstrom," another farm worker, was born in Sweden in about 1861. He lived and worked at the Nils Brattlund farm in 1885.

In 1886, Nils and Marie Brattlund left their homestead and moved to Willmar, changing church membership from the Lake Florida Mission Church, Lake Andrew Township, to the First Covenant Church in the city. Within one year, Nils was the chair of his family's new congregation and served in this leadership role for nine years. Nils and Maria lived on 4th Street until their deaths. However, the Brattlunds maintained their connection to Lake Andrew Township with ownership of a lot, Section 34, on the south shore of Lake Florida.

Caroline Brattlund & Christian C. Selvig

The families of the four farms celebrated the marriage of Caroline Brattlund and Christian C. Selvig on November 3, 1882. Christian, his siblings, and his parents, Bernt (1823-1891) and Hanna (Christenson) Selvig (1828-1908), were from the Selvik farm, Hurum Parish, Buskerud, Norway[3]. This Selvig family left Hurum in April 1868, and arrived in Quebec, Canada. Soon they were in Kandiyohi County and claimed a small homestead in Fahlun Township (118N 34W, Section 18, W ½ of SW ¼). By 1880, the family lived in Section 21 (NW ¼) of Lake Andrew Township, having purchased the 160 acre farm from A. E. Rice. Their neighbors to the west were the Brattlund family. Bernt and Hanna Selvig sold their farm in 1889 to William Larson and moved to Tacoma, Washington. Bernt and Hanna had 12 children (most are buried in Tacoma, Washington):

1. **Ole** (1851-1907) married Mary Johnson
2. **Karen Marie** (1853-1933)
3. **Haldor** (#1; 1854-1860)
4. **Ragnhild** (1856-1941) married Niels Iverson
5. **Christian** (1861-1922) married Caroline Brattlund
6. **Caroline** (1863-1949) married Ole Tofte
7. **Bernardine** (1864-1967) married James Garness
8. **Haldor** (#2; 1866-1940)

---

2 Findagrave.com; ancestry.com; NARA RG 49; Norway Church Records; *Illustrated History of Kandiyohi County*; *West Central Tribune* 15 December 2015; Willmar City Directories, 1927, 1932. Pittsburgh City Directories, 1912, 1948. Kandiyohi County Recorder.

3 The family took the surname which honored their Selvik farm in Norway, with a slight variation in spelling.

9. **Harold** (#1; 1867-1868)
10. **Mina** (1869-1960) married Theodore Johnson
11. **Harold** (#2; 1871-1953)
12. **Einar** (1875-1939)

For the first two years after their marriage Caroline (1851-1919) and C.C. (1861-1922) rented the Mankell homestead, only ½ mile west of her parents and one mile west of his parents. In the early 1880s, the Mankell family lived in Willmar, so their house was available to the neighbors. (The farmland was rented to another person.) The Selvig family then moved to Willmar where C.C. was a merchant and had a hardware store. For many years he was the chief of the Willmar Fire Department. The family lived at 714 Seventh Street, close to the future locations of Rice Park, Rice Hospital and Selvig Park, established later by the Rice family and their son Edwin Selvig who was Willmar's mayor, 1926-1931. Edwin and another son Albin (wife Juliet and children) continued to live in their parents' home after the elders' deaths. C.C. and Caroline Selvig are buried at Fairview Cemetery in Willmar.

Children of Caroline and C.C. Selvig:
1. **Edwin** (1883-1972) Vice-President of the Bank of Willmar and mayor of Willmar, 1926-1931.
2. **Walter A.** (1886-1972) married Mary Kean. They lived in Pittsburgh, Pennsylvania, for more than 60 years. He was a chemist with the U.S. Bureau of Mines.
3. **Victor H.** (1888-1938) married Minnie Hedin. The family lived in Mankato, Minnesota, in the 1920s and 1930s, where he was an inspector for the Hubbard Milling Company. Minnie was the daughter of Nils Otto and Maggie Hedin, from the small hamlet of Jericho (Arctander Township), west of the four farms.
4. **Harriet** (Hattie, 1890-1960) married Victor E. Vickstrom and lived in Duluth, Minnesota, where he worked for the Northern Pacific Railway as an engineer.
5. **Albin** (1892-1950) married Juliet Signal. The family lived in Willmar where he worked as an engineer for the Great Northern Railway. Their son Donald served in the Navy during WWII.

NORMAN FARM[4]

The decade began with a relative from Sweden living with and working for the Norman family: Anders J. Ramsin, a nephew of Johannes and Marie. In the 1880 census, he was listed as a farm laborer. Anders was the son (possibly a step-son) of Marie's sister Maja Stina and her husband Johan Ramsin. The family lived in Håkantorp Parish, Skaraborg. Anders left Sweden on April 3, 1880, and arrived in Philadelphia twenty days later. Soon he was at the Norman farm with his extended family. Ramsin returned to Skaraborg Sweden where he married Emma Andersdotter on June 17, 1884. Ramsin died in 1929 at Segerstad Parish in Skaraborg.

---

4 *Willmar Gazette* 18 September 1884; findagrave.com, ancestry.com; Swedish Church Records;

Norman Family Death

Johannes Norman died from tuberculosis on September 15, 1884, the second death of the immigrant settlers. Johannes was 56 years old. His widow and four adult children, ages 17-28, mourned his death and adjusted to farm work without him. He was buried at Lake Florida Mission Church cemetery, 2.5 miles southeast from his farm. His death notice was printed in the *Willmar Republican Gazette*.

> *We are sorry to inform our readers that one of our oldest and most respected citizens, Johannes Norman, died last Monday from consumption, after an illness of two months. Mr. Norman was born in Skaraborgs Lan, Sweden, and was fifty six years of age. He always was a very industrious man, and had thus accumulated considerable property. His death will be mourned by the entire community.*

Following Johannes' death, ownership of the farm appears to be with his widow and children until probate resolved ownership to widow Marie in 1890. Son Gustav Albert operated the farm until his death in 1893.

MANKELL HOMESTEAD[5]

H. W., Elizabeth, and their six unmarried children temporarily moved to Willmar during or before 1880 and returned to the farm about five years later. Mankell owned property in the county seat, having purchased two lots from the St. Paul and Pacific railroad (Lots 8 and 9 of block 25, between 2nd and 3rd streets, Ward 3) in 1870. The family moved to Willmar, 15 miles south of the homestead, so that the children could receive an education that offered more than their township school. Soon son Oscar took business classes at the Willmar Seminary after it opened in 1883. It is believed that H. W. wanted to open a carpentry store where he would make cabinets and other types of furniture. He had a ready supply of timber (like oak and maple) at the lots he and Elizabeth owned in section 3 of Lake Andrew Township (between Lake Andrew and Middle Lake) and Section 5 (north side of Norway Lake). The family owned several lots west of Willmar Seminary in the 1880s and 1890s (Block 4, Lots 2, 3, 4, 5 in Thorpe and Lien's Addition). He also built a house close to Willmar Seminary. It is not clear if the family lived in this house (Block 3, Lot 1—address is 629 7th St. NW, Willmar), but with some of their children studying at the Willmar Seminary, the family logically would have lived nearby.

Willmar seminary c1900.
(*Illustrated History of Kandiyohi County* p. 408)

---

5 Mankell Family Collection; *Illustrated History of Kandiyohi County*, p. 408-409. "Willmar Seminary Papers, Student Roster" Norwegian American Historical Association. *Willmar Republican Gazette*, 13 April 1882, 18 September 1884, 4 April 1889; *Willmar Tribune*: 8 November 1899; 22 December 1915, 16 January 1936; moms.mn.gov; ancestry.com (Minnesota State Census, 1885 and 1905; US Federal Census, 1920, 1930); findagrave.com; *Niederasphe to Norway Lake*;

Willmar Seminary served to educate young men and women to enter the workforce. It was a joint venture of the Norwegian Lutheran Synod, local businessmen, and civic leaders. After a decade of several failed attempts at securing funding and a location, the Minnesota Lutheran Seminary and Institute was incorporated in 1882 and opened on October 16, 1883. Within five years attendance exceeded 280 students. Three Mankell siblings attended Willmar Seminary: Oscar in the first year, 1883; Sophia, in the third year, 1885; Otto in its seventh year, 1889.

Mankell Weddings

Two daughters of homesteaders H. W. and Elizabeth Mankell married during this decade.

Mary Mankell & John Young

Mary Mankell married John Young (1854-1930), a Swedish immigrant on March 17, 1881 in Kandiyohi County, probably at the Mankell homestead. Mary Mankell (1860-1887) was born in Northfield, Minnesota, the second child of H. W. and Elizabeth. John and Mary owned Young's Flowers, a store in Minneapolis, Minnesota, on 36th Street, near Lyndale Avenue; the family lived next to the corner store. According to Minnesota State census data Mary and John had three children:

1. **Frank Edward** (1881-1952) married Inga Kajsa (Carrie) Johnson.
2. **Esther** (1884-1967) married Thomas Moore and lived in Washington State.
3. **Jennie** (1885-?)

Amanda Mankell & Julius Landquist

The next year on April 9, 1882, Mary's younger sister Amanda married Julius W. Landquist, a Swedish immigrant born in Gothenburg, who was living and working in Willmar. The couple lived in Willmar for several years after their marriage. Here is the description from the *Willmar Republican Gazette*.

> *Mr. J. W. Landquist, deputy clerk of court, was married Sunday Evening to Miss Amanda Mankel, daughter of Mr. H. W. Mankel, at the residence of Mr. A. F. Nordin* [a judge in Willmar]. *The wedding ceremony was performed by Rev. D. T. Booth, and was witnessed by a large assembly of the relatives and friends of the contracting parties. They have already gone to housekeeping in their own house, recently purchased by Mr. Landquist, and the best wishes of a large circle of friends attend them.*

Amanda and Julius Landquist (1861-1939) had five children. The family moved from Willmar to Minneapolis in 1892. Julius left Amanda when the children were young. (He remarried in 1900 and moved to Washington State.)

1. **Alfred** (1883-1934) married Alma Helling.
2. **Lillian** (1884-1963) married M.E. Trainor.
3. **Austin** (1887-1942)
4. **Helen** (1889-1936)
5. **Herman J.** (1891-1960) married Ellen Christopherson from Arctander Township.

CH 4: 1880-1889

In 1899 Amanda filed for divorce and on November 8, 1899, the *Willmar Tribune* wrote

> *Among the divorce cases as cited by the daily papers is an action entered in the Hennepin county courts by Mrs. Amanda Landquist, of Minneapolis, against Julius W. Landquist. The defendant, it is claimed, has large interests in a mining company in the state of Washington, and a large amount of alimony is asked.*

Amanda's children financially supported their mother; it appears that neither Helen nor Herman graduated from high school because they had to work to support their mother. Amanda died at the age of 82 and is buried at Lakewood Cemetery in Minneapolis. Julius, died in 1939 and is buried at Woodland Cemetery, Woodland, California.

Mankell Farm Laborers

The Mankell farm had different people renting the house and/or working the land in the 1880s. There is some overlapping of years, so the times of arrival and departure are not always clear. While the Mankell family lived in Willmar, renters C. C. and Caroline (Brattlund) Selvig were on the farm, 1882-1884. H. W. and his family had recently returned from Willmar, having live there for about five years. Upon their return they had a young man named "J. Halstenson", born c1865 in Norway, who lived and worked at the farm in 1885. It is possible that he was the brother of Norwegian immigrant Halvor Halstenson (born 1858), a farm laborer at the Johannes Quam farm in 1880. The Quam and Mankell families were neighbors and related through the 1879 marriage of their children Anna and Nels (and a few years later between Sophia Mankell and John Quam). At the same time that Mankell had J. Halstenson at the farm, he also leased his farm acreage to a man named Per Hoej, an immigrant from Denmark, during the years 1884-1888. He rented the acreage, but it is not clear how long he lived at the farm, because the family returned to the farm from Willmar in 1885.

Mankell Family Deaths

At the end of the decade the Mankell family mourned the deaths of two family members.

Mary (Mankell) Young, the second child of H. W. and Elizabeth, died in 1887, six years after her marriage to John Young. Her husband John was left a widower with three young children. In 1915 John Young purchased property from his brother-in-law Nels Quam (also a widower) in New London, Minnesota. John left Minneapolis, moved to New London, and worked as a mason at a cement business, owned by Nels Quam. It appears that John took ownership of the business in the 1920s when Nels moved to Minneapolis. Mary and John Young are buried in the Crystal Lake Cemetery in Minneapolis.

The April 1, 1889 death of **Herman W. Mankell** was the last major event in the 1880s for the four families. His obituary was published in the *Willmar Republican Gazette* on April 4, 1889:

> *An old settler of the county, Mr. H. W. Mankel [sic] of Lake Andrew passed to eternal rest on Sunday last. He had been sick but a short time, and his death was rather sudden, although not entirely unexpected. Mr. Mankel was fifty three years of age: he came to*

America thirty three years ago and has been a resident of this county twenty three years. He leaves a wife and family of eight grown up children. Funeral services will be held today.

H. W. was the first of member of the Mankell family to be buried at the Lake Florida Mission Church cemetery. Over many more decades his wife and three additional generations of Mankell family members would be laid near him.

Flowers at the funeral of H. W. Mankell, 1889.

ARCTANDER & LAKE ANDREW MUTUAL FIRE INSURANCE COMPANY[6]

Influenced by the Granger Movement, the late 1800s witnessed a powerful cooperative movement in Minnesota, with the development of mutual owned businesses: insurance companies, creameries, telephone companies, and union stores. Founded in Minnesota in 1867, this Granger Movement found its way to Lake Andrew Township, to the Swedish and Norwegian immigrants, and to the four farms. Here are a few of the Granger Movement characteristics:

- Coming together as customers, farmers owned and managed the business. Farmers only; no investors.
- Spreading and sharing financial burden due to loss. Mutual aid in the community.
- Democratic operation. One person, one vote.
- Political neutrality.
- Response to exploitation in the monopolistic markets with a unified voice.
- Divided into local units, each called a "Grange".

The concept of mutual insurance coverage—where people voluntarily pool their money (via membership fees and premiums) to protect each other against severe property loss—began with Benjamin Franklin in Philadelphia in 1752. The concept of township mutual insurance companies was received with skepticism in the 1870s by many in the insurance industry, including the Minnesota Insurance Commissioner, Andrew R. McGill, who received political pressure from the leaders of stock insurance corporations to not allow mutual insurance companies. McGill worked to defeat legislation in 1873 and 1874 which would have allowed the creation of mutual insurance companies. He has been quoted as saying that these companies would be "failures" because "there is very little chance of these township mutuals ever surviving." He

---

6   www.mafmic.org/mission-history, including correspondence with the association's Vice President Dan Rupp, June 2018. "Survival of Minnesota Township Mutual Fire Insurance Companies" *Journal of Cooperatives*, 2015. *Illustrated History of Kandiyohi County*; Wikipedia.com; *Willmar Tribune*, 23 August 1911; Minnesota House and Senate bills #18; Keillor, *Cooperative Commonwealth: Co-ops in Rural Minnesota, 1859-1939*

CH 4: 1880-1889

thought that the mutual insurance companies would not have enough assets for farmers who claimed loss due to fire. His 1875 attack failed with the passage of Minnesota House and Senate Bill #18. More than 140 years later, the mutual insurance companies thrive and continue to provide policies to farmers.

In the early 1880s, several townships in Kandiyohi County, allowed by the 1875 Minnesota law, created mutual insurance companies for the farmers in the townships, providing fire insurance to their members. A mutual insurance company is owned entirely by its policyholders in the townships—the farmers. The company offered policies against loss or damage by fire, lightning, building collapse, livestock death, and more. Swedish and Norwegian immigrant farmers in Lake Andrew Township, including men from the four farms, were a part of this cooperative movement. Together they created the Arctander & Lake Andrew Mutual Fire Insurance Company which organized on April 7, 1881. Business commenced on August 17, 1881 with the first policy issued to Anders P. Skoglund. The first loss ($7.00) was claimed in 1882 by Reier Thorson due to a house fire. Other township mutual insurance companies formed in the county included Dovre-Mamre (1880), Acton-Gennessee (1880). This cooperative movement provided protection to farmers, so important for their economic survival.

One of the voting members in the April 1881 organizing procedure was from the four farms: Johannes Norman. Other original voting members included men connected to or soon to be connected to the four farms:

- Nels Quam, a future son-in-law of H. W. Mankell, and President of the company in the 1890s
- Members of the Gordhamer family in Arctander Township who were related to Mankell's daughter, Jennie (Mankell) Gordhamer
- Hans Christenson, father of one of the four farms' men who joins this story in the 1890s

The following is the list of signers of the Articles of Incorporation represented by both townships (*first board members; four farms in bold). Also included are the townships (Arctander and Lake Andrew) and location of the farms by section number.

Martin Aasen	AR16	John Lungstrom	LA22
Hans Christenson	LA16	Martin A Mostue	LA30
Christopher H Engen	AR12	Arne P Mostue	LA30
O. A. Erickson	LA30	Ole H Negaard	AR30
John H Gordhamer	AR34	Lewis Nelson [Louis]	LA22
Martin H Gordhamer	AR34	**Johannes Norman**	**LA17**
John Halvorson	LA18	Nels Quam	LA19
Lars Hedin	LA28	Torsten N Rosby*	AR36
Andrew Hedin	AR13	John A Skoglund*	LA22
John L Hjelle	AR26	Carl A Syverson	LA30
Syver Iverson	AR16	Simon A Syverson*	AR26
John Johnson	AR6	Reier Thorson*	LA22
Ole Knudson*	AR2		

H. W. Mankell was not in the original group who voted to start the Arctander & Lake Andrew Mutual Fire Insurance Company.[7] He and his family were living in Willmar in the early 1880s, so, due to distance, he may not have been available to officially join with his (temporarily) former neighbors in this endeavor of cooperation and support. In later years, H.W.'s son Oscar Mankell, grandson Herman Mankell, and great-grandson Orlynn Mankell all served in leadership roles of this mutual insurance company. Oscar and Herman sold policies to their neighbors. Generations of men from the four farms were involved for many decades as leaders of the Arctander & Lake Andrew Mutual Fire Insurance Company.

By the early 1910s, the Arctander & Lake Andrew Mutual Fire Insurance Company expanded its business area, serving farmers in several more townships: Burbank, Colfax, Dovre, Green Lake, Mamre, New London, and Norway Lake. It was also authorized to conduct business in parts of Swift County to the west: Hays, Kerkhoven and Pillsbury townships. Yet, with this expansion there was little added cost to the company. The officers conducted business out of their homes, so no offices needed to expand or be built. The expansion of territory brought in more policyholders and spread the financial risk among more people. In 2013, the Arctander & Lake Andrew Mutual Fire Insurance Company merged with the Crate Farmers' Mutual Insurance Company in Clara City, to form Prairie West Mutual Insurance Company with offices in Clara City, Minnesota. Arctander & Lake Andrew Mutual Insurance Company served its farmers for more than 130 years with a name tied to its geographical roots.

NORWAY LAKE BASEBALL PLAYERS[8]

While the first official Norway Lake Baseball Team organized in 1891, local men from Lake Andrew and Arctander Townships were playing baseball in 1889. Several players were connected to the families of the four farms, or would become connected to the four farms within a few years:

- Lewis Christopherson, from Arctander Township. His niece Cora would later marry Herman Mankell, the son of Oscar
- Gustaf Albert Norman, son of settlers Johannes and Marie Norman
- William Larson, husband of Johanna Norman and brother-in-law of Gustav Albert Norman.
- Oscar Mankell, son of settlers H. W. and Elizabeth Mankell
- Otto Mankell, son of H. W. and Elizabeth Mankell
- Mons Olson, future brother-in-law of Martin Reierson
- Nels Quam, brother-in-law of Oscar and Otto Mankell

---

7 It's possible that H. W. Mankell was one of the main voices encouraging his fellow farmers to join in this cooperative effort to help those affected by fire. In the late 1850s, before living in Northfield, the Mankell family lived in Vasa. H.W. had a carpentry business and helped build the Vasa Lutheran Church (second church building). But his business burned in a fire. Minnesota's first farm mutual insurance company was Vasa Farmers Mutual Insurance Company, founded in 1860 by Swedish immigrants (allowed before the 1875 law). These Swedish immigrants in Vasa also created a co-op store and a cooperative to get higher market prices for their wheat. While H. W. was framing the church building, did he have conversations with these Swedish policyholders about their newly formed mutual insurance company?
8 A 1939 article in the August 25 issue of the *Willmar Tribune* dated the team to 1889. *Centennial of Kandiyohi County*, p. 147, 323;

- John Quam, future brother-in-law of Oscar and Otto Mankell
- Swen Swenson, from Jericho in Arctander Township. His sister Minnie was the future wife of Oscar Mankell

1889 Baseball Team.

**Front row: Christian Rustad, Oscar Anderson, Gustav Albert Norman, Martin Peterson, John Quam, Ole Rustad, Oscar Mankell, M. O. Rustad.
Second row: Lawrence Hedin, Otto Mankell, Swen Swenson, Ole Haugan, unidentified, William Larson, Joseph Rustad.
Third row: Olavus Gordhamer, Nels Quam, Mons Olson, Andrew Henjum, Lewis Christopherson, John Forshager, Akan Nelson, Otto Sell.
Two boys in the back, far right: Andrew Gordhamer and John Gordhamer.**

(*Willmar Tribune,* August 25, 1939)

Other members of this first baseball team included men from area townships.
- Oscar Anderson, Arctander
- John Forshager, Arctander
- Oliver (Olavus) Gordhamer, Arctander
- Ole Haugen, possibly from Stearns County
- Lawrence Hedin, Lake Andrew

- Andrew L. Henjum, Arctander
- Akan Nelson
- Martin Peterson, Lake Andrew
- Four Rustad brothers who were sons of Pastor Lars and Mari Rustad, Lake Andrew
  - Christian Rustad
  - Joseph Rustad
  - Mathias O. Rustad
  - Ole Rustad (later a laborer at the Mankell farm)
- Otto Sell, possibly from McLeod County who later lived in Chippewa County

The team played on a ball diamond created in the farm field of Gabriel and Wilda Stene who lived on the east side of Lake Mary, in section 19 of Lake Andrew Township. As described in a newspaper article about the 1889 team,

> *the players have no gloves, no mask, no body or knee protectors. A foul in those days was often just too bad for the catcher. A broken nose or broken fingers were common. It was common practice for the catcher to step back a ways and catch the ball on the bound* [sic bounce] *for the first two strikes, coming up behind the batter to take his punishment for the third strike. In the course of time catchers were provided with a padded finger glove with sole leather tips for the left hand. It would be interesting to see the ball player of today take a hot liner with his bare hands.*

The first Norway Lake Baseball Team, officially created in 1891, played for about five years, was later re-organized as the Norway Lake Lakers, and played for many decades.

CHAPTER 5:
1890-1899

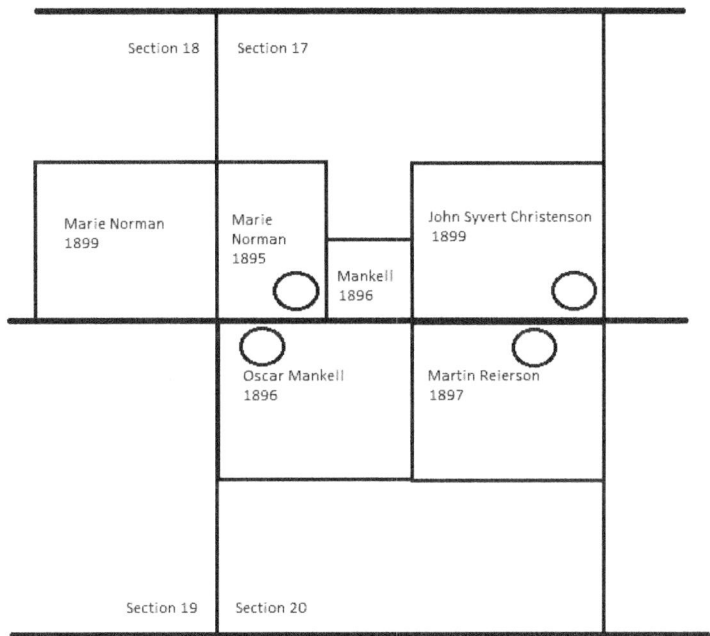

HIGHLIGHTS

- Farm transitions: transitions of farm ownership occurred for all four farms due to sale, transfers to family members or marriage
- Business: the Norway Lake Creamery was formed, involving all four families
- Community activities: the Norway Lake Band and the Norway Lake Choir were formed
- Neighborhood schools play a prominent role

TRANSITIONS

The decade of the 1890s brought transition of ownership to the next generation. Neighbors began to call the farms by the names of the new owners. The Stenseth farm became the Christenson farm; the Brattlund farm became the Reierson farm. The Mankell farm continued to be called the Mankell farm, through the transition from widow Elizabeth to her son Oscar Mankell. Even though, at the end of the decade, the Norman farm had new owners with the last name Larson, the farm continued to be called the Norman farm. William and Johanna Larson owned another farm, one mile to the east, which the neighbors called the Larson farm. To keep a clearer reference to these two farms, the Norman farm retained this moniker for a few more decades.

STENSETH/CHRISTENSON FARM[1]

The decade began with Nicholas N. Stenseth (aka Nicolai) running the farm for his widowed mother, though he suffered from health issues caused by tuberculosis. By 1894, these family and work dynamics would change.

1894
Carrie Stenseth & John Syvert Christenson

Two of the children of Karen and Nils Stenseth married in the 1890s. First, was daughter Carrie (aka Karen Dorothy, 1868-1904), who married a neighbor, John Syvert Christenson on September 6, 1894. Carrie and J. S. briefly lived with his parents, Hans and Lena Christenson, before moving to the Stenseth farm.

As mentioned in the grasshopper section of the 1870s chapter, a boy named John Syvert Thori was adopted (or fostered) by Norwegian immigrants Hans and Lena Christenson and grew up on a farm in Section 16, about a mile east of the Stenseth homestead. The couple also fostered Magdalena Nary. John Syvert's biological parents were Paul Christopherson Thori and his wife Oline/Elen, who were from Granite Falls in western Minnesota. She died in 1873 a few months after giving birth to John Syvert. Paul Christopherson Thori later lived in

Carrie Stenseth, c1890.

Lake Andrew Township and was a member and leader of the Nannestad Lutheran Church in Arctander Township, where the Stenseth family were members. He became destitute due to the aftermath of the grasshopper infestations. He mortgaged his property near Norway Lake, his wife had died in 1873, and he had two young sons. The Christenson couple adopted John Syvert, the younger of the two boys.

John Syvert Christenson and his family remained connected to the four farms story for many decades to follow.

---

1 *Willmar Tribune*, 29 March 1899, 26 Apr 1899, 5 March 1902, 19 November 1902; Findagrave.com; ancestry.com; *Willmar Republican Gazette*; *Illustrated History of Kandiyohi County*, p. 119, 307; Christenson Family Collection.

1896
Nicholas N. Stenseth & Hilda Hanson

Nicholas married Hilda Hanson on June 24, 1896, at St. Paul's Lutheran Church, Minneapolis, Minnesota. In 1894 or 1895, Nicholas had moved to Minneapolis where he worked as a street car conductor. With Carrie's marriage to neighbor John Syvert in 1894 and because the couple lived at the Stenseth farm, Nicholas made changes in his life. He knew that his mother, deaf sister Maren, and the farm were cared for so he moved for other work opportunities.

After their marriage, the couple lived in Minneapolis where son Leslie was born in 1898. In 1900, Nicholas returned to Kandiyohi County, with his family, and settled in Mamre Township. Daughter Cora Jeannette was born after they arrived in the county. Nicholas owned a general merchandise store located next to the Mamre Creamery in Section 14, northwest of Mamrelund Lutheran Church.

1892-1899
Teachers at School Districts 25, 16, 69[2]

J. S. and Carrie Christenson taught at three area schools throughout the 1890s. At that time, school terms lasted about five months, October through February. J. S. taught at School District 25, in 1892 and 1899. At that time located in the southwest corner of Section 21. During 1893, 1894, 1895 and 1897 he taught at District 69, located ½ mile north of Jericho in Arctander Township.

Before and briefly after her marriage, Carrie (Stenseth) Christenson taught local children in both District 25 and District 16. During the years 1887 and 1895 she was the teacher at District 16, the school she attended in the 1870s and 1880s. (This was before part of Section 17 was redistricted to District 25.) Her classmates included the Norman children, her brother Nicholas, and the Reierson siblings who grew up in Section 15. She was the teacher at District 25 in 1893-1894. From partial enrollment records, neither J. S. nor Carrie taught children from the four farms at District 25. Later in this decade, when other teachers were at District 25, one child from the four farms, Ludvig Stenseth, attended.[3] There were no children at the Reierson farm and no school-age children at the Norman or Mankell farms. Within the next ten years, more children of the four farms would be attending District 25.

The school in the community

The school districts celebrated the end of the school terms with programs for families and neighbors. Here is an example of one celebration after the 1894-95 term when J. S. Christenson was the teacher. From this *Willmar Tribune* article, it is evident how he brought his other interests (such as music, religion, and community leadership) into this event.

---

2 *Illustrated History of Kandiyohi County*, p. 278. *Kandi News*, March 2012, June 2015; *Willmar Tribune*: 12 March 1895, 20 Dec 1899, 3 January 1900.

3 There are no records to indicate how Ludvig was related to the Stenseth family. According to census data, Ludvig was born c1884 in Minnesota. He was possibly a nephew of Nils Stenseth. From *Willmar Tribune* information he later lived in Minot, North Dakota, and would return to Lake Andrew Township to visit family.

> *The school in district No. 69, town of Arctander, closed with a very successful entertainment Saturday evening, with much credit to the teacher, Mr. J. S. Christenson, and scholars. The meeting opened by a piece from the Norway Lake Brass Band, then a few recitations and dialogues were very ably delivered; the Norway Lake choir gave a song; the last issue of the* Jericho North Star *(a weekly paper published by the scholars of district 69) was read. The entertainment was closed by speeches of Rev. D. C. Jordahl [Pastor of First Lutheran Church]. Our county superintendent, B. S. Covell, gave a very able address on schoolwork and duties of parents and teachers to scholars. This was followed by remarks of Rev. R. K. Fjelstad [Pastor at East Norway Lake Lutheran Church] and farewell address by J. S. Christenson. Rev. Jordahl closed with prayer.*

In 1899, Christenson hosted a party to raise money for the District 25 school library. While there is no record of which families and neighbors attended, the party was described in two issues of the *Willmar Tribune*:

> *J. S. Christenson, one of the leading teachers of the county, has also arranged for a basket party to take place Friday evening, Dec. 22. The proceeds will go to a library. Everybody interested in the welfare of the young people should make it a point to attend and give the good work a helping hand. Schoolhouse in District. No. 25.*

> *The closing entertainment and basket party in Dist. 25 last night was a perfect success, and for the well-rendered program the teacher, Mr. J. S. Christenson, and the scholars deserve great credit. Whatever J. S. undertakes he is right in it with both hands and feet. To judge from last night's party it takes Lake Andrewites to make a successful one, not only in liberality but also in decent and good behavior. The baskets sold brought $16.56. Well done.*

Three neighboring school districts are indicated in a portion of the 1900 plat map: #25, #69 and #16. The Christenson farm in Section 17, the residence of two teachers, Carrie and J. S. Christenson, is marked. Families in Section 20 and the southern half of Section 17 were assigned to District 25.

When teaching at District 69 in Arctander Township, Christenson taught children who lived west and northwest of the four farms community. However, during the years he was at District 25, he taught children of the four farms area and others in this central part of the township. The District 25 School was located in the southwest corner of Section 21. (In 1912, a new building was erected south, across the road in Section 28, where it would stand for 100 years.)

1899

In 1899, J. S. Christenson purchased the 160-acre farm from his mother-in-law, widow Karen Stenseth, for $3,000. One of the first things he did was to purchase a windmill from Ole Stene who lived about two miles west, on the east side of Lake Mary and move it to his newly purchased farm. This farm would remain in the family until the mid-1940s.

J. S. and Carrie Christenson had two children, before her death in 1904.

1. **Harvin** (1897-1971) married Sigrid H. Larson on June 29, 1925 in Chicago. The family would later live at the farm where he was born.
2. **Clara** (1899-1955)

J. S. married Mina (Minnie) Engen in 1905 and they had two children:

1. **Clarence** (born and died in 1907)
2. **Hedvig** (1908-1989) married Chris Knutson in 1931. They are buried at Glen Abbey Memorial Park in Bonita, California.

Clara and Harvin Christenson, c1904.
(image courtesy of the Christenson Family)

BRATTLUND/REIERSON FARM[4]

1897

In October 1897, Sophia (Brattlund) Rice sold the Brattlund farm to Martin and Anna (Alvig) Reierson for $2,500. This change in ownership of the Brattlund farm is noteworthy because the new owner was not related by blood or marriage.

Nils and Marie Brattlund had been living in Willmar since 1885 (on 4th Street, between Trott Avenue and Minnesota Avenue) and maintained ownership of the farm until 1896 when daughter Sophia Rice took ownership. There is no documentation of anyone renting the farm between the time the Brattlunds moved to Willmar in 1885 and the 1897 sale 12 years later. However, Nils Brattlund maintained his connection to the township with his ownership of other property: one lot in Section 34, on the south shore of Lake Florida.

---

4 *Willmar Tribune* 5 Oct 1897; Kandiyohi County Recorder; glorecords.blm.gov; ancestry.com

Martin Reierson, 1894.
(image courtesy of the Burton Berry family)

The new owner, Martin Reierson (1870-1966), was the son of Bjorn Reierson and Sigrid Olsdatter who homesteaded 160 acres in Section 15 of Lake Andrew Township in the mid-1860s. Bjorn emigrated in about 1861 from Norway with two young children from his deceased first wife, Ragnild Helgesdatter. One of these daughters died on the journey and was buried at sea. Soon after arriving in the Midwest Bjorn married Sigrid Oldsdatter and they came to Kandiyohi County. This couple had eight children. Bjorn and Sigrid are buried in the cemetery at East Norway Lake Lutheran Church, where Bjorn was a founding member and trustee.

On May 31, 1894, Martin married Anna Martine Berthina Alvig at East Norway Lake Lutheran Church in Arctander Township, the home congregation of the Reierson family. About 40 horse drawn buggies brought the guests and bridal party to the church.[5]

Anna (1876-1951) was the daughter of Ole and Britha (Flatebo) Alvig who farmed in Section 8 of Dovre Township, south of Lake Andrew Township. Her parents emigrated about 1868 from Kvamme (Kvam) Parish, Hordaland, Norway and were members of Vikor Lutheran on the eastern shore of Solomon Lake in the township. Ole and Britha are buried at the church cemetery.

Martin and Anna had no children, though two young nieces lived with them at different times in the decades to follow.

NORMAN FARM[6]

During the 1890s, the Norman family was in transition. After Johannes Norman's death in 1884, son Gustaf Albert operated the farm for a few years until his death in 1893. Johannes' widow Marie Norman celebrated marriages of three children, and mourned the deaths of one son and one daughter. In addition, the farm witnessed a series of moves by family members, to and from the Norman farm. Here is a chronology of these transitions.

1890

The family built a new farm house in 1890, which remained on the farm for more than 100 years. The original log house stayed standing for a time after the new white farm house was constructed.[7]

---

5   Martin and Anna's wedding ceremony was a double wedding with Rev. R. K. Fjelstad, officiating. The other couple was John E. Roisom and Gemine Nygaard. An additional 40 rigs brought guests. Post ceremony parties were held at the brides' homes. *Willmar Republican Gazette*, 7 June 1894
6   Burial records of Lake Florida Mission Church; Ancestry.com. Swift County Plat Map, 1915; findagrave.com; moms.mn.gov; *Willmar Tribune*; *To God Be The Glory, 1875-1975*; findagrave.com; Riksarkivet.se; moms.mn.gov; Canada Census, 1911, 1916, 1921; plat maps of Lake Andrew Township; Norman Family Collection; Swedish Church Records. Kandiyohi County Recorder.
7   The Norman farm house, built in 1890, remained on the farm until about 2010 when the New London Fire Department scheduled a burn to train their firefighters.

1892
Widow Marie Norman witnessed the marriages of three of her children during 1892.

Clara Mathilda Norman & Peter Dahlstrom
The first to marry was her daughter Clara Mathilda (Tilda) who wed Swedish immigrant Peter Halvorsson Dahlstrom on January 21, 1892, in Kandiyohi County. Peter (born Per, 1866-?) was from the Dalby Parish, Värmland County, Sweden and emigrated in 1889. After their marriage, Tilda and Peter lived with at the Norman farm with her widowed mother. They assumed duties at the farm after Gustaf Albert's 1893 death.

John Andrew (aka J. A. & Andrew John) & Christine Sampson
On July 2, 1892, in Swift County John Andrew Norman married Christine Sampson. Christine was born in Iowa, the daughter of Norwegian immigrants, Jorgen Samson and Marta Ericksdotter Helleland, later known as George and Martha Sampson. George had an 80-acre homestead, Section 26 of Hayes Township, Swift County and also had 120 acres in neighboring Section 27. John Andrew and Christine lived in Swift County during their first years of marriage, returned to the Norman farm in 1895, and later moved back to Hayes Township, Sections 11 and 12.

Johanna Norman & William Larson
One week after her brother John Andrew's wedding ceremony, Johanna Norman (1863-1947) married neighbor William Larson (1857-1911) on July 9, 1892, in Kandiyohi County, possibly at Lake Florida Mission Church where both families were members. The bride and groom were Swedish immigrants and both were from Håkantorp Parish, Skaraborg County. It is certainly possible that the families knew each other and attended church services together when living in Sweden. The Norman family left Sweden in 1869; Larson family members left during the years 1879-1882.

William Larson, his siblings, and parents immigrated to the U.S. in different years. Most resided in Lake Andrew Township.

- 1879: **William Larson** (born Wilhelm Larsson) arrived in New York City on the ship "City of Montreal". He soon arrived in Kandiyohi County and briefly lived with the Nils Brattlund family.

- 1880: **Herman Larson** (born Tell Herman Larsson) arrived and lived with his brother William, possibly in Section 16. In 1906, Herman married Alfrida Stenberg. They had 3 children (Elsie, Reynold, and Elmer). A few years later their parents—Herman's widowed mother Katherine Johnson and Alfrida's parents, Andrew and Maria Stenberg—joined this growing family in Section 29.

- 1881: **Bolla Mathilda** immigrated. A sister of William and Herman she soon married Charles Swedberg and lived in Redwood Falls, Minnesota.

- 1882: The parents of William, Herman, and Bolla—**Lars Johan Larson** (aka L.J. 1825-1890) and **Katherine Andersdotter** (aka Anna Katerina, 1821-1914)—left Håkantorp Skaraborg in June 1882 with their youngest child, 18-year-old daughter **Augusta**.[8] Upon their arrival parents L.J. and Katherine used the surname Johnson, a reference to his patronymic Swedish name (Johansson). Lars Johan and Katherine Johnson lived in with their son William Larson. Later widow Katherine lived with son Herman Larson in the township and used the Larson surname.

Many members of the extended Larson, Johnson, and Stenberg families are buried at the Lake Florida Mission Church cemetery. L.J. and Katherine are buried with the last name "Larson" on their gravestones.

With the 1892 marriage of Johanna Norman and William Larson came their joint connection to two farms, one mile apart, in Lake Andrew Township. William owned 160 acres in the northwest corner of Section 21 which he purchased from Bengt Selvig in 1889. With the marriage to Johanna Larson, he became part of the Norman farm in Section 17.[9] Their four children were born in the 1890s:

1. **Oscar Leonard** (1893-1974) later owned the Section 21 farm, previously owned by his father William. Later in life he lived near Lake Andrew. Oscar is buried at Lake Florida Mission Church cemetery.
2. **Lillie Alminda** (1896-1910) is buried at Lake Florida Mission Church cemetery.
3. **Victor Herbert** (1897-1909) is buried at Lake Florida Mission Church cemetery.
4. **Edith Wilhemina** (1899-1996) was born October 9, 1899, at the Norman farm. She married Edwin H. Railson from Lake Andrew Township on April 8, 1925. This couple later owned the Norman farm. They are buried at First Lutheran Church of Norway Lake

1893

Gustav Albert Norman ran the family farm after his father's 1884 death. In March 1892, Gustav became the sole owner of the family's 160 acres in Section 18, directly west of the original 80-acre Norman farm, which was then owned by extended Norman family members. The death certificate for Gustav Albert noted that he died from "consumption" (tuberculosis) at age 25 on January 18, 1893, less than a year after ownership of his 160 acres, and less than ten years after the death of his father, Johannes. These 160 acres were in probate until Marie Norman became the owner in 1899.

---

8 No record found as to where Augusta lived.
9 Larson also purchased 40 acres in Section 16 from Sophia and A. E. Rice in 1893. These 40 acres were northeast of and contiguous to his Section 21 farm.

1894

Clara Matilda "Tilda" Dahlstrom.
(image courtesy of Christy Hicks)

Clara Matilda (Tilda) Norman, her husband Peter Dahlstrom, and their daughter Lydia moved to the Norman farm after the death of her brother, Gustav Albert. The plan was for Peter to operate the farm, but the death of Tilda on October 13, 1894, changed everyone's plans. She died from complications after a tooth extraction during pregnancy. Tilda and Peter were members of Lake Florida Mission Church until her death. Tilda is buried at the church cemetery.

Widower Peter moved west to Swift County where he briefly rented the farm of his brother-in-law, John Andrew Norman, (Hayes Township, Sections 11 and 12). In 1896, he married widow Annie Ostlund (nee Anderson; widow of Nels Ostlund). Peter and his family lived in Mamre Township just south of Lake Andrew Township. By 1910, they were living in Alberta, Canada, where son Floyd was born. The family soon moved to Saskatchewan. Here are the children in this blended family (birth years are approximate):

Child of Tilda (Norman) and Peter Dahlstrom:

1. **Lydia Josephine**, 1892. Married Lewis Evenson in 1911 and Sigurd Otheim in 1922. She is buried at Concordia Cemetery in Crosby, North Dakota.

Children of Annie (Anderson) and Nels Ostlund, and step-children to Peter:

1. **Levi**, 1890
2. **Clarence**, 1893
3. **Eddie**, 1895

Children of Annie (Ostlund) and Peter Dahlstrom:

1. **Ruth**, 1897
2. **Myrtle**, 1898
3. **Martha**, 1900
4. **Hazel**, 1902
5. **Arnold Wilfred**, 1904
6. **Peter Walton**, 1904
7. **Francis**, 1907
8. **Floyd**, 1910

Several members of the extended Dahlstrom family are buried at the Hillside Cemetery, Medicine Hat, Alberta, Canada.

1895

Martin Evenson lived at the Norman farm in 1895, according to census data. He was a farm laborer for widow Marie Norman, though it is unknown how many years Martin was with the family. He was born in 1872, the son of Tosten and Mari (Roa) Evenson, Hayes Township, Swift County. Tosten and Mari were 1867 immigrants from Norderhov Parish, Buskerud, Norway. Martin's connection to the Norman family was probably through John Andrew Norman who lived in Hayes Township soon after his 1892 marriage. Martin Evenson died in 1900 and is buried at Monson Lake Lutheran Church cemetery near the graves of his parents.

1895-1897

After his 1892 marriage, John Andrew Norman and his wife Christine lived about ten miles west in Hayes Township, Swift County, where their first child Albert was born. Then in the spring of 1895, after Gustav Norman's death, the John Andrew Norman family moved back to the Norman farm, and to his widowed mother, where their second child, Mabel, was born. Mabel was baptized at East Norway Lake Lutheran Church, one mile west of their home. In 1895, after John Andrew and his family moved back to Kandiyohi County, his brother-in-law and widower Peter Dahlstrom and his daughter moved to John Andrew's farm in Hayes Township where they lived for a short time, prior to his second marriage.

In 1897, the John Andrew Norman family returned to his Swift County farm where seven more children were born and were baptized at Kerkhoven Lutheran Church. John A. Norman died in 1913 and is buried at the Monson Lake Cemetery in Swift County about a mile north of his farm in Sections 11 and 12 of Hayes Township. In March 1919, his widow Christine moved to Saskatchewan Canada. In July 1919, she married Matthew Sybouts, an immigrant from the Netherlands. Christine Norman Sybouts died in 1952 in Saskatchewan, Canada. She is buried at Monson Lake Lutheran Church cemetery near the plot her first husband. Eight of John Andrew and Christine's nine children moved to Montana in the 1920s and 1930s. The four youngest later moved to Canada.

1. **Albert Cornell** (1893-1943) married Helga Rigg
2. **Mabel Josephine** (1895-1959) married Nestor Lesteberg
3. **Emma Elizabeth** (1897-1999) married Baard Bringedal
4. **Ella May** (1897-1985) married Carl Hagen
5. **Blanche Sophia** (1902-1945) married Herbert Wirtzberger
6. **Leonard Julius** (1904-1977)
7. **Walter Melvin** (1907-1999)
8. **George Wilton** (1909-1979) married Annie Kline/Klein
9. **Lillian Victoria** (1912-1980) married Jacob F. Klein

Mabel Norman, the daughter who remained in Swift County, married Nestor Lesteberg in 1915. They had at least four children. Daughter Elaine married Charles Edman from Kandiyohi County in 1951.

Charles' grandparents, Henry and Nellie Swenson, rented the Norman farm for about 15 years, beginning in 1910.

1898
In 1898, Marie lived at the farm without other family. Marie's son John Andrew and his family had moved back to Swift County in 1897. Marie's daughter Johanna and her husband William Larson lived in Section 21 and but would soon move to Marie's farm in 1899. Her two other children had passed away. It's highly probable that a farmhand lived with her because she needed assistance with the chores and caring for a farm. Martin Evenson who lived at the farm in 1895 may have remained at the farm for a few more years.

1899
In March, Johanna and William Larson moved from his farm in Section 21 to her family's Norman farm in Section 17. By 1899, widow Marie Norman was the owner of the original 80-acre farm in Section 17 and the 160 acres in Section 18 after probate following her son Gustav's death. She lived at this farm with her daughter Johanna, son-in-law William, and their growing family. Having moved one mile west, William rented his Section 21 farm to Fred Amundson and his family, also from Lake Andrew Township. This arrangement lasted for one year until April 1900 when the Larson and Amundson families switched farms. Marie Norman moved with her daughter and lived with the Larson family until her death in 1906.

MANKELL FARM[10]

After H. W. Mankell's death in 1889, the farm ownership was shared by his widow Elizabeth and all their children. In the 1890s, oldest son Oscar acquired portions of the farm from his mother and his siblings and became the sole owner. The family had three weddings during this decade and a death of one new bride.

1893
Hulda Mankell & Hans Melgaard[11]
Four years after H.W.'s death Elizabeth hosted another family wedding when their daughter Hulda married Hans Melgaard on Syttende Mai (May 17) in 1893 (Norway's Constitution Day). Their courtship began in 1891.

In the summer of 1890, a year after her father's death, Hulda sailed to Gothenburg, Sweden, where she visited with many relatives. She also traveled to Stockholm, the home of her uncle and artist, Otto A. Mankell. When Hulda left on this voyage she was engaged to a businessman (Charles Reese) from Minneapolis. When she returned to the U.S. in August 1891, still engaged to Charles, she fell in love with another man, Hans Melgaard, a Norwegian whom she met on board the steamer ship, S.S. Bothnia.

---
10 Much of the Mankell family information is from mankell.org and Mankell Family Collection. Records of the Kandiyohi County Recorder; *Willmar Gazette*, 19 January 1894.
11 Pejsa, *Hans and Hulda Mankell: The One Hundredth Wedding Anniversary Book*.

Hans had been living in Argyle, Minnesota, where he was a banker[12], having emigrated in 1882 from Sør-Fron, Oppland, Norway (the Gudbrandsdal Valley).

Hans wrote to Hulda in September 1891:

> *I shall never forget the ocean trip on the "Bothnia"... I enjoyed your company so much, and the time seemed to pass away so fast and pleasantly that I was almost wishing that the voyage would last twice as long as it did.*

Hulda remained engaged to Reese for a time after her return to the U.S., but Hans continued his courtship of Hulda and they married in May 1893 at the Mankell farm. Their granddaughter, Jane Hauser Pejsa wrote about their wedding:

> *The marriage was performed by Mr. Gjertsen, "Minister of the Gospel." Witnesses were A. H. Gordhamer, husband of Hulda's sister Jenny, and Nels Quam, husband of her sister Annie.*

> *The wedding trip took them to the newly opened Columbia Exposition in Chicago. This grand festival and exhibition celebrated the four hundredth anniversary of Columbus' 'discovery' of America in 1492. However, the opening of the exposition had been delayed until 1893. From Chicago, the couple returned to Minnesota and to Argyle. Hulda arrived as wife of Argyle's most prominent citizen and mistress of the grandest house in town. The house even carried its own name "Bothnia"!*

Hulda and Hans had six children:

1. **Agnes** (1894-1984) taught art at William and Mary College. She died in Los Angeles, California and is buried at Lakewood Cemetery in Minneapolis near her parents' graves.
2. **Irene** (1896-1990) married Walter Hauser (1894-1975). They had two daughters, Susan and Jane. The family lived in Minneapolis, Minnesota.
3. **Ruth** (1898-1994) married Frederick Deveber Sill (1885-1962). They had two children, Mary and Frederick, both born at the Panama Canal Zone.
4. **Mildred** (1901-1996) married Caradoc Rees (1896-1989), an immigrant from Wales. The family lived in Los Angeles, CA. They had two sons, Thomas and John. Thomas Mankell Rees was a California congressmen (1967-1977) who shared the stage with Robert Kennedy at RFK's final speech, June 5, 1968, at the Ambassador Hotel. Minutes after the speech, RFK was shot.
5. **Harold** (1903-1986) married Josepha Knutson (1905-2001). They family lived in Hennepin County, Minnesota, and had three children: Hans, Mary and Marcia. Harold and Josepha are buried in Lakewood Cemetery, Minneapolis, Minnesota.
6. **Carmen** (1912-1999) married Leon Holman (1911-1979) and lived in San Diego and Texas. They had at least one child, Leon Holman Jr.

---

12 Hans Melgaard organized the Farmers and Merchants Bank of Argyle in 1886, the first bank in Marshall County.

1893
Sophia Mankell & John Quam[13]

Sophia Mankell (1870-1894) was born on the family homestead in Kandiyohi County. She married John J. Quam at her home on June 6, 1893. John was the son of Johannes and Anne Kvam, Norwegian immigrants who had a farm southwest of the Mankell homestead. In the 1890s, he was the Postmaster of Jericho (aka Norway Lake).

Wedding of Sophia Mankell and John Quam at the Mankell homestead, 1893.
(image courtesy of the Mankell Family)

1894

The Mankell and Quam families, their neighbors and friends mourned the untimely death of Sophia Mankell Quam who died on January 6, 1894, one day after the birth of her daughter, Sophie. Her obituary was printed in the *New London Times* and the *Willmar Republican Gazette*.

> *Mrs. Sofia Quam, wife of John Quam of Norway Lake, aged 23 years, 1 month and 17 days, died at her home Jan. 6th, 1894. On the day before she gave birth to a girl baby, who survives her. She [Sophia] was married last spring. Her death casts a gloom over the whole community. Fate seems to have cast her lot into one of those series of unfortunate circumstances against which human effort contends in vain. When she was confined, and it was seen that medical aid was necessary, the roads were almost impassable. When the doctor finally got there he found embolism of the pulmonary artery. The child was saved but the mother, in spite of all effort and some slight remission of the symptoms, gradually sank, dying at 11 o'clock a. m. Saturday. A very large number of people from far and near attended the funeral Thursday in spite of the severe weather.*

---

13 Ancestry.com; Mankell Family Collection; *Willmar Gazette*, 19 January 1894; *History of New London*

> *To mortal ken the loss to husband, child, parent, brothers and sisters is sad—the loss of one so good, so kind, so noble in all the womanly graces, and with such bright prospects in life before her, and just as she had realized the ideal of true womanhood—the joy of maternity. But if we could look behind the veil, we should no doubt see her—not dead, for the good never die—but as the guardian angel ministering to the loved ones left behind.*

Sophia Quam is buried at East Norway Lake Lutheran Church. Widower John Quam married Tilda Christianson on August 1, 1897. They lived for many years in New London, about nine miles east of the four farms, where he was mayor of the town, 1904-1905, following his brother Nels' term in office. Later they moved to Washington State.

John and Sophia Quam had one daughter: Sophie Leontine. After her mother's death, Sophie was raised by her aunt and uncle, Anna (Mankell) and Nels Quam who lived in New London. Sophie married Andrew Danielson, the son of Swedish immigrants Anders and Mari Danielson who settled in Section 35, south of Lake Florida. Sophie and Andrew's son, Andrew W. Danielson, was a former United States Attorney and a Senior Judge of Hennepin County District Court.

1895
Oscar Mankell & Minnie Swenson[14]

Minnie Swenson (1875-1959) was the oldest daughter of Norwegian immigrants Gunder and Gemine (Negaard) Swenson who lived on their homestead located on the eastern edge of Arctander Township on the south shore of Lake Mary, about two miles west of the Mankell farm. Gunder emigrated with his parents, Sven Gunderson Borgen and Margit from the Numedal Valley, Buskerud, Norway, in 1857. The Østerdal Valley in Hedmark Norway was the home of Gemine and her parents, Halvor Olsen Negaard and Martha Haraldsdatter. The Negaard family left Norway in 1870 arriving in the United States from Quebec.

While they attended different churches, Oscar and Minnie were members of the Norway Lake Choir. These two young adults would have crossed paths in the community of Jericho where they would shop and get mail at the General Store.

In February 1895, only a few months before his marriage to Minnie, Oscar Mankell was in Minneapolis for about two weeks, visiting his sister (probably Amanda Lundquist) and staying at 916 14th Ave South. He wrote a letter to his "Dearest Minnie" who was living in Willmar at the home of "Miss Anna Carlin" and working as a dressmaker. He asked her to write and visit soon. In his letter, Oscar made reference to family—siblings Hulda and Esther, and Minnie's Aunt Tomine. Oscar's friends Oliver Halvorson, Elmer Railson, and Elmer Reese are also mentioned in the context of wanting to attend a famous criminal trial in Minneapolis.

---

14 *Willmar Tribune*, July 9, 1895. Hauge's Lutheran refers to the Nannestad Lutheran Church. The Norwegian violinist was Prof. Eivind Aakhus (1854-1937), an expert with the Hardanger fiddle.

CH 5: 1890-1899

Minneapolis, Minn.
February 21, 1895

Dearest Minnie, You must excuse me dear for not writing you before but have been so taken up down here that I have not taken time. I have enjoyed myself better than I had expected since it has been such nice weather all the time. Elmer R [Railson] was with me down but went home on Monday. I had expected to go home on Friday eve so as to get home on Sat. but they are teasing me to stay over Sun. and pray do so. Was to St. Paul Thursday and returned yesterday.

Was in to see your Aunt Tomina but she had not arrived at the store I guess for it was quite early as I wanted to be back here in time to be at the great "Hayward trial" but didn't come in time anyway as there were many hundred people that could not be admitted. Have been there one day with Oliver H. Elmer Reese went to the sheriff and got a pass for us as they will not admit you without having one. Will try and have him get a pass for me this afternoon.

Dear Minnie, how I wish you would be down here so I could take you to some entertainments. I am all alone here and don't feel like going anywhere as Esther works so far from here that she has only been here once since she came down but will come tonight and we are going to the Swedish Tabernacle as I have never been there before.

Should also like to go to the "Salvation Army Hall" one evening but can't go alone or rather don't like to go alone. I just wish you were working down here Dear so I could go and see you every eve. Then it wouldn't be so lonesome down here and would be liable to stay longer too.

The mail carrier just came now and had a letter from Hulda. She is very anxious to have me come that way before I go home. This is the third letter she has written since I came down here but have said I haven't twenty dollars to pay out in RR fare. So she says now that she will see to that, but I am not going now anyway since I can't stay away from home so long. She says if I don't come now I will never come and that may be so too. Am going up to see Otto Monson this afternoon and tomorrow I intend to take my photo as I never took one before.

Now "dear Minnie" I want you to send me a letter before I go home, address to 915 14th Ave S. Suppose Miss S has found another partner for tomorrow eve since I couldn't promise for sure to come. Too bad that I shall miss such "en gylden auledning" [a golden opportunity].

Must close my letter with a half a Doz. kisses to my Dear little Dressmaker at Willmar. Be sure to mail your letter before Sun. Eve.

Ever Yours, Oscar.[15]

---

15 Mankell Family Collection. References to Oliver Halvorson, who ran the General Store in Jericho; possibly neighbor Elmer Railson. Harry T. Hayward, "the Minneapolis Svengali," was hanged in December 1895 for the 1894 contract killing of dressmaker Catherine Ging. Hayward had convinced Ging to name him as the beneficiary in her life insurance policy. He hired Claus Blixt to commit the murder. murderbygaslight.com/2010/05/minneapolis-svengali.html

Oscar married Minnie Swenson on June 29, 1895 at the Nannestad Lutheran Church, west of Jericho in Arctander Township, with the reception at her parents' home.[16]

Miss Minnie Swenson, one of our brightest and high esteemed young ladies, was married to Mr. Oscar A. Mankel, a young respected farmer of Lake Andrew, on Saturday, June 29th, at the Hauge's church in this town, by Rev. B. Reitan. After the ceremony the guests, consisting of 30 or 40 well filled rigs, proceeded to the home of the bride's parents, Mr. and Mrs. Gunder Swenson, where an elegant dinner was served. The afternoon was very pleasantly spent with songs by the choir and music by the Norway Lake band. Also some excellent solos by the great violinist, Prof. E. Aakhus, who happened to be present. Speeches were made by Rev. B Reitan and Mr. Landal. Many and costly were the presents received by the young couple. After a bountiful supper had been served the crowd, with many well-wishes to Mr. and Mrs. Oscar Mankel, left for their several homes feeling that they had spent a day long to be remembered.

Wedding picture of Oscar and Minnie (Swenson) Mankell, June 29, 1895.
(image courtesy of the Mankell Family)

After their marriage Oscar and Minnie lived at the Mankell farm. Widow Elizabeth Mankell and her two youngest children, Otto and Esther who both were in their early 20s, remained on the farm with Oscar, Minnie, and their growing family. Oscar and Minnie had three children, all born at the Mankell farm:

1. **Herman** (1896-1985) married Cora Christopherson (1903-1963)
2. **Edna** (1898-1987) married Alvin Halvorson (1894-1950). He was the son of Hans and Margit (Thorson) Halvorson who farmed 1.5 miles northeast of the Mankell farm. Alvin's parents, immigrants from Oppland and Buskerud Norway, were neighbors of the Stenseth family.
3. **Alice** (1903-1991) married George Alvig (1903-1992). Alvig was the son of Nels and Bella (Reierson) Alvig who farmed in Dovre Township, Lake Andrew Township's neighbor to the south. George was a nephew of Martin Reierson.

Oscar's sister, Esther, kept diaries during the late 1890s, where she reflected on several aspects of her life: farm life, the weather, music lessons, working as a housekeeper in Willmar, activities of her mother and siblings, visits with her sister Jenny Gordhamer and niece Dena, her courtship with Gustave Erixon, and her feelings of loneliness and sadness.

---

16 Why Nannestad Lutheran Church and not East Norway Lake Lutheran Church, of which Gemine's father Gunder was a founding member? The mid 1880s was a turbulent time for East Norway Lake, with the creation of First Lutheran Church due to the conflict at ENL. Gunder was one of the men holding the majority at ENL which ultimately saw the resignation of Pastor Lars Markhus. Tensions between the two congregations remained for decades. It's possible that Gemine and Oscar, with friends from both East Norway Lake and First Lutheran, as well as his family's Lake Florida Mission Church, preferred to have the ceremony at a more neutral location.

CH 5: 1890-1899

Esther's diary entries in 1898 were brief. She mentioned a few times that the Mankell family visited Marie Norman—for parties and for coffee. In her entries Esther also noted visiting the Brattlunds who lived in Willmar. Sharing coffee was an activity that brought families together for a moment of rest in a busy day. One can envision two widows and neighbors, Marie Norman and Elizabeth Mankell, visiting with each other over hot cups of coffee, remembering their deceased husbands who they missed, and sharing stories about their children and grandchildren. These two immigrant women spoke Swedish to each other and probably worked to improve their English language as well. Here are Esther's entries relating to visits with the Normans and Brattlunds.

January 19, 1898
Mamma and Otto went to Normans for a party; I did not go. Minnie and Oscar did not visit. [This was two days before Minnie gave birth to her second child, Edna, on January 21.]

January 27
Very windy; hope it won't snow; been to Normans for coffee.

January 29
Alone home; fine weather; Mamma and Oscar went to Willmar. Mamma went to Brattlund; he is very sick. [Both Nils and Marie Brattlund were ill in 1898 and living in Willmar. Marie was recovering from a stroke.]

February 3
Baked forenoon; went to Normans for coffee;

August 19
Went to New London; Gustave [Erixon] *and myself came to town; had a ride with Larson home. Walked from there, home; feel tired;* [Possible reference to William Larson, husband of Johanna Norman]

At the time of her niece Edna's birth in 1898, Esther wrote entries in her diary reflecting on the events at the homestead house. She also shared some of her activities and emotions which show her loneliness, some immaturity and selfishness.

January 21, 1898
Been up since three o'clock this morn. Minnie is sick. Otto went for Mrs. S [probably Minnie's mother, Gemine Swenson], *Forenoon washed clothes; afternoon baked a cake and ...worked very hard. How I wished I was not at home. Why did I not stay away. I dread this night. If I could rest in Gustave arms. 8pm*

January 22
Slept about two hours all night; so frightened I am almost sick. Minnie got a girl and very very sick. I helped to dress baby, but wished I was away. How long this night has been and how long these weeks shall seem.

January 23 *(Sunday)*
Weather is fine. Wished Dena would come. I am so very lonely. Going to write to Gustave this pm; got a letter yesterday. Feel very tired; cannot practice my lesson on account of Minnie. Hope I can take my lesson next Monday; shall take only one a week.

> **January 24**
> *Washed clothes forenoon. Mrs. Swenson came to help. Jennie called in the forenoon. I saw Minnie and the baby. Wished people would stay away. I am disgusted with them; take the life out of me; wished I was away.*
>
> **January 25**
> *Baby good all day; worked for myself; wish D* [Dena Gordhamer] *would call. No letters today; fine weather. Oscar went to New London. Annie* [Esther's sister, in New London] *speaks foolish as usual; good I don't see her.*

1895[17]

The Minnesota Census for 1895 registered Ole Rustad as a laborer at Mankell farm and he lived with the family. Ole O. Rustad was the son Lars O. and Mari Rustad, a Norwegian immigrant family who lived on the south shore of Lake Mary, about ½ mile southwest of the Mankell farm. Lars and his family immigrated in 1869, with Ole born prior to their travels across the ocean from the Gudbrandsdal Valley in Buskerud, Norway. Lars was the pastor of the newly organized Nannestad Lutheran Church in Arctander Township, of which the Stenseth family were members.

Later Ole worked as a carpenter. In 1900, he is recorded as living and working as a carpenter with Hans and Eli Ostenson in Arctander Township; then in 1905, for the Lars H. Larson family, neighbors to the southeast of the Mankell farm, also in Section 20. He married Anna Halvorson in 1906. They had two children and lived in Minneapolis, where Ole was a motorman for a streetcar. He died between 1930 and 1940.

1896-1897[18]

In August 1896, Oscar Mankell became sole owner of the farm: 160 acres of the Section 20 homestead and the 40 acres directly north, in Section 17, from his mother and siblings. During the 1890s, he also became sole owner of four contiguous lots in Willmar's First Ward, north of the railroad tracks—the Thorpe and Lien's Addition, Block 4, Lots 2, 3, 4, 5 in Lot 1—on Olaf Avenue directly west of Willmar Seminary. These inherited properties were transferred from his mother and siblings to Oscar. These lots were owned by his father H.W., purchased in the 1880s when they lived in Willmar and children attended Willmar Seminary. In August, 1896, Oscar sold Lots 4 and 5 of Lot 1 to Andrew Nelson. In May of 1897 Oscar Mankell sold the remaining 2 lots in Willmar: Block 4, Lots 2 and 3 of Lot 1. The buyer was P. O. Larson.

1899
Esther Mankell & Gustave Erixon[19]

On June 8, 1899, Esther, the youngest of H. W. and Elizabeth's children, married Gustave Erixon (1872-1928, born Gustav Erickson) at the Mankell homestead. His parents, Erick Erickson and Charlotte

---

17 Ancestry.com; findagrave.com; moms.mn.gov
18 Kandiyohi County Recorder; *Willmar Tribune* 18 May 1897, 11 August 1896; Mankell Family Collection.
19 Erick Erickson's younger brother was Lars Magnus Ericsson, inventor and founder of the telephone equipment manufacturer Ericsson Company in Sweden. Ancestry.com; transcripts of Esther's diaries are at mankell.org; *Willmar Tribune*, 14 June 1899;

Hedberg, were Swedish immigrants and had a homestead in Section 18 of Irving Township on the eastern edge of Kandiyohi County. Here is an excerpt from the *Willmar Tribune*, describing the event.

> *The beautiful home of Mrs. Elizabeth Mankell, in the town of Lake Andrew, was the scene of a pleasant gathering last Thursday, the occasion being the wedding of her youngest daughter, Ester, to Mr. Gustave A. Erixon, of Irving. About fifty guests responded to the invitations, among them being a number from Willmar.*
>
> *It was a little after two o'clock when the bridal pair descended the stairway and marched into the parlor where the Rev. W. Frykman, of Mamre, was in waiting to pronounce them man and wife. After the brief but impressive marriage service had been read, the happy couple received the congratulations of those present. The bride was mostly attired in a gown of military blue, with satin and passamentrie trimmings. After the ceremony a sumptuous wedding dinner was served on the lawn...*
>
> *The bridal pair is well and favorably known in this county. The groom was for some time a law student in the office of A. F. Nordin at Willmar, later on engaging in the collection business, with headquarters at New London. He has lately accepted a position as agent for the medical book publishing house of the F. A. Davis Company of Philadelphia, and will make his headquarters at Brainerd [Minnesota]. The bride has a host of friends who have known her from her childhood, the early years of which were spent in Willmar. She will make an excellent helpmeet for the husband she has chosen. The TRIBUNE joins with their friends in wishing them much happiness in their new home at Brainerd, for which place they left last Monday.*

Esther and Gustave Erixon, c1899.
(image courtesy of the Mankell Family)

Before their marriage both had worked in Willmar—Esther worked in people's homes; Gustave, studied law. After the wedding, according to the newspaper article, the couple moved to northern Minnesota; however, within a year they returned to Willmar where Gustave was a salesman. Their two daughters were born in Willmar. The family moved to the Oklahoma Territory and by 1905 were in Guthrie, two years before statehood. In 1915, the family moved to Oklahoma City. Esther Erixon died October 21, 1915 a few days after surgery at a Guthrie, OK, hospital. She is buried at the Summit View Cemetery, Guthrie, OK.

Esther and Gustave had two daughters:

1. **Lillian Evangeline** (1900-1994) was born in Willmar. She married Lewis Meyer in 1918 in Arkansas; they lived in Tulsa, OK. Louie's father Leo Meyer played an important role in the politics and creation of the State of Oklahoma in 1907.

2. **Florence Mercedes** (1904-1994) married Frank Adelbert Hoshall at her sister Lillian's home in Tulsa in 1928. She studied art at the University of Oklahoma with artist Oscar Jacobson. After graduating in 1926, she joined the faculty of the same university and taught art for nine years. She painted with water colors and pastels, and also worked in woodcuts. In 1934, Dr. Hoshall opened his orthopedic medical practice in Charleston, SC.

BUSINESSES & ACTIVITIES

NORWAY LAKE CREAMERY[20]

The Norway Lake Creamery Association organized on February 8, 1896, with the building and ice house constructed in the spring by Martin Walby. A typical creamery in Kandiyohi County cost about $2,300 to build and included the separators, large butter churns, engines, and ice houses. Butter production began at the Norway Lake Creamery on June 4, 1896. It was one of several co-operative creameries in Kandiyohi County and in Minnesota. In Kandiyohi County, 18 of 24 townships had a creamery which started in the late 1890s to early 1900s.[21] The state had 560 cooperative creameries in 1898.

These "one-man, one vote" co-operative endeavors were a response to the Panic of 1893, an economic depression which lasted until about 1897. During this economically difficult time, land value and grain prices, specifically wheat, plummeted. Many farmers began to move toward dairy farming and they had an increasing supply of milk. The co-operative creamery movement began in Denmark and migrated across the ocean to the east coast and the Midwest and provided farmers with a way to make money from their milk, specifically the cream. Prior to the co-operative creameries, farm wives made the butter in a time-consuming and labor intensive process using the butter churn. Farm-produced butter varied in quality and taste and was generally used for their families. Sometimes the farm women sold extra butter to neighbors or at local markets.

Technological changes in the 1880s were also available to make this co-operative effort profitable as centrifugal separators (primarily the Alfa deLaval Separator) were faster than gravity when separating cream from milk. Railroads transported butter to markets as far away as New York City. "Minnesota 13" was a new corn variety suitable to the state's short growing season and eaten by the farmers' livestock, including the milk cows. So the farmers moved away from wheat-focused farming toward dairy and the hope of making money by using a business model that pooled together supplies of cream and created a standardized product for the growing market.

Creameries throughout Kandiyohi County were located in the townships at crossroads communities, like Jericho, which had other businesses and organizations, such as: post office, general store, feed mill, church, cemetery, and blacksmith shop. This allowed for patron farmers to take care of other errands

---

20 "Norway Lake" is not a reference to Norway Lake Township, rather to the community of Jericho, also known as "Norway Lake" in its early years. Arctander Township had another creamery, West Lake Creamery, on the far west side in the community of Negord, which also served farmers in Hays Township in Swift County. Wikipedia.org; *Minnesota: A History of the State*, p 397-98; Peterson, Cynthia L, *Little Dairy on the Prairie*; Minopedia.org. Keillor, *Co-operative Commonwealth: Co-ops in Rural Minnesota, 1859-1939*, p. 100-141; *Willmar Tribune*: 10 March 1896, 26 May 1896, 9 June 1896, 27 Feb 1901, 2 October 1901, 19 March 1902, 2 April 1902, 8 August 1903, 9 September 1903, 21 Nov 1903, 19 Dec 1904, 9 Jan 1907, 12 Jan 1910, 24 May 1911, 24 April 1912, 26 Feb 1913; mankell.org; "From Churns to Butter Factories"; 1907 Biennial Report of State Dairy and Food Commissioner p. 152.

21 The 18 Townships with names of creameries if different from the Township name: *Arctander* (West Lake and Norway Lake), *Burbank* (Georgeville), *Colfax* (Scandia), *East Lake Lillian*, *Gennessee* (Atwater), *Green Lake* (Hub), *Harrison*, *Irving*, *Kandiyohi* (Kandiyohi Central), *Lake Elizabeth*, *Lake Lillian*, *Mamre*, *New London*, *Roseland* (Winfield), *Roseville* (Lintonville), *St. John's* (Pennock), *Whitefield* (Svea), *Willmar*. *Illustrated History of Kandiyohi County*, various pages.

Norway Lake Creamery, c1900.
(image courtesy of the Kandiyohi County Historical Society)

after delivering their raw supply to the creamery. It would also be a time for the men, women, and children to visit, share stories, and hear local news. This social time gave the men and women time away from home, providing a break from their daily chores.

At each of these co-operative creameries, farmers pledged their cows' milk or cream and they purchased shares, at about $25 for each farmer. Farmers owned the creamery and employed a butter maker and a business manager. Some creameries accepted the cream; others, the raw milk and then provided the separation process, with cream as the product and skim milk the byproduct. Each creamery had a schedule to accept the milk or cream from the farmers: daily, twice a day, or twice a week, for example. Butter was the product for sale—to the farmers, neighbors, and to larger markets. If the creameries were successful, the farmers shared in the profits. If not, then they shared in the losses. These creameries were usually profitable, though the Norway Lake Creamery was not as successful as hoped because not enough farmers were patrons/shareholders.

The Norway Lake Creamery and its ice house were located in the community of Jericho (aka Norway Lake), on the eastern edge of Arctander Township and one to two miles from the four farms. Farmers from Lake Andrew and Arctander townships were part of this co-operative. The creamery was open six days a week when milk was plentiful. (In January, 1898, the creamery closed briefly due to lack of milk.) Each March the ice house was filled with ice harvested from local lakes and covered with sawdust to reduce melting. The ice kept the final product—butter—cool through the warmer months before selling to customers or transporting to the local railroad. Men connected to the four farms (noted in bold) served as officers and shareholders, along with several of their neighbors from Lake Andrew and Arctander Townships:

John Syvert Christenson
Christopher H. Engen
Martin H. Engen
  (father of Mina Christenson)
Andrew H. Gordhamer
  (brother-in-law of Oscar Mankell)
Hans A. Halvorson
John Halvorson

Severin Hatlestad
C. K. Lund
Oscar Mankell
E. O. Negaard
Mathias O. Rustad
Christian T. Skindelien
Gabriel Stene
Simon A. Syverson

Creamery staff, shareholders, and farmers were proud of the creamery's butter. Buttermakers at creameries from across the county and state entered butter scoring competitions at local fairs, state fairs, and dairy conventions to show off their skills to fellow buttermakers, and earn bragging rights with neighbors and friends. The competitions helped communities learn more about the importance of the dairy industry. These men earned diplomas and state licenses from the State Agriculture Society. Buttermakers at the Norway Lake Creamery included these men:[22]

- Oliver Halvorson (1896-1900) was born in Lake Andrew Township; also the postmaster for the Jericho (aka Norway Lake) community
- Ludvig M. Steberg (1901) came from Swift County
- Louis Toveson/Tuveson (1901), who came from Atwater, soon left to work at the Mamre Creamery
- O. Gordhamer (1902)
- David J. Ostlund (1902-1903) was born in Mamre Township
- Oscar Hallquist (1903-1904) moved to Rice County where he was a buttermaker and food inspector
- David J. Ostlund, (1904-06) returned to the creamery; he later worked in Minneapolis as a buttermaker.
- A man from Vernon County Wisconsin (1909-?)

In 1902, the creamery became a stock company known as the Norway Lake Creamery Company. However the company was not successful. The Norway Lake Creamery ceased production after about 15 years of service to area farmers. The equipment was sold at a public auction on May 26, 1911. There was an unsuccessful attempt at restarting the creamery in 1912. The property was sold in February 1913 to its neighbor Henry Hande who built a shed from lumber of the dismantled building. Without the local creamery, farmers brought their cream product to other area creameries, including New London.

---

22 Years at the creamery are approximate.

PASTIMES

MUSIC[23]

Many of the young adults of the four farms were part of a growing musical community—a band and a choir—which appears to have begun in the mid-1890s and lasted for several decades. Members of two area churches (East Norway Lake Lutheran Church and Lake Florida Mission Church) combined to create the **Norway Lake Choir**, led by John Syvert Christenson. Members of the 1894 choir which connect to the four farms included the following:

- J. S. Christenson
- Carrie Stenseth, married J. S. Christenson in 1894
- Minnie Swenson, married Oscar Mankell in 1895
- Mina (aka Minnie) Engen, the 2nd wife of J. S. Christenson, after the 1904 death of Carrie
- Louisa Engen, niece of Mina Engen

Norway Lake Choir, c1894.

Front row: Matilda Slattum, Minnie Swenson, Carrie Stenseth, Minnie Engen, Thilda Christianson, Hilda Slattum, and Esther Mankell.
Second row: Oscar Mankell, Ole Rustad, John Quam, Clara Swenson, Minnie Slattum, Louisa Engen, and Lina Swenson.
Back row: Christian Engen, Albert Slattum, J. S. Christenson (leader), Carelius Thori, Christian Rustad, and Swen Swenson.

---
23 *Keeping the Faith*, p 55; *Willmar Tribune*, 23 April 1895, 4 June 1895 and an undated (probably 1944) Eben E Lawson article.

- Esther Mankell, sister of Oscar Mankell
- Oscar Mankell
- John Quam, husband of Sophia Mankell
- Swen Swenson, brother of Minnie (Swenson) Mankell

Other members of the 1894 choir:
- Thilda Christianson, later the second wife of John Quam
- Ole Rustad
- Christian Rustad
- Albert Slattum
- Hilda Slattum
- Matilda Slattum
- Minnie Slattum
- Carelius Thori, possibly related to J. S. Christenson (born J. S. Thori)

This group was truly a community choir, with choir members from Sections 17, 19, 20, and 30 on the western edge of Lake Andrew Township and members from Section 24 in eastern Arctander Township.

There are newspaper accounts of the **Norway Lake Band** existing in 1895 and 1896. This group presented concerts and played at events in Sunburg, Willmar, New London, and at Lake Andrew before the existence of Sibley State Park.[24] Here is an 1895 article recalling the event on the northern shore of Lake Andrew. Did these neighbors gather at the same location later designated as Sibley State Park, established by the State Legislature in 1919? The writer noted this location's beauty and a place for fun, picnics, and recreation—as it has been for 100 years.

> *The picnic at Lake Andrew Sunday was, we believe, as far as a general good time was concerned, a great success. Together with the fact that it was a splendid day for such sport, a cool, shady and beautiful spot on the north shore of the lake had been chosen for the place of fun, enjoyment and recreation. The picnic was gotten up for no special purpose except to give the people a chance to come together for a day of association with each other, and they certainly took advantage of the occasion far and wide, to which the crowd that was there is sufficient testimony. Eloquent addresses were made by Prof. B. S. Covell* [Burton S. Covell, businessman from Willmar] *and Dr. Johnson* probably Dr. Christian Johnson, of Willmar and New London] *and music, both vocal and instrumental, was furnished in great plenty by the Norway Lake Quartette and the Norway Lake Cornet*

---

24 Sibley State Park was established in 1919. Peter Broberg, the only family member who survived the Monson Lake killings in the Dakota War of 1862, provided the funds necessary to purchase the land for Sibley State Park development. In 1935 the Veterans Conservation Corps, a group of about 200 men, built the park's buildings, roads and trails, using granite from central Minnesota. stateparks.com/sibley.html; Wikipedia.org;

Band. The crowd stayed until late, evidently being loath to leave. But when it did leave, it could and we believe it did leave with the conviction that they had spent the day very profitably and that the picnic of Lake Andrew would long be remembered.

The Norway Lake Band and Choir, in April 1895, joined the festivities celebrating the 25th wedding anniversary of Rev. and Mrs. R. K. Fjelstad, the pastor at East Norway Lake Lutheran Church. Two months later the two groups provided music and celebrated the marriage of two of their members: Oscar Mankell and Minnie Swenson. The Band also played for the neighbors who gathered at the Even Railson farm in 1896 to celebrate the Fourth of July.

CHAPTER 6:
1900-1909

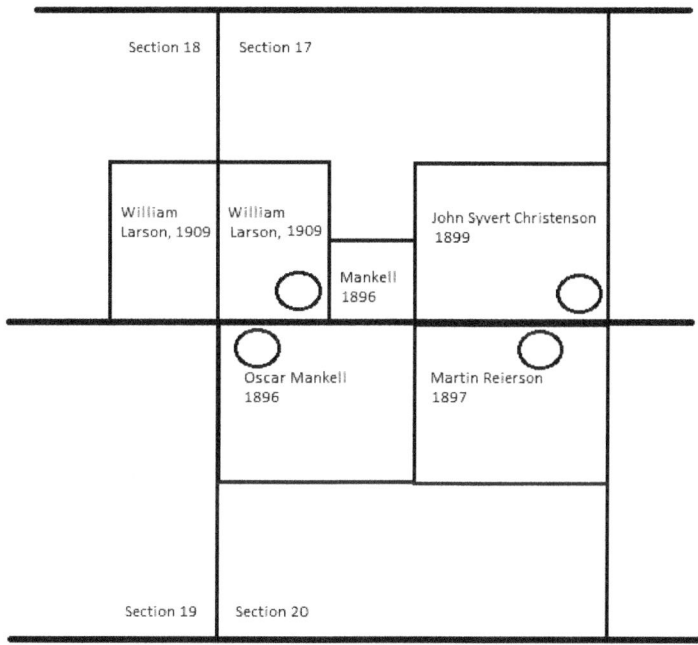

HIGHLIGHTS

- The last of the four immigrant settler men on the mile died; three of the four women settlers died
- Jericho continues to be a business center for the community
- New technologies arrived—cars and telephones
- One farmer had agricultural patents accepted
- All children on the mile now attend District 25 school

STENSETH/CHRISTENSON FARM[1]

Three generations of the Stenseth and Christenson families lived at the farm at the beginning of the century: Widow Karen Stenseth and her daughter Maren Stenseth; J. S. Christenson, his wife Carrie (Stenseth) and their children, Harvin and Clara. By the end of the decade Karen and her daughter Carrie would be dead and John Syvert would marry again and have more children. He also received two patents for his agricultural inventions.

1900

Here is a drawing of the farm as it appeared at the beginning of the decade. This drawing recreates the diagram hand drawn by Harvin Christenson, son of J. S. and Carrie Christenson.

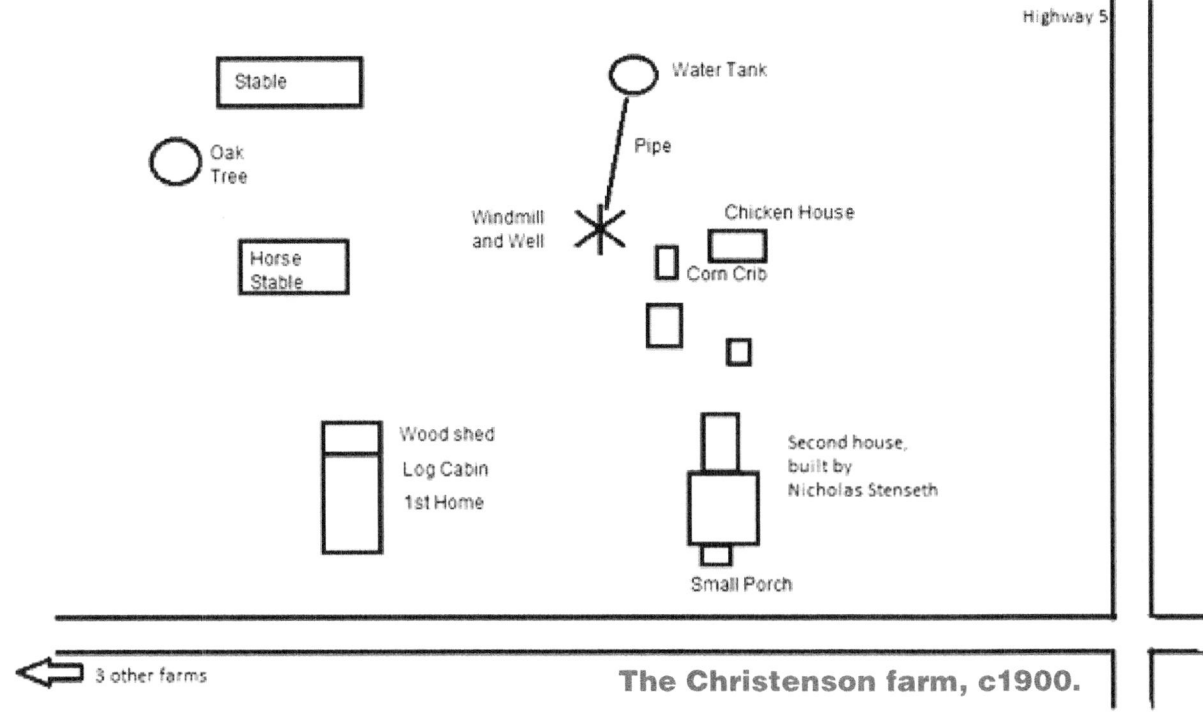

The Christenson farm, c1900.

1902

Deaths of young adults were not unusual during this time period. Tragedy struck the Stenseth family when Nicholas and Hilda (Hanson) Stenseth, living in Mamre Township, died within months of each other—both from tuberculosis, then called "consumption"—leaving two children under the age of five. The couple had been married less than six years. They married in Minneapolis and lived in the city for four years before moving to Mamre Township where Nicholas operated a mercantile store near the Mamre Creamery.

---

1 *Willmar Tribune*, 5 March 1902, 4 May 1904, 10 May 1905, 17 May 1905, 27 Nov 1907, 8 April 1908, 13 May 1908, 20 May 1908, 6 January 1909, 3 February 1909, 1 September 1909, 9 September 1909, 15 December 1909. *Willmar Gazette*, March and November 1902, December 1909; moms.mn.gov; ancestry.gov; findagrave.com. United States Patent Office, No. 922,457 and No. 897,271; Christenson Family Collection; Ronning, *Bethesda Children's Home*. Kandiyohi County Recorder.

Husband Nicholas Stenseth died in Mamre Township on March 4, 1902, and is buried at Nannestad Church Cemetery (also referred to as the Hauge, Hauge's or Haugean Church) in Arctander Township—the church of his parents, Nils and Karen Stenseth. His mother Karen Stenseth mourned for her son and his family. Here are two obituaries published in the *Willmar Tribune* and the *Willmar Republican Gazette* which described Nicholas, his life, and his death:

Death at Mamre

N. N. Stenseth of Mamre died yesterday. Deceased had been suffering for many years form consumption; a bad cold brought a sudden turn for the worse and the end soon came.

Mr. Stenseth was born at the Stenset [farm in Nannestad] Norway, in 1864. He came to America with his parents about thirty years ago. The family lived in Fillmore County for two years, and then moved to this county, where they settled on a farm in [the] town of Lake Andrew. Some eight years ago Stenseth went to Minneapolis, where he held a position as street car conductor until his failing health forced him to retire. In the fall of 1900 he came to Mamre and opened a store at the creamery.

He leaves a wife and two children, his aged mother and two sisters to mourn his early death. The sympathy of the entire community goes out to the family in their sad affliction. Funeral services will be held at the Hauge church, town of Arctander, on Friday afternoon, and the remains will be interred in the cemetery adjoining that church.

N. N. Stenseth, the storekeeper near the creamery, died last Tuesday morning after a lingering illness of the dread disease consumption. The funeral arrangements have not been made at this writing but it will occur from Hauge church, town of Arctander. Deceased was about thirty-seven years of age and leaves a wife and two small children. He came to Mamre a year and a half ago and entered the mercantile business in which he was engaged at the time of his death. An aged mother who lived in Lake Andrew survives him. While here he made many friends and was honored and respected by all who knew him.

Following Nicholas' death, his widow Hilda operated the store with her brother George C. Hanson. Born in 1876, Hilda died in November, only eight months after Nicholas' death, also from tuberculosis. George Hanson soon sold the business following the death of his sister. She is buried next to her husband at the Nannestad Church Cemetery in Arctander Township. Her death notice appeared in the *Willmar Republican Gazette*:

Died of Consumption

Saturday, at her home in Mamre town, occurred the death of Mrs. N. N. Stenseth. Mrs. Stenseth has been suffering from consumption for some time past and the end, while it was not unexpected, brings sorrow to a large number of friends. Mrs. Stenseth's husband died early last spring and two small children are orphaned by her death. Funeral services were conducted the first of the week by Rev. Hansen of Spicer.

Following Hilda's death, the two young children—son Leslie, age 4, and daughter Jeanette, age two—were orphans. Maternal grandparents George and Jonette Rebecca Hanson took the children with them to their home in Minneapolis. Soon after, four-year-old Leslie was sent to the Bethesda Children's Home, an orphanage in Beresford, Lincoln County, South Dakota. This orphanage, which began in 1896, was affiliated with the Haugean Norwegian Lutheran Synod, and supported by congregations in South Dakota, Minnesota, and Iowa and also supported by individuals. Its mission was mercy, by offering care, education, music, sports, and religious instruction to orphaned or neglected children, numbering from 50 to 75 at any given point in time. The boy's grandparents were members of St. Paul's Lutheran Church in Minneapolis. In addition, Leslie was baptized at this congregation. St. Paul's may have had ties to this orphanage in South Dakota. Leslie was at the orphanage from 1902, and left soon after 1910. This orphanage experienced two epidemics, typhoid and diphtheria, in 1908. All children and all staff, except one, contracted the diseases. Leslie was one of those who became ill. His little sister Jeanette stayed with her maternal grandparents in Minneapolis. However, her grandmother Jonette Rebecca died in 1909, leaving this young girl with another loss. In 1910, Jeanette was sent to the orphanage. Leslie and Jeanette possibly overlapped their stays at the orphanage during that year. By the 1920s, both siblings were living and working in Minneapolis and they remained in the city until their deaths. Leslie died in 1976 and Jeanette in 1982. Both are buried at Lakewood Cemetery, Section 15, Lot 47A, in Minneapolis.

1903

At the end of 1903, John Syvert Christenson began working in New London where he sold lumber. The family moved to New London; sadly, Carrie was ill by this time.

1904

Two years after the Stenseth and Christenson families mourned the death of Nicholas and his wife, the family faced the death of Carrie Stenseth Christenson, wife of J. S. Christenson, on April 28, 1904. She was ill from stomach ulcers and tuberculosis of the blood (aka pernicious anemia), left behind two young children, and is buried at the Nannestad Church in Arctander. The *Willmar Tribune* and two other newspapers published her obituary; these accounts contained some discrepancies regarding her birth year, location of death—in New London or at the Lake Andrew Township farm—and her husband's employment. J. S. was the lumberman in New London at the time of his wife's death

> *On Thursday morning occurred the demise of Mrs. J. S. Christenson at her home in the town of Lake Andrew. Deceased had been a patient sufferer for about eight months and death came as a great relief from all earthly afflictions. Death was due to ulcer of the stomach and anemia.*
>
> *Mrs. Christenson was born at Highland Prairie, Fillmore County, January 1, 1868, and was at the time of death 36 years of age. In 1870 she moved to Kandiyohi County with her parents and was a resident of Lake Andrew ever since.*
>
> *The following immediate relatives are left to mourn her death. Her husband, a son aged 8, a daughter, aged 5, one sister, Miss Mary Stenseth and her mother 79 years old. Deceased will be remembered by old schoolmates in this city under the maiden name of Miss Carrie Stenseth, being in her girlhood days a pupil of the Willmar public schools and later a student at the Seminary. Growing to womanhood she became a devout Christian*

and an ardent worker in the church and will be greatly missed by many co-workers and friends.

The funeral took place on Monday, Rev. Joe Halvorson of Spicer officiating. The remains were taken to the Hauge's church cemetery at Arctander for interment.

From two undated New London newspapers:

Died: Mrs. Carrie Dorthea Christenson at Lake Andrew, Thursday, April 28th, of tuberculosis of the blood.

The deceased was the wife of Mr. J. S. Christenson our new lumber merchant. She has been suffering for a long time with the disease which ended her life. Mrs. Christenson was born in Fillmore County this state on New Year's Day, 1867 [sic 1868]. When she was three years of age, her parents moved to this county. September 6th 1894 she was married to the husband who now greatly mourns her untimely demise. The union was blessed with two children, a boy of 7 and a girl of 5 who are now motherless. The mother, Mrs. Carrie [Karen] Stenseth, about 80 years of age, is yet living and one sister yet survives. The funeral took place Monday from the Nannestad church at Norway Lake and was conducted by Rev. Halvorson, of Spicer.

Mrs. Christenson Dead.
Gloom hangs heavily at the home of Mr. J. S. Christenson in the village of New London. Last Thursday afternoon Mrs. Christenson died after a short illness of complications of stomach troubles. The funeral was held Monday from the Hauge Lutheran Church in the town of Norway Lake [Jericho] and the interment was at the [Nannestad] church cemetery.

Deceased was one of the best known of the younger residents of the town of Lake Andrew, where the Christensons made their home prior to going to New London last winter. She had resided there from her childhood and as she grew to womanhood her circle of friends grew with her. She was born in Fillmore County January 1, 1868, and came with her parents to this county a few years afterwards. Her early schooling was received in the Lake Andrew and New London schools. Later she taught in North Dakota. Ten years ago she was married to Mr. J. S. Christenson, at Lake Andrew, and two children came to bless their union. One boy, Harvin, aged 8 and a daughter, Clara, aged 5, besides her husband are left to mourn her death.

The bereaved husband and his little ones will have the sympathy of all who know them in their affliction. Mr. Christenson started in the lumber business at New London a short time ago and had just become settled there as the hand of death devastates his home. The scenes at the funeral were sad in the extreme. A large number of friends from outside points attended the funeral.

1904-1905

After his first wife's death Christenson quit the lumber business. He finished building a barn on the Section 17 farm, using the lumber from his closed business in New London. The old barn had been north of the farmhouse. The new barn was closer to the north-south Highway 5. The barn's foundation had begun in 1903, with the construction completed in 1905.

1905

A year after the death of his wife Carrie, John Syvert Christenson married again, to Mina Engen on May 7, 1905. Mina (1870-1955) was the daughter of immigrants, Martin and Helene (Skindelien) Engen from Lund Parish, Oppland, Norway. The Engen family lived in Section 12, Arctander Township, to the west of Norway Lake. J. S. brought his wife and children back to the farm in Lake Andrew Township. They lived with his first wife's mother, Karen Stenseth, and Carrie's sister, Maren.

J. S. and Mina had two children; one died as an infant:

1. **Clarence H. M. O. Christenson** (1907-1907)
2. **Hedvig Oline Christenson** (aka Hedviq, 1908-1989) was baptized at the Nannestad Church. She married Chris Knutson (1896-1982) on July 18, 1931, in Kandiyohi County.

John Syvert and Mina married at her parents' home in Arctander Township. One day after their marriage, the couple was serenaded at their home in Lake Andrew Township by their fellow musicians of the Norway Lake Band. With the unusual band instruments used for this occasion, the serenade probably brought the neighbors to the farm to share the enjoyment. Here is a description (with some humor) of the event, as printed in the *Willmar Tribune*.

> *An unusual occurrence took place last Monday night, which caused quite a sensation in the whole neighborhood. Nervous women took it to be an earthquake, but men who thought they understood a little about it said it must be the strikers, police force and bums from Chicago. But others said it was only the Lake Andrew music band serenading the newly married couple, Mr. and Mrs. J. S. Christenson. Their musical instruments consisted of cow bells of every variety, old boilers, circular sawblades, dynamite "and other articles too numerous to mention" which filled the air with the most beautiful chimes until daylight the next morning. Nor had the serenaders forgotten to lay in an ample supply of Milwaukee champagne, which they intended to make the groom pay for. They were freely treated to cigars, but the groom refused to pay for the beer, which caused the repeating of the performance several times throughout the week. It is safe to say that every member of the band feels proud of his occupation. It has been suggested that the band wagon from Willmar be obtained and the boys taken down there to give a free exhibition in the courthouse yard.*

1907

In 1907, several area farmers worked together to more efficiently drain water from farmland, north to Norway Lake. Farmers routed their ditches to a slough in the northwest part of J. S. Christenson's 160-acre farm, then to the Johannes Halvorson farm, and finally to Norway Lake. One ditch was from Martin Reierson's slough in Section 20 to Christenson's slough. Another ditch was from Christenson's slough to Johannes Halvorson's slough. Halvorson had land in Section 17 (north of the Norman farm) and in Section 8, on the south shore of Norway Lake. The final ditch was from Halvorson's slough to Norway Lake.

Reierson had agreed to pay $35 to Christenson for cutting a ditch through his land, but Reierson did not pay. Christenson hired an attorney from Willmar to take care of the matter and the situation was resolved, with Reierson paying the $35. According the Christenson family, this situation strained the relationship between the two families.

The Christenson family faced another death in 1907. Clarence H.M.O. Christenson, son of J. S. and Mina died one month after his May birth. His tombstone at the Nannestad Cemetery has this inscription: "*Likkelig du lille*" (Your little one).

1907

In 1907, J. S. Christenson arranged for the Nannestad and East Norway Lake congregations to have a joint Christmas festival—with a combined choir and combined Sunday school providing most of the program. Christenson was the Superintendent of the Nannestad Sunday School and leader of the choir for many years. Here is a description from the *Willmar Tribune*:

> *The joint Christmas tree festival at the East Norway Lake church last Thursday evening was a success from start to finish. The money taken in at the door amounted to $56.80. A well rendered program was given to an audience that eclipsed any previous gathering at a festival in the church. The children's part of the program, about 15 numbers of declamations and songs, was given in a very creditable manner. The joint choir of 25 singers sang in a way that reflected great credit on them. The committee on arrangements feels very grateful towards Hon. Elias Rachie of Willmar, Rev. J. S. Halvorson of Long Lake and the local pastor, Rev. Sotendahl, for their valuable assistance in making the festival one of the finest ones in this vicinity.*

1908

Six months after burying his son, John Syvert buried his mother, Lena Christenson, an immigrant and pioneer of Lake Andrew Township who now lived in New London. As mentioned in an earlier chapter Lena and her husband Hans adopted John Syvert Thori when he was a young child. Here is her obituary from the *Willmar Tribune*:

> *Another pioneer of Lake Andrew, Mrs. Hans Christenson, lately of New London, answered death's summons on the evening of December 28. She had been very sick for a long time, and death surely came to her as a kind reliever. She was a friend to everybody, a devoted Christian and a loving wife. With her husband she settled down in Lake Andrew about 35 years ago and with the other pioneers struggled thru those days of hardship fully realized only by the pioneers. About eight years ago they sold their old homestead and bought property in New London, where she resided till her death. The funeral took place last Saturday at the Hauge church, of which she had been a faithful member ever since its organization. The last sad rites were conducted by Revs. Halvorson and Nordberg. Mr. and Mrs. Hans Christenson had no children, but two adopted children, J. S. Christenson of Lake Andrew and Mrs. Edward Johnson of Willmar, to whom she was a faithful mother and their interests were always hers.*

One year after the death of infant Clarence, J. S. and Mina welcomed the birth of their daughter, Hedvig, on May 3, 1908.

Mina with young Hedvig, c1910.
(image courtesy of the Christenson Family)

1908-1909

In addition to being a farmer, church leader, and musician, John Syvert was also an inventor, having received two patents from the United States government.

Grain-Cleaner for Wild Pea and Cockle

On September 1, 1908, Christenson received a patent for the Grain-Cleaner For Wild Pea and Cockle (Number 897,271). Christenson invented a grain cleaner in response to two problematic weeds found in the farmers' grain, with the goal of separating the weeds from the good grain. The cockle plant was probably the invasive, common, and poisonous corn-cockle plant. It quickly grew with the wheat plants, seeded, and was inadvertently harvested and resown during the next spring's planting season. The wild pea plant was probably the toxic Wild Sweet Pea plant, which is a perennial, fast-growing plant found throughout North America. Christenson exhibited his invention at the 1908 Minnesota State Fair. J. S., Mina, and Harvin took the train from Willmar to St. Paul, which left at 3:00 in the morning. The family stayed with Christenson relatives and J. S. returned home. (Later in this chapter is Gabriel Stene's story about how John Syvert, Stene, and a friend returned home from the State Fair to the township.)

Here is Christenson's description of his device, which included a tilted frame, side boards, conveyor belts, a fly wheel, rollers, and hopper, working together to separate wild pea weeds and cockles from the grain:

> *My invention relates to grain cleaning machines, and more particularly to devices for separating from wheat and other grains, wild peas and cockle. The wild peas have especially of late years become a serious trouble to farming of wheat, rye, barley, oats and the like, and as the size of these peas is such as to permit them to go through any strainer through which the wheat will pass, the separation of the peas from the grain has at least as far as I know been impossible by any device heretofore constructed. ...*

A grain cleaning machine comprising in combination a supporting frame, a tilting frame normally laterally inclined frame hinged at one side therein, and means for changing the inclination of said frame, one or more endless conveyer belts or aprons mounted on and driven by rollers in the tilting frame, means for rotating said rollers so as to move the conveyers, a rock-shaft journaled at one side of the tilting frame and operatively connected with the driving mechanism of the rollers, a pan fixed on the rock-shaft for each conveyer belt and projecting in over the upper run thereof, a hopper mounted on the tilting frame, spouts extending from said hopper one into each pan, and means for regulating the passage of grain through each spout, said spouts having each an elongated outlet by which to spread the grain upon the bottom of the pan.

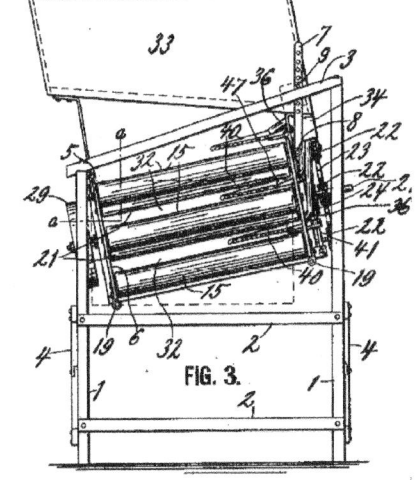

Grain-Cleaner for Wild Pea and Cockle, Patent No. 897,271.

Christenson applied for his patent in March 1908, with Nels Quam as a witness, and soon after took his new machine to his neighbors, showing them how it worked, and probably shared his excitement of applying for and waiting for his patent which he received several months later. One wonders if his neighbors bought this invention from him.

Tank Heater and Feed Cooker

Tank Heater and Feed Cooker, Patent No. 922,457.

On May 25, 1909, Christenson received a patent for the Tank Heater and Feed Cooker (Number 922,457). One of his witnesses was Nels Quam, his witness to the earlier invention. This new invention, which heated or even cooked the feed for pigs, stood on legs and included a furnace, water tank, fire box, dampers, and smoke flue. Christenson's patent for the device which consumed less fuel than the typical heater of this time period, included this statement from the inventor:

My invention relates to improvements in water tank heaters and feed cookers for the class of tanks used to water cattle, sheep etc. on large farms, ranches or other places where stock is kept. The object of the invention is to provide a new and improved device of said class, which is simple and durable, easily operated and of a minimum cost to construct.

As he did with his Grain Cleaner, Christenson demonstrated his device to his neighbors and solicited orders, with the help of neighbor and friend, Gabriel Stene. In the summer of 1909, Christenson sold his patent to a Minneapolis business, which named it the Zenith Tank Heater.

1909

Karen Stenseth (aka Karine Larsdatter), widow of Nils Stenseth, died on Monday, December 13, 1909. Her funeral was on December 17, probably at the Nannestad Church in Arctander Township. She is buried at the church cemetery next to her husband. Karen was a founding member of this congregation and was active with the Ladies' Aid Society, hosting the church women at her home. Prior to her death she had mourned the deaths of four of her children, a grandson, and her daughter-in-law. Two Willmar newspapers wrote about her death.

From the December 15, 1909, issue of the *Willmar Tribune*:

> It is also our duty to chronicle the death of another early pioneer. Mrs. Karen N. Stenseth, who died Monday morning last at 4:30 from old age. She reached the good old age of 85 years. She had been suffering a good deal from asthma which was the immediate cause of her death.

From the *Willmar Gazette*:

> Mrs. Karen Stenseth died at the home of J. S. Christenson of town of Lake Andrew, on Monday of last week, at the advanced age of 85 years. Mrs. Stenseth was one of the pioneers of that township. Her husband and four children have preceded her in death, the only survivor of the family being one daughter.

FARM LABORERS & BOARDERS

During this first decade of the 20th century, J. S. and Mina Christenson had at least two laborers who worked and lived at the farm, per the Federal and State census information. It isn't clear how long each of these men lived and worked at the farm. The family also had a boarder.

In 1900, Ole Kallevig worked for Christenson. Born in 1878, Kallevig was a Norwegian immigrant, having arrived in 1893. Five years later he was working in Arctander Township, at the home of Rev. Mons and Berthe Sotendahl. Mons was a pastor at West Norway Lake and East Norway Lake Lutheran churches in Arctander Township.

Following Kallevig at the Christenson farm was Irish immigrant Mike Shields. He was born about 1874 and immigrated in 1888. Shields worked for the Christenson family until about 1907. During the 20+ years he lived in the township, Shields worked for other area farm families including Hans and Margit Halvorson also in Section 16. By 1910, he was living with the Reese family by Lake Florida. By 1920, Shields rented a place in Section 16, ¼ mile east of the Christenson farm. Johanna Larson owned these 120 acres (S ½ of SW ¼; SW ¼ of SE ¼).

A woman named Selma Regina Farmen was a boarder for about 2 years, beginning in late 1909. She was a teacher at District 25. Farmen arrived at the Christenson farm after Karen Stenseth's death and stayed in the matriarch's bedroom at the front of the house. Selma married Christian Karelius Christianson on Christmas Day, 1911. Both were from Cerro Gordo Township in Lac qui Parle County, Minnesota. The couple later lived in Montana and Oregon.

BRATTLUND/REIERSON FARM[2]

1900

The decade began with the death of Nils Brattlund on November 20, 1900. He and his wife Marie had moved to Willmar, the county seat, in 1886. Nils was the last surviving man of the initial immigrant settlers in the four farms community. His obituary was in the *Willmar Tribune*:

> **Death of Nels Brattlund**
> **One of the Early Settlers and Respected**
> **Citizens of the County Passes Away.**
> **Stricken by Paralysis**
>
> *Nels Brattlund, an old and respected citizen of this place, died yesterday morning at 3:30 of hemorrhage of the brain. Deceased was stricken with paralysis last Wednesday and his death was momentarily expected. He was 81 years and 7 days of age.*
>
> *Mr. Brattlund was one of the early settlers of the county, and removed here from Lake Andrew to make his home with his two daughters, Mrs. A. E. Rice and Mrs. C. C. Selvig. The demise occurred at the home of the latter, with whom Mr. and Mrs. Brattlund have resided for a number of years. The deceased leaves a widow in feeble health, besides four daughters, to mourn his departure. The two daughters residing at outside points are Mrs. Marie Beckstrom of Oakland, Nebraska, and Mrs. Johanna Olson of Clinton, Minn.*
>
> *The funeral will take place tomorrow (Thursday) at 9 o'clock a.m., from his late home. After a brief service at the house, conducted by Rev. Anderson, the remains will be taken to Lake Andrew for burial. Service will be held in the Swedish Mission church* [Lake Florida Mission Church] *at that place, Rev. Frykman officiating.*

1905

Five years after Nils Brattlund died, his widow Marie Brattlund died. She had suffered from a series of strokes in 1897 previous to the one that led to her death in September 1905. The Brattlund property on 4th Street between Trott and Minnesota Avenues, which included a house, barn and three lots, were for sale two months later. Marie's daughter Caroline Selvig and her family had been living with Marie for several years. With the sale of the house, Caroline and CC Selvig and family moved a few blocks west and north to 7th Street and Litchfield Ave. Marie's obituary was in the *Willmar Tribune*. The tribute poem was written by Ida Mae (nee Wortman) Styles, her neighbor and friend.

> **Answers Death's Summons**
>
> *Another of the early residents of Kandiyohi County has answered the last roll call. Mrs. Maria S. Brattlund died at four o'clock last Thursday morning, Sept. 7. She had been rather feeble for a long time on account of old age. Nine weeks ago she suffered a paralytic stroke in her right side that rendered her entirely helpless.*
>
> *The funeral took place last Saturday. Rev. A. N. Osterholm conducted short services at the residence, and read a poem composed by Mrs. Styles in memory of the deceased. The remains were then taken to the Lake Florida church for interment by the side of her husband. At the church, services were conducted by Rev. I. N Nelson of Ellsworth, Wis., and an address was made by Rev. Osterholm.*

---

2 *Willmar Tribune* 21 November 1900, 13 September 1905, 20 March 1907; 14 August 1907; 16 Sept 1908, ancestry.com;

Maria S. Brattlund was born in Elfsbacka parish, Vermland, [Värmland] Sweden, April 26, 1817, and had therefore at her death reached the ripe old age of 88 years, four months and seventeen days. In 1838 [sic 1840] she was united in marriage to Nils Brattlund. Nine children blessed the union, of which four are still living—Mrs. Maria Beckstrom of Oakland, Neb; Mrs. Sophia L. Rice, Mrs. Caroline Selvig and Mrs. John Olson, of Willmar.

The Brattlund family emigrated to America in 1865, first settling in Moline, Ill. A year or two later they moved to this county and settled on a farm in [the] town of Lake Andrew. Twenty years ago the old folks moved to Willmar and built a residence on Fourth Street, where they spent the rest of their days. The husband died in Nov., 1900.

Mrs. Brattlund was a devoted and earnest Christian and was a member of the Mission church here, where she took an active part in the church work as long as she had the strength to do so.

IN MEMORY OF MOTHER BRATTLUND
"But the pathway of the just is as the
shining light, that shineth more and more
unto the perfect day." Prov. 4-18.

The mother gone—our lonely hearts
Can but miss her from her place
But can we grieve that now with Christ
She sings Love's story—"saved by grace."

"Min Käre Jesus!" was her cry
Her soul beat hard its fleshly bars
As up she looked with longing eyes
To her dear Home beyond the stars.

"Earth goes to earth, and dust to dust"
I hear God's minister declare—
'Tis the worn garment seamed and just
Too frail, for such a soul to wear.

Oh! lonely hearts, look up! look up!
From earthly mould and upturned sod
She wears the robe of spotless white
Reserved alway for saints of God

How sweet the thought—O! blest estate,
Her soul out-grown its earthly clod
Has winged to Him its eager flight—
She's with her God! She's with her God!

No barrier there of language strange
In that dear land of love and light
To mar the perfect interchange
In all that heaven born souls delight

But often here I tried to grasp
The meaning of each burning phrase
As patient face and upward glance,
Bespoke her walk in Godly ways.

We praise Thee Father that thy power
Upraised for us from common dust
Such sweet and patient holy lives—
To tread "the pathway of the just."
We thank Thee, too, that o'er that "way."
Thy glory shows the "perfect day."

Farewell, dear saint, and "aurevoir—"
Now home and mother waits on high.
To welcome there each child and friend
When their departure draweth nigh.

Saviour, divine, oh! give us grace
To wait, in us. Thy perfect will;
Give us "clean hands, and purer hearts"
To all Thy righteousness fulfill!

So when our time to meet Thee comes
Like her to "lay us down to sleep"
Trusting a tender Father's care,
Our never dying "souls to keep."

Lovingly
Sept. 8, 1905. IDA M. STYLES

Martin & Anna Reierson

Not much is recorded as to what happened at the Brattlund/Reierson farm in Section 20 during this decade though there are a few items of note.

1905

Martin and Anna Reierson did not have children. However, by 1905 their niece Birdie Alvig, then age 11, was living with them. Birdie Sophia Alvig (1896-1931) was the daughter of Bella Reierson (sister of Martin) and Nels Alvig (brother of Anna). Twice, there was an Alvig-Reierson marriage. The Alvig family connects to the Mankell family, with the marriage of Birdie's brother George Alvig to Alice Mankell in 1931. The Alvig family was from the Ålvik farm, Kvam Parish, Hordaland, Norway. Immigrant grandparents of Birdie and George, Ole and Britha (Fladeboe) Alvig, homesteaded in Dovre Township, Section 8.

Birdie lived with her aunt and uncle for only a few years. She probably left prior to the fall of 1907 as the student lists for School District 25 did not include her name. After living with the Reiersons she moved to Buffalo, South Dakota, to live with her parents. Birdie did not marry and died at the age of 34. She is buried by her parents at the Vikor Church Cemetery on the eastern shore of Solomon Lake in Dovre Township.

1907

During the spring and summer, Martin built a new barn.

1908

In September, Martin Reierson and William Larson helped their neighbor to the west, Gabriel Stene, with threshing of flax.

NORMAN FARM[3]

1900

The Norman farm, owned by Marie Norman, had tenants during this decade. As William and Johanna Larson moved between the Norman farm and the farm they owned in Section 21, this allowed for renters at the unoccupied locations.

Frederick & Gunda Amundson, renters

In the spring of 1900, two families 'switched farms.' William and Johanna moved from the Norman farm in Section 17, to William's farm in Section 21, one mile to the east. William's renters at the Section 21 farm, Frederick and Gunda Amundson, moved to the Norman farm.

---

3   Findagrave.com; ancestry.com; moms.mn.gov; *Family maps of Kandiyohi County, MN*; *Willmar Tribune*: 13, June 1906, 20 May 1908, 3 March 1909; Christenson Family Collection. Information about Severin Hatlestad can be found In *Keeping the Faith… Sharing the Faith*, pages 69, 75-78. The Norwegian Boarding School closed in 1924; *New London Times*, 9 December 1909.

Frederick Amundson (1870-1944) was the son of Norwegian immigrants, Andreas (Andrew) Amundson and Marin (Maren) Kasparsdatter, who homesteaded in Section 14, SW ¼. Frederick married Gunda Hagen on August 31, 1892. She was the daughter of Martin and Berte Hagen from Dovre Township. Fred and Gunda had several children (dates approximate):

1. **Harry** (1892-1959) served in WWI
2. **Della** (1894-1988) married Christian Ulrickson
3. **Melvin** (1897-1976) married Thalia McSweeny
4. **Lillian** (1899-?)
5. **Frances Mae** (1902-1977) married James Hosek
6. **Curnel** (1904-1904) is buried by his maternal grandparents at Lake Florida Mission Church cemetery
7. **Clara** (1905-?)
8. **Pearl** (1909-?)
9. **Hazel** (1910-?)

1901 November

Frederick Amundson and his family lived only a short time at the Norman farm. In November 1901, about 18 months after arriving in Section 17, the family moved to the C.W. Odell farm south of Foot Lake. Another family soon rented the Norman farm.

1904
Lars & Caroline Hatlestad, renters

Lars Hatlestad married and Caroline Tollefson on December 3, 1903. Soon after the wedding they rented the Norman farm from Johanna and William Larson. Caroline was a niece of the previous renter, Frederick Amundson. Caroline (known as Lena) was the daughter of Thor Tollefson and Gunvor Amundson and grew up on her parent's farm in Section 14, which had been the farm of Gunvor's father, Andrew Amundson. For a few years, Caroline's younger sister, Clara, lived with Lars and Caroline.

Lars had emigrated from Norddal, Møre og Romsdal, Norway, in 1882, when only a few months old. Lars and his parents, Severin and Pernille Hatlestad, arrived in Lake Andrew Township in 1883. The Hatlestad family lived ½ mile west of the Mankell homestead, having purchased about 20 acres in Section 18, from another Norwegian immigrant, Even Railson.

The family did not farm initially. Severin worked for two Norwegian Lutheran churches in the area: East Norway Lake Lutheran, where he and his family were members after their immigration, and then at First Lutheran Church of Norway Lake, where he served as secretary and klokker (cantor and musician). He was also a school teacher and administrator at the First Lutheran's parochial school. The Norwegian Boarding School was located in the basement of the church. This school was in session primarily during January and February when the township schools were closed. In the late 1890s and into the early 1900s, Severin conducted parochial classes for a few terms at these school districts in Arctander Township: District 54, located in Section 30, District 56 in Section 26, and District 69 in Section 12, which also had children from Lake Andrew Township. These classes were extensions of his parochial school teaching; he was not a teacher of these school districts. Severin would fit these sessions of parochial schools around the terms of the township schools and the Norwegian Boarding School. Students attending this parochial school, where classes were taught in the Norwegian language, were primarily from the local Lutheran congregations. Thus many of the same children in the local farms changed from public school lessons to religious school lessons during the school year. One of more interesting lessons learned from Severin Hatlestad was very practical for a farming community. Here is one student's recollection:

> *We practiced penmanship. First we wrote a line with our right hand and then with our left hand.* [Mr. Hatlestad] *explained that should we ever lose the use of our right hand it would be handy to be able to write with our left hand.*

Severin and Pernille Hatlestad had nine children:
1. **Lars** (1882-1961) married Caroline Tollefson (1882-1918)
2. **Martin** (1884-1963)
3. **Lena** (1886-1965) married Sivert Selvag (1879-1950)
4. **Hannah** (1890-1929) married Sam Henjum (1881-1945)
5. **Cornell** (1893-1981) married Geoline Rood (1897-1975)
6. **Othelia** (1893-1981) married Henry Nash (1892-1957)
7. **Sverre Lawrence** (1896-1955)
8. **Nellie Luella Amalia** (1901-1918) died during the flu epidemic
9. **Arthur** (1903-1987)

In later years, as Severin's children grew to adulthood, the Hatlestad family began farming and purchased more acreage in the township, including acreage from the Norman and Larson families. Today's descendants of Severin and Pernille Hatlestad are active farmers in Lake Andrew Township; their land still includes the farm in Section 18. Severin (1857-1934) and Pernille (1861-1943) are buried at First Lutheran Church cemetery with several of their children, spouses, and grandchildren.

Lars and Caroline Hatlestad had several children; the oldest five children were born at the Norman farm:
1. **Pearl** (1904-2001) married Herman Westergard
2. Infant died two days after June 1905 birth
3. **Myrtle** (1906-1986) married Melvin Larson
4. **Luella** (1907-1999) married Levine Erickson
5. **Selmer** (1908-1998) married Bernice Rasmussen

6. **Florence** (1911-2003) married twice: Oliver Olson and later George Dahlberg
7. **Alf** (1915-1991)
8. **Clarence** (1918-1960) was a WWII veteran

Lars and Caroline lived at the Norman farm until 1910 when the family moved south one mile to the Ole Slattum farm. Norwegian immigrants Ole and Marie Slattum moved to Sacred Heart, Renville County in 1909.

After the Hatlestads moved out, another family arrived to rent the Norman farm: Henry and Nellie Swenson. Henry was a son of Gunder and Gemine. His sister, Minnie Swenson, had married Oscar Mankell in 1895. These siblings became neighbors.

After living at the Slattum farm, the Lars Hatlestad family moved north to Colfax Township. Caroline (Tollefson) Hatlestad died on November 3, 1918, three days after giving birth to Clarence. The cause of death was pneumonia. This may have been a complication from influenza which was prominent in Kandiyohi County during the fall of 1918. Caroline is buried at First Lutheran Church. The infant son, Clarence, was baptized the same day the family buried his mother. Lars died several decades after his wife and is also buried in the same cemetery.

William & Johanna (Norman) Larson

Because the Norman farm was now rented, Johanna and William returned to their farm in Section 21 where they raised their children. In the late 1920s, their daughter Edith would return to the Norman farm in section 17 to raise her family; widow Johanna would soon live with her. Here are some of the events which affected the Norman and Larson families during the first years of the 20th century.

1906

Marie Norman, one of the immigrant settlers, died on June 7, 1906. She is buried at the Lake Florida Mission Church Cemetery next to her husband, Johannes. Her obituary was in the *Willmar Tribune*, June 14, 1906:

Marie Norman, c1900.

> **Death of Lake Andrew Pioneer.**
> *Another of the pioneers of Lake Andrew Township has laid down the pilgrimage staff. Mrs. John Norman Sr. died at the home of her daughter, Mrs. William Larson, last Thursday evening, June 7, the cause of death being old age. She has been in a feeble condition, physically and mentally, for some years and during the last year was confined to her bed most of the time, so death came as a welcome relief from her sufferings. She had reached the age of 80 years. The funeral occurred Saturday and the remains were interred at the cemetery of the Lake Florida Swedish Mission church, Rev. N. Frykman officiating. Mr. and Mrs. Norman came here in the spring of 1870 [sic 1869] and*

took a homestead. Mr. Norman died in 1886 [sic 1884], *a son Albert died in 1892,* [sic 1893] *and a daughter, Mrs. P. J. Dahlstrom, died in 1894. All are buried in the cemetery where Mrs. Norman is now resting.*

1908

In the summer of 1908, carpenter Martin Walby of the Jericho community, finished the construction of a new house for William Larson and his family on the Section 21 farm. According to Harvin Christenson, their neighbor and friend of their son Victor, William built this house so his two sick children could live more comfortably prior to their imminent deaths. Three people died in this new house within the next three years.

1909

Ownership of the Norman farm changed at the end of this decade—the 80 acres in Section 17 and the 160 acres in Section 18. After the deaths of Marie Norman in 1906 and her son Gustav Albert Norman in 1893, descendants and other extended family members owned the two parts. In 1909, the transfers of ownership of the 80 acres and the 160 acres were complete. William Larson became owner of the 80 acres in Section 17 and the eastern half (80 acres) of the Section 18 property. The western half of the Section 18 property, contiguous to the Severin Hatlestad farm, was sold to Severin.

Three years after her mother Marie's death, Johanna (Norman) Larson mourned the death of her young son Victor who died at the Larson farm in Section 21. The cause of his November 27, 1909 death was complications from diabetes. Harvin Christenson, son of J. S. Christenson and Carrie Stenseth, and Victor's friend and neighbor, served as a pallbearer at the funeral service. Victor is buried at the Lake Florida Mission Church cemetery. J. S. Christenson wrote a lengthy and emotional obituary, published in the *New London Times,* for this young boy. He wrote about the importance of newspapers printing sad news, Victor's faith and last days, and the difficulty when facing the death of a young person. Perhaps Christenson reflected on the many deaths his family had faced earlier in the decade. Perhaps Christenson placed himself in the shoes of neighbor William Larson because John Syvert's son Harvin was the same age as Victor.

> *Time and again, it is the lot of this paper to bring to its many readers the sad news that the angel of death has overshadowed the thread of life. Sometimes of the dear little one in the arms of a beloved father or mother; sometimes that of a boy or girl, who so many times have gladdened the home with their innocent childish plays and acts of kindness, who are tied to father and mother, brother and sister, with the most pure, most upright bounds of love. Sometimes that of the young man or woman in the spring of life, with all the bright future ahead of them—with all their promising usefulness to everything which is high, noble and good, and whom we think are indispensable to the good and advancement of the home, the neighborhood, the church and the state, and sometimes that of the weary worn and, after life's battle for rest—longing for old age. But, thanks ever be to God for that, as this paper time and again must narrate the sad work among us of the angel of death, it in many instances can and does with well-rounded reason speak of the hope for a glorious resurrection awaiting the dear ones gone ahead of us.*

> *This time this paper must bring to its many readers and friends the sad tidings that at 8:30 am, Nov. 27, the angel of death called at the so pleasant home of Wm. Larson of Lake Andrew and took from their midst, that of the Sunday School and neighborhood dear, little Victor Herbert. No pen can describe, nor words can tell, how sad it was to have to speak, from the heart of dear father and mother, brother and sister, relatives and neighbors, never more to see his smiling face and how he strived to do good and be kind to everybody. Be the night of sorrow and sadness be ever so dark in the Larson home, the Sunday School and the neighborhood after Victor has left, there is amidst the deepest of sorrow, great reams of joy and hope, as we know from his own words that he is now with Jesus and is in that great gathering dressed in pure while constantly praising God, who, the Apostle of John saw and speaks about in his revelation. The day before Victor died he said, "Tomorrow I am going to Jesus." The morning he died he said goodbye to his father and mother, brother and sister, prayed for them and himself. He then asked his little sister with whom he had played so often: "Do you know Jesus, Edith?" Having asked this question several times he began to sing about how glorious it shall be when Jesus comes to gather him home and he sang until his mind failed him, yes right into the jaws of death. Dear friends who may read these lines, is your end going to be like Victor's? Victor will never be forgotten by father, mother, brother, sisters, relatives or neighbors. Thanks for what Victor was! Victor Herbert Larson was born April 17, 1897, died Nov. 27, 1909, hence 12 years, 7 months and 10 days.*

Victor's death was the first of three in a three-year period, with a sister Lillie and their father William dying in 1910 and 1911. These three deaths would leave Johanna Norman Larson a widow with two young children.

MANKELL FARM[4]

Here is a chronology of some events at the farm in this decade. Those living at the farm were widow Elizabeth, her son Oscar, his wife Minnie, and their children.

1903

Minnie and Oscar's youngest child, Alice, was born on April 8, 1903. After graduating from New London High School in 1921, Alice attended St. Cloud Teachers' College and taught in various St. Paul schools (c1926-1931). Alice married George Alvig on June 30, 1931 at the Lake Florida Mission Church. The couple lived in Montevideo in western Minnesota where George owned Alvig Motor Sales. Alice and George later lived in Spicer and then California where they lived until their deaths. They are buried at Greenwood Memorial Park in San Diego. They had two children, both born in Montevideo:

1. **Bette** married Milton William (Bill) Huff on June 24, 1956, in Kandiyohi County.
2. **Delphi** married Robert (Bob) Ballinger on June 8, 1961 in Spokane, Washington.

1905

The farmhouse received a new roof.

---

[4] *Willmar Tribune*: 15 June 1904, 14 June 1905, 3 May 1905, 11 April 1906, 19 June 1907, 10 July 1907, 4 Dec 1907, 17 June 1914; Mankell.org; *Warren Sheaf*, 25 March 1909; moms.mn.gov; ancestry.com.

1907

In June, a straw shed at the farm collapsed onto a herd of cattle. Ten of Oscar's herd died in the event or were killed later due to major injuries. The cause was attributed to heavy spring rains. Several neighbors helped the family recover from this financial loss, by giving the family $50.00. Two of Oscar's milk cows were killed by lightning during a July storm.

Oscar built an addition to the barn. This was probably the portion of the barn on the south side of the main structure.

1908

Neighbors Matthias O. Rustad and Oscar jointly purchased a manure spreader. The northeast corner of Rustad's farm in Section 19 met the southwest corner of Oscar's homestead.

LOCAL BUSINESSES

Jericho (aka Norway Lake)[5]

Jericho is located primarily in the southeast corner of Section 13 and with a small part of the community in the northeast corner of Section 24, on the eastern edge of Arctander Township which borders Lake Andrew Township. This crossroads community, only 1-2 miles west of the four farms, provided various services for area farmers and their families as illustrated on the next pages.

Local Blacksmith, Swen G Swenson[6]

The services of Jericho's local blacksmith were critical for area farmers to repair machinery and tools, fix buggies and wagon wheels, craft horseshoes, and more. Swen G. Swenson (1872-1942) served his neighbors, family and the farmers of Lake Andrew and Arctander Townships. His shop was across from the General Store and Post Office. Swen maintained detailed expense and payment ledgers documenting the work he did for his customers. Here are excerpts from Swen's entries for farmers of the four farms (owners and renters) and the Norway Lake Creamery for the years 1902-1914. These entries provide a glimpse into everyday life in this farming community.

Fred A. Amundson

Casting on mower fixed.................$ .35	Pump hook.................$ .35
2 shoes set, stone shoe nails.................$ .35	Buggy brace fixed.................$ .25

---

[5] *Illustrated History of Kandiyohi County*, p. 114; mankell.org. This crossroads community was officially called "Norway Lake" and had the Norway Lake Post Office until about 1930, but was locally called Jericho, probably to reduce confusion with and distinguish itself from Norway Lake Township to the north and the lake called "Norway Lake" to the northeast. In this book, this area is called Jericho.

[6] This extant ledger has been preserved and shared by Lynn Geer Pryor, great-granddaughter of Swen Swenson. In about 1920, Swen served as the local mail carrier. By 1930 he and his family were living at a farm with acreage in both Lake Andrew Township and Colfax Township, east of Games Lake. Swen and Guri (Hande) Swenson are buried at East Norway Lake Lutheran Church cemetery.

J. S. Christenson

Runner fixed	$ .20
Mower fixed	$1.55
Sickle fixed	$ .10
6 sets of stone wedges	$ .50
8 bolts made 7 in. long by 1/2	$ .50
1 eyebolt hook and staple	$ .20
Windmill braces fixed	$2.20
Chain guard for mower fixed	$ .60
Bundle carrier fixed	$ .85

Lars Hatlestad

Plow lay painted	$ .75
Six shovels fixed	$ .60
Pump handle fixed	$ .70
4 shoes sharpened and set	$ .80
2 plows sharpened	$1.20
Sleigh bolster fixed	$ .25

William Larson

Horseshoeing	$1.30

Oscar Mankell (brother-in-law of Swen)

Wire stretcher fixed	$ .15
8 shoes sharpened and set	$1.60
8 new shoes put on	$2.00
Repairs to the track	$2.50
Buggy fixed	$1.50

Martin Reierson

Plow fixed	$1.50
2 rings made for plow	$ .25
Pick-ax fixed	$ .50
One coulter stand fixed	$ .25
Plow lay painted	$1.50
4 Bolts for Barn	$ .50
Wheels babbited	$1.00
Drag Tether sharpened	$1.45

Henry G. Swenson (brother of Swen)

Buggy cover arm fixed	$ .20
Shoes plugged and set	$ .80
Buggy tongue Brace	$ .25
8 shoes calked and reset	$1.60
Buggy stubbed bottom fixed	$5.20
Grain wheel on Binder fixed	$ .50
Plow Lay sharpened	$ .60
6 new shoes	$2.40

Norway Lake Creamery

Milk vat soldered	$ .10
Strainer fixed	$ .10
Wheel barrow fixed	$ .50
Work on well	$ .50
Pump fixed and bolts	$1.25
Churn fixed	$ .35
Whistle and hand ax fixed	$ .40

NEW TECHNOLOGIES

Lake Andrew & Dovre Telephone Company[7]

The first phones in Kandiyohi County were installed in Willmar in 1880. This new communication system spread throughout the county over the subsequent decades and used the manual system (as opposed to the dial telephones which arrived in the 1950s). The early years of this decade were witness to the development of rural co-operative telephone companies, including the Lake Andrew & Dover Union Telephone Company in the southern part of Lake Andrew Township and the northern part of

---

[7] *History of New London, 1865-1965*, p. 116, 121; *Centennial History of Kandiyohi County*, p. 184, 274; *Willmar Tribune* 24 June 1903, 2 March 1904, 5 April 1905, 28 Feb 1912; 27 Jan 1915; *Illustrated History of Kandiyohi County*; kevinskoglund.com/familyhistory/skoglund2.html.

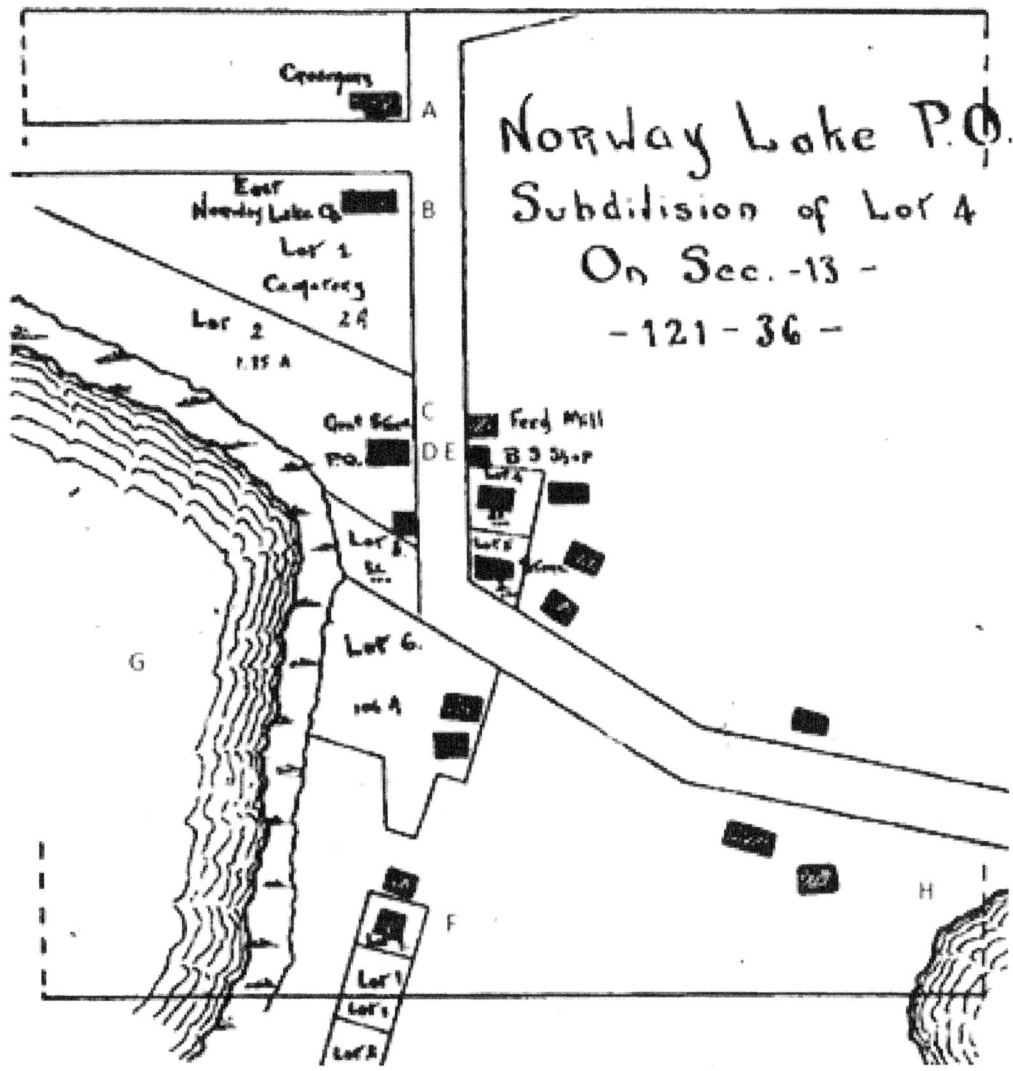

Hand-drawn map of Jericho (c1900) which identifies the locations of the church, homes, and former businesses. The horizontal line at the base indicates the division between Sections 13 and 24.

A. Norway Lake Creamery
B. East Norway Lake Lutheran Church and cemetery
C. Feed Mill
D. General Store and Post Office
E. Swen G. Swenson's Blacksmith Shop
F. Home of Swen and Guri Swenson
G. Slough
H. Home of Andrew and Jenny (Mankell) Gordhamer, with Lake Mary to the east at the Lake Andrew Township line

(1905 Illustrated History of Kandiyohi County, p. 114)

Dovre Township in 1904 and the Union Star Telephone Company in the northern part of Lake Andrew Township in 1905. The Lake Andrew & Dovre co-operative connected to the phone system in New London in 1905.

Here is a list of Kandiyohi County's telephone co-operatives, established from about 1903 to 1905.

Arctander Central	New London	Sunburg
Diamond Lake Union	New London-West Lake	Sunburg-Brooten
Harrison Union	Nickel	Sunburg-Carlson
Kandiyohi Union	North Star (Arctander)	Union Start
Lake Andre & Dovre Union	North Star (Irving)	Western Union
Mamre & Pennock	Norway Lake-Sunburg	Willmar & St. Johns
Mamre & Pillsbury	Ringville	
Minnesota Central	Spicer Willmar Union	

The first officers of the newly formed Lake Andrew & Dovre Telephone company were K. T. Rykken, President; Gabriel Stene, Vice-President; Peter Skoglund, Secretary; L. Nelson, treasurer; Lars H. Larson, Nels Quam and G. A. Peterson, Trustees. There were 30 stockholders during the early months of the company, with 30 miles of wire from Norway Lake (probably a reference to Jericho) to New London. A second line connected the Lars H. Larson farm (SE ¼ Section 20) with Willmar phone lines. The switchboard was located in the Peter Skoglund home on the north shore of Lake Florida until 1912, when it was transferred to the John Nelson farm next to School District 25.

The Skoglund family has shared memories of their ancestors' early years with the telephone company:

> *Peter Skoglund was a man of many talents...[Peter]* and his brother John Alfred began to organize and interest local farmers in building their own telephone line. On February 27, 1904, they set up a county phone system. For decades, Peter served as the first secretary and maintained the central switch in the Skoglund home. Weather forecasts were given out by a general telephone call each morning. Sometimes, on winter evenings when nearly every home was snow-bound, Peter's children would entertain with music and songs over the telephone. The farmers loved their telephones, but were still a bit cautious. Once when four children in one family died from a contagious disease, a neighbor telephoned Peter and advised him not to let his children take any calls from that home as the neighbor feared that germs might travel over the phone wire.

By 1915, J. S. Christenson and Oscar Mankell were part of the leadership of this company. Mankell was elected as a collector, so he would go to the farm families and collect the payments from members for telephone service.

THE AUTOMOBILE[8]

In 1908, J. S. Christenson and two of his friends had a ride in one of the first automobiles in the county. This automobile was owned by Lars Halvorson, an inventor and mechanic. Halvorson was a president, manager, and stockholder of the Willmar Gasoline Engine Works.[9]

On Sunday, September 6, 1908, Halvorson found himself a chauffeur for three men from Lake Andrew Township who were returning from the Minnesota State Fair: J. S. Christenson who had exhibited a model of his new invention (Grain-Cleaner for Wild Pea and Cockle), Carl A. Syverson who had exhibited his butter, and Gabriel Stene—friend, neighbor, and the author of the following article. The men had taken the train from St. Paul to Willmar, but then had to find a way to travel the final 15 miles north to Lake Andrew Township.

> Last Sunday morning bright and early, while returning from the state fair, J. S. Christenson, C. A. Syverson and ye scribbler were parading the streets of Willmar working on the conundrum how to get home. The puzzle was soon solved and we were carefully stowed into a cozy place, left to the mercy of the driver of Halvorson's Queen with but a faint idea of the effect of the first ride over the road in an automobile. Inexperienced as we were, we looked for a fine ride, but it was not long till we looked for a chance to get our hands clutched fast to anything available. Taking a glance at the situation, I could see Syverson displaying a coat tail like a monster turkey over a piece of red flannel, and with a peculiar expression on his features like a go-to-church face, while Inventor Christenson was in full motion in a peculiar way of pounding a beefsteak on the sides and the ends (patent likely applied for), and ye scribbler had his thoughts concentrated and set on his new hat, which was secured to his head by the aid of two good hands, all trying to get an occasional chance to breathe enough to keep life going. At first chance, and at the time the conductor was to collect the fares, a reorganization took place, when we congratulated each other upon our safe arrival, having made the trip from Willmar to Norway Lake in 40 minutes.

Lars Halvorson's Queen automobile, c1908.
(Image courtesy of the Kandiyohi County Historical Society)

The first automobile seen in New London was in September 1901. The first owner of an automobile in Willmar (and possibly Kandiyohi County) was Samuel Osmundson, the County Recorder. Sam was the oldest child of Thomas and Bergit Osmundson, Norwegian immigrants and one of the earliest settler families in Lake Andrew Township. Sam was also the cousin of Minnie (Swenson) Mankell, wife of Oscar. Sam's first car was the Locomobile Steam Car which was 5 horsepower and cost $600. Another early car owner in Willmar was Sophia Rice, daughter of Nils and Marie Brattlund, from one of the

---

8   U.S. Patent Office No. 600147; *Willmar Tribune*: 9 March 1897, 29 July 1908, 9 Sept 1908; 13 June 1962; *Digest of United States Patents of Air, Caloric, Gas, and Oil*. Volume 2. *History of New London, 1865-1965*, p. 116. In 1912, Oscar Mankell purchased a Maxwell automobile.

9   Willmar Gasoline Engine Works existed from 1898 to 1905; U.S. Patent Office No. 600147. Halvorson received patent #600,147 for his "Explosive Engine" (later known as a carburetor) which was patented on 8 March 1898. Lars, Ingeborg and their family lived in Willmar.

four farms. Here is a list of those in Willmar who owned "gasoliner" cars in 1908, noting each person's car model and the price, as published in the *Willmar Tribune*[10]:

A. A. Anderson	Gale	$ 650	Henry Osmundson	Ford	$ 750
Ben Benson	Rambler	$ 750	G. W. Ostlund	Auto Car	$1,100
Dr. Bernt J. Branton	Ford	$ 800	George H Otterness	Rambler	$ 800
A. O. Bryant	Moline	$2,500	Dr. J. R. Peterson	Maxwell	$ 850
John Dale	Buick	$ 250	S. B. Qvale	Ford	$ 900
Dr. Harold E. Frost	Holsman	$ 900	**Mrs. Sophia Rice**	**Ford**	**$ 850**
Lars Halvorson	Queen	$ 900	George S. Stewart	Buick	$ 250
Frank G. Handy	Winton	$2500	David N. Tallman	Pierce	$4,500
Dr. Christian Johnson	Maxwell	$ 950	David N. Tallman	Auto Car	$2,750
Dr. Christian Johnson	Holsman	$ 700	J. H. Wiggins	Tribune	$ 650
John Madison	Rambler	$ 850	George Wilson	Buick	$ 500
Jacob F. Millard	Buick	$ 250	George Wilson	Rapid Sight Seer	$ 700
Emil and Sigfrid Nelson	Rambler	$ 750	20th Century Wheel and Tire Company	Rambler	$ 250
F. F. Nelson	Falls	$1,500			

The *Willmar Tribune* added the following information regarding automobile expenses, giving the impression that these automobiles were a novelty, not yet a necessity:

> Willmar now has 32 automobiles, representing an investment of $35,500. Add to this the cost of two garages, $10,000 and you have a neat sum of $46,500 invested in pleasure vehicles and their maintenance…All of the automobiles are "gasoliners," no steamers or electrics having so far been found practicable for this section of the country…It may be interesting to know that these cars consume about 900 gallons of gasoline per month, which means $200. The repair bills easily amount to twice this sum, which means that every month 32 persons spend about $500, or $20 each, just to "move fast."[11]

SCHOOL DISTRICT 25[12]

Children of the four farms families attended District 25.[13] The following list names the children *(with parent name in italics)* registered at the school during the fall 0f 1907. Those highlighted are from the four farms (Amundson had been a renter, but at this time was living in the southern part of the township). Their teacher was Henrietta (Etta) B. Davenport in 1907.

---

10 Interestingly, the newspaper article states that there were 32 automobiles in Willmar. However, the article lists 27 cars. Sam's Locomobile is not in this list, which did not include steam cars. By 1908, he may no longer have owned the vehicle. Sam Osmundson owned one of the two automobile garages in the city. It was located on Fifth Street, across from the Opera House. *Willmar Tribune* 30 October 1907, 29 July 1908.
11 *Willmar Tribune* 29 July 1908.
12 *Willmar Tribune* 7 October 1908, 17 March 1909; *Illustrated History of Kandiyohi County*, years 1872, 1896, 1898, 1903 ; KCHS, extant enrollment records begin with 1909; Mankell Family Collection; ancestry.com.
13 Before c1900 those living in Section 17 attended District 16. Following redistricting all children on the mile attended District 25.

Amundson: Della, Melvin, Lillian *(Fred)*
Bengtson: Leonard *(Carl)*
Christenson: Clara, Harvin *(John Syvert)*
Erickson: Oscar, Mabel, Edwin *(Maria)*
Hegstrom, Albin *(Elisa)*
Larson: Edith, Lillie, Victor, Oscar
   (William)
Larson: Grant, Agnes, Hattie *(Lars H.)*
Larson: Walter *(Dick)*
Linnerud: Minnie, Mabel, Olaf *(Carl O.)*
Lundin: Mabel, Paul *(John)*
Mankell: Edna, Herman *(Oscar)*
Nelson: Agda *(John)*
Railson: Mabel, William, Edwin, Lawrence
   (Oluf B)
Rustad: Bennie, Sophie, Manda, Leonard *(M.O.)*
Skaalerud: Harry, Edwin *(Jens)*
Skoglund: Walter *(John A.)*
Skoglund: Esther *(Peter)*

There are two items of interest in regard to these students.

- Edwin Railson enters the Norman farm story when he marries Edith Larson, also a pupil in the above list, in the 1920s.
- Nine-year-old Mabel Lundin died in September, 1908, from appendicitis. Services were held at Lake Florida Mission Church with burial at the cemetery. Several of her friends and schoolmates provided the special music and acted as her pallbearers—girls who were 8-12 years old. One of these pallbearers was Edna Mankell, daughter of Oscar and Minnie. Lillie Larson also served as pallbearer for her friend, less than two years before she herself would face a similar fate—to be carried into and out of the same church, buried in the same cemetery, and mourned by the same schoolmates. Here is an excerpt from Mabel's obituary:

> At the church songs were sung by the Swedish Sunday school class of which she was a member, and also a song by Miss Lawler's school in Dist. 25, her schoolmates, the parting hour being extremely sad for her small schoolmates. The pall bearers were Hattie Larson, Lillie Larson, Mabel Railson, Mabel Skoglund, Lillian Skoglund and Edna Mankell, all small girls of her age.
> When father and mother, sister and brothers look for the last time upon the beautiful face of their darling daughter and sister who has been called from earth just as the tender plant of her girlhood is budding into the flower of womanhood, it is sad indeed. However, they have a blessed consolation of knowing that while their poor hearts are bursting with grief, the melody of heaven is sweeter by having added to that great angelic choir the voice of their precious child and sister.

Changes were coming for District 25 School. By the end of the decade the Lake Andrew Township officials and families realized that the school and the Township needed a new building. In addition, the township had recently voted to add another country school (District 104) which was to be located 2 miles west of District 25, on the Lake Andrew/Arctander township line. Some students from District 25 and some from Arctander School District 56 would be redistricted to District 104.

GOVERNMENT, POLITICS & THE FARMERS[14]

The school district building was also the Town Hall for Lake Andrew Township, a place where residents voted and conducted township business. Following in the footsteps of the pioneer settlers who helped organize the Lake Andrew Township government in the 1870s, several men of the four farms community were active in township government during the early 20th century. These men and their elected offices were the following:

Oscar Mankell:
1901, Supervisor
About 1903, Constable
1907, Pathmaster (concerned with conditions of local roads, culverts, and bridges)
1910, Clerk
1912, Assessor
1915, Supervisor
1918-1921, Supervisor

John Syvert Christenson:
1901, Assessor
1904, Justice of the Peace
1905 or soon after, Clerk Dist 25
1912-1914, Clerk

Frederick Amundson (renter of the two farms owned by William and Johanna Larson):
About 1904, Constable
1910, District 2 Road Overseer

Emil Peterson (father of Earl Peterson who enters the four farms story in the 1940s):
1910, Constable

Herman Larson (brother of William Larson):
1913-1915, Treasurer
1918, Treasurer

O. B. Railson (father of Edwin H. Railson who married Edith Larson):
About 1902, Constable
1912, Supervisor

Mike Shields (laborer for Christenson and other neighbors):
1912, Constable

For some of these men, their involvement with local politics led to activities within political parties during the next 25 years.

In 1900, Oscar Mankell was active with the People's Party—an agrarian, populist movement which grew in the 1890s, with the goal to represent the common folk including the farmers, against corporations, bankers, and other powerful and wealthy special interest groups. He was a delegate to their fall convention in Willmar. The local party's convention platform included the following:

1. Bringing the government nearer to the people
2. Supporting Williams Jennings Bryan, candidate for US President in the 1900 election
3. An American system of finance

---

14 *Willmar Tribune*: 3 October 1900, 20 October 1920, 20 February 1918, 19 June 1918, 11 December 1918, 14 May 1924; Wikipedia.org; ancestry.org

4. No government beyond the constitution
5. Restriction of corporate greed
6. Freeing of the producing classes from the trust Hydra [a reference to multi-headed snake in Greek mythology]
7. Election of U.S. Senators by direct vote of the people
8. Temperance reform and fighting the illegal liquor trade
9. Opposition to the county paying for bonded Road No. 1 [Foot Lake dump]

The People's Party, because it was so similar to the Democratic Party, did not survive long after the 1900 election. It folded somewhat into the Progressive movement which was active in the coming decades.

J. S. Christenson was active in local and state politics as a member of the Republican Party. In 1900, Christenson attended the Republican County Convention with his father Hans Christenson, his brother-in-law Edward Johnson, and other neighbors: Rev. Jordahl, pastor at First Lutheran Church, and Lars Nelson. At the 1908 Republican County Convention J. S. was a member of the Resolutions Committee and selected as a delegate to the State convention. In the next decade J. S. Christenson would leave the Republican Party.

CHAPTER 7:
1910-1919

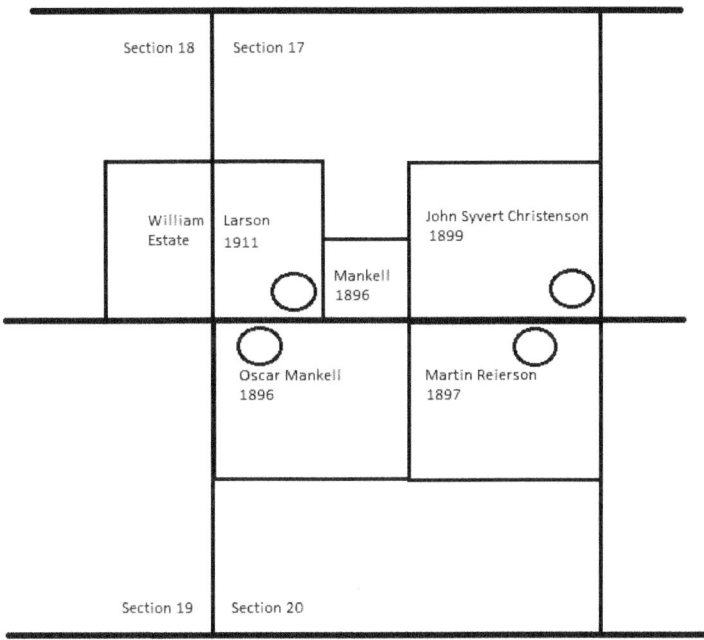

HIGHLIGHTS

- A new District 25 school building was completed and celebrated.
- Local men were involved in politics, government, and improvements to a key local road
- Farms changed with new renters, relatives moving in, and additional land purchased
- World events affected the township: war and influenza epidemic
- Activities: Music continued to bring joy to members of the four farms

STENSETH/CHRISTENSON FARM[1]

John Syvert (J. S.) & Mina Christenson

During this decade, those living on the Section 17 farm were Maren Stenseth, John Syvert Christenson and his second wife Mina Engen and children: Hedvig, Harvin and Clara.

Owner of the farm, J. S. Christenson, expanded and enhanced this farm and acquired new properties during this decade. It appears that J. S. and his family remained on the Stenseth farm until the early 1920s. Here are the identified transactions and activities which give a small glimpse into the life of a religious farm family who celebrated music.

1910

For the first worship service of the year, the Nannestad Lutheran Church families met at the Christenson home because it was too cold to clear snow and warm the church building for services.

1911

In November Mina Christenson hosted the Ladies' Aid of the Nannestad Lutheran Church. The guest speaker was Anna Lee, a missionary in China.

1912

Christenson purchased about 122 acres and buildings on the southeastern shore of Norway Lake in Section 8 (SE ¼) from Christian and Maria Solberg for $8,800. Neighbors Elmo and Alvin Halvorson purchased an additional 160 acres (Section 17 NE ¼) from Solberg. Because Christenson's farm abutted the lakeshore, the family, especially Harvin and his friends, did a lot of fishing—catching sunfish, pike and muskellunge (aka muskie).

Christenson also purchased a seven-acre wood lot from Solberg (Section 4, SW corner) located between the eastern side of Norway Lake and Middle Lake. In later years, this location would become the home for J. S. and Mina.

Christenson kept steers and hogs at the Solberg farm. By 1918, Harvin worked for his father at the Solberg farm. Two young men from the Township, Cornell Thorson and Christian Korsmo worked for Christenson. Thorson worked for part of 1913 and Korsmo worked during 1913 and 1914 when he fed the livestock and planted corn at Christenson's two farms. By 1917, Korsmo worked for both Christenson and Oscar Mankell; in the 1920s he worked for Edwin C. Railson[2]. In 1928, Christian Korsmo married Lena Swenson, niece of Oscar's wife, Minnie. In the 1930s, this family rented William Larson's Section 21 farm and later owned a farm in Section 22.

---

1   *Willmar Tribune*: 27 Nov 1907, 1 Jan 1908, 8 April 1908, 13 May 1908, 6 January 1909, 29 Nov 1911, 24 December 1913, 30 September 1914, 30 May 1917, 11 July 1917, 28 Aug 1918, 26 March 1919, 23 April 1919; Norwegian Church Records on dagitalarkivet.uib.no; findagrave.com; Christenson Family Collection; ancestry.com; Mankell Family Collection; *To God be the Glory*, p. 29.

2   This was not Edwin H. Railson, married to Edith Larson. Edwin C. Railson (1870-1934) was the son of Andrew and Bertha Railson. Edwin H. Railson (1897-1968) was the son of Oluf and Nellie Railson and grandson of Even and Mathea Railson. Both men lived in Lake Andrew Township.

The Stenseth farmhouse was shingled and a large porch was added to the front.

For many years Christenson had been an active leader at the Nannestad Lutheran Church, both with the music program and as Sunday School leader. John Syvert's father Hans Christenson and the Stenseth family had been a part of this congregation's leadership from its development in the 1876. After 40+ years this congregation of sold their building in 1912 to the Church of God congregation in Willmar, though there at least two special services for the Nannestad families in following years. This transition meant that families went to other congregations. The John Syvert and Mina Christenson family became involved with East Norway Lake Lutheran Church and was very active in the music program. Mina served as the church organist, c1912-1913.

**Stenseth house c1920, with the large front porch.
Left to Right: Clara, Hedwig, Mina, J. S., and Harvin Christenson.**

1915
Christenson built a new kitchen on the north side of the farmhouse at the Stenseth farm.

1917
Christenson built a new granary and added a new silo on the Stenseth farm. This silo was inside the barn, allowing for the silage to stay fresher into the winter months. Hans Holter helped with the construction. Before then, the Christensons used the original log home, built by Nils Stenseth, as the granary.

1918
Farm worker Christian Korsmo laid drainage tile near the barn at the Solberg farm. Christenson purchased a "Waterloo Boy" tractor. Son Harvin farmed the Solberg farm until 1918 and then his father rented this farm to brothers-in-law Elmer Nelson and Tom Kvamso. Tom was married to Elmer's sister Selina. The Kvamso and Nelson families lived together at the Solberg farm. Elmer and Selina's mother was Caroline Reierson, sister to Martin Reierson. She married twice: to Lars Nelson and then to Mons T. Olson.

1910-1911
Harvin Christenson (son of J. S. Christenson) was a close friend of Herman Mankell (son of Oscar and Minnie) who were teenagers during this decade. They fished at the Solberg farm, traveled to Montevideo, and even got into a bit of mischief in 1910 when they found a boat on Christenson's slough which belonged to the Gordhamer twins, Axel and Eddie, who lived in Jericho and were Herman's cousins. Herman's aunt Jenny (Mankell) Gordhamer was the mother of these twins. Herman and Harvin speared

holes into the twins' boat. In the spring of 1911, Harvin repaired the boat and used it to hunt muskrats. Soon the Gordhamer twins came to claim their boat.

1917-1919

Son Harvin lived on and farmed the Solberg acres on the southeastern shores of Norway Lake. He raised turkeys and grew wheat. Harvin bought his first Ford Model T car for $418, which he owned for two years. As the war grew in Europe and the United States entered the war in 1917, Harvin, then age 20, claimed exemption from military service by completing paperwork in Willmar. His request was granted. His reason was because he was farming. In his diary he stated that "I feared to die." By August 1918 he had registered in the draft as all men of age 21 were required to do.

1919-1922

Son Harvin felt called into ministry and attended the Red Wing Seminary on his journey to becoming an ordained minister. His parents, J. S. and Mina, would soon follow him to Red Wing on the Mississippi River. When Harvin was to leave for Red Wing, Minnesota, in the fall of 1919, he sold his Model T for $418, the same as his purchase price.

Maren Stenseth

Maren Sophia Stenseth died April 12, 1919. The obituary describes her physical challenges, the family's immigration, and that Maren outlived her parents and her siblings. The pall bearers included neighbors from the four farms: Oscar Mankell and Martin Reierson. The choir included people from the neighborhood and probably her brother-in-law J. S. Christenson.

> At 10 clock on April 12 occurred the death of Miss Maren Sophia Stenseth at the home of J. S. Christenson in the township of Lake Andrew, where she had made her home since the death of her only brother and sisters and parents. She was born Dec. 27, 1856 in the farm called Stenset in Ullensaker parish, [Akershus] Norway.
>
> In 1867 she immigrated with her parents Nels Nelson Stenseth and Karen Stenseth to America and arrived safely at North Prang, Fillmore Co Minn. In 1870 she arrived with the rest of the Stenseth family to Norway Lake, Kandiyohi Co Minn. Where they were received hospitably by the then established Iver Stene family. Out of their kindness the said family let the Stenseth family have the use of one much needed room. While the family thus was protected from sleet and storms.
>
> Maren's father entered the homestead of the SE ¼, Sec 17 Lake Andrew. By the fall of 1870 he had completed his first and only mansion on this earth. Just before Christmas that year the Stenseth family moved into this mansion. Maren being the oldest and willing was a great help to her folks in their pioneer days. But she being a mute was deprived of all the pleasures we who can hear and talk enjoy. She entered the Minnesota Institute for deaf and dumb from where she graduated with good standing in 1876. In spite of this her great defect she was deprived of the pleasure of her folks as death took one by one till she was the only one left of the Stenseth family. May all our recollections about Maren's disadvantages by her being a mute awaken us to being more thankful for being blessed with our full five senses.

The remains were laid to rest in the Hauge cemetery [Nannestad Lutheran Church] *Norway Lake, April 16, 1919. Rev. Sotendahl and Rev. Njus officiated assisted by the Norway Lake male choir. The pall bearers were J.* [John?] *Halvorson, M. B. Reierson, Oscar Mankell, G. Stene, M. O. Rustad and Herman Larson.*

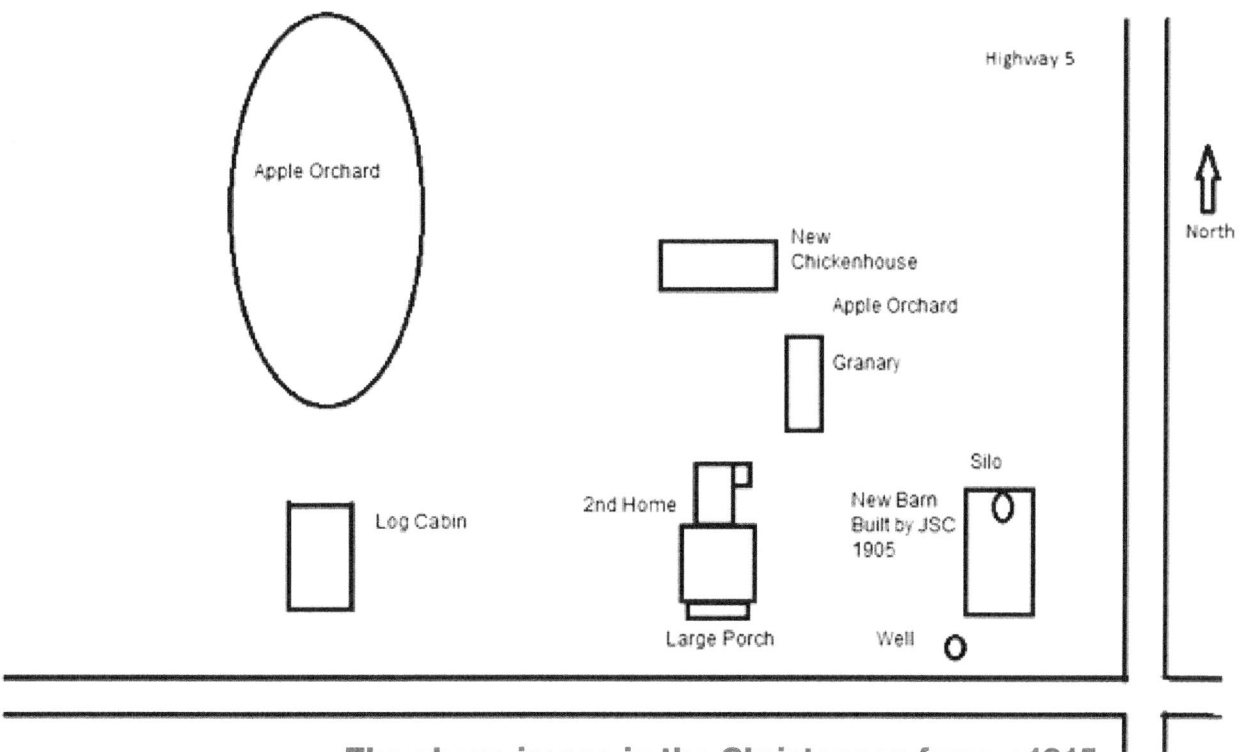

The above image is the Christenson farm, c1915, including the silo inside the barn.

BRATTLUND/REIERSON FARM[3]

A few years after their niece Birdie Alvig left the care of her aunt and uncle, the Reiersons welcomed another niece to their farm. From 1913-1919, a young girl named Stella Ruby Berry lived with Anna and Martin Reierson. Stella, the daughter of Olina Reierson (sister of Martin) and Edward Berry, was born in 1904 in Kandiyohi County, but by 1909 the family was living in South Dakota. During the years she lived with her aunt and uncle, Stella attended District 25 with children of neighboring farms.

In 1927, Stella married Andrew W. Rasmussen, also from Kandiyohi County, in Chicago. They had six children and lived in Illinois, New York, Canada, and Washington State. She died in Vancouver, British Columbia, Canada, in 1965. She is buried at Mountain View Memorial Park, Pierce County, Washington.

---

3 Ancestry.com; District 25 school records at Kandiyohi County Historical Society; *Willmar Tribune*: 6 March 1912, 9 October 1912, 14 February 1914, 27 Sept 1916; 2 April 1919; *New London Times*, 8 June 1944; findagrave.com;

During this decade the Reiersons enjoyed raising their niece and yet the family also faced loss. Bjørn Reierson, the father of Martin, died on March 25, 1917, and is buried at East Norway Lake Lutheran Church where he was one of the first Trustees of this congregation. Martin's farm was two miles west of his parents' homestead in Section 15.

Here are some of the known events at the farm during this decade.

1912
In October, Martin purchased a new car: a five-passenger Reo.

During the summer Martin built a new two-story house. This home remains on the farm in 2019.

1916
Anna Reierson hosted the monthly meeting of the Ladies' Aid of East Norway Lake Church in October,

1917
In the spring, Martin bought two lots in New London from his parents for $1,500. Martin and Anna moved to New London in the mid-1920s and this may be the location of their home.

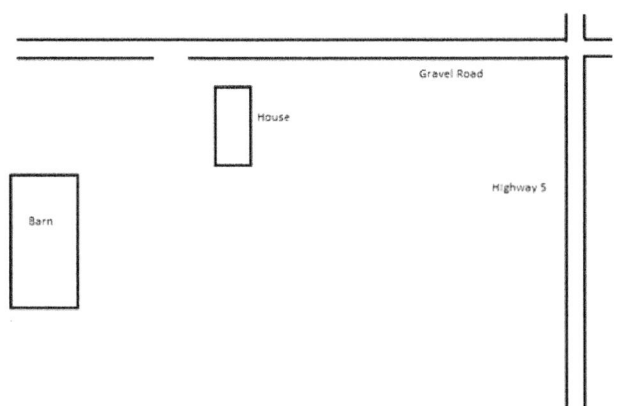

Diagram of the Reierson farm with the house built in 1912, and the barn built in 1907. There may have been some smaller buildings such a shed or granary.

In 1944, when Martin and Anna celebrated their 50th wedding anniversary in New London, Minnesota, Stella (Berry) Rasmussen shared a song she wrote to honor her aunt and uncle, sung to the tune "Count Your Many Blessings." With her imagery we see the life and love which Martin and Anna shared during their 50 years of marriage, on a farm in Lake Andrew Township and later at their home in New London.

GOLDEN MEMORIES

As I'm sitting thinking of the days upon the farm
Where the birds were singing,
As they filled the air with charm,
There the flowers blossom,
There they blend their hue
And the morning grass was, often wet with dew.

Oh, the golden sun would set at night,
Oh, the golden hours would make the night seem light,
Golden mem'ries light your path today
God bless you, on this your Golden Wedding day.

Once there was a cottage, just a little home,
Here Martin brought his fair young bride, his very own.
Here Annie made you welcome, then the table spread,
And we all had coffee, cake and jam and bread.

When I think of Martin, how he toiled all day
He must plow and sow the seed, no time for play.
Annie worked right with him, 'til the setting sun.
One could never say they left a task undone.

By and by they built a home, a mansion fair.
It was big and beautiful and rather square.
Here they lived together, near the old oak tree.
How my heart would leap for joy that oak to see.

Years have come and years have gone, for time marches on.
All hard work is over, for they live in town.
They are loved by hosts of friends, neighbors and kin.
As our memories travel back, our eyes do dim.

May God richly bless you, is my daily prayer
And we'll meet together in our home over there.
We must all be ready, when the time does come,
And the Lord will give us then a welcome home.

Stella Rasmussen

DEATHS

Two daughters of Nils and Marie Brattlund, the original Section 20 homesteaders, died during this decade: Sophia Rice in 1914 and Caroline Selvig in 1919. After their marriages both of these women lived in Willmar. Here are their obituaries, published in the *Willmar Tribune*.

Sophia Rice

Mrs. Sophia L. Rice, wife of our distinguished citizen, Hon. A. E. Rice, passed away from the scenes of this world at the Rice mansion on Third Street last Thursday morning, Feb.12, at the age of sixty years and 12 days, cause of death being anemia. Mrs. Rice had not been well for several years. She has been critically ill several times, but her strong power of mind held the malady at bay and she would partially recover at times. Her death came as a shock to the people of city and county, for no other woman in the county has become so well known to the people as she, thru an active participation in educational and cultural circles for a period of forty years. And in the pall of sadness which her death cast over the hearts of many friends is a deep feeling of sympathy for the lonely life companion whose true help-meet and comrade she has been during all these years.

The only son, Capt. Cushman A. Rice, was not at home. Since retiring from the army service, he has made his residence at Camaguey, Cuba. It seems that about the first of the year he joined a party that went on a prospecting and hunting trip into the mountainous parts of Cuba, and since that time he has been out of touch by mail or wire. Letters to his mother have come at stated intervals, one arriving two days after her death, but all messages and letters sent to him have remained uncalled for and have failed to reach him. When the final summons came to the mother, messengers were employed to penetrate the wilds of Cuba and attempt to bring the sad news to Capt. Rice, but up to this time he has not been heard from.

Biography

Mrs. Sophia Lavinia Rice was born at Brattfors, Varmland [Värmland], Sweden, Jan. 31, 1854. She was the daughter of Nils and Maria Brattlund. When Mrs. Rice was a girl of ten years the family emigrated to America, first locating at Rock Island, Ill. In a few years, however, the Brattlunds concluded to come to the Minnesota frontier and join the flourishing settlement of pioneers within the present boundaries of Kandiyohi County who came from the picturesque province of Varmland, Sweden. The father staked out his homestead claim in the present township of Lake Andrew on what is now the farm home of Martin Reierson, in Sec. 20. The girl, Sophia, had made the most of her opportunities to attend school in Illinois. Soon after arriving to Minnesota she attended the State Normal School at Winona, from which institution she graduated in one year. She returned to this county to teach, and held the second first-grade certificate issued in the county. She first taught in the old Syverson schoolhouse in Dist. No. 25 of Monongalia county, and then in Dist. No. 16, the Railson schoolhouse. In 1874 she came to Willmar and taught in the village school, becoming its superintendent. In January of 1877, she married Hon. A. E. Rice, then state senator from this county. On March 15, 1878, the only son, Cushman, was born. Mrs. Rice's duties as wife and mother, however, did not cause her to relinquish her interest in the public welfare.

Educational Activities

She served on the Board of Examiners for the Willmar schools from 1879 to 1884, when she was elected as a member of the Board of Education and served as its clerk from 1884 to 1899, a term of fifteen years. She was for years the president of the oldest literary society of the city, and served as secretary of the Woman's Improvement League which did much to bring about sentiment for the beautifying of the city. In 1903, when the public library was established, she was appointed member of the governing body of that institution and took an active interest in the management of the same. She continued as secretary of the Library Board until her death. She was treasurer of the local Red Cross society. She followed the work of her husband in public life as senator, lieutenant governor, and member of the Board of Regents of the State University with the most lively interest, and was ever his true confidante and counsellor until the last.

As a girl Mrs. Rice was confirmed in the Lutheran faith by Rev. Erik Hedeen and became a member of the Swedish Lutheran Augustana church.[4] On coming to Willmar, there being no church of that denomination at Willmar at that time, she attended the Episcopal Church and became active in the work of the same.

Besides husband and son, the deceased leaves to mourn her death two sisters and their husbands, Mrs. C. C. Selvig, and Mrs. John Olson of this city; brother-in-law, John Beckstrom of Oakland, Neb.; a number of nephews and nieces—Rev. Adolph Holt of Omaha, Neb. Mrs. (Rev.) S.L. Wilson of Ironwood, Mich. Mrs. (Prof.) F. E. Peterson of Minnesota College, Minneapolis Mr. Paul Holt and Lydia Holt of Rock Island; Atty David Beckstrom, county attorney of a county in Kansas; Atty. Warner Beckstrom of Chicago Walter Selvig of Pittsburgh, Pa.; Mrs. Victor Vickstrom, Duluth; Adolph Olson of Virginia, Minn; Robert, Myrtle and Cecelia Olson and Edwin, Victor and Albin Selvig of this city and one brother-in-law, Mr. Olof Holt of Rock Island, Ill.

The Obsequies

The funeral occurred last Monday. Services were held at the late residence at 1:30 o'clock by Rev. W. E. Pearson, of the Bethel Lutheran Church. Rev. Pearson sang "Nearer My God to Thee," led in prayer, read the 130th Psalm and used that as the subject for a brief discourse. He spoke of the life of the departed and addressed words of comfort to the mourners. The funeral cortege then proceeded to St. Luke's Episcopal church, where the impressive funeral ritual and lesson was read by Rev. E. R. Todd, the rector. The

---

4   Reference to Lake Florida Mission Church which was part of the Augustana Lutheran Synod until 1879.

vested choir sang several selections and Miss Esther Larsen sang, "In the Sweet Bye and Bye." At the close of the service, a chance was given to view the earthly remains of the departed and several hundred people passed silently by the bier and cast a last look at the well-known features. The cortege left the church for Fairview cemetery, where the casket was placed in the receiving vault. The active pallbearers were six G.A R. [Grand Army of the Republic][5] comrades of Gov. Rice—M. D. Manning, A. H. Sperry, E. M. Stanford, J. B. Boyd, W. E. Roberts and John Costello. The honorary pallbearers were Mr. C. Hennings, of the G. A. R. Post, and Messrs. L. O. Thorpe, Alton Crosby, Chas. Johnson, C. B. Carlson and S. B. Qvale, members of the Public Library Board. The floral offerings were most profuse and beautiful. There were no less than forty different pieces. The offering sent by the members of the Board of Regents of the U. of M. alone sufficed to cover the casket. Handsome pieces were also there from the Red Cross society, The Housekeeper's Club, the Library Board, the Ladies' Guild, Mt. Nebo Chapter No. 63, the Baptist church, Col. Heg Post G. A.R. Monday Afternoon Club and the B. P. O. E. The remainder were contributed by relatives and friends of the departed. Among those from a distance who attended the funeral were Mrs. F. E. Peterson of Minneapolis and Mr. and Mrs. C. E. Hornbeck of Superior, Wis. Mrs. Hornbeck was a very close friend of the deceased.

Mayor E. C. Wellin of the City of Willmar issued a proclamation reading as follows:

The City in Mourning

Mrs. A. E. Rice passed away at her home in this city in the morning of February 12th, 1914. On that day hand of death touched her and she sleeps. Never before has death caused so universal, so sincere, so heartfelt an expression of sorrow, and there is mourning, genuine and unaffected in our city. With loyal and loving heart, and with purest hands she faithfully discharged the duties of daughter, sister, wife and mother. She was pure of soul, kind of heart, generous disposition, devoted and faithful to all public trust. This brave and tender woman, this oak and rock, this vine and flower has passed to silence and pathetic dust, to that glorious world, where there is no more night, and where the sunbeam of love is eternal.

The funeral of Mrs. Rice will take place at 1:30 o'clock in the afternoon on Monday, February 16, 1914. Therefore, as this hour is given to contemplate the grand example, a rich inheritance, a noble life worthily ended, I, E. C. Wellin, Mayor of the City of Willmar, Minn., hereby request and direct that all factories, shops, stores, offices and all other places of business be closed and remain closed on Monday, February 16, between the hours of 1:30 o'clock p. m. and 4:00 o'clock p. m. of that day, And I respectfully urge that every citizen of Willmar abstain from work on that day between the hours named, And that those who are unable to accompany the remains to its last peaceful resting place, there to say farewell for a very little while to Mrs. Rice, that they observe that hour in their homes and bend with solemn thoughtfulness and render there the offerings of a faithful tear. Yet let the tribute be in silence between God and our soul. Dated at Willmar, Minnesota this 14th day of February, A D. 1914. E. C. WELLIN, Mayor. This proclamation was generally observed by the business houses of the city. At the hour of the funeral, 1:30 o'clock p. the Mayor's proclamation was read

---

5   Grand Army of the Republic was a fraternal organization comprised of veterans of the Union military who served in the Civil War.

to the pupils of the public schools by the teacher of each room, supplemented with a statement of the services rendered by Mrs. Rice to the schools of the city in the past. The flag on the city hall was placed at half-mast as a further token of respect.

 E. C. Wellin, Mayor

Five years after Sophia Rice's death, her sister Caroline Selvig died. Her obituary was published in the April 2, 1919, issue of the *Willmar Tribune*.

Mrs. C. C. Selvig

Tomorrow afternoon the earthly remains of Mrs. Caroline Selvig, beloved wife of C. C. Selvig and one of Willmar's well known and respected women, will be laid at rest at the Fairview cemetery. She died last Monday, March 31st, at her home at 714 Seventh Street South, death being caused by a stroke of paralysis which she suffered four days previous.

Mrs. Caroline (Bratlund) Selvig was born July 28, 1851, [sic June 27] at Brattfors, Karlstads Län, Värmland, Sweden. At the age of fifteen she came with her parents, Nils and Marie Bratlund to America. They resided two years in Rock Island, Ill. And in 1868 came to Kandiyohi County, being pioneer settlers of Lake Andrew Township. The deceased was married to Christian C. Selvig of Willmar in 1882. Their children are Edwin Selvig of Willmar, Walter Selvig of Pittsburg [sic], Pa., Victor Selvig of Mankato, Mrs. Harriet Vickstrom of Duluth, Alvin Selvig of Willmar. There are four grandchildren. She is also mourned by one sister living, Mrs. John Olson of Willmar and a number of other relatives. One of the four sisters who have gone before was the late Mrs. Sophia L. Rice of Willmar.

The funeral will be held from the Bethel Lutheran church tomorrow (Thursday) afternoon. Brief services will be held at 2 o'clock at the house and 2:30 at the church. Rev. Jesper Holmquist will officiate.

The sorrowing husband and children have the sincere sympathy of all in this their sudden bereavement in the loss of a true, kind and loving wife and mother.

NORMAN FARM[6]

Henry & Nellie Swenson

Renters Lars and Caroline Hatlestad left the Norman farm in early 1910. New renters Henry and Nellie Swenson arrived on the Section 17 farm in March 1910 and resided there until about 1926. Henry and Nellie were from the area and both were connected to residents of the four farms, by friendship or relation. Henry and Nellie married on November 19, 1904 at East Norway Lake Lutheran Church. (It was a double wedding; Nellie's sister Clara wed Sam Mikkal Engen.) Henry and Nellie Swenson had six children; two died as newborns:

1. **Harriet** (1905-1905) lived 5 days
2. **Miranda** (1906-1989) married Roy Edman
3. **Wallace** (1909-1984) married Edna Anne Larson

---

6 Kandiyohi County Recorder; 1927 plat map; *Willmar Tribune*: 23 Nov 1904, 6 Nov 1907, 27 Nov 1907, 16 Mar 1910, 22 Mar 1911. Lars H. Larson was not related to William Larson. Lars' parents were Norwegian immigrants; William, Swedish.

4. **Eleanor** (1914-2006) married Bennie Edman
5. **Gordon** (1923-1923) lived 1 day
6. **Henry, Jr.** (aka Lolly, 1925-1995) married Madelyn Thostenson

Henry Swenson was the son of Gunder and Gemine Swenson, Norwegian immigrants who lived on the southern shore of Mary Lake which shared the border between western Lake Andrew Township and eastern Arctander Township. The Swenson family lived about a mile west of the Norman farm. Henry's sister, Minnie, married Oscar Mankell in 1895 and lived across the road at the Mankell homestead. Further, the Swensons were friends and fellow musicians of the farm family to the east, John Syvert and Mina Christenson. Gunder Swenson hosted choir rehearsals of the Nannestad and East Norway Lake church choirs when preparing for special holiday music. Several of Gunder and Gemine's children sang in the Norway Lake Choir with J. S. Christenson in the 1890s. Three of Henry's brothers (William, Melvin and Gerhard) were in the 1914 Norway Lake band with Harvin Christenson, John Syvert's son.

Henry was a mail carrier and for about seven years prior to the move to Lake Andrew Township his postal route covered the Negord business community, located in the western edge of Arctander Township (Section 19, aka Goldbug). He ended his work as a mail carrier when the family moved to the Norman farm.

Nellie (Larson) Swenson was the daughter of Lars H. and Helena Larson and grew up on a farm in Lake Andrew Township (SE ¼, Section 20, which bordered the Brattlund homestead).

Given these family and neighbor connections, it is not surprising that, when a farm so central to this community of families became available, Henry and Nellie would rent it for several years. Many of the Swenson and Larson extended families are buried at the Lake Florida Mission Church Cemetery.

Johanna & William Larson
Owners of the Norman farm, Johanna (Norman) and William Larson, lived a mile from the farm which they rented to the Swenson family. William and Johanna had mourned the death of son Victor in 1909. The decade of the 1910s brought more loss to this family, leaving Johanna a widow with two children: Oscar and Edith.

1910-1911
A few months after burying Victor, Johanna and William Larson buried their 14-year-old daughter Lillie. Peritonitis, an inflammation of the tissue lining the abdomen, was the cause of death in the obituary, though Harvin Christenson later recalled that she died from what was then called "menstruation poison," though this cause of death is not listed as a disease in today's medical books. She died from a massive infection and is buried next to her brother at Lake Florida Mission Church Cemetery. Her obituary appeared in the April 27, 1910 issue of the *Willmar Tribune*:

> *The home of Mr. and Mrs. William Larson has again been visited by the grim reaper death. It is our sad duty to chronicle the death of their beloved daughter, Lillie, 15 years*

of age [sic 14]. Lillie attended school and played for the last time with her schoolmates last Monday and this Monday lies cold in death. What makes the sorrow doubly great is that it is the second child they have lost in four months. Victor, age 17 [sic 12], passed away the last week in November last. The funeral will be held tomorrow, Tuesday. The last sad rites will be conducted by Rev. Franklin, at the home at 1 p.m., and at the Florida church at two where the remains will be laid to rest by the side of those of her favorite brother who so shortly before preceded her.

J. S. Christenson wrote Lillie's obituary which was published in the *New London Times*, just as he had done for her brother Victor in 1909. This man, a father of young children, wrote about the death of another child who was a friend of his children. In Lillie's obituary Christenson asked the unanswerable questions which many ask during their sorrow.

Saturday evening, April 23, at about 10 o'clock occurred the death of one of the most promising and highly esteemed young ladies, Lillie Alvida Larson. As we look upon what happens to ourselves and others, we are often asking the questions: Why shall it so be? Why should this happen? And as we now look upon the death of Lillie Larson these questions come to us with special weight. Why should she at this time be torn by the cold arms of death from a home that gave her anything and everything she wished, and from a mother and father who showed no pains in bringing her up to be an excellent young lady, morally, mentally, and as a Christian.

Lillie, after having attained to an ideal daughter, to be for mama for papa, for the interest of the home, for the advancement of everything so greatly needed, yes indispensable, these questions roll up for us: Why and wherefore shall Lillie now sleep in the churchyard? This question causes our tears to flow and makes us feel as though our hearts would break.

But here again amid the deepest and darkest cloud of sorrow comes the soothing ray of hope and consolation which is that again one of our dear ones has been safely harbored into the eternal rest, protected so safely from all the dangers of sin by singing His praise, who prepared a home beyond. And right hear what a great stepping stone is not this death to even more than ever draw mama, papa, sister, brother, and so many relatives and friends of Lillie hereafter to live more than ever for to enter the eternal joy and happiness. When the shepherd is especially anxious that the sheep shall follow Him even more closely. He comes and goes the lamb with him.

Lillie Alvida Larson was born at her home in Lake Andrew, Feb. 6, 1895 [sic 1896] and died at the same place, April 23, 1910. She attended school Monday the same week she died. Coming home from school that day she complained of a slight headache. Tuesday she was a little worse, and on Wednesday she complained of acute pains in her abdomen. The doctor was called at once, but it was found that nothing could be done for her. Three doctors were in attendance but she grew worse till Saturday evening when at 10 o'clock she passed away, having been sick only four days. The cause of her death was peritonitis.

She said goodbye to the family and then said, "I do not need to say goodbye to Victor as I will meet him soon." (Her brother Victor died last November.) What was it not for Lillie and Victor to meet in Heaven and what a meeting shall it not be when their dear ones come after to join them on that beautiful shore which Lillie used to sing of while she was yet with us.

> *No one can fill Lillie's place and all her dear ones and friends should so live hereafter, that when our time on earth is ended we may meet dear Victor and Lillie. Friends and readers let us live ever most for the hereafter. Dear Lillie rest in peace till we are permitted to meet again never to part.*

On March 9, 1911, William Larson died with his obituary published in the *New London Times*. Christenson wrote the obituaries for William's two children, and given the flavor of this obituary, he probably wrote this one, too—one final way to honor his friend and neighbor.

> *It is our sad duty this week to report the death of one of the highly respected citizens of Lake Andrew, Wilhelm Larson, better known as Willie Larson who died at his home last Thursday [March 9th, 1910] afternoon from Pernicious anemia after being sick for about 3 months. Wilhelm Larson was born in Hokenthorp, Westergotland, [Västra Götaland] Sweden, September 28, 1857. He came to this United States in 1876 [sic 1879], and at once settled in the town of Lake Andrew, where he has ever since resided. In 1893 he was married to Miss Hilda [Johanna] Norman. To the union, four children were born, of which only two are living, the other two, a boy and a girl having just recently passed to the great beyond. Mr. Larson is survived by his wife, two children, Edith, eleven years old and Oscar, aged seventeen years, one brother, Herman Larson also of Lake Andrew and one sister, Mrs. Chas. Stenberg of Walnut Grove, Minn., besides his aged mother who resides in the town of Lake Andrew, and who has passed her 90th birthday. In the death of Mr. Larson, the community in which he lived, will mourn the loss of a good citizen and kind and generous friend. He lived a Christian life and was a member of the Swedish Mission Church. The funeral took place on Monday afternoon. Services were first held at the home at 1 o'clock and at the Lake Florida Mission Church at 2 o'clock, Rev. Franklyn conducting the lasts rites. The sympathy of the entire community goes out to the bereaved family in this their hour of sorrow.*

With the death of William, the 160-acre farm in Section 17 was in probate and finally in 1921 went to his daughter Edith Larson. William's son Oscar became the owner of William's Section 21 farm. Widow Johanna became the owner of 120-acres in Section 16 (directly north of the Section 21 farm) which had also been owned by William.

MANKELL FARM[7]

During this decade the following members of the Mankell family lived at the farm: immigrant Elizabeth, her son Oscar and his wife Minnie Swenson, and their children Herman, Edna and Alice. Here are a few events surrounding the Mankell family.

1910
A storm with very strong winds struck the area in early March. Windmills collapsed at Lake Andrew Township farms, including the Mankell farm.

---

7   *New London Times*, 11 June 1914, 13 June 1914; *Willmar Tribune* 16 Mar 1910, 13 Dec 1911, 3 Jan 1913, 27 May 1914, 4 November 1914 3 November 1915, 20 Mar 1918, 8 October 1919, 30 Nov 1921; Christenson Family Collection; mankell.org. *History of New London, 1865-1965*, p. 38; *Lakes Area Review*, 7 June 1914.

1911-1917
Herman Mankell attended school in New London (with several others from the Township). He graduated at the age of 21; his high school education may have been intermittent due to farm work responsibilities. When attending school, he stayed in New London during the week with his aunt, Anna Quam, and her family and then came home on weekends. Because Herman was no longer available to help with the farm work, Oscar hired Tom Larson as a farm laborer in the winter of 1911-1912. While workers often lived with the Mankell family, there is no record that Larson stayed with the family.

1912
Oscar purchased a Maxwell Touring Car.

Herman, Alice, and Edna enjoying the new family automobile, a Maxwell Touring car.

1913
Oscar Mankell upgraded the barn by installing swinging stanchions, which allowed the cows more freedom to move their heads when getting milked.

1916
There were no marriages between the four farm families, not during this 100 year history, or to date. However, according the Harvin Christenson's written log of events, he dated Edna Mankell in 1916. Driving his father's Ford car, Harvin took Edna to the Willmar Fair (possibly the Kandiyohi County Fair) where they enjoyed a ride on the Ferris wheel. Here is Harvin's recollection of a brief conversation during that ride:

> *Harvin: "Edna, I love you"*
> *Edna: "Hush! Hush! Somebody might hear you!!"*

1918
Oscar Mankell was elected Lake Andrew Township supervisor for a three-year term.

1918-1921
Oscar and Minnie's youngest daughter Alice was a student at the New London High School. After graduation she attended St. Cloud Teachers' Training College.

1919
Brothers Oscar and Otto Mankell sold 40 acres of land in Mamre Township, the SW ¼ of the SW ¼ in Section 14, for $3,200.

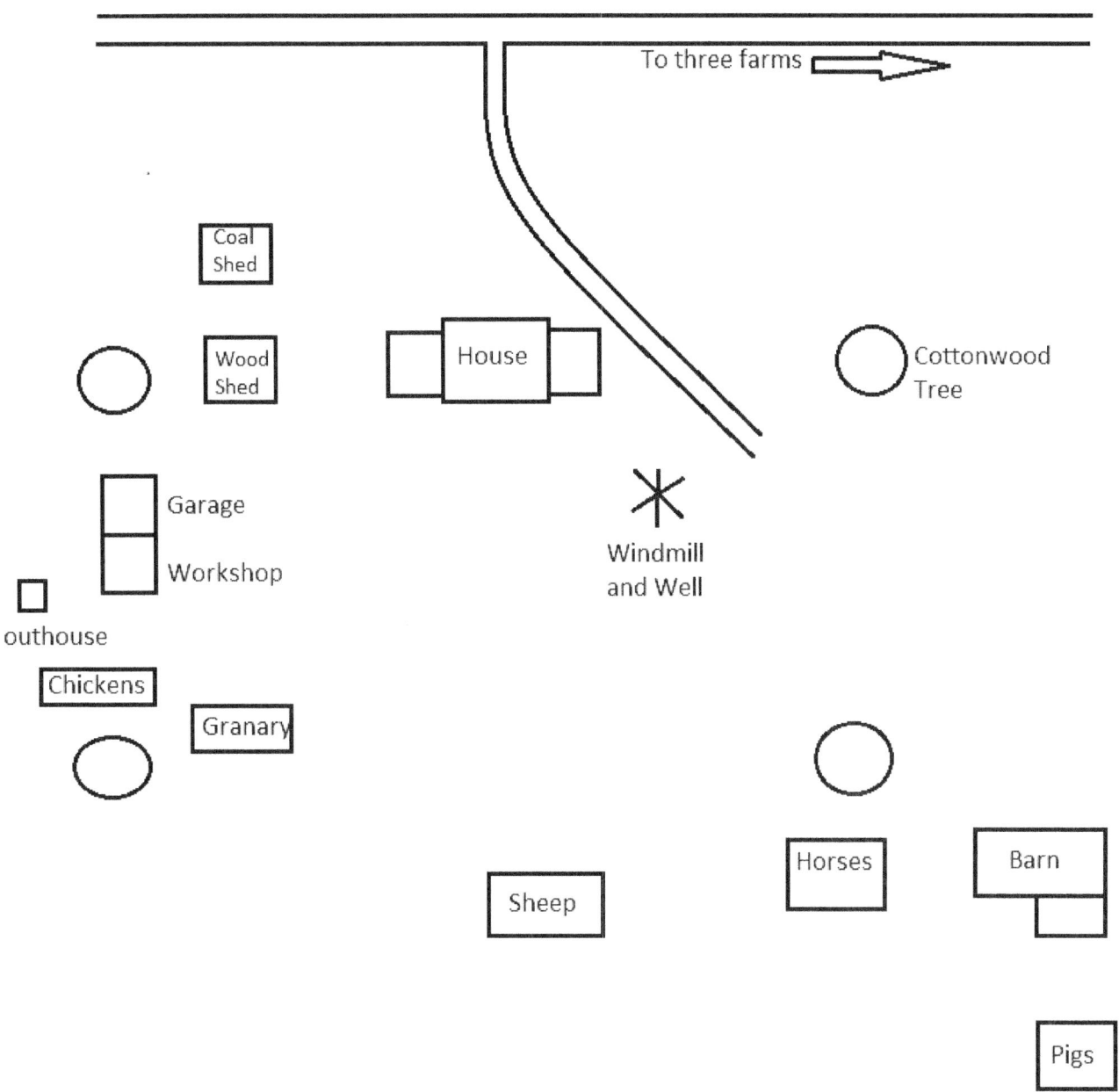

Mankell farm, about 1915.

DEATHS

The Mankell family mourned the deaths of three women in the family. Anna Quam and Elizabeth Mankell died in 1914; Esther Erixon in 1915.

MRS. NELS QUAM

Mrs. Nels Quam of New London is no more among the living. Death came to her last Saturday May 23rd, and though not unexpected, for she has been sick a long time, the news cast a gloom of sorrow over all her host of friends thruout the county. In Kandiyohi County she had lived for fifty years, nearly all her life, and by her cheery disposition, vivacious and lively nature and helpful ways had won the love of all.

Mrs. Anna Augusta (Mankell) Quam was born at Northfield, Minn. on the 24th of December, 1862. In 1863 her parents, Herman Wilhelm Mankell and Elizabeth Mankell, moved to St. Cloud and the following year located at Lake Andrew in this county. Here she spent her girlhood days receiving a common school education in the frontier schoolhouse. In 1879 she was married to Nels Quam. They continued their residence in the Norway Lake community until 1895 when they moved to the village of New London. Here she worked hard for many years conducting a boarding house and later as landlady of the Great Northern hotel. About two years ago however, her health began to fail her and the hotel was sold. Later it was declared by the physicians that she was suffering from cancer. Thru her long suffering, however, she has born up with remarkable fortitude. Besides the grief-stricken husband she leaves to mourn five children, Andrew Neptune, merchant at New London, John William, concrete worker, New London, Edward Lawrence, postmaster at Spicer, Estella Amanda, now Mrs. H. Johnson of Kerkhoven and Oscar Arnold, farmer at New London. She also leaves her mother, Mrs. Elizabeth Mankell of Lake Andrew, two brothers, Oscar of Lake Andrew and Otto of New London, three sisters, Mrs. Jenny Gordhamer of Norway Lake, Mrs. Amanda Landquist of Minneapolis, Mrs. Esther Erixon of Guthrie, Okla. several grandchildren and a large number of other relatives.

The funeral takes place this afternoon at the Norwegian Lutheran church at New London, Rev. E. M. Hanson, local pastor and Rev. J. J. Daniels of Duluth officiating. The pall-bearers are Dr. C. Johnson, Harold Swenson, T. J. Lawson, Wm. Olson, Oliver Larson and J. M. Monson. The earthly remains will be laid to rest in the Oak Hill cemetery. Thus a useful life has ended and a true and good woman passed to her Heavenly reward. Her memory will be blessed.

Five months after Anna's death, immigrant settler Elizabeth Mankell died on October 25, 1914. Elizabeth was the last of the eight immigrants who settled on these four farms to pass away. With her death, first-hand accounts of immigration from Sweden for the Mankell family also passed.

MRS. H. W. MANKELL

Another of our worthy pioneers left this earthly home on Sunday, October 25th, when the death of Mrs. Mankell occurred at the home of her son, Oscar Mankell, after an illness of only three weeks.

Mrs. Mankell was born June 30th, 1832, [sic June 29] at Hollered Socken Goteborgs Lan, Sweden and thus had attained the ripe old age of eighty-two years, three months and twenty-five days. She came to America in 1857, locating first at Red Wing, Minn. Later she has made her home at Northfield and St. Cloud. At the latter place she resided until after the Indian outbreak in 1867 [sic 1866] *when she came to Kandiyohi County, settling on a homestead in section 20, town of Lake Andrew where she lived until her death. Her death was caused by congestion of the lungs resulting from chronic heart trouble. She was married to Herman W. Mankel in 1857. Her husband died April 1st, 1889. She leaves to mourn her departure, six children, Mrs. A. H. Gordhamer, Norway Lake, Mrs. A. Landquist, of Minneapolis Mrs. H. L. Melgaard of Argyle, Minn. Oscar, who resides on the home farm, Otto of New London and Mrs. Gustave A. Erixon of Guthrie Okla., of whom all were present at the funeral but Mrs. Erixon. She also leaves one sister, Mrs. Mathilda Widdich of St. Paul, and one brother, who lives in Sweden, thirty-six grandchildren and 27 great grandchildren.*

The funeral was held at the Lake Florida Mission Church, Thursday, October 29th, Rev. G. T. Moline, officiated. The pall bearers were Axel Hedin, John Holmdahl, John Olson, Herman Larson, Gunder Swenson and S. [Severin] *Hatlestad. Interment was made in the Lake Florida cemetery.*

On October 22, 1915, one year after her mother's death, Esther (Mankell) Erixon died. The following obituary and service notice were from the Guthrie Oklahoma newspaper and reprinted in the *Willmar Tribune*.

MRS. GUSTAVE A. ERIXON.

Esther Erixon, wife of Gustave A. Erixon, an attorney of Oklahoma City, formerly of Guthrie, died at the Methodist hospital at 9:45 last night. Mrs. Erixon underwent an operation at the hospital last Monday morning and was apparently on a fair road to recovery when a sudden relapse took place about 7 o'clock last evening, at which time, the physician and nurses in charge notified Mr. Erixon at Oklahoma City. Mr. Erixon and daughters, Lillian Evangeline and. Florence Mercedes, arrived at the hospital in their automobile about midnight, but too late to be with his wife and their mother during her last moments.

Mrs. Erixon, nee Mankell, was born at Willmar, Minnesota, and would have been forty years old on the 31st of this month. Besides her husband and daughters, she leaves surviving her, the following immediate relatives: Oscar Mankell and Otto Mankell, brothers at Norway Lake, Minnesota; Mrs. Hulda Melgaard, sister, Argyle, Minnesota; Mrs. Amanda Landquist, sister, Minneapolis, Minnesota; and Mrs. Jennie Gordhamer, sister, of Norway Lake, Minnesota. The funeral will be held at the First M. E. Church tomorrow at 10 o'clock. Interment will be made in Summit View cemetery. Guthrie, (Okla.) Daily Leader, Oct. 22. Mrs. Esther Erixon, who died at the Oklahoma Methodist hospital on Thursday, was conveyed to her final resting place in the Summit View Cemetery Saturday morning.

The funeral services were conducted at the First Methodist Church at ten o'clock Rev. T. S. Pittenger officiating. Besides Mr. Erixon and his daughters, several hundred friends of the deceased had gathered at the church. The services were very impressive and the floral display was unusually elaborate. Many flowers were sent by friends in Oklahoma City, Guthrie and elsewhere. A beautiful bouquet of roses has been sent by the Oklahoma City Bar Association of which Mr. Erixon is a member. Rev. Pittenger delivered a glorious tribute to the memory of the deceased. The pall bearers were R. M. Chilcott, Jack Langston, C. C. Clothier, C. A. Marr, N. E. Wallace and J. S. Shearer. Mr. Erixon and daughters returned to their home in Oklahoma City Saturday evening.—Guthrie (Okla.) Daily Leader, Oct. 23.

Another death occurred in the extended Mankell family in late 1914. Six weeks after Elizabeth Mankell's death, her sister Mathilda Wittick (Wittich/Widdich) died after being hit by an automobile in St. Paul. Because of her injuries, she was unable to provide her name and it took several days before family knew of her death. She is buried at Lake Florida Mission Church Cemetery near Elizabeth's grave.

POLITICS & GOVERNMENT[8]

J. S. Christenson had been an active member of the Republican Party at the turn of the century. About ten years later J. S. Christenson shifted his politics from the Republican Party to the growing Non-Partisan League, which had its political roots in North Dakota. Christenson joined with at least one other neighbor, Herman Mankell, as members of this new political party in 1918. In his early 20s, Herman Mankell, son of Oscar Mankell, was active in the NPL in Kandiyohi County. Christenson—a farmer, an inventor, and a student of politics—was a candidate for State Senator on the NPL ticket, but was unsuccessful.

Membership of the Non-Partisan League were farmers and laborers who joined together to promote common interests. The Non-Partisan League was a strong progressive, political force in Minnesota politics in 1917-1918 when the state's farmers came together to promote their economic rights. These farmers represented 48 of the state's 87 (present-day) counties. With fewer farmers, the urban and iron range counties were not part of this movement. The farmers were upset with receiving low prices for the grain and livestock which they sold, yet believed they paid high prices for their purchases. The NPL campaign showed a divided state at a time when the world was at war and the US would soon enter the war. NPL leaders faced violence and arrest as they campaigned in the state. Urban and local newspapers vilified NPL leaders and members. The Minnesota State legislature declared "war" on the NPL, with plans to suppress legislators of the NPL party.

On Friday, June 14, 1918, the Kandiyohi County chapter of the Non-Partisan League had a parade—from Svea to New London, with stops at several towns along the route. Here is a description from the *Willmar Tribune*. As is evident by this description the newspaper owners and editors supported the NPL political movement and the attendees appreciated the support. Parade participants, including J. S. Christenson, and attendees witnessed vocal protestors and took precautions to avoid violence.

> *The Non-Partisan League parade through the county last Friday was something unprecedented in the political history of the county. The impression made upon the spectators as mile after mile of automobiles passed loaded with quiet but determined country people, and decorated with flags and banners, cannot be described. It was soul gripping. To such people as have been led to believe that the farmers' movement is based on disloyalty, the sight was of course exasperating, and led them to say and do many things they otherwise would not have thought of saying or doing. But even on such, the presence in the parade of the leading and best known successful farmers of the county*

---

[8] ancestry.com; mnopedia.org /group/nonpartisan-league; http://collections.mnhs.org/MNHistoryMagazine/articles/34/v34i06p221-232.pdf; Wikipedia.org, *Willmar Tribune*, 1918: 20 Feb, 3 April, 10 April, 24 April, 5 June; 19 June; 1919: 8 January; 1920: 20 Mar, 5 May, 10 May, 20 Oct.

CH 7: 1910-1919

had a cooling effect, for it began to dawn upon them that after all they might not have understood the matter correctly.

The parade started from Svea for Raymond. The committee in charge of the same was C. F. Kragenbring, Roy Bingham, P. M. Burns and F. W Gratz. At this place a meeting was held which was addressed by Messrs. A. O. Nelson, J. B. Bosch and John Wicklund. A farmers' band of twelve pieces from north of Raymond accompanied the tour and played at the various stopping places. The parade left Raymond for Pennock 110 autos strong. The meeting at Pennock was addressed by J. S. Christenson, A. O. Nelson, Bosch, and Wicklund.

When the parade arrived at Willmar there were over three hundred autos in line. No stop was made owing to threats which had been made and circulated as to what would happen here. It was thought best to avoid trouble if possible, so the cars sailed right thru and left no spoken message in Willmar. A number of people disgraced themselves by pulling off banners and hurling jibes at the paraders. The parade was joined here by a large number of cars that had been assembling in town during the morning.

The next stop was made at Kandiyohi. Here the farmers were nicely treated, and coffee was served to them, as they ate their dinners. Speeches were made on the Ed Currence lawn. A collection was taken for the band, which amounted to about $50. The parade started for Atwater at two o'clock, and was of such length that the first cars arrived at Atwater seven miles distant and the speaking began there before the last cars had left Kandiyohi.

At Atwater, Rev Fred Stromberg delivered a speech to the paraders. Increasing in numbers all the time, the parade started north from Atwater thru Harrison and Irving townships to Hawick. People at the various farm homes saluted the paraders as they passed. A brief stop was made at Hawick and then the tour proceeded to New London [where] people report that over seven hundred cars were counted in the line as it reached New London. This made the parade from nine to ten miles long.

At New London a large meeting was held on Main Street which was addressed by J. B Bosch, John Wicklund, A. O. Nelson, J. S. Christenson and others. The parade then disbanded one contingent going south thru Spicer to Willmar.

Every car carried a Lindbergh banner and was decorated with flags. Many mottos, as "United, we Stand, Divided we Fall" loyalty expressions, etc. were in evidence. The participants enjoyed the trip thru the county immensely. That the farmers have put every available field into crop this year was evident, even breaking up the roadsides in some places in order to raise as much foodstuffs as possible. The remark was jokingly passed around that the only unproductive field passed was the golf links at Spicer.

The editor was called to his office at eight o'clock and found a large crowd of tired but happy paraders who proceeded to unload lists of subscriptions pledged to the Willmar Tribune *taken on this trip. Additional pledges and subscriptions have been received at the office ever since. This unexpected help in the editor's exchequer was indeed welcome and we certainly appreciate the kind boosting that was done for the paper on this trip. Thank you, boys.*

The participants in the parade whom we have since talked with are unanimous in saying that they had a lot of fun on this trip.

Charles A. Lindbergh (father of the aviator) was a farmer from Little Falls and U.S. Representative from the State's 6th District. He was the NPL party's candidate for governor in 1918. Lindbergh lost in the primary and died soon after.

Christenson was a delegate to the state NPL convention in March 1920. Here is part of their platform in 1920.

1. A belief in the democratic process of reform by the ballot
2. A belief that people must preserve their constitutional rights of free speech, a free press, and peaceful assemblage
3. Demand that taxes on large incomes and excess profits be continued and increased
4. Endorsement of the programs of the Minnesota farmer and labor organizations

When elected, the leaders pledged to:

1. Enact and enforce net profits tonnage tax on iron ore
2. Stand for the eight-hour day in all industries except where, as in farming, natural conditions will not allow its establishment
3. Ensure the State guarantee of bank deposits
4. Revise grain grading and inspection rules
5. Provide workmen's compensation for injury or death in industry
6. Recognize the right of workers to organize and deal collectively
7. Protect and encourage co-operative enterprises
8. Secure full equality under the law for men and women

Within the NPL, the Farmers' wing promoted the following:

1. Exemption of farm improvements from taxation
2. Rural credit banks operated at cost
3. State grain elevators, warehouses flour mills, stockyards, packing houses, and creameries
4. State hail insurance

The Labor wing of the NPL promoted the following:

1. A minimum wage, which will maintain workers in health and comfort without labor of mothers and children
2. Abolishment of unemployment through government work in periods of depression

3. Public ownership and operation of railways and public utilities; nationalization of basic natural resources
4. Extension of soldiers' life insurance by the government without profit
5. Equal Pay for men and women doing similar work
6. Academic freedom and economic independence for teachers

Many of these reforms predated or paralleled issues on the national level, including women's rights, child-labor laws, the FDIC, and social programs enacted during or after the Great Depression. Some of these issues, such as equal pay for equal work, remain issues in the 21st century. Though the NPL declined in the 1920s, members fought for their ideas and the NPL was a forerunner of the Minnesota Farm-Labor and the Democratic Farm Labor parties and the progressive era.

Christenson stayed active in politics and promoted the needs of fellow farmers. In 1924, when living in Red Wing, Christenson ran unsuccessfully for the position of Lt. Governor of the State of Minnesota. He lost in the Farm-Labor primary, having received 35,966 votes.

SCHOOLS, BUSINESSES, & EVENTS

SCHOOL DISTRICT 25[9]

One of the decade's highlights for several farm families in the central part of Lake Andrew Township was the new schoolhouse, built and dedicated in 1912. Children over several decades of education witnessed changes in locations for their school buildings. As described in the 1860s chapter, the Mankell homestead provided the first classroom for students. This was followed by a few months at the Amund Syverson farm and then the log school at the Ole Slattum farm.

The next school building (1881-1912) was located at the intersection of Highway 5 and 29 on the Nelson farm, the southwest corner of Section 21. Extant enrollment records for 1909 include these children from the four farms: Harvin and Clara Christenson; Edna and Herman Mankell; Edith, Lillie, and Victor Larson (they lived at the Section 21 farm at this time). Another student, Edwin H. Railson, would become part of the four farms story about 15 years later when he would marry Edith Larson and then live on the Norman farm.

District 25, about 1910.
(*Kandi Express*)

---

9   Mankell.org; Mankell Family Collection; Kandiyohi County Historical Society; *Willmar Tribune*, 22 Nov 1911; 14 Feb 1912, 28 Feb 1912, 10 April 1912, 11 Sept 1912; *Kandi Express*, June 2015.

Teachers at the 4th location of District 25 are listed below, with known dates of teaching. This list includes John Syvert (J. S.) Christenson.

Jessy Henderson, 1882	**John Syvert Christenson**, 1892 Spring	Lina Slattum, 1902F, 1903, 1904 Fall
John Patterson, 1883	J.W. Johnson, 1892 Fall	Ellen Shipstead, 1904 Spring
Bergitta Bratberg, 1884	Charles A. Nelson, 1894 Fall	Nora Odell, 1905 Spring
Anna Hanson, 1885	Nora Odell, 1895	Ida Lorentzen, 1905 Fall
A.O. Morwatt, 1886	Julia Halvorson, 1896	Etta Davenport
Susan Berndon, 1887	Mathilda Slattum, 1898-1899	Frances Lawler
John Quam, 1888	**John Syvert Christenson**, 1899	Clara Everson
Otto Monson, 1889	Emma Peterson, 1900	Regina Farmen
Elias Mostue, 1890 Fall	Theodora Ellefson, 1901	Amanda Johnson
Lillian Moor, 1891 Fall	Anna McManus, 1902 Spring	

Discussions for two new schoolhouses began in the fall of 1909—for District 25 and for the newly established District 104. Officials with the Lake Andrew Township decided that a bigger building was needed to both better educate their children and serve the township board. So a building project began with a new building site for District 25 in the northwest corner of Section 28, directly south from the existing school. The District 104 building was to be built 2 miles west and serve children from families on the western edge of Lake Andrew Township and the eastern edge of Arctander Township.

J. S. Christenson designed both buildings: the new building of District 25 and the school building for District 104. Construction of the new District 25 building began in the spring of 1912, with its dedication in the fall. Sand from Lake Florida was used for the foundation's cement blocks. Neighbors responded to a call for hauling sand, with this announcement in the February 14, 1912, issue of the *Willmar Tribune*:

> The School Clerk of District No. 25 [J. S. Christenson] *issued a general call over the 'phone last Saturday, ordering everyone in the district who possibly could to assist in hauling sand from Lake Florida, to the new school house site, where cement blocks will be made next spring, from which the intended school house is to be built. The school house which is to be erected in District No. 104 next spring is to be built of cement blocks, too.*

In April 1912, the Building Committee received bids for the construction of the new building. The specifications included a basement, furnace, and bathrooms with toilets. The approximate cost of the building was $3,000. Farmer Herman Larson donated a few acres of his land for the building site in Section 28.

The school building was dedicated at 3:00 on Sunday afternoon, September 8, 1912, with Minnesota Governor Adolph O. Eberhart and State Superintendent of Schools C. G. Schultz, and County Superintendent of Schools W. D. Frederickson in attendance. These men made several stops that fall day to meet constituents during the election year: Sunburg, the District 25 dedication, New London, and

Willmar. Here is an excerpt from the September 11, 1912, issue of the *Willmar Tribune* and a portion of Frederickson's speech at the dedication.

> *...From this picnic* [at Glesne's Grove near Sunburg] *the gubernatorial party left for Lake Andrew where they had lunch at the residence of Lars H. Larson. About three o'clock dedicatory exercises of the new school house in District 25 took place. There were violin solos by Prof. Swalin, piano solo by Miss Nelson and duet by Mesdames Nelson and Nordgren. State Superintendent Schultz was introduced by Superintendent Frederickson and made a speech pertaining to school matters. He complimented the district by saying that this was the finest one-room school house he had yet seen in the state of Minnesota. The Governor then spoke, giving an address along educational lines. An historical sketch of school district number 25, written by Ole Newman, was read by J. S. Christenson. The dedicatory address by the county superintendent gave the district credit for its enterprise and progressiveness in providing such a fine edifice for the education of its children. The cost of the building and improvements will be close to $3,000.*

The dedication speech by W. D. Frederickson:

> *Man is a social being. He has his highest development in a free and friendly, social and* [illegible] *course where intelligence and justice prevail and determine every act. To develop and maintain these social qualities in the highest degree schools are established and churches are instituted.*
>
> *The people of District 25, mindful of their duty and responsibility to the coming generations, has caused this beautiful place of learning to be erected and which we dedicate today. To the boys and girls of this school district, these precious buds of humanity that shall bloom into manhood and womanhood to adorn their country, we dedicate this building.*
>
> *To the ambitious youth and the aspiring maiden who are seeking the avenues to a useful and noble life, we dedicate this building. To truth, justice and good will among the people, we dedicate this building.*
>
> *And lastly to the service of the people, of our country and our God, we dedicate this building.*

The new school building, c1912. Note that the entrance door is located on the north side of the building. The entrance was later moved to the south side.

Here is the list of teachers who held classes in the last building of School District 25, with some years identified. This school and many other county schools consolidated with the New London-Spicer School District in 1959 and closed its doors in 1963.

Emanual Franklin
Johanna Mittvet, 1913-1914
Horace Reese
Ellyn Anderson
Alphia Olson, 1917-1920 (later, Mrs. A. C. Gustrud who taught 1951-1960)
Alma Bratberg, 1921-1922
Anna M. Johnson, 1922-1923
Alice Kruger, 1923-1924
Myrtle Heimdahl, 1924-1928
Eunice Peterson, 1928-1930

Esther Njus, 1931
Margaret Olander, 1931-1932
Elvera Skavdahl, 1933-1934
Viola Newstrom, 1934-1936
Harriet Reese, 1936-1937
Mrs. Frances Klein, 1937-1938
Florence Jendro, 1938-1939
Mrs. R. Shelman, 1939-1940
Lillie Jensen, 1940-1941
Ida Amundson, 1941-1943
Rhoda Railson, 1944-1945
Manda Swenson, 1944-1945

Ella Holmgren
Delores Thompson
Luella Fredrick
Arlene Nygard
Alphia (Mrs. Arnold) Gustrud, 1951-1960 (she also taught, 1917-1920, Alphia Olson)
Mrs. Richardson
Mrs. Donald Birkland (1961-1963)

Enrollment during the decade of the 1910s averaged 25 children, with a high of 30. Some years had fewer students when some older students traveled to New London for high school, including Herman and Alice Mankell. Some older children stopped attending school after they reached their teen years in order to work, marry, or move away from the township. Also affecting attendance at District 25 was the 1919 establishment of another country school—District 108—directly east, in Section 23.[10] Families from the eastern edge of 25 were redistricted to this new school.

Students from the four farms identified in enrollment records in the 1910s for District 25 include: Harvin, Clara, and Hedvig Christenson; Stella Berry (niece of Martin and Anna Reierson); Miranda and Wallace Swenson (parents Henry and Nellie Swenson rented the Norman farm); and Edna Mankell. One family, who lived in Section 26 north of Lake Florida, who had been at District 25 were redistricted to School District 108. The older daughters (Viola, Florence, and Eunice) of Emil and Anna Peterson first attended District 25. Later the Peterson siblings, including Earl Peterson, attended District 108. Earl enters the four farms story in the 1940s.

---

10 Alice Mankell was a teacher at School Districts 108 and 104 in the 1920s.

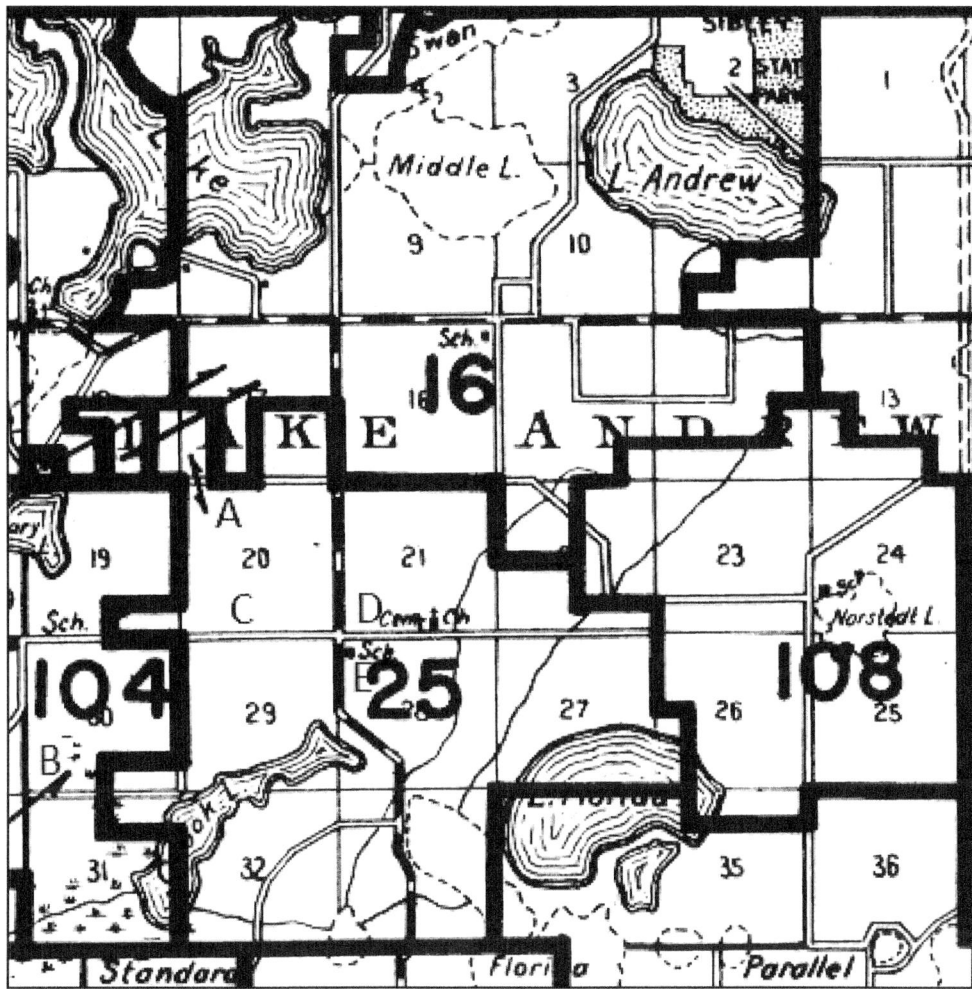

Lake Andrew Township with the boundaries of District 25 and those districts on its border, dated approximately 1950. Portions of Districts 104 and 108 had been part of District 25 (1860s-1910s). These are the locations where children attended school:

A. **1868:** Mankell homestead, northwest corner of Section 20.
B. **Late 1868 or early 1869:** Amund Syverson homestead, southwest corner of Section 30.
C. **1869-1881:** Log building located on the southern edge of Section 20.
D. **1881-1912:** Framed school, southwest corner of Section 21.
E. **1912-1963:** Framed school with bell tower, northwest corner of Section 28. After the building was no longer used as the school, it remained the Township Hall and voting place until 2012 when the township built a new Town Hall at the same location. The new owners of the old school building then moved it one mile north to the southeast corner of Section 17—at the site of the Stenseth/Christenson/Peterson farm.

(image courtesy of the Mankell Family)

LAKE ANDREW & DOVRE HORSE COMPANY[11]

In the spring of 1911 several farmers in the area formed the Lake Andrew & Dovre Horse Company. Families from at least two of the four farms connected to this business. Here is the announcement which appeared in the May 3, 1911, issue of the *Willmar Tribune*:

> *A number of the progressive farmers of Lake Andrew and Dovre Townships organized a horse company last Thursday, and purchased the choice imported Belgian Stallion, the dapple bay Duc de Braine, whose imported number is 52,214, from W. A. Lang and Company of Greeley, Iowa, thru their salesman J. C. Marlow. These farmers believe in raising the best possible horses, and hence have purchased this fine draft house to improve the breed. Mr. Marlow is the head salesman for the company. Like the lightning rod business, which in itself is a legitimate business but has come into disrepute thru unscrupulous men in the business, the stallion business has suffered much thru schemers in the same. But the contract made by this firm thru Mr. Marlow is such that the interests of the purchasers are fully protected.*
>
> *John Nelson of Lake Andrew is the president of the newly organized Lake Andrew & Dovre Horse Company; A. E. Gynild, vice president; O. B. Railson, secretary; C. S. Solberg, treasurer: C. J. Johnson, Gust Rudeen, and Melvin Swenson, directors. Other stockholders are Oscar Mankell, Thosten Larson and E. O. Dengerud [sic A. O. Dengerud]. The company will have an ad in our next issue.*

The above article includes the names of the men involved with this new business. The following list notates where they lived.

Lake Andrew Township:
August O. Dengerud, Section 20
Arnt E. Gynild, Section 15
Carl J. Johnson, Section 23
Oscar Mankell, Section 20
John Nelson, Section 21
Oluf B. Railson, Section 22
Christian S. Solberg, Section 8
Melvin Swenson, born in Arctander Township,
   Section 24 and lived in Arctander Township.
   He may have lived in Lake Andrew Township
   at the time that this business organized.

Dovre Township:
Thosten Larson
Gust Rudin/Rudeen

The goal of this company was to breed the draft stallion, Duc de Braine, with mares from local farms. The farmers brought their mares to the stallion and paid a "stud fee" to the Horse Company. Belgian horses, like the Percherons, were strong draft horses which pulled plows and large wagons. Tall (usually 16-17 hands in height; 1 hand = 4 inches) and muscular, with a stature for pulling heavy loads, these horses were the workhorses on the farms. Often weighing 2,000 pounds, with a work-life span of 20

---

11 Connor, *National Register of Belgian Draft Horses*, volume 4. *Willmar Tribune*: 3 May 1911, 24 May 1911, 8 May 1912, 9 Oct 1912; 15 July 1914; *1915 plat map*. Wikipedia

Horse Company advertisement.
(*Willmar Tribune*, May 3, 1911)

years, these large draft horses did not have to be shoed when they worked in the softer dirt of the fields.

Duc de Braine, a Belgian horse, had a star on its forehead and foaled in 1907 in Braine-le-Comte, Belgium. He was imported into the U.S. in 1911 by W. A. Lang & Company. His sire was Avenir C and his dam was Princesse de Braine. Initially, Duc de Braine was boarded at the farms of the men who were part of this new business. Here is an ad which appeared in the *Willmar Tribune*, in May and June 1911, which identifies those farmers.

DUC De BRAINE
Imported Belgian Stallion

The fine Dapple Bay, whose imported Registry No. is 52,214, purchased recently from W. A. Lang & Co. of Greeley, Ia, will stand during the season as follows:

Mondays and Tuesdays at Carl J. Johnson's place in Lake Andrew.
Wednesdays and Thursdays at John Nelson's place in Lake Andrew.
Fridays at Thorsten Larson's place in Dovre.
Saturdays at Gust Rudeen's place in Dovre.

TERMS ARE $20 TO INSURE

Lake Andrew & Dovre Horse Company

By 1912, the stallion was boarded at the Kelly & Sanderson's Livery Barn in Willmar (later called Downs and Sanderson). This breeding business lasted three years until the draft stallion was sold in the summer of 1914 at public auction at the Nelson farm.

HIGHWAY 5 IMPROVEMENT[12]

While maintenance of the roads in the county and Lake Andrew Township was necessary over the decades, the middle of the 1910s saw quite a bit of activity on Highway 5, the main road from the four farms and other farms in the Township, to Willmar, the county seat. Kandiyohi County established the Highway Department in 1915. This was part of a larger movement in the State of Minnesota to improve major roadways and to bring major highways to standard size, as determined by the State Highway Commission.

Kandiyohi County officials and business leaders worked to improve the streets of Willmar and the main highways which primarily connected to this growing city Commerce was a major factor. Businesses needed goods from the farmers, but hauling produce and goods several

Split-Log Drag.
(*Willmar Republican Gazette*, October 12, 1911)

miles to Willmar proved to be physically difficult and slow. Mud holes and ruts in the dirt or clay roads caused problems and slowed down commerce. Also, there were more people driving automobiles and trucks were replacing horses for commercial transportation. The roads were too narrow for vehicles to meet. In 1911, the *Willmar Republican Gazette* wrote about road conditions in Kandiyohi and nearby counties, as observed by a committee from an automobile club:

---

12 *Willmar Tribune*: 3 Feb, 10 Feb, 14 July, 13 October, 22 Dec 1915; 2 Feb, 2 Aug 1916; 17 Jan, 23 May, 11 July 1917; 16 Jan 1918; 15 Jan 1919. *Centennial History of Kandiyohi County*, p. 304.

> ...The road to Wright County, generally speaking, showed a lack of maintenance. While in places where work had been done they were permitted to deteriorate to such an extent that the good effect was almost entirely lost...
>
> The roads of Meeker county plainly show the fault of the present township system of supervision as in places the roads are good while in others they show a deplorable lack of attention....There is apparently a good supply of suitable soil and gravel...
>
> Kandiyohi County showed the same general neglect as Wright. Its roads are rough, the weeds grow to the roadway and farmers are permitted to plow the road to the wheel tracks which prevents drainage and destroys the work previously done. This is a fault evident all over the state and should be remedied. Those who plow up portions of the road thereby spoiling the road bed should be prosecuted. Until this practice is stopped it is useless to attempt road improvement work.
>
> Swift County showed a noticeable neglect of maintenance throughout the entire distance. From Kerkhoven to Benson heavy black clay roads were passed which were devoid of attention. No drainage was provided and the weeds were permitted to grow to the center of the road...
>
> Some of the worst roads encountered on the entire trip were found in Chippewa County. They were apparently generally neglected. Culverts were not kept in repair and that there were no accidents was due more to the care exercised by drivers than through any conditions of the roads. However citizens are realizing the importance of better thoroughfare and we hope in the near future to see great improvement...
>
> If overseers can be induced to buy or to build drags, and use them frequently, especially when the roads are soft, most of the present objections can be overcome. The general fault is neglect which, in most instances, is inexcusable.

The county's farmers provided much of the manual labor to construct and improve these roads. Using horse or tractor pulled drags, narrow dirt roads became wider gravel roads with more culverts and bridges. Laborers also laid culverts over the low wet sections and built bridges. They used their horses or tractors for scraping, dragging, leveling, and grading. The men hauled and shoveled gravel onto the improved road surfaces.

Road improvement in Dovre Township with Peter and Melvin Alvig using a grader in 1916.
(image courtesy of the Kandiyohi County Historical Association)

CH 7: 1910-1919

The roads selected for improvement in the county included the following:

- Willmar northeast to Stearns County line *(Highway 1, later numbered State Road 24 and then numbered US 71/SR 23 to SR 23)*
- Atwater south to Lake Lillian *(Highway 2, remained County Road 2)*
- Willmar southwest to Raymond *(Highway 3, later SR 49 and then SR 23)*
- Willmar south to the Renville County Line *(Highway 4, later portions of US Highway 71)*
- Willmar north to Norway Lake *(Highway 5, remains known as County Road 5)*
- Meeker County line to Swift County line *(Highway 6, later SR 10 and then US 12)*
- Pennock north to Pope County Line *(Highway 7, later County Road 1)*
- Atwater to Spicer *(Highway 8, later County Road 2)*
- Eagle Lake Road *(later part of US 71 and County Road 9)*

In 1914, about $24,000 was allocated for improving these roads; including $4,000, for the Highway 5 project. Several men connected to the four farms worked to improve the portion of Highway 5 in their township in 1914-1916. Here are those farmers/laborers from the four farms identified as having been paid for their labor on the Highway 5 improvement project:

Martin Reierson Oscar Mankell Henry Swenson
Herman Mankell J. S. Christenson

Other Lake Andrew Township farmers who worked on the road improvement projects included: Martin Hatlestad, O. B. Railson, Edwin Railson, August Dengerud, Lars H Larson, Christian Linnerud, Alvin Halvorson, Carl Mostue, John Nelson, Mike Shields, Mathias O. Rustad, and Gustaf Nordin. (These men joined with men from Norway Lake and Dovre Townships to improve Highway 5). Payments ranged from $4.00 to $60.00 determined by status as laborer or foreman, or if horses were provided.

Time marched forward. In 1922, Highway 12, from Atwater west to the Swift County line, was upgraded from gravel to concrete paving. Trucks and motor-powered equipment replaced men and horses when working on road repair and maintenance issues.

NORWAY LAKE BAND[13]

Young men in the communities across the county joined together for music, with choirs, orchestras, and bands. Men from the Lake Andrew and Arctander townships had a band for a few years in the late 1890s and ended in 1901. The group re-organized in September 1914, led by the efforts of Henry Halvorson who played the trumpet. Joe Birkemeyer was the director and he lived near Pennock. The musicians were from the local area (four farms men are in bold) and included:

---

13 Christenson Family Collection. *Centennial History of Kandiyohi County*, p. 147, 184. Mankell.org. *Willmar Tribune*: 16 September, 1915, 9 December 1914, 5 May 1915, 9 June 1915,

Ludwig Boe
Harold Bolstad
Harvin Christenson, drums and trumpet
Henry J. Halvorson, trumpet
Herman Mankell, piano and Jew Harp/
 harmonica (possibly)
Arthur Reigstad
Sidney Reigstad
Bennie Rustad
Henry Scott
Edwin Skaalerud
Archie Stene
George Stene
Johnny Stene
Oliver Stene
Gerhard Swenson
Melvin Swenson
William Swenson

This group called themselves the Norway Lake Band and played at local functions and celebrations, continuing a tradition from the 1890s. In June 1915, they played at the wedding of Adella Sundstrom and Elmer Stene (his brothers played in the band) in Arctander Township. The band also performed several concerts at East Norway Lake Lutheran Church, where several of the players were members.

This re-iteration of the band lasted only a few years. Several players were drafted early into the army including Harold Bolstad, George Stene, and Melvin Swenson, though not all served during the war later known as World War I.

THE GREAT WAR[14]

There are no records indicating that any men from the four farms served during the Great War. As required by law, adult men ages 21-30 registered with local draft boards on June 5, 1917. They answered questions to determine if they would be subjected to the draft for service in the war. During the summer of 1917, many from the first list were selected to be physically examined for military service. Fifty-eight men from Lake Andrew Township came to the draft board for registration and this group included names familiar in this project: Oscar L. Larson, Herman W. Mankell, Cornell Thorson, Christian Korsmo. The person designated as Registrar for Lake Andrew Township was C. A. Syverson. The initial quota for Kandiyohi County was 140 men. In 1918, having reached the age 21, Harvin Christenson registered. Not all men who registered actually served in the military. Men were allowed to request exemption from service. Some requests were granted; others denied. Reasons included farming, supporting dependents, and religious objections.

Enlisted men from Kandiyohi County were trained at several camps, including Camp Dodge, Iowa; Camp Grant, Illinois; Camp Wadsworth, South Carolina; Fort Riley, Kansas; Fort Forrest, Georgia; and Fort Cody, New Mexico. Those from Lake Andrew Township who served in the military during the war and/or soon after the Armistice included these men: Harold Bolstad, Orlean Christian, Carl Danielson, Victor Danielson Albert Eckman, Edwin Erickson, Alfred Halvorson, Carl Hegstrom, Christian Linnerud, Olaf Linnerud, Edwin Nelson, Harry Skaalerud, and Walter Skoglund. Soldiers from

---

14 *Willmar Tribune*: 1917: 2 May, 23 May, 20 June, 25 July, 1 Aug, 26 Sept. 12 December; 1918: 2 Jan, 20 February, 27 Feb, 24 April, 1 May, 22 May, 10 July, 17 July, 11 September, 9 Oct, 6 Nov, 13 November, 20 Nov, 4 December, 18 December; 1919: 1 Jan, 8 Jan, 15 January, 22 January, 23 July. Christenson Family Collection. Centennial p. 102-103; ancestry.com; findagrave.com.

nearby Arctander Township included twins Axel and Eddie Gordhamer who were friends of Harvin Christenson and cousins of Herman Mankell. Harry E. Amundson, a former neighbor and schoolmate of Harvin and Herman at District 25, served overseas with Company A of the 49th Infantry, U.S. Army. (His parents, Fred and Gunda Amundson rented the Norman farm for about 2 years, 1900-1901, moved to the southern part of Lake Andrew Township, and later moved to Renville County.)

Area soldiers died in battle: Pvt. Oluf O. Finstad from Norway Lake Township, Lewis Larson from Colfax Township and Pvt. George H. Olson from Dovre Township.

Families in Lake Andrew Township showed their support for the war effort by raising money for the Red Cross and honoring area soldiers with speeches, patriotic songs, prayers, and farewells with cash gifts. In addition, local families raised money for the American Red Cross at various social events and purchased Liberty Bonds. J. S. Christenson was one of three men in Lake Andrew Township designated as Township Solicitors. The other two men were Rev. H. J. Strand and Emil Peterson. Oscar Mankell was on the committee promoting investments in War Savings Stamps.

The county had local Red Cross chapters which raised money and had service projects which supported the troops. J. S. Christenson was the treasurer of the Lake Andrew/Norway Lake chapter. Newspaper reports show that people from the four farms were part of this war effort, including J. S. Christenson, Martin Reierson, Miranda Swenson, and Minnie, Alice, and Edna Mankell. Activities and participation across the county included:

- Women knitted for the Red Cross. They created "Trench Socks" made from heavy amoskeag yarn. Women created refugee garments, too. (There were mandatory allotments.)
- People cheered the soldiers when they left on trains for military camps and soldiers from other areas of Minnesota when trains passed through local towns.
- Children collected magazines and books for soldiers and sailors.
- Money was raised at auctions, concerts, dinners, picnics, and ice-cream socials.
- Red Cross work days were held on Wednesday afternoons. Women prepared surgical dressings and "Front Line Packets" which had gauze, compresses, and bandages. Local communities were required to provide these packets. Willmar had to provide 400 in April 1918.
- People attended funerals of soldiers.

The Norway Lake/Lake Andrew area chapter of the American Red Cross (A.R.C.) was the beneficiary of a fund-raiser picnic held on the Fourth of July, 1918, at J. S. Christenson's Solberg farm property on the southeast shore of Norway Lake. He described this perfect summer day in Lake Andrew Township, published in the *Willmar Tribune*:

> "Providence had blessed us just the night before with a light sprinkling rain that settled the dust and enriched the fragrances of the flowers, the shrubs, and the trees, and the day of the 4th with a clear blue sky here and there dotted with clouds and a gentle northwest breeze fanning the water, the leaves, the heated brow of the merry partakers."

About 1,500 attendees cheered for the boat and foot races, ate picnic lunches, heard speeches and music—all to celebrate the country's birth and raise money for the war effort. As Christenson wrote for the *Willmar Tribune*: "Keep the fire for the A. R. C. burning higher yet that our boys over there may suffer less."

At the end of the war, November 11, 1918, Willmar Mayor E. C. Wellin ordered the fire house whistle blown at 5:00 am. Railroad whistles soon followed, with continuous noise for about an hour. The county celebrated for days with parades, train whistles, church bells, and closed stores. These celebrations helped people temporarily forget about another great worry—the influenza pandemic which sickened and sometimes killed people in the township, the county, the state, the nation, and the world.

INFLUENZA PANDEMIC[15]

Concurrent to and following the Great War was the influenza pandemic of 1918-1920. A world destroyed by a war was also ravaged by the flu. Two-thirds of all deaths occurred within a few weeks in the fall of 1918. Estimates for deaths across the globe are between 50 and 100 million, with 675,000 in the United States. These numbers are far higher than the 117,000 American service members who died in the war.

Epidemiologists have identified Kansas as the location of the first influenza infections—first in Haskell County and then in Fort Riley. From the Midwest the disease and deaths then spread to other military camps and across the Atlantic Ocean with the military to Europe. The first outbreak in Europe occurred in April 1918, in Brest, France, after American troops disembarked at the harbor. Another wave, a more deadly strain, of the epidemic returned to the United States with the soldiers coming home from the war. The disease knew no political boundaries. People fighting and enduring the war's destruction on both sides of the conflict suffered from influenza. It spread within the United States—to military camps, cities, and rural areas. War was the primary reason for the pandemic's rapid geographic progression. Fighting and winning the war were of more urgency than fighting a growing flu pandemic. The U.S. military needed soldiers so men were transported between military camps and across the ocean—even if they were sick—which led to more military illnesses and thousands of American deaths. Military camps were overcrowded due to the need for soldiers. The medical field was aware of how the disease spread and the need to quarantine. However, military quarantines occurred too late to quell the epidemic at the camps. Several soldiers and sailors from Kandiyohi County died when training at military camps across the United States. Newly enlisted soldiers from Kandiyohi County primarily received military training at Camp Grant in Rock Island, Illinois. Autumn 1918 deaths from influenza at Camp Grant, include these men from the county who had just arrived at the camp about a month earlier:

- John Peter Soderlund of Lake Andrew Township, died October 6
- Harry Paulson of St. John's Township, died October 5
- Herman Skutle of Dovre Township, died October 4

---

15 While called Spanish Influenza, the disease was initially identified in the United States, China, and France, not Spain. The Spanish press was the first to write about the illness. Barry, *The Great Influenza*; *Willmar Tribune* 1918: 9 October, 16 October, 23 October, 30 October, 20 November, 27 November, 18 December; 1919: 22 January, 7 May; 1920: 7 January, 26 May; Washington Post 8 November 2018, p. Q6; *New London Times*, 2 January 1919; Leite Family Collection; Brandt Family Collection

- Andrew Lundgren of Colfax Township, died October 6 immediately after his transfer from Camp Grant
- Iver Cornell Dunham of Norway Lake Township, died October 4
- Christian Evenson of Norway Lake Township, died October 6
- Willard Doss of Raymond, died September 30
- Floyd Wessels of Raymond, died October 5

On October 8, the military leader of the Camp Grant, Colonel Charles Hagadorn, received a report which stated that more than 500 of his men died from the flu including young men from Kandiyohi County. Hagadorn recognized his part in ordering the overcrowding of Camp Grant and initially ignoring quarantine advice from the medical personnel until it was too late. Minutes after receiving the report Hagadorn killed himself with his gun.

This strain of influenza, spread in the air and by touch, primarily killed young and strong adults, ages 20-35; 40% of the death were in this age group. Previous flu epidemics took the very old or very young. The average age at time of death in the 1918 epidemic was 34 years. The victims were called "doubly dead"—the death of the person and the death of the person's future. The immune system in these previously healthy adults mounted a rapid response to target the virus which had invaded the lungs. Literature states that it was the body's immune system which killed the young adults—not the influenza infection by itself.

The majority of influenza victims recovered. The majority of pneumonia victims recovered. Some had a mild infection; some more severe. They were sick for about ten days and experienced bad headaches, body aches, sore throats, fever, exhaustion, and coughs. But for some—millions across the world—their infection did not follow normal patterns.

Those who had the most virulent strain faced death. Some were dead only a few hours after experiencing their first symptoms. For others death was within 24-48 hours. Here are the severe to lethal symptoms which victims faced as they fought the disease:
- Blood loss from nosebleeds
- Blood loss from the ears
- Coughed up blood
- Coughed so hard that abdominal muscles and cartilage tore
- Painful headaches
- Intense body aches
- Vomiting
- Fingertips and lips tinged with blue

- Cyanosis: Skin turned unusual colors, including shades of blue to almost black due to lack of oxygen in the blood.
- Hemorrhagic lungs: Within 24-48 hours the lungs filled with blood and the victim could not breathe.

Many of those who had severe infections also suffered from lingering brain and nervous system complications: muscle twitching, depression, delirium, hallucinations, confusion, forgetfulness, psychosis, schizophrenia, and even suicide.[16]

The flu arrived in Kandiyohi County in the fall of 1918 and stayed for about two years, occurring in waves. Records show no deaths occurred at the four farms due to influenza. However two women and one man died from the flu who were connected to the families: a sister of a renter, a woman who was a neighbor and former classmate, a brother to a farm wife.

Nellie Luella Amalia Hatlestad died on December 4, 1918, at the age of 17. She was the youngest daughter of Severin and Pernille Hatlestad and a sister to Lars Hatlestad, renter of the Norman farm. Nellie died

> from a two days' illness of the influenza… At the time of Nellies' death the mother was at the New London Hospital too weak to be told. She has since, however, improved and has been informed of her bereavement.

One month prior to Nellie's death, the family had buried another woman, Caroline (Tollefson) Hatlestad, wife of Lars, and the mother of seven children. She had given birth to her youngest son just three days prior to her death. Caroline's obituary stated the cause of death was from pneumonia, which was often a complication of influenza. Born in 1882, she died in 1918 at the age of 36 and is buried at First Lutheran Church of Norway Lake cemetery. Her funeral services were conducted outside of the home and then outside of the church building due to the flu epidemic. When gathered together, people were concerned about enclosed spaces where they believed people could fall ill.

Nellie Hatlestad, 1901-1918.
(image courtesy of Marlin Henjum)

---

16 Western leaders who met in Europe to finalize the peace treaty suffered from influenza, including President Woodrow Wilson and his staff. There is a strong argument that because of his decreased mental abilities due to his severe flu infection, his missed meetings, and his sudden reversal in negotiations, Wilson conceded to European leaders in their need to punish Germany with severe reparations. This rapid reversal in negotiations laid the groundwork for a nationalistic Germany to arise in the 1920s and 1930s. A severely weakened and diminished man, Wilson soon suffered a stroke—or it was additional complications from his severe influenza from which he never fully recovered.

Agnes (Larson) Knutson on her wedding day in 1919.
(image courtesy of Loretta Brandt)

Agnes (Larson) Knutson died the following spring. She was the daughter of Lars H. and Helene Larson, and born on July 6, 1888. She grew up on the farm in Section 20 (SE ¼) and worshiped at Lake Florida Mission Church where she attended Sunday School and was confirmed. She attended District 25 School located across the road from her parents' farm. Her former classmates from the four farms families included Harvin and Clara Christenson; Herman, Edna, and Alice Mankell; Edith, Lillie, Oscar, and Victor Larson; and Stella Berry. Expecting their first child, Agnes married Elmer Knutson on April 14, 1919 and she fell ill days later, after their arrival at their new home in Granite Falls in western Minnesota. Her death came one week later, on April 23.

While on their wedding trip she was taken ill. Mr. and Mrs. Knutson had reached Granite Falls when she fell victim to influenza pneumonia which resulted in death. Her mother was the only one who had time to reach her bedside before she passed away.

Pallbearers at her funeral included former classmates from the four farms: Herman Mankell, Harvin Christenson, and Oscar Larson. Wearing her wedding dress, she and her unborn child are buried at Lake Florida Mission Church cemetery.

One year after the death and burial of Agnes Knutson, another death affected the four farms community, specifically the Christenson family. Casper Engen, the brother of Mina Christenson (Mrs. J. S. Christenson), died on May 15, 1920, at the age of 35. The son of Martin and Helen Engen, Casper was born on May 7, 1882. "He fell victim to the dreaded plague influenza, and having a weak heart that disease affected this important organ and caused his death." He is buried at East Norway Lake Lutheran Church cemetery.

Casper Engen 1882-1920.
(image courtesy of Marlin Henjum)

In Kandiyohi County and Lake Andrew Township, the residents responded to calls for aid and restrictions on activities. Beginning in the fall of 1918, the county Health Officer, Dr. J. M. Rains, placed bans on public gatherings such as movie theaters and churches. These bans lasted about five weeks. He also closed Willmar public schools. Those who had recovered from influenza were asked to wear masks. School District 25 was closed for about a week in October 1918.

During 1918, the Health Officer for the county reported 38 deaths from influenza and various complications, including pneumonia. One of those deaths in the county was a Hilda (Haramoen) Espelien. Her parents were Norwegian immigrants who settled in Section 35 of Norway Lake Township. Her husband Adolph Espelien was from a farm about a mile away, in Section 25. They married in 1906, lived in Norway Lake Township early in their marriage, and were members of First Lutheran Church of

Norway Lake. By 1910, the growing family lived in New London and later returned to the Espelien farm in Norway Lake Township. Hilda was 33 years old, a mother of six children (ages 2-12) and pregnant with her seventh, when she died from pneumonia, a complication from her flu infection. According to her obituary, her illness was brief as were many deaths from the lethal form of influenza. She was buried at Oak Hill Cemetery in New London. Hilda's oldest child, Viola Myrtle (Espelien) Skare, was 12 years old when her mother died. Several years later she reflected back on her mom, life in the household, fears about the flu, and that difficult time for her, her siblings, and her father.

> *My mother was a sweet, lovely person. She was tall and slim and had lots of long, auburn hair and she wore it in a pug on the top of her head. She was a milliner and seamstress so she made beautiful hats, wedding gowns, and confirmation dresses, etc. She worked for Mary Peterson in New London, a milliner and seamstress who taught sewing. She [Hilda] taught me to sew when I was about five and I wasn't too enthused about it then. She made me sew my doll dresses by hand, and if she thought I could do it better, she made me take it all up again and again until it got nice. I might as well have done my best the first time. The same thing with reading. We had to learn our ABC's long before we started school and our Katikismus [catechism]. We used to have a whole month of Norwegian school every year and had to memorize most of the Bible history...and even Norwegian hymns.*

> *My mother died on Christmas Eve, December 24, 1918, at 12 o'clock. She died with an unborn baby from the flu which had turned to pneumonia. Everybody was so scared of the flu that year that nobody but our dad, aunt, and my sister and I went to the funeral. There were a few who met us at the grave. She was buried in New London. Our home was broken-up and we all went to live with neighbors and relatives.*

NEAR EAST RELIEF & ARMENIAN GENOCIDE[17]

While people across the globe faced war and its aftermath and the ravages of the world's influenza pandemic, others suffered for different reasons. Americans, including those in Lake Andrew Township, responded to the call to help those in need, hoping to alleviate people's suffering with humanitarian aid. Refugees in the Near East suffered as a consequence of the Great War and the Armenian genocide which happened concurrent to the war. Armenians fled their homeland after loved ones were massacred by the government of Turkey, which had aligned with Germany during the war. At the end of the war Turkish leaders were held accountable for the atrocities, though never admitting to genocide. However, suffering and starvation of the Armenian people continued. They were refugees in countries of the Near East, including Syria, Greece, Syria, Russia, and the Holy Land.

In November 1918, President Woodrow Wilson called on his fellow Americans to continue their efforts in saving lives and restoring homes, with the establishment of the Near East Relief Fund. An estimate of more than 4 million people were displaced and faced death and the loss of an ancient peoples if humanitarian relief was not offered.

---

17 Near East Relief ended in 1930. *Willmar Tribune*, 8 January 1919, 10 December 1919, 14 January 1920, 17 March 1920, 21 December 1921; Armenian-Genocide.org

> *I, therefore, again call upon the people of the United States to make even more generous contributions than they have made heretofore to sustain through the winter months those, who, through no fault of their own, have been left in a starving, shelter-less condition, and to help reestablish these ancient and sorely oppressed people in their former homes on a self-supporting basis.*

In addition to raising money and supplying food, the Near East Relief drive answered additional needs by establishing hospitals, vocational training centers, refugee camps, and orphanages. Children at the orphanages had lost parents in the massacres, the war, disease, or from other causes. In addition, these orphanages housed unwanted children who were the result of rapes and forced marriages endured by Armenian women.

In early 1919, the residents of Kandiyohi County, including families of Lake Andrew Township, responded to the congressionally mandated Near East drive and continued these fund-raising efforts for a few years. One year after President Wilson's declaration, the county exceeded their goal of $5,700 by raising $6,300. Each township board appointed a committee to address this need. Oscar Mankell was one of several men in the township who collected funds from their neighbors. Other men included Elmer Halvorson, Knute H. Nelson, Olaus Reierson, and Gabriel Stene. Families donated money and farmers donated surplus corn to help those who faced starvation. Grain elevators and train companies donated their services to move the grain.

The decade of the 1910s ended with the hope of better things to come. The war was over and the flu epidemic was diminishing and would soon end in 1920.

CHAPTER 8:
1920-1929

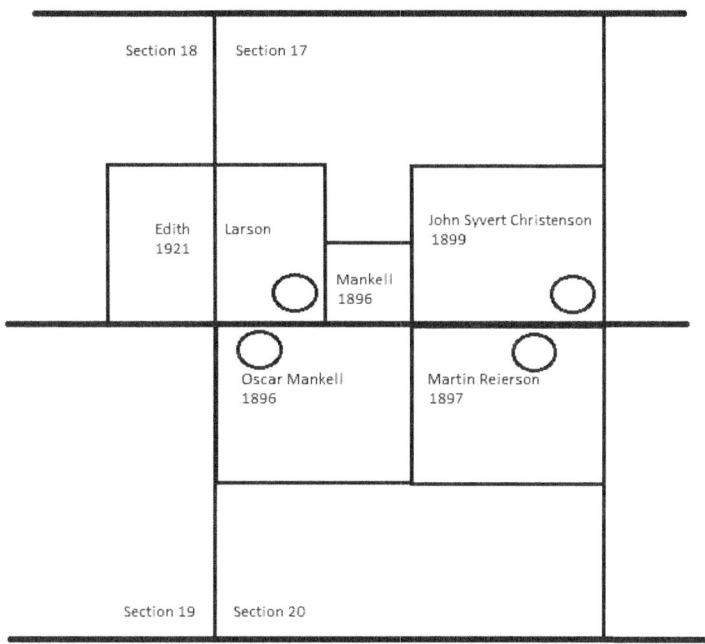

HIGHLIGHTS

- The farms were in transition: new renters and a new owner
- The community celebrated their school and local church

STENSETH/CHRISTENSON FARM[1]

During the 1920s, the Christenson family managed two farms, even during the three years they lived near Red Wing. The farms had renters. Here is a chronological list of events in the family.

1922
John Syvert (J. S.) and Mina Christenson, with their daughters Hedvig and Clara, moved to Red Wing, Minnesota, on the Mississippi River. The family lived with one of the Red Wing Seminary faculty members, Librarian and Professor Edward O. Ringstad. Their son Harvin was a student at Red Wing Seminary, a religious institution connected to the larger Haugean Lutheran church body. (Nannestad Lutheran Church was a Haugean Lutheran congregation.)

1922
With the family in Red Wing, Christenson rented the Stenseth farm to Elmer and Clara Skindelien who moved to the farm in November 1922. Elmer had married Clara Rood in May of the same year, and they soon moved to Lake Andrew Township from Arctander Township where they both were raised. Elmer was a cousin of Mina Christenson's mother, Helene (Skindelien) Engen. Elmer and Clara lived at this farm for about a year and later lived in the Sunburg and Arctander areas where their children were born.

1924
When in Red Wing, John Syvert maintained his interest in politics. He ran for Lieutenant Governor, but lost in the May 1924 primary race. J. S. and family returned from Red Wing to Lake Andrew Township and lived at the family's Solberg farm at Norway Lake (Section 8). Ole Aasen and his family had been renting the Solberg farm prior to the Christenson family's return. Ole was married to Hanna Engen, the daughter of Hans and Beata Engen. Hans was a brother of Mina Christenson. Thus Christenson rented this farm to his extended family. The Aasen family left the Section 8 farm and later lived in Norway Lake Township.[2]

1925
John Syvert built a new barn at his Section 8 property.

1925
On June 29, one month after graduating from Red Wing Seminary Harvin married Sigrid Harriet Larson at Ebenezer Lutheran Church in Chicago, Illinois. Sigrid was the daughter of Louis Larsen and Hilda Clausen, both Norwegian immigrants. Soon after their marriage Harvin entered Luther Theological Seminary in St. Paul. He and Sigrid lived with a professor from the seminary. By 1926, Harvin and Sigrid had left St. Paul to live with Sigrid's widowed mother in Chicago. Hilda's husband Louis died in 1920 from a kidney ailment, leaving his wife Hilda and nine children. Harvin and Sigrid had their first child when in Illinois.

---
1 Christenson Family Collection. ancestry.com; *Willmar Tribune* 6 Nov 1922, 14 May 1924.
2 With J. S. and family at the Section 8 farm and not at the Section 17 farm, one can assume that there were renters at the farm, but the author has found no documentation as to the identity of this renter, prior to the arrival of Gustav Swenson in 1930.

1927-1928

By late 1927, Harvin and his family were back in St. Paul so Harvin could continue his Seminary studies. Their second child was born while they lived in St. Paul. After his ordination in June 1928, the family soon moved again as Harvin was to serve as pastor at congregations near Frederick in Brown County, South Dakota, and later in Douglas County, also in South Dakota. Four more children were born in South Dakota. The family returned to Lake Andrew Township in 1936.

REIERSON FARM[3]

Martin and Anna Reierson moved to New London in 1922 or 1923. Martin and Anna had purchased property in the town in 1917 so this may be where they lived—Block One of the Larson Addition on the north side (today it is the NW corner of Ash St. and 2nd Ave NE). Martin stopped farming and owned a trucking business in town. He worked as a dray trucker, transporting cargo on regular routes. Though they left the township, they maintained contact with people living near their farm, especially the Christenson family. Martin and Anna attended tent meetings led by Pastor Harvin Christenson. J. S. Christenson was one of the guest speakers at their 50th wedding anniversary celebration in New London in 1944.

1922

The Reiersons retained ownership of their farm in Section 20 and rented to two families in the 1920s. The first family, John Gunder and Ellen (Monson) Johnson and their son Gordon, arrived in September 1922. This family had been living with Ellen's parents, John (aka Jonas) and Johanna Monson, in Section 36 of Lake Andrew Township. Ellen's mother emigrated from Kronoberg, Sweden, to New London in 1887 at about the age of 25 and was an active member of the historically Swedish Lebanon Lutheran Church in New London until her death in 1922. For two years, 1927 and 1928, Gordon attended District 25 with other children from the area. After leaving Lake Andrew Township the family continued to farm, first moving to New London Township and then to Cosmos in Meeker County.

1925

Martin's mother, Sigrid Reierson, died on September 22, 1925, at the home of another son, Olaus Reierson who also lived in the township. After services on September 25 at East Norway Lake Lutheran Church, she was buried in the church cemetery.

1928

Soon after the Johnson family left the Reierson farm, another young couple arrived. Walter and Lillian (Bergman) Carlson moved to Section 20 soon after their April 7, 1928, marriage, and rented the farm for about 10 years. Walter and Lillian both grew up in Dovre Township, south of Lake Andrew Township.

---

3   *Willmar Tribune*: 4 April 1917, 9 August 1922, 23 Sept 1922; District 25 enrollment records at Kandiyohi County Historical Society; *History of New London, 1965-1975* p. 169. *Anniversary Album, 1959-1944, Lebanon Lutheran Church*, p 141; *New London Times*: 24 September 1925, 8 June 1944; 8 March 1951; ancestry.com. Interview with Wendell Carlson.

Walter was the son of Edward and Caroline Carlson. Lillian also grew up on Dovre Township, and was the daughter of Jonas and Lena Bergman. Martin's wife, Anna (Alvig) Reierson grew up in Dovre Township, so it is possible that the Alvig, Bergman, and Carlson families knew each other.

NORMAN/RAILSON FARM[4]

**Second house on the Norman farm, built in 1890.
Norman, Larson, and Railson families (and several renters) lived in this house.**
(image courtesy of the Norman Family)

1921
Edith Larson became the owner of the Norman farm in 1921, following probate after her father William Larson's death: 80 acres in Section 17 and 80 acres in Section 18. The acreage in Section 18 had been in the Norman family since 1874 when Johannes Norman purchased 160 acres. The land was passed to son Gustav Albert, then his siblings. By the 1920s, only 80 acres of Section 18 land remained in the family.

1920-1926
Henry and Nellie Swenson and children Miranda, Wallace, Eleanor, and Henry, Jr. (Lolly) rented the Norman farm in 1910 and lived there until about 1926, with older children Eleanor and Wallace attending District 25. In 1929, Henry Sr. purchased a farm in Section 4, east of Games Lake in the northern part of Lake Andrew Township. After the family moved, their youngest son Henry Jr. attended District 16.[5]

1926
Nellie's mother, Helena Larson, died on July 27, 1926, from diabetes. Helena and her family lived in Section 20 (SE ¼) and was a neighbor to the four farms, with the property adjacent the Reierson farm. Helena and her family lived southeast from daughter Nellie and her family. Helena's obituary was published in the *Willmar Tribune*. Those attending included her neighbors from the four farms. Three men from the four farms were her pallbearers: John Syvert Christenson, Oscar Mankell and Martin Reierson. The flower girls included one of her granddaughters.

---

4 Attendance records of School District 25, Kandiyohi County Historical Society; ancestry.com; Willmar City Directory, 1927; Norman Family Collection. *Willmar Tribune*, 20 March 1918, 5 Aug 1926; Plat maps: 1886, 1900, 1905, 1915, 1927, 1932. Kandiyohi County Recorder's Office; *New London Times*, 5 August 1926.
5 Where did the Swenson family live in 1927 and 1928? It's possible the family rented the Section 4 farm prior to purchase.

CH 8: 1920-1929

Mrs. L. H. Larson Has Passed Beyond
Came to America in 1870 at the Age of Ten Years and Has Lived Here Many Years

An unusually large gathering of sympathizers gathered last Friday afternoon to pay tribute at the funeral of Mrs. L. H. Larson who passed away Tuesday evening, July 27th. That she was highly esteemed, loved and respected by all was fully attested to by the large gathering present. She was a faithful companion, a loving mother, hard worker and faithful to her domestic duties, a true Christian, always a member of the Swedish Mission Florida church, always active in the promotion of same in all its branches.

She was present at the funeral of Mrs. Frank Eklof and when asked by Rev. Anderson how she was getting along, she answered: "My turn is next," and just one week to the day she passed over the Valley of Death. Interment took place at the Florida Mission church which always was her church home.

Mrs. Helena (Eliason) Larson was born in Vermland, [Värmland] Sweden, January 13, 1860. Emigrated with her parents to America at the age of 10 and settled down on Section 33, Lake Andrew, in 1870, later moving to Grant, S. Dak.

She was united in marriage to Lars H. Larson Sept. 17, 1881. Besides her husband, L. H. Larson, she leaves behind her loving children: Clara, Mrs. M. M. Engen of Arctander; Nellie, Mrs. Henry Swenson of Lake Andrew; Esther, Mrs. Edwin Gadney at home; Hattie, Mrs. Herman Strand, Lake Andrew; Agnes, Mrs. Elmer Knutson preceded her in death in 1919; and Anna staying home; three sons, Lawrence, George, and Grant; also one brother, Joseph Eliason of Grand County, So Dak. ; a large number of nieces and nephews and 18 grandchildren.

The pall bearers were Herman Larson, Oscar Mankell, J. S. Christenson, Martin Reierson, John Nelson, Peter Skoglund. The flower girls [carried the flowers which covered the casket] *were Eleanor Swenson, Kathy Eliason, Eunice Reece and Harriet Reese....*

This obituary stated that Helena was "faithful to her domestic duties." Evidence of this characteristic was highlighted in the previous chapter: in 1912 Nellie Larson hosted Adolph Olson Eberhart, Governor of Minnesota, and others for lunch prior to the dedication of the new building for School District 25.

1925-1926

Edith Larson, who grew up at her parents Section 21 farm, married Edwin Railson in Willmar on April 8, 1925, and lived for a short time in Willmar at 809 Lake Avenue. Their first child, Robert, was born on February 6, 1926 when the family lived in this county seat. Edwin was a driver for the Handy-Lewis Motor Company on Litchfield Avenue, which sold and serviced automobiles. Edith's brother Oscar L. Larson worked at this company for several years. Edwin and Edith Railson arrived at the Norman farm in 1926, after the Henry Swenson family left. Edith was returning to the Lake Andrew Township and to the Section 17 farm

Edwin and Edith Railson, c1925.
(image courtesy of the Norman Family)

which had been in her family for two previous generations: her parents Johanna and William, and her maternal grandparents Johannes and Marie Norman.

Born in 1897, Edwin Herbert Railson (aka Herbert Edwin) grew up in the township in Section 21, on the east side of Lake Florida Mission Church. His parents were Oluf B. and Nellie (Nelson) Railson, the earliest pioneers of the Township. Their roots were with First Lutheran Church of Norway Lake.

MANKELL FARM[6]

The decade began with Oscar and Minnie and their three children, Herman, Edna and Alice, living on the Mankell farm. By the end of the decade, son Herman was married with two young children and was operating the farm. Oscar and Minnie lived in Willmar. Daughter Edna was working in Minneapolis and would later join her parents in Willmar. Daughter Alice finished her education at the St. Cloud Teacher's College and worked in various St. Paul schools until 1931.

Herman, Edna, and Alice Mankell, c1925.

Other Mankell properties

In the 1920s and 1930s, Oscar owned properties in other areas of the township, the City of Willmar, and the county. Here is a list of the known properties:

- 200 acres in Lake Andrew Township on the four farms mile: Section 20 (NW ¼, 160 acres) plus Section 17 (SE ¼ of the SW ¼, 40 acres)
- Co-owner of 166 acres with L. H. Larson on the northwest shore of Lake Florida, Sections 27 and 28. The previous owner had been Swedish immigrant Charles Peterson, whose grandson Earl becomes part of the four farms story in the 1940s. Following the 1936 death of Oscar and the 1940 death of Lars, the new owners were Oscar's widow Minnie, and Clara Engen, daughter of Lars Larson.
- House in Willmar, 910 West Litchfield Avenue. Oscar and Minnie lived in this house for many years.
- 160 acres in Burbank Township, Section 15 (NW ¼), originally the homestead of Martin Halvorson. Oscar owned this property from 1920-c1935.
- Lot on the northwest shore of Green Lake
- Lot on the eastern shore of Games Lake

---

6   Mankell.org; Mankell Family Collection; *Willmar Tribune* 30 November 1921, 3 November 1926, 6 November 1929; *West Central Tribune* 5 April 2006; ENL history, p 16; Plat Maps: 1905, 1915, 1927, 1932; mncourts.gov; Kandiyohi County Recorder.

CH 8: 1920-1929

1926

On October 30, 1926, Herman Mankell married Cornelia (Cora) Christopherson at the Lake Florida Mission Church. Two families from Lake Andrew and Arctander Townships were brought together with this marriage. Here is the summary from the *Willmar Tribune*:

> A very pretty wedding took place Saturday afternoon at 3 o'clock at the Lake Florida Mission church when Cornelia Bernice Christopherson, daughter of Mrs. Bastine Christopherson of Arctander Township, and Herman Mankell, son of Mr. and Mrs. Oscar Mankell, of New London, were united in marriage.
>
> The bride was attired in white georgette over satin and carried a shower bouquet of pink roses, white pom-poms and baby breath. Her veil was arranged in bandeau effect with sprays of orange blossoms. The bride was attended by her sister, Millie Agnes, as maid of honor, gowned in pale green Elizabeth crepe and wearing a corsage of pink roses, white pom-poms and baby breath. The bridesmaid was Edna Mankell, sister of the groom, who wore tan net over lavender georgette and also wore a corsage. Little Gloria Bernice Myrhe, niece of the bride, in an attractive flesh colored georgette dress over satin, carrying a basket of flowers, acted as flower girl.
>
> The groomsmen were Herman Landquist, a cousin of the groom, and Otto Christopherson, brother of the bride. The ceremony was performed before a triple arch of white. Potted plants and ferns banked the altar.
>
> After the playing of Lohengrin's Wedding March by Edna Hjelle, "At Dawning" was sung by Miss Rebecca Grefe. The impressive ring ceremony was performed by Rev. Anderson of Litchfield. Immediately after the ceremony a five o'clock dinner was served to 35 guests at the home of the bride. Guests from a distance attending the wedding were Millie A. Christopherson, Ellen Christopherson, Julius Christopherson, Herman Landquist and Otto Mankell, all of Minneapolis; Alice Mankell and Rebecca Grefe of St. Paul; and Mrs. Evenson of Battle Lake.
>
> During the evening a large number of friends and relatives of the newlyweds gave a shower of many beautiful and useful gifts for the bride. After a short wedding trip to Minneapolis and northern Minnesota, the young couple will make their home on the Mankell farm near New London.

Herman and Cora Mankell, 1926.

Cornelia (Cora) Christopherson was born and grew up on the Christopherson homestead in Arctander Township (Section 26), just one township west of Lake Andrew Township, and about four miles from the Mankell farm. Cora's parents, Bastina Hjelle and August Christopherson, were immigrants from Norway who met and married in Kandiyohi County. August, his siblings, and parents Lars and Anna Christopherson immigrated in 1868 and had a homestead in Arctander Township. Lars paid for Bastina's 1888 voyage and she then worked for the Christopherson family. She later married August, one of their sons. Bastina was from the Hjelle farm south of Fåvang and north of Lillehammer. The Christopherson family's roots were in Nannestad and the Holter farm in Ullensaker, Norway. August Christopherson died in 1906, so Bastina was a widow by the time of her daughter's marriage.

1929

Oscar, Minnie, and Edna moved from the farm to Willmar in 1929 and lived at 910 W. Litchfield Avenue. The 1930 census states that Oscar rented this home for $40 per month. (They owned the home at a later date.) They moved to Willmar because Oscar was named Register of Deeds by the Kandiyohi County Commissioners. He completed the unexpired term of his predecessor. After completing the term he did not seek election to another term, but the family remained in Willmar. Here is an excerpt about his appointment from the *Willmar Weekly Tribune*:

> A special meeting of the board of county commissioners was held Monday afternoon at the court house to appoint a Register of Deeds because of the vacancy caused by the death of August Lundquist. . . . Several applications were in for this position but after a short deliberation Mr. Oscar Mankell of Lake Andrew township was appointed. Mr. Mankell assumed his new duties at the courthouse this morning.
>
> Oscar Mankell has been a lifelong resident of this county, having been born in Lake Andrew Township. He has held a number of offices in that township and at the present time is chairman of the town board and has held several other township offices. He has also been treasurer of school district No. 25 and at the present time is president of the Arctander and Lake Andrew Fire Insurance Co. . . . Mr. Mankell is 61 years old, married and has three children. For the present his family will remain on the farm home but may move to Willmar at a later date.
>
> The new register of deeds is a son of Herman Wilhelm Mankell, a native of Stockholm, Sweden, who arrived to this county in 1865 and shortly thereafter located the homestead claim in the Norway Lake community which has been the home of son Oscar since the death of his father in 1889. The father was very active in the organization and development of the early community.

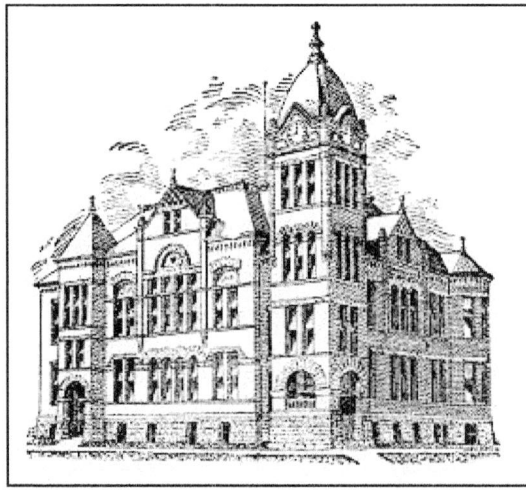

Edna lived with her parents for a while in the early 1930s where she was a Deputy Register of Deeds.

Herman, Cora, and their growing family remained on the homestead. Oscar continued to own the farm until his 1936 death. By 1937 Herman owned the farm.

Drawing of the old Kandiyohi County Courthouse. Built in 1890, this Victorian Romanesque style building, with a tower and clock, was razed in about 1966. This image appeared on the letterhead for Oscar Mankell, Register of Deeds.

1928-1929

By the end of the decade Herman and Cora had two children. Their son Orlynn was born in 1928; their daughter Marjorie, in 1929. Cora's mother Bastina and Bastina's sister Martha Hjelle were local midwives, birthing many children in the Lake Andrew and Arctander Townships. It is highly probable that Bastina helped with the deliveries of Cora's children—Bastina's grandchildren. Martha lived on a farm next to Bastina and August's farm in Arctander Township. She died one month after Marjorie's birth, so this may have been the last birth for which Martha was the midwife.

Marjorie "Marge" Mankell was born August 6, 1929, attended School District 25 and New London High School. She graduated from St. Cloud State University with a Bachelor of Science degree and taught in the public schools. She married Billie "Bill" Larimer on August 2, 1958, at the New London Covenant Church. Bill's parents had a resort on the south shore of Norway Lake in the 1950s and later lived in New London. Bill was a graduate of the University of Minnesota and worked as a data processor and in computer management. They lived in St. Paul, MN; Long Lake, MN; Wahpeton, ND; Fargo, ND; Duluth, MN; and finally in Rochester, MN. They had three children and four grandchildren.

Marge died on April 2, 2016, in Rochester, Minnesota with funeral services at the Rochester Covenant Church on Friday, April 8. The Rev. Joel Johnson officiated. His grandfather Rev. Jerry Johnson married Marge and Bill in New London decades earlier. Here is a portion of her obituary.

> *Marge was born at home on August 6, 1929, on the Mankell family homestead near New London, Minnesota, to Herman and Cornelia (Christopherson) Mankell. She was confirmed in the Christian faith on Pearl Harbor Day, December 7, 1941, at the Lake Florida Swedish Mission Church. Marge attended rural school and finished high school in New London, later graduating from St. Cloud State University. She taught elementary school in Clara City, Montevideo, Roseville, St. Louis Park, and Alexandria. Over one summer break, she pursued her Great Adventure: a two month solo trip around Europe, with just an overnight case. Marge married Bill Larimer on August 2, 1958, and after raising her family she was a substitute teacher for many years. Marge always made guests welcome at her home. She was a member of Rochester Covenant Church and several Covenant ministries, and enjoyed time with family, painting, traveling and camping, and hiking outdoors.*

COMMUNITY PRIDE

The 60th Anniversary Celebration of School District 25[7]

On July 1, 1928, the community came together to celebrate the 60th anniversary of School District 25. Here is the address given by former student, Gabriel Stene. Written at the age of 72, he notes the generations of families who attended this country school, those who attended the celebratory picnic, early pioneers, life in the township 60 years earlier, and other observations about the neighborhood.

---

[7] *Willmar Tribune*, July 1928.

Address Given at the Second Annual Reunion Picnic of School Dist. No. 25 Delivered on the Picnic Grounds at the Crook Lake Grove on Sunday July 1.

Assembled Friends from Far and Near. We extend a hearty welcome to you all. The picnic grounds are yours. Make yourselves at home!

When I take a look at these modern vehicles, automobiles and enclosed sedans, my mind reverts to recollections and memories of pioneer days. Then it was difficult for a young man to get a girl partner out for a joyride, as they would rather walk than ride on a lumber wagon, seated upon a rough board laid across the box, and the rig drawn by oxen. There is many an episode connected with early frontier life. The first spring seat in the county was home-made by Lars Nelson.

When Henrick Nary got married to Miss Karen Skaalerud they settled down to housekeeping on what is now the home of Jens Skaalerud. Henrick had a yoke of oxen, I had a pair of mules. For the accommodation of taking home bride and house equipment he got my mules, as he could speed them a little faster than the oxen.

You young people do not know who Mr. and Mrs. Nicholas Blom were, but Lars Nelson does. They erected a little log cabin on a high naked hill where there was not a single twig of bush of a tree. They sold out and left. The log cabin has dwindled away, giving place to a modern building. The hill cannot be noticed now for it is hidden in a beautiful grove at the fine home of Oscar Larson.

Peter Warholm was a bachelor living in a little log cabin by the roadside. Not a bush planted on the naked prairie. He married a widow and got two big boys on the deal. They sold out and left. The place is now the beautiful farm home of John Nelson.

Another bachelor lived on what is now the Lars H. Larson place. He could get no girl, school ma'am nor widow, so he sold his claim to Christen Lien. $150 was the price. Lien sold it to Henrik Larson for $300. The air was then sounding and resounding over such ungodly profit, but if you ask Commissioner Larson to price it today, he will eclipse anything in sight. The pioneer shack has disappeared, and a modern house is hid in the beautiful grove.

Another homestead bachelor, Peter Odell, pioneer sheriff, picked up Miss Karin Reese. Their daughter, Miss Nora Odell, was one of the esteemed and faithful school ma'ams holding down the chair in Dist. No. 25 for several terms.

Now I must close this survey and come down to the program of this present day. Midsummer time! Cheerful midsummer time! When Mother Earth is dressed in her pride and beauty, her green carpet so lovely displayed and dotted with an abundance of roses and flowers. Trees loaded with unusually heavy foliage of shady leaves, under whose limbs are gathered a bunch of satisfied neighbors and friends with smiling countenances! Modern automobiles and glass-enclosed sedans parked everywhere! Birds in the treetops exclaiming their joy and cheer with thrilling songs, in midsummer time!

The word 'picnic' has a wonderfully attractive sound, especially when it is a school district picnic. It brings back a person's memory to the innocent days of childhood. To youth and school grounds! Happy, happy schooldays, when you and I were young! Last year we had a lovely picnic and a good time on this same grounds through the efforts of the citizens—parents, pupils and teachers of School District No. 25. Today we are again gathered on the same place with the same joy and happiness rampant. It is our sincere wish that it will become a permanent midsummer picnic for years to come.

The picnic today marks the sixtieth anniversary of the organization of District No. 25. It was organized in the spring of 1868, when the first little schoolhouse was erected on Section 20. The first enrollment of 32 kids included myself who was initiated then into the mystery of school craft.

Sixty years is a long time. Changes have come in many different ways. Happiness and sadness go hand in hand. Today happy, and tomorrow disappointed and sad! Such is life! The old pioneers of sixty years ago are not with us today. They did not respond to the call. The history of those riding in "kubbe-rullers" and lumber wagons belong to the past. Also the oxen. When I take a scrutinizing look at this audience today, I am almost at a loss to locate myself. Nearly all are strangers to me. But there lingers a hope of pride that they are the descendants from the sturdy old pioneers.

An example of a primitive "kubbe-ruller" or ox cart, also spelled "kubberollar" in Norwegian and "skrikkäran" in Swedish. The kubberollar had wooden wheels, sections of a tree trunk. Image courtesy of Vasa Lutheran Church and Vasa Museum in Vasa, MN.

I must make a detour over the different cemeteries where blocks are placed in rows. There I find carved in the marble and granite those names so dear and familiar to me. They are at rest. Their hovels, dug-outs, sod housed, shanties, and small log cabins have disappeared. Elegant dwellings, modern farm houses, country dotted with groves, cemented and graveled roads—All you can recognize the country now by is the lay of the ground which has not changed in sixty years. The majority of the early pioneers including the first teachers of sixty years ago have disappeared. Probably most of them lie in their last resting places. Of them it may be said:

> They grew together side by side,
> They filled our home with glee;
> Their graves are severed far and wide
> By mount and stream and sea.

Generations come, and generations go. We keep the traditions of ye olden times unchanged in District No. 25. Parents, grand-parents, great grand-parents! They will keep the school going continuously. School ma'ams come and go in order. Especially now when the young men shine around in glass enclosed sedans. No wonder the school ma'ams disappear. But schools and picnics will function and follow, like the shadow the body. Picnics do not run themselves automatically. The idea is generally conceived in the mind of some lady with pep and energy. It is whispered, and talked about, and agitated and the result is a good get-together picnic at midsummer time.

Keep your eyes and ears alert next summer. Something will drop, and we will meet again at the beautiful picnic ground of Dist. No. 25.

The only ones left now in the immediate vicinity are Julia and Arnt P. Reese, Lars Nelson, Engeborg Nelson (Mrs. John A Halvorson): Johanna Norman (Mrs. William Larson): Jennie Mankell (Mrs. A. H. Gordhamer): Bertha Rustad (Mrs. Magnus Olson); Otto Hedin, Ole Stene, Carl Syverson, Albert Syverson, Martin Syverson—all members of the first enrollment of 1868, myself included. The memories of the companionship of youth are written in indelible letters which don't fade away. Happy school days, when you and I were young.

G. Stene

Lake Florida Mission Church[8]

On June 30, 1929, the Lake Florida Mission Church families, former members, and neighbors met for an all-day celebration of activities. Local historian Gabriel Stene[9] wrote this article for the *Willmar Tribune*:

Lake Florida Had Homecoming Day

Sunday, June 30, was a big day at the Lake Florida Swedish Mission church, being its homecoming day. It was a beautiful morning and the day proved ideal. The same Christian spirit of sixty years ago is still manifest among the descendants of the early Swedish pioneers. Forenoon and afternoon sessions were held.

The nicely kept cemetery looks like a lovely little park. The graves adorned with roses and flowers makes a visitor feel that a deep feeling of love and respect for the departed pioneers who sleep there lives in the community. The nicely parked automobiles have taken the place of the oxen and lumber wagons. Smiling faces and friendly greetings were in evidence just like sixty years ago among the charter member who with H. W. Mankell and John Lungstrom as leading architects erected the building.

The yard was soon filled with smiling faces and friendly people. The ladies were busy stowing away their baskets, boxes and packages. The meeting was in [the] charge of the pastor, Rev. John Anderson, who proves to be a genuine scion of the early settlers' creed and mission doctrine. With my good friend, Mr. Emil

Lake Florida Mission Church, c1960.
(image courtesy of the Mankell Family)

---

8 *Willmar Tribune* August 1929; Boyd; *Illustrated History of Kandiyohi County*, p. 278, 282.
9 While Stene was of purely Norwegian heritage, it is evident from his many articles in the *Willmar Tribune* that his love of community extended to Swedes as well.

Schedeen, by my side, I was placed where I could face the audience. The church was filled to its fullest standing capacity. But the faces so familiar to me in early days were missing. They have not responded to the announcement of this homecoming day. Where are the pioneer trail blazers, the charter members of this church—Johan Lungstrom, Ahlberg, Skoglunds, Rodlunds, Nord, Nygrens, Elliassens, Hedins, Danielsons. Warholm, Nicholas Blom, Brattlunds, Normans, Mankells? I came to the conclusion that the only survivor of the charter members is Emil Schedeen. But the meeting was conducted in the old pioneer style.

At noon the ladies were all Marthas [a Biblical reference], *busy to see that all received their share of a free dinner—chicken, watermelon, and other good eatables, more than I can enumerate.*

The church being too small to accommodate all, the seats were all placed under the trees in the open outside. The speakers of the day were Revs. J. J. Daniels, L. P Kretz, Chester Dahlberg, C. H. B. Peterson and the local pastor, Rev. John Anderson.

General satisfaction of having spent a happy day prevailed among those present, as the homecoming days came to a close.

A feeling of sadness overcame me when I saw the granite and marble monument blocks with the names of those so familiar to us. Long live the memory of those early pioneer church members, so honest and sincere in the days of early hardships! May their descendants be as loyal to their little church as their fathers and mothers were.

In his newspaper article Stene listed the charter members and mentioned the many tombstones in the cemetery. There are discrepancies between Stene's list of charter members, those listed in the 1905 *Illustrated History of Kandiyohi County*, and those cited by a former pastor. Whether charter members or not, these are the earliest members and their wives. While men were listed as the charter members, their wives were not so named, as was customary at the time. Here are the names of those Swedish immigrants who were the earliest members of the congregation, with the section number of their farms in Lake Andrew Township. (There are variations in spellings of surnames and given names.) Twelve men marked with * are listed by former Pastor Theo Paulson, citing church records, as charter members.[10]

Buried at Lake Florida Mission Church

Appelgren, Gustav A. (Section 22)
***Brattlund, Nils and Maria (Section 20)**
Danielson, Anders and Maja
   (Andrew and Maria, Section 35)
Eliasson, Nils (Section 32)
*Hedin, Lars and Anna Maria (Section 28)
*Hedin, Andrew (Section 18)

*Jansson, O. aka Ole Johnson (Section 24)
*Larson, N. Nels (section 26)
Lungstrom, John Andrew and Amanda Sophia
   (Section 22)
Mankell. Herman Wilhelm and Elizabeth, (Section 20)
Norman, Johannes and Maria, (Section 17)

---

[10] "The 70th Anniversary of the Lake Florida Mission Church" *Willmar Tribune*, 10 August 1945. J. A. Skoglund died in 1867, prior to the first worship service. "Nord" could refer to two men connected to the early formation of the church. J. N. Nord (1809-1869) is buried at Lake Florida Mission Church Cemetery, and Johan N. Nord (1835-1903) emigrated from Sweden in 1869 and was received into the congregation in 1870. Given that Theo Paulson uses the Americanized name of "John Nord", it was probably the latter.

Nygren, Olof and Elizabeth, Dovre Township, (Section 4)
*Rodlund/Rodlun, Lars Nilsson (Section 26)
Rodlund, Olaf L (Section 26)
*Skoglund, Anders Peter and Christina (Section 26)
*Skoglund, J. A. (Section 22)

Not buried at Lake Florida Mission Church
*Blom, B. N. (Bengt Nicolas) and Sarah (Section 21), buried Lindsborg, KS, Elmwood Cemetery
*Håkanson, Hemming and Anna Maria (Section 30), buried Traverse County, Minnesota, Sharon Mission Covenant
*Nord, Johan N. and Lovida, (Section 28), buried Wheaton, Minnesota, Zion Mission Cemetery
*Warholm, P. E. and Christina (Section 21), buried Wheaton, Minnesota, Bethlehem Covenant

CHAPTER 9:
1930-1939

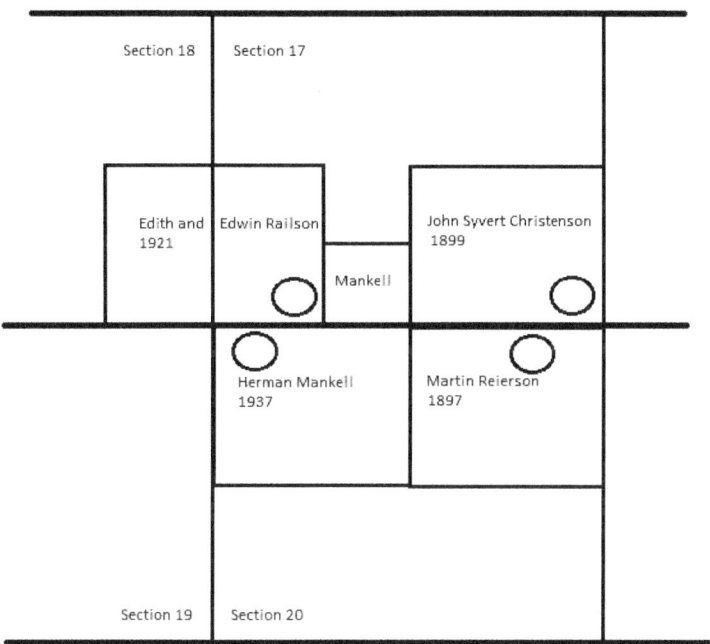

HIGHLIGHTS

- A new renter arrived at the Christenson farm
- Natural Disasters: a drought
- Pastimes: Area residents enjoyed a local baseball team
- New technology: Electricity arrived in Kandiyohi County

STENSETH/CHRISTENSON FARM[1]

This decade began with John Syvert (J. S.) Christenson, his wife Mina, and their daughter Clara living at their Solberg farm property by Norway Lake and J. S. renting out his farm in Section 17. In this decade Harvin Christenson returned home with his family to Lake Andrew Township, at which time three families connected to the Stenseth/Christenson farm had a series of moves with families "rotating" homes. In this decade the Christenson family celebrated a wedding and mourned a death of an elder.

1930

Hans Christenson, the adoptive father of J. S. died October 18, 1930, in Minneapolis, Minnesota, where he had been living with his daughter. Here are excerpts from his obituary which tell of an interesting immigration journey of the man who farmed in Section 16 of Lake Andrew Township and the adoption/fostering of two children:

> *Hans Christenson Harstad…passed away at the home of his foster daughter and son-in-law, Mr. and Mrs. Edward Johnson, Minneapolis. Funeral services were held at Barney Anderson's Funeral Chapel, Minneapolis…On October 22 the remains were brought by hearse to the East Norway Lake church. There funeral services were held…Rev. H. N. Christenson of Frederick SD, a grandson of the departed, paid a beautiful tribute… Interment was made at Nannestad Church cemetery.*
>
> *Hans Christenson Harstad was born on August 19, 1841 at Nannestad Parish, Norway. He, together with his wife, Lena, launched out for America in a sailing vessel in 1870. The trip was not promising all the way, when they were in sight of the Newfoundland shores an adverse wind came and drifted them back so they saw England, but with firm determination, peculiar to the Norsemen, the ship landed at Quebec after 11 weeks of sailing. From Quebec Mr. and Mrs. Christenson continued their journey to Kandiyohi County…*
>
> *Having no children of their own and possessed with a zeal to help the needy, they adopted into their home two motherless children. Magdalena Nary (Mrs. Edward Johnson) and John Syvert Thori, who is better known as J. S. Christenson…Mrs. Christenson passed away December 28, 1908. At that time they lived in New London. In 1920 he [Hans] married Mrs. Anna Peterson of Willmar, who preceded him in death by four years….*

In 1930, new renters arrived at the Stenseth/Christenson farm: Gustav (Gust/Gustaf) and Petra Swenson, and their seven-year-old son Donald who joined neighborhood children at School District 25. Within a few years Donald (1924-2017) became friends with Orlynn Mankell and his younger brother Sherman—friendships that lasted throughout their lives. The Swenson family stayed at this farm in Section 17 until 1938, though their connection to another Christenson property extended into the 1950s.

On May 23, 1923, Petra Stulen married Gustav A. Swenson in Kandiyohi County. Petra (1903-1995) was born in Stavanger Norway, the daughter of Peder O. Stulen and Johanna Jacobina Asbjornson. Accord-

---

1 Christenson Family Collection. KCHS: District 25 and 16 enrollment records; *Centennial History of Kandiyohi County*, p. 148, 157, 171; plat maps of Dovre Township; Kandiyohi County Recorder; *Willmar Tribune*, 7 November 1930; findagrave.com; ancestry.com; *Anniversary Album 1959-1944, Lebanon Lutheran Church* p. 147, moms.mn.gov.

ing to census data, Peder immigrated in 1886 and Johanna followed in 1892. They lived in Hamilton County, Iowa, for several years where four children were born. In about 1900, the family returned to Norway, where two children were born, including Petra. Peder returned to the U.S. first; Johanna and six children joined him in 1905 in Illinois. Two more children were born in Illinois; and one in Nobles County, Minnesota. By 1920, the family was living in Kandiyohi County, first in New London Township and then in Green Lake Township, south of Spicer. The family attended Bethany Lutheran of Long Lake and later Green Lake Lutheran Church, south of Spicer. Both churches were of the Haugean Lutheran tradition, similar to Nannestad Lutheran church which connected to the Stenseth and Christenson families. Petra and Gustav may have known the Christenson family through their church activities. Many Stulen family members are buried at the Green Lake Lutheran Church cemetery.

Gustav (1900-1965) was the son of Nils and Anna Mathilda (Olson) Swenson who had married in Kandiyohi County in 1891 and lived at the farm of her parents in Section 36 of Lake Andrew Township. Nils was a Swedish immigrant. Anna was the daughter of Norwegian and Swedish immigrants, Arne Olson Sagaholt and Anna Swenson. Gustav's parents are buried at Lebanon Lutheran Church cemetery in New London.

1931

The daughter of J. S. and Mina, Hedvig Christenson married Christian Knutson on July 18, 1931, at East Norway Lake Lutheran Church, located two miles west of the Section 17 farm. The bride's brother Harvin officiated. After the 1912 closing of Nannestad Lutheran Church, East Norway Lake Lutheran became the church home of the Christenson family.

Christian Knutson was the son of Cornelius and Christine (Olson) Knutson and lived in Section 25 of Norway Lake Township; they were members of First Lutheran Church of Norway Lake. Christian was a banker. Both enjoyed music, with Hedvig on the piano and Christian on violin. They lived in San Diego, California, for many years. Hedvig died in 1989 and Christian in 1982. They are buried in Glen Abbey Memorial Park, San Diego County, California.

1936

In the summer of 1936, Harvin Christenson, his wife Sigrid, and their children left South Dakota and returned to Lake Andrew Township. For a few months they lived at his father's Solberg farm on the southeastern shores of Norway Lake, and a few months later they rented from Adolph Highstrom, near Games Lake.

1938

In the fall of 1938, the two Christenson families and renters Gustav and Petra Swenson rotated homes.

1. Renters Gustav and Petra Swenson, with son Donald, moved 1.5 miles north, from the Stenseth farm to J. S. Christenson's Solberg farm on the southeast shores of Norway Lake in Section 8. Donald was soon enrolled at District 16. They lived at this farm until 1951.

2. Harvin, his wife Sigrid, and their growing family moved from the Highstrom house by Games Lake to the Stenseth farm, where he had grown up. Harvin farmed and continued his ministry, speaking at tent revival meetings and congregations in Wisconsin, South Dakota and Minnesota. One child was born when the family lived at the Section 17 farm.

3. John Syvert, his wife Mina, and daughter Clara moved from the Solberg farm to a seven-acre lot in the southwest corner of Section 4, on the small strip of land which divide Norway Lake and Middle Lake. In preparation for this transition, the family had moved a small cottage from the Solberg property in 1937 to this new location, about ½ mile north and winterized it for the family. The Christensons called their new home "Hollywood." At this property J. S. had cows, chickens, and goats.

J. S. Christenson and his goats, c1950.
(image courtesy of the Christenson Family)

BRATTLUND/REIERSON FARM[2]

As mentioned in the previous chapter, Martin and Anna Reierson lived in New London where Martin had his trucking business. Their renters, Walter and Lillian Carlson, arrived in 1928 and rented the 160-acre farm for $300 per year. Two of their four children were born at this farm. The oldest, Wendell, attended District 25 in the 1937 and 1938 school years. He became good friends with his schoolmates, including Donald Swenson and Orlynn and Sherman Mankell—friendships which lasted for many decades.

---
2 Interview with Wendell Carlson, 2018; ancestry.com

During a drought of the mid-1930s, Walter had no money to pay the rent, so he "paid" Reierson in corn at a value of 5 cents per bushel. Reierson then sold the corn for 10 cents per bushel.

In 1938, the family left Section 20 and moved to a farm in Section 8 in Dovre Township. This farm on County Highway 5 had been owned by one of the Alvig families from the Township. It is at this Dovre farm where Walter and Lillian lived for many more decades and saw their four children become adults. Two lived at nearby farms; two in Willmar. The family maintained contact with Lake Andrew Township, as members of Lake Florida Mission Church and as very good friends of the Mankells. Walter, Lillian and other family members are buried at Clover Leaf Cemetery in Willmar.

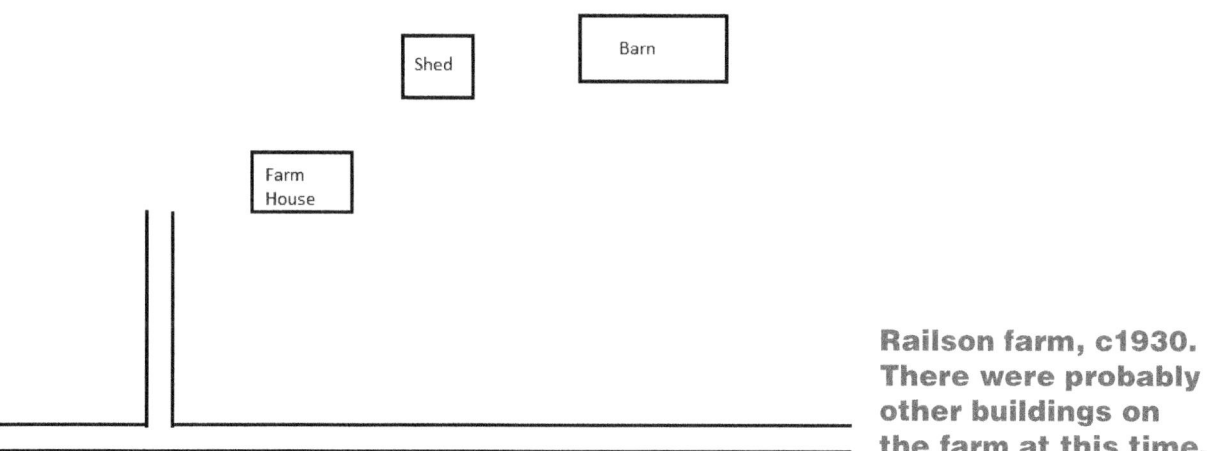

Railson farm, c1930. There were probably other buildings on the farm at this time.

During this decade Edith and Edwin Railson welcomed two more children, to join their oldest son Robert. Here is a summary of the three Railson siblings.

- Robert Waldo Eugene Railson was born February 6, 1926. He married Dorothy Rhymer on January 6, 1951, and they had five children. Robert served in the U. S. Army during the Korean War. This family became the owners of the "Larson Farm" in Section 21—the farm which had been owned by Robert's grandfather William Larson, prior to and after his marriage to Johanna Norman, and then by Robert's uncle Oscar Larson. Robert died on July 25, 1991. This part of his obituary provides a brief summary of his work and interests.

    > He farmed in the area and he also worked as a carpet layer for Erickson furniture for many years, retiring in 1988. He was a U. S. Army veteran of the Korean War and was active with New London American Legion Post 537. He was also a past commander of the Sunburg VFW.

---

[3] *Willmar Tribune*, 9 June 2015, 4 August 2015; moms.mn.gov; Norman Family Collection. Kandiyohi County Recorder.

- On May 8, 1932, Richard Orlando Railson (aka Wayne) was born. A soldier in the U. S. Army, Wayne served after the Korean War. He then returned home and continued to live and work on the Norman/Railson farm until the last years of his life.
- Joyce was born on May 20, 1938. Joyce married Lloyd Vern Johnson on August 15, 1959, and they had one daughter. The family lived in Willmar. Joyce died at her home in Willmar on May 30, 2015. Here is portion of her obituary which sheds light on her politics and other interests.

She was a resident of Willmar for almost 60 years. She worked as a Weight Watcher Leader traveling to clients throughout Western Minnesota. Joyce loved many things but most of all, her animals and the dozens she rescued over the years. She was a member of the Democratic Party (DFL) and never missed a vote since 1960. She was proud of her personal signed cards from President Barack Obama, President Bill Clinton, Vice President Al Gore, Senator Paul Wellstone, and of course Vice President Hubert Humphrey. And finally, she also loved anything Scandinavian, especially sweets. She was a lifelong Lutheran and a member of Vinje Lutheran Church.

Three women from the four farms, c1930. Left to Right: Edith Railson, Alice Mankell, (possibly) Petra Swenson. Picture was taken at the Mankell farm, with the windmill in the background.

MANKELL FARM[4]

At the beginning of the 1930s, Herman and Cora Mankell lived on the farm with their two young children and in 1934 and 1937 the family welcomed two more children (and three more children in the 1940s). In 1937, Herman acquired ownership of the farm from his mother and siblings, who each inherited partial ownership after Oscar's death in 1936. Herman continued his service to the Lake Andrew Township government where he held several positions, including Township Clerk, from the 1930s to the 1970s. The Mankell family celebrated weddings and births, but also mourned the deaths of loved ones. The family continued to worship at Lake Florida Mission Church, the location for several family weddings and funerals. Here are the major events for the family during this decade.

---

4   Mankell.org, Mankell Family Collection; *Willmar Tribune* 5 September 1936, September 1959; *New London Times* 26 August 1939; *San Diego Tribune*, 11 April 2004

1931

Alice Mankell, the younger daughter of Oscar and Minnie, married George Alvig on June 30, 1931, at the Lake Florida Mission Church. George grew up in Dovre Township, just south of Lake Andrew Township. His parents Nels and Bella Alvig were both born in Minnesota, though for a few years the family lived in South Dakota. In addition to his connection to the Mankell farm, George was also connected to the Reierson farm as he was a nephew of Anna (Alvig) Reierson. Prior to their 1931 wedding, George was living in Montevideo, in western Minnesota, where he owned Alvig Motor Sales. After their marriage Alice and George lived in Montevideo, then Spicer, and later California where they lived until their deaths. They are buried at Greenwood Memorial Park in San Diego. They had two children.

Hulda (Mankell) Melgaard

Oscar's sister Hulda Melgaard died on December 25, 1931, eight years after her husband Hans Melgaard. Both are buried at Lakewood Cemetery in Minneapolis. The family had lived many years in Argyle, Marshall County, Minnesota, and later in Minneapolis, where he was a banker. The Great Depression affected Hulda financially after her husband's death. Their granddaughter, Jane Pejsa, wrote about Hulda's last years:

> *Hulda's financial situation had been deteriorating for two years, and along with it her health. In a decline that began soon after the stock market crash of 1929, Hans' banks, his land, and his farms were all in foreclosure. Worse yet, even Hulda's Minneapolis home and her cottage at Maple Lake were in jeopardy. Still, she continued to put up a brave front as the hostess with the mostest. Especially at Christmas, Hulda still included into her "Swedish Jul" celebration all the lonely and abandoned ones from her large friendship circle. In early December of 1931, Hulda suffered a massive stroke. She lived a number of days after that, but was fully paralyzed on one side. On Christmas Day, Hulda Mankell Melgaard died at home. Her last words were, "Be sure to have Christmas here and invite those who are alone."*

1934

During the first years of the 1930s, Edna, the older daughter of Oscar and Minnie, worked as a housekeeper in the Kenwood area of Minneapolis and later at the Kandiyohi County Courthouse in Willmar, Minnesota. On September 18, 1934, she married Alvin Halvorson who grew up in Section 16, 1.5 miles from the Mankell farm. Born in 1895, Alvin was the son of Hans A. and Margit (Thorson) Halvorson, both Norwegian immigrants who arrived in the U.S. as children and married in 1881.

After their September 18, 1934, marriage Edna and Alvin lived and worked on his family's farm. Alvin had a brother, Elmo, who owned a store and bait shop on the south shore of Norway Lake, and three sisters, Annie, Alma, and Clara. In 1950, Alvin died, leaving Edna a widow for more than 35 years. They had no children. Edna's mother Minnie Swenson lived with Edna for several years. Edna did not remain a member of the Lake Florida Mission Church after her marriage. She and Alvin were members of First Lutheran Church of Norway Lake, the congregation of his parents and grandparents. For the last three years of her life, Edna was a resident of Glen Oaks Nursing Home in New London, Minnesota. She died in 1987. Edna and Alvin are buried at First Lutheran Church of Norway Lake, New London, Minnesota, where several generations of Halvorsons are buried.

Herman and Cora's third child, Sherman, was born in 1934. Sherman married Bette Mattson in 1963, in Kensington, Minnesota, where she was born and grew up. Now retired from farming, Sherman and Bette live on the farm previously owned by his aunt and uncle, Edna and Alvin Halvorson, 1.5 miles from the Mankell homestead. It is on this farm that Sherman and Bette have raised their three children and enjoy their 12 grandchildren.

1936

Oscar and Minnie Mankell had moved to Willmar in the late 1920s. They lived west of downtown on Litchfield Avenue between 9th and 10th streets. Oscar died on September 2, 1936, in Willmar after suffering a stroke. Minnie remained in Willmar for several years after his death, taking in boarders for more financial security.

Oscar's pall bearers included his brother-in-law and former blacksmith, Swen Swenson, and many Lake Andrew Township neighbors—men with whom he had grown old, laughed over coffee, spoken Swedish, experienced the ups and downs of farm life, and to whom he probably sold insurance products. His obituary was published in the *Willmar Tribune*.

Oscar Mankell (1868-1936)

Oscar August Mankell, a resident of Kandiyohi county all of his life, was born May 26, 1868, in Lake Andrew township. His boyhood days were spent on the home farm, and at the age of 12 years he came with his parents to Willmar. The elder Mankells came to this city to educate their children. Oscar attended the Willmar Seminary and when he completed the business course at that school he worked for a short time in this city. He was confirmed by Rev. D. T. Booth of St. Luke's Episcopal Church in Willmar.

When the family returned to the farm home in Lake Andrew Township, he returned with them and continued to reside in that community until the year 1929, when he was named register of deeds by the county board to complete the unexpired term of the late August Lundquist. Upon receiving that appointment, Mr. Mankell moved to Willmar, purchasing a residence at 910 West Litchfield Avenue, and here he resided until his death.
Mr. Mankell was not a candidate for the office for which the commissioners selected him, and upon completing the term he retired from public life. Since that time he has been associated with various insurance companies.

His kindly nature, his business ability and honesty endeared him to all in the community in which he lived, and he was called upon to fill many positions of trust. He served as a member of the town board and on the school board. June 1, 1902, he was named a director in the Arctander and Lake Andrew Insurance Co., and he remained a director until 1926, at which time he was named president, a position he held at the time of his death. He was for many years a director of the Farmers State Bank of New London, holding this position at the time of his passing. Always interested in cooperatives, he was a director for a long period in the New London Co-operative Creamery.

On June 29, 1895 Mr. Mankell and Miss Minnie Swenson were married at the home of the bride in Arctander, and they made their home in the Lake Andrew community until seven years ago, at which time they come to Willmar. Surviving are his widow and three children: Herman, who lives on the home farm; Edna (Mrs. Alvin Halvorson) of Lake An-

drew; and Alice (Mrs. G. M. Alvig) of Montevideo. Four grandchildren survive, as does one brother, Otto of Lake Andrew and two sisters, Mrs. Jennie Gordhamer of Arctander and Mrs. Amanda Landquist in Minneapolis.

Mr. Mankell was possessed of a quiet and retiring nature. Never pushing himself forward, he possessed many sterling qualities which were recognized by all with whom he came in contact, and his friends were legion. He had not been in the best of health for several years, and his death came as a result of a stroke suffered the evening of August 27. Funeral services were held from the residence Sunday afternoon, August 30, with Rev. C. H. B. Peterson of the Willmar Mission church and Rev. C. B. Dahlberg of the Florida Mission church officiating. Rev. and Mrs. Dahlberg sang a duet at the home, and at the church both pastors spoke and a duet was sung by Rev. and Mrs. Dahlberg and a solo by Miss Adeline Sundberg.

So large was the attendance of friends at the services at the church that the service was brought to them out of doors, by means of loudspeaking equipment installed for the purpose.

Burial was in the church cemetery. Honorary pallbearers were Swen Swenson, J. S. Christenson, M.O. Rustad, L.H. Larson, K.H. Nelson, and Martin Hatlestad. Active pallbearers were Emil Peterson, Oscar Larson, Henry Swenson, Carl Danielson, Paul E. Anderson and Elmo Halvorson.

Relatives from a distance at the funeral included Mrs. Amanda Landquist, Austin and Herman Landquist, Mrs. Dena Tjosvold, Mrs. L.A. Tjosvold, Harry Gordhamer, Miss Florence Swenson, and Mrs. C.H. Brace, Mr. and Mrs. Nels Quam, Mr. and Mrs. Oscar Quam and Eddie Quam, all of Minneapolis; Mrs. Marie Negaard, Mr. and Mrs. A.W. Danielson and son Danny of St. Paul; Mr. and Mrs. Gilbert Anderson of Granite Falls; Nordahl Alvig of Montevideo; Mr. and Mrs. Joseph Gordhamer of Belgrade; Mrs. Minnie Hagen of Murdock; Mrs. Amanda Negaard, Arnold Negaard and children, Dr. and Mrs. S.C. Leuben, Dr. and Mrs. Hans Johnson and children of Kerkhoven.

1937

Mary Ann Mankell was born on October 7, 1937, attended School District 25, graduated from New London High School, and graduated from the University of Minnesota. On June 13, 1962, she married Jim Petteway who had graduated from the University of Washington and was an architect. She moved from San Diego to Seattle, Washington, in 2003 to be near her two children and four grandchildren. Mary Ann died in 2004 and here is a section of her obituary which describes her education and life and also captures her spirit and interests.

Born October 7, 1937 in New London, Minnesota, Mary Ann grew up on a farm with her three brothers and two sisters. After graduating from the University of Minnesota with a Bachelor's degree, Mary Ann moved to San Diego, Ca, and married James Elliott Petteway, architect, in 1962. They lived in Mission Hills in a home designed by her husband, and had two children. Mary Ann earned her Master's degree in liberal arts with an emphasis in writing. During her 43 years in San Diego, Mary Ann worked as a medical technician for Sharp Hospital, UCSD Medical Center, and the American Red Cross before retiring in 2003, when she moved to Seattle to be near her family.

Mary Ann traveled extensively and was an active member of the Sierra Club. She was very involved in her church, Grace Lutheran, where she found such comfort. She was an enthusiastic reader and participated in a book club that has met consistently for over 30 years, and she loved theater and opera and was a subscriber and donor to both for decades.

1939

Otto Mankell, the younger brother of Oscar, died at a hospital in Minneapolis on August 9, 1939. Otto had lived in various locations in Minnesota during his lifetime. In 1900, soon after he left the Mankell farm, he lived in Willmar with his sister Esther and her husband Gustave Erixon and worked at a lumber yard. From 1901-1904, Otto worked at the New London Milling Co. and probably lived in New London. In 1905, he became a partner with his cousin, Andrew Quam to create Quam & Mankell, a general merchandise store. During some of the time when he was in partnership with Quam, Otto no longer lived in New London. In 1909, Otto Mankell moved near Argyle, in northern Minnesota where he worked for his brother-in-law, Hans Melgaard, husband of Hulda Mankell. Otto was in charge of Melgaard's Springbank farm east of Argyle.

In June 1914, Otto Mankell retired from his business in New London. The Quam & Mankell store dissolved its partnership, though the store continued with its sole owner, Andrew Quam. Otto's pet squirrels were a local novelty in the store and were "greatly missed by a good many" when Otto sold his pets to people in Willmar. The store, located on Main Street, remained in business until 1932.[5] In 1918, Otto purchased a lot on the northern shore of Norway Lake (Section 5) though he lived in New London for a few years and then in Minneapolis, where he worked for the Minnetonka Creamery Company. Otto built a cabin on this lot at Norway Lake. In 1925, Otto sold part of his lot to Herman Landquist, married to Ellen Christopherson who was a sister of Cora Mankell. One of Otto's great nephews remembered Otto as a loveable eccentric who built many bird houses, a brewer of beer, an inventor, a businessman, a friend, and helper to all he met. Otto did not marry and is buried at Lake Florida Mission Church.

Otto's obituary was published in the *New London Times*. The list of honorary and active pallbearers were his friends, neighbors, family, or fellow baseball players on the 1889 team. Several men connected to the four farms were included in this list: Henry G. Swenson rented the Norman farm; Gustav Swenson rented the Stenseth farm; J. S. Christenson owned the Stenseth farm; Martin O. Rustad was a laborer on the Mankell farm and fellow baseball player; Oscar Larson was the brother of Edith Railson, owner of the Norman farm.

Otto Mankell, c1920.
(image courtesy of the Mankell Family)

---

5   The building, originally known as the Samuel Adams Building, later housed a jewelry store and then the New London Variety Store. The building was demolished in the late 1970s to make room for the expansion of The Big Store.

Otto Mankell (1872-1939)

The funeral of the late Otto H. Mankell was held August 12 at the Lake Florida Mission church, the service being conducted by Rev. Theo. Paulsen of Minneapolis. Burial was in the Lake Florida cemetery. Honorary pallbearers were George Torison of Brooten, H. G. Swenson, J. S. Christenson, Herman Strand, Anton Jacobson, M. O. Rustad, L. H. Larson of New London and Dr. Hans Johnson. Active pallbearers were H. J. Landquist of Minneapolis, Herman Mankell, Austin Gordhamer, Elmo Halvorson, Gust Swenson and Oscar Larson, all of New London.

Otto Herman Mankell was born May 20, 1872, in Lake Andrew Township. His death occurred August 9 from asthma and heart complications. He had been ill about three months. He attended common schools and the Red Wing Seminary. In Willmar he worked for the New London Milling company and he was in business at New London under the firm name of Quam & Mankell, a general merchandise store. For several years he resided in the northern part of the state.

For the past 20 years he had resided nearly all of the time in his cabin on the north shore of Norway Lake. He never married. Surviving are two sisters, Mrs. Amanda Landquist of Minneapolis and Mrs. Jennie Gordhamer of Arctander Township, as well as a host of nephews and nieces.

SCHOOL DISTRICT 25[6]

These are the children from the four farms who attended District 25 during all or part of this decade:

Donald Swenson: He attended through 1938.
Helen, Jeannette, Harvey, Martin, Grace, and Harold Christenson: Their first enrollment year was in 1939.
Wendell Carlson: He attended during 1937 and 1938 and then attended school in Dovre Township
Robert and Wayne Railson
Orlynn and Marjorie Mankell

The older children of Lena and Christian Korsmo, a farmhand for John Syvert Christianson in 1918, also attended District 25 in the 1930s. The Korsmo students were related to the Mankell classmates through their mother Lena (Swenson) Korsmo.

---

[6] District 25 enrollment records at KCHS

NATURAL DISASTER—THE DROUGHT[7]

In the mid-1930s, the central prairies of the United States experienced extreme drought and dust storms, what became known as the Dust Bowl. Communities experienced dense black clouds of dirt, sometimes called a "black roller," that blocked out the sun. These intense winds spread massive amounts of soil from the prairies to the east, even to the Atlantic Ocean. Crops shriveled. Cattle died of starvation or thirst. Farmers moved cattle to greener areas. States opened up some state lands for cattle grazing. States and their residents suffered from drought, defined with having an annual rainfall of less than 85% of a normal year. In 1934, Minnesota joined 18 other states as being in a major drought year. Some states suffered for several years; others, one or two years.

Minnesota was officially in a drought during 1933 and 1934. The year 1934 was a very difficult period for Kandiyohi County. Here is an excerpt from the county's 1970 centennial history book which describes the effects:[8]

> *Signs of the coming drouth in 1934 were apparent in 1933, the year of far less rainfall that summer and far less snow in the winter. Then came that summer of 1934 which will never be forgotten by those who were around at that time. It reminded them of the year 1876 and also 1877 when the grasshopper hordes wiped out the crops in the county.*
>
> *Shallow lakes completely dried up. Foot Lake north of Willmar, too; you could walk across it. Children doing so found buffalo heads in the lake bed. Even Green Lake showed the effects and sand bars were noted just below the water level.*
>
> *The dust storms of that summer. Clouds of dust as dark as the heaviest rain clouds, but it was all dirt. Farmers told of how the horses refused to go into the fields and face the blizzards of sand and soil. The scene looked like a desert with crops burned to a frazzle not to mention all the lawns and sprinkling forbidden and water supplies serious. Tumble weeds never before seen except in the desert rolled across the land. There were folks who believe that our area had become a part of the Southwest desert and even had planned to leave this area and never return, that our area had "gone to the dogs".*
>
> *The matter of feeding cattle on the farms was critical. Many cattle were shipped up north. Farmers drove long distances to get wheat straw as feed. Some cattle survived by eating slough grass where found and basswood sprouts. On many farms cattle stood so weak they could not even bellow. Many had to be shot. The Atwater Commercial Club bought 150 tons of hay from Oklahoma at $12.50 a ton to feed starving cattle in the Atwater area.*
>
> *The courage of the farmers and the townspeople during this trying year was a symbol of fortitude in history. They took it on the chin when perhaps others in other places might have been faint of heart. They carried on into the years when Mother Nature was more kindly.*

---

7 In 1934, 19 states were in a drought: Minnesota, Iowa, Missouri, North Dakota, South Dakota, Nebraska, Kansas, Oklahoma, Montana, Wyoming, Colorado, New Mexico, Arizona, Utah, California, Michigan, Indiana, Ohio and Kentucky. Bill Rowley, *Major Drought Years. Centennial History of Kandiyohi County*, p. 310. *Pine River Journal* 6 Aug 1936; Minnesota Historical Society: Executive Council, Drought Relief Applications 1933.

8 "Drouth" was a common spelling in the 1930s. The text is quoted as printed and includes incomplete sentences.

Farmers suffered during the drought because crops did not grow. While having less food for their livestock the farmers also did not have a supply of seed grain to plant the next spring. Farmers from across state applied for relief from the Minnesota government. There are no records of applications from farmers of the four farms. However a previous renter applied. On September 23, 1933, Lars Hatlestad applied for 400 bushels of oats. His application was approved. Widower Lars Hatlestad was living near Sunburg, rented a farm of 323 acres, and reared several children following the death of his wife Caroline 15 years earlier. His livestock consisted of 25 head of cattle, 37 hogs, and 7 horses.

By 1936 rains had returned to the central states, alleviating drought conditions and leading a better growing season and greener pastures. However, the drought was not over in many other states.

BASEBALL AT NORWAY LAKE & ON NORWAY LAKE[9]

Baseball returned to Lake Andrew Township in 1934 when the amateur team formed once again after a hiatus of a few years. It was part of the new amateur Corn Belt League, which existed until 1965. There were eight teams—from seven towns plus one rural team. Teams in the Corn Belt League were from Benson, De Graff, Kerkhoven, and Murdock in Swift County; Lake Andrew Township, Raymond, and Willmar in Kandiyohi County; and Clara City in Chippewa County. The team from the township called themselves the Norway Lake Lakers and played at a diamond near the lake from which they took the name. Over the years most of the players were from Arctander Township, west of the adjacent Lake Andrew Township. The men were primarily farmers who worked Monday through Saturday. Sunday was a day of rest and relaxation—and baseball during the summer. Teams played each other twice during the normal rotation, plus the playoffs. Working on the farm made these men strong and fast. In addition to planting and harvesting crops and milking the cows, they threw bales, removed large rocks out of the fields, mucked out the barns, chased cattle, and lifted heavy loads.

While these Sunday outings were enjoyable for players, fans, and communities, they also brought emotional relief from worries and concerns during the drought years in the county, the state, and the Midwest. Neighbors played with neighbors. Spectators watched games with their fellow neighbors. Attending games was a family activity, with a ticket price of 20 cents in the 1930s. Attendance reached 100-200 people, or more if the teams were rivals. Geographically the teams were not too far apart so fans traveled to the local ball diamond and often to the nearby communities to watch their favorite teams. Farmers in Lake Andrew Township were no exception. Herman Mankell would drive to the Lakers' ball field at Norway Lake and other ball diamonds to cheer local players (and in the 1950s, one of his sons).

---

9   The team played in Lake Andrew Township, but most of the players were from Arctander Township, to the west. Centennial Book, p 147, 323. Conversations with several people from Arctander and Lake Andrew Townships whose relatives played on the team. *Lakes Area Review* 21 July 2018; Lilly, Mark. "Rural Baseball and the Community: West Central Minnesota and the Corn Belt League." Ruth Sorenson collection at Kandiyohi County Historical Society. Minnesota Department of Transportation, 1940 map.

1938-1940 Norway Lake Lakers.

Back row: Herbert Henjum (outfield, 1st base), Darwin Roisum (3rd base), Kermit Reigstad (2nd base), Willard Reigstad (pitcher), Ernest Henjum (utility), Julian Henjum (outfield).
Front row: Oliver Reigstad (Manager), Earl Huseby (catcher), Henry Roisum (shortstop and lead-off batter), Orville Henjum (utility), Basil Sims (centerfield), with Ardell Knutson as the batboy.

(image courtesy of Marlin Henjum)

With the drought affecting lakes as well as crops and cattle, the Norway Lake Lakers moved to a new, though temporary, ball diamond. During the years of the drought Norway Lake had lost more than 60% of its size, and exposed the lake bed. So the team created a new ball diamond near Tom's Resort[10] on the southern shore of the lake. However, this ball diamond, with bleachers, was on the lake bed, not next to the lake. The team played on this temporary diamond from 1939-1942. Rains returned to the Midwest and to Lake Andrew Township, so the team's ball diamond gradually became submerged. Without this diamond, the team played for two years at a ball field in Belgrade, to the north. The team did not play for three years, 1945-1947. The team then played on a new ball diamond less than ¼ mile south of Norway Lake along the road approaching from County Highway 40.

---

10 Owned by Tom Kvamso, previously known as Halvorson's Beach and later called Ken's Kamping Kove.

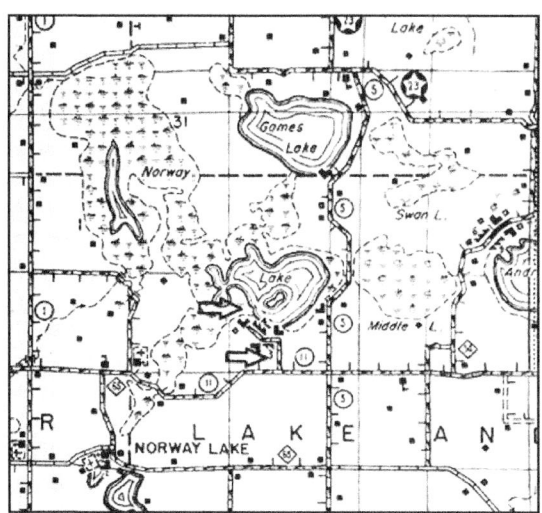

This 1940 map shows the reduced size of Norway Lake. The team played on the lakebed, marked with the upper arrow. The team's regular ball diamond is marked with the lower arrow.
(Map printed with permission from the Minnesota Department of Transportation.)

The Norway Lake Lakers continued to play amateur baseball through the 1940s, 1950s, and to 1965 with players from Arctander Township and Lake Andrew Township, including one young man from the Mankell farm who played for about 10 years—Sherman. Willard Reigstad, an outstanding pitcher from Arctander, played with the Lakers from 1937-1964, except for one year. In 1946 he played organized baseball in the Northern League with a team in St. Cloud. The team won their championship that year, with pitcher Willie Reigstad.

When the land under the ball diamond on the south side of Norway Lake was sold in the 1960s, the team left its home in Lake Andrew Township and moved to a ball diamond in Sunburg, Norway Lake Township, today known as Willie Reigstad Field.

ELECTRICITY ARRIVED IN THE TOWNSHIP[11]

On October 25, 1939, a switch was flipped and electricity came to farms across the county. Life was about to change for area farm families which had been without electricity, though their Willmar neighbors had access to electric power since the 1890s and New London neighbors had a local light plant since about 1921. The entire town of New London was connected to electric power in the 1930s, with a hook-up to the Public Service Company in St. Cloud. Even the small crossroads community of Jericho, west of the four farms, had a small "electric plant" at East Norway Lake Lutheran Church in 1929.

The effort to bring electricity to rural farms was part of President Franklin Roosevelt's New Deal initiative. The Rural Electrification Administration (REA), signed into law on May 11, 1935, allowed for federal loans to encourage businesses and co-operatives to bring electricity to rural areas across the county. These loans were also available to farm families to upgrade their homes and outbuildings. As part of the New Deal, the government hoped that using these funds to make major upgrades in households

---

11 Some farms had generators prior to electricity. *Illustrated History of Kandiyohi County*, p. 403, 433; *Centennial History of Kandiyohi County*, p 296-197. *Willmar Tribune* November 1939; *To God Be the Glory, East Norway Lake Lutheran Church, 1875-1975*. p. 25; http://www.mnopedia.org/thing/rural-electrification-administration-minnesota; *History of New London 1865-1975*, p. 124, 133-135.

would stimulate the economy, which was coming out of the Great Depression of the 1930s. Here is a brief summary regarding Minnesota's availability of electricity prior to the establishment of the REA:

> The 1930 census reported 185,255 farms in Minnesota with 895,349 people living on them. Of that number, 23,342 farm homes had gas or electric lighting. Most families used kerosene lanterns in the house and in outbuildings and lived without indoor plumbing. Even so, by 1934, 6.8 percent of Minnesota's farms had central station electrical service.
>
> Commercial power companies showed reluctance to pursue rural customers due to the high cost of building power lines. They believed that rural electrification would not be profitable. Farms with central station service paid a high price for electricity. Average rates ranged from ten cents to fifteen cents, per kilowatt hour for lighting, and ten cents for farm power service, beyond the reach of many farm families in the Great Depression. As a result, less than 11 percent of American farms had electric service in 1935 compared with 90 percent of city residents...
>
> The lack of support from commercial power companies prompted groups of farmers to work together to organize electric cooperatives. Each co-op's board of directors drew up articles of incorporation and bylaws and registered with the State of Minnesota...
>
> Once established, the co-ops applied for long-term loans from the REA. The funding covered the construction of generating plants, transmission lines, and wiring of homes and outbuildings. Farmers could use the money to purchase milking machines, cream separators, bale lifters, and other electric equipment and tools. The loans also covered the installation of indoor plumbing and the purchase of such labor-saving household items as refrigerators, washing machines, and electric irons.

Kandiyohi County responded to this new federal program. The first meeting for the farmers was held in October 1935. At the meeting they learned and discussed specifics, such as construction, equipment, and financing the project. Farmers were encouraged by other farmers to become members of the co-op. Some farmers wanted to join in the progress while others were skeptical and concerned about a new federal program during the time when communities and farms faced financial problems associated with the Great Depression. Members of the co-operative would have paid $2-$5 per share plus the power usage fees. Some were concerned as to whether this new technology would work or was necessary at their farms.

Township committees were soon formed with two men assigned from each township. Their duty was to answer questions and to convince neighbors to join in this endeavor with their fellow neighbors. The two men assigned from Lake Andrew Township were Carl Danielson (Section 30) and Herman Mankell (Section 20). Herman was a logical choice for several reasons. First, the Mankell farm already had electricity from a generator. So Herman could share direct knowledge of how farm life changed because of electricity. Second, he was active with the Lake Andrew Township government which meant that neighbors may have shown him more respect and looked to him for guidance on Township issues. Third, he sold insurance to his neighbors and had already built relationships apart from farming. And finally, because of his experience selling insurance products, he knew how to make a successful sale's pitch.

Farmers throughout the county voted overwhelmingly in favor of creating the electric co-operative, called the Kandiyohi County Electric Power Association, at a meeting on November 12, 1935. (Neighboring Meeker County organized the first REA co-op in the state.) This new co-op held meetings, enrolled new members, established office space, purchased equipment and worked with farmers who had to cede rights of their land for the electric poles. The dream became a reality when electricity came to 120 members' farms, along 98 miles of line on October 25, 1939, called "Christening Day". These first power lines stretched to almost all townships in the county. New London had one of the sub-stations. Farm families were periodically added to the growing list of customers, with the goal of bringing electricity to all the farm homes. Families updated their homes and farms to accommodate this new technology. For the four farms along the gravel road, the power lines came from New London on their way to Jericho, where the electric lines would then branch out into Arctander Township. The first transmission lines were place along the roads by the farms of the two men who encouraged fellow farmers to join in the co-operative endeavor: Herman Mankell and Carl Danielson.

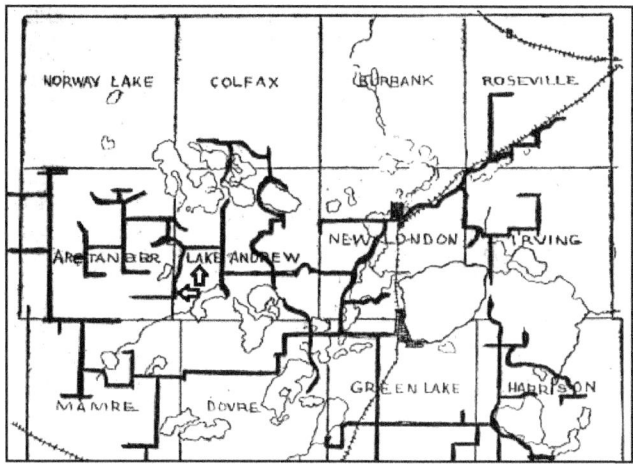

Map of the 1939 electric transmission lines in the northern half of the county. Portions of these lines followed the roads by farms of Herman Mankell and Carl Danielson, the two men from the township who talked to their neighbors and encouraged them to become members of the new Kandiyohi County Electric Power Association co-operative. Added to this published image are two arrows which mark the Mankell and Danielson farms—Mankell at the letter "A" of "Lake Andrew" and Danielson to the southwest, at the township line. A map of the entire county is in Appendix 1.
(*Willmar Daily Tribune*, November 10, 1939)

The decade of the 1930s ended with electricity at many farms in the county and in the Township. But another war raged in Europe and Asia. Soon the United States would enter that war, with soldiers and families from the county worried about the growing threat.

CHAPTER 10:
1940-1949

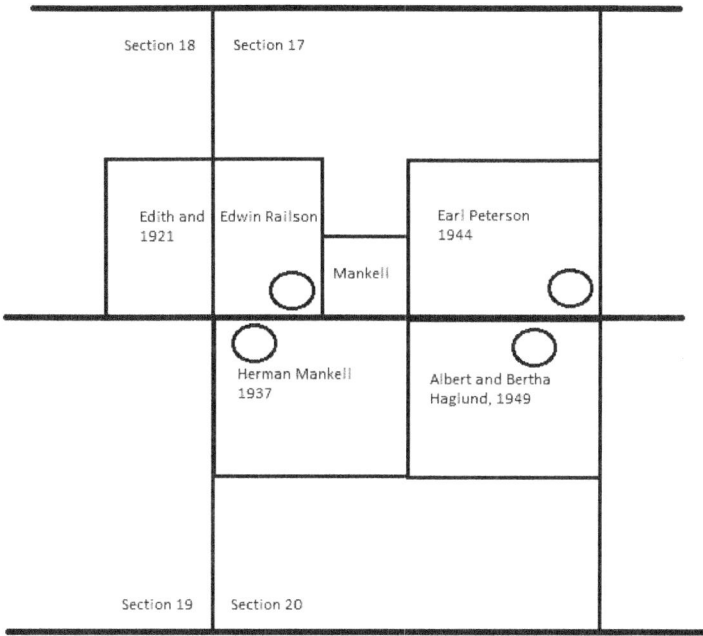

HIGHLIGHTS

- Farm transitions: two farms were sold, with new families arriving which had no family connection to the 160-acre homesteads; another owner had a separate job meaning more hired hands
- National events: two families celebrated a religious milestone on December 7, 1941; America goes to war
- Community: a church building is razed

STENSETH/CHRISTENSON/PETERSON FARM[1]

After seven decades of ownership within one extended family, this farm, located on the corner of Highway 5 and the gravel road which connects the four farms, had new owners in 1944.

1940-1944
Harvin & Sigrid Christenson

For the first half of this decade Harvin Christenson, his wife Sigrid and their children lived at the farm in Section 17. Harvin and his family had returned to Lake Andrew Township and the family farm after several years of ministry in South Dakota. Several of their children attended School District 25 through the 1944 school term. Here is a list of Harvin and Sigrid's children.

1. **Helen Catherine** (1926-2017) was born in Chicago, Illinois, and married twice. In 1962 she married Pastor Karl Berg in Salem, Oregon. Her second marriage was to Dale Johnson in 1989. She died in Woodburn, Oregon.

2. **Jeannette Cora** (1928-) was born in Minnesota and married Stanley Onerheim in 1948. They had six children. A widow, she lives on the family farm in Frontier, Saskatchewan, Canada.

3. **Harvey** (1930-2011) was born in South Dakota, married three times and had three children. He was an officer in the U.S. Navy. He died in Woodburn, Oregon.

4. **Martin Luther** (1931-) was born in South Dakota and married Arlene Gilbertson. They had five children. He later married Sylvia Christenson. A Lutheran Pastor, Martin lives in Frontier, Saskatchewan.

5. **Grace Signe** (1933-) was born in South Dakota. She married Lloyd Ashland (1919-1973) in 1954. They had nine children. She later married Harry Burr (1926-2006) in 2002. A widow, she lives in Woodburn, Oregon.

6. **Harold Raymond** (1935-2008) was born in South Dakota and married Evelyn Benner in 1959. They had two children. A Lutheran pastor, Harold was a manager of Christian radio stations in Seattle, Washingington, (KGDN/KTW) and Minot, North Dakota, (KHRT). After serving a parish in New York he retired to Woodburn, Oregon, where he died.

7. **Blanche Beverly** (1937-) was born when the family lived at the Highstrom farm in the northern part of Lake Andrew Township. She married John (Jack) L. Rasmussen in 1960. They had five sons. Widowed, Blanche lives in Twin Falls, Idaho.

8. **Ruth** (1939-) was born at the Christenson farm and married William Bleasner in 1962 and adopted two children. They live in Spokane, Washington.

9. **Dorothy Joan** (1941-) was born at the Christenson farm married Thomas Thompson in 1964. They had three children and later divorced. She lives in Phoenix, Arizona.

10. **Karen Lee** (1945-2006) was born in St. Paul, Minnesota, and married David Gilson. She died in Lake Oswego, Oregon.

---

1 Christenson Family Collection, moms.mn.gov, Kandiyohi County Recorder; ancestry.com;

The Christenson children attended School District 25 for the first half of the decade. The following farm kids often walked to school together during the 1940s:
- Martin, Grace, Harold, and Blanche Christenson; Helen and Jeannette were attending high school in the early 1940s.
- Orlynn, Marjorie, Sherman, Mary Ann, and Douglas Mankell
- Robert, Wayne, and Joyce Railson

In early 1945, Harvin and his family moved briefly to St. Paul and then Saskatchewan, Canada. Harvin was a pastor and had several congregations requiring him and his family to move. In 1948, the family moved to Woodburn, Oregon, where they lived for many more years, though in later years he no longer served in congregations.

1944-1949
Peterson Family

The next owners of the farm were Earl and Eldora (Anderson) Peterson who married June 9, 1945. This couple began their lives together at this farm which remains in the family for more than 70 years.

Earl (1916-2007) grew up in Lake Andrew Township. He was the son of Emil and Anna (Thorson) Peterson who lived at a farm in Section 26 of Lake Andrew Township. Earl attended School District 108, just north of his parents' farm. Emil was the son of Swedish immigrants, Charles and Inga Christina Peterson; Anna, the daughter of Norwegian immigrants, Thor and Kari Thorson. Several members of Earl's Swedish ancestors are buried at Lake Florida Mission Church cemetery. His Norwegian ancestors are buried at First Lutheran Church of Norway Lake.

Eldora (1919-2011) was from Kandiyohi Township in the eastern part of Kandiyohi County where her Swedish immigrant ancestors settled on farms in Sections 12, 16, and 20. She was the daughter of Harry and Hilma (Noid) Anderson. Many of her ancestors are buried at Tripolis Lutheran Church located in Section 27 in Kandiyohi Township. Other family members are buried in Atwater Union Cemetery.

Earl purchased the farm in 1944, prior to his marriage. After their marriage the farm was jointly owned by Earl and Eldora. Soon after moving to the farm, Earl removed the old barn (built in 1905 by John Syvert Christenson) and built a new barn, located on the south side of the silo. The couple had five children, with the two oldest born in 1946 and 1949.

Wedding day of Earl and Eldora Peterson: June 9, 1945.
(image courtesy of Lorna Peterson)

BRATTLUND/REIERSON/HAGLUND FARM[2]

1940-1945
Strand Family

During the first five years of the decade, Martin Reierson rented his farm to Harold and Valborg (Knudson) Strand. The family was renting the farm by 1940, having moved to the farm soon after the Carlson family left in 1938. Harold and Valborg, married in 1937, had five children, with the oldest two children born while at the Reierson farm. The family left in about 1945, when the Haglund family arrived. The Strands moved to Section 12 of Arctander Township, close to other Strand family living across the township road in Section 7 of Lake Andrew Township.

Harold and Valborg were descendants of two pioneer families in the northwestern part of the county. Harold was the great-grandson of Even and Mathea Railson, immigrants from Norway, who were two of the earliest pioneers in Monongalia County (the previous name of the northern half of Kandiyohi County). The Strand family homestead is in Section 7 of Lake Andrew Township. Valborg was the granddaughter of Ole and Aase Knudson, also Norwegian immigrants, who homesteaded in Section 2 of Arctander Township. The family's log cabin exists today and is a part of the Norway Lake Lutheran Historical Association. Having arrived in about 1860, the Railson and Knudson settlers were part of the Norway Lake Settlement and were witnesses to events of the Dakota War of 1862 and the subsequent evacuation and return of immigrant settlers.

1945
Haglund Family

After having renters for two decades, Martin and Anna Reierson sold their farm in 1949. The new owners of the Reierson farm arrived about 1945: Albert and Bertha Haglund. The family purchased the farm in 1949, so it appears that the Haglunds rented from the Reiersons for their first years at the farm. For Bertha, born in 1921, this was coming home because she grew up 1.5 miles east in Section 22. She was the daughter of Cornell and Beda Thorson. Generations of Thorson family and extended family are buried at First Lutheran Church of Norway Lake.

Albert was born in 1918 in Rockford, Illinois, the son of Swedish immigrants Algot Haglund and Anna Murath, who emigrated in c1883 and c1891, respectively. Algot and Anna married in Chicago in 1907 and lived in Chicago for a few years, where Algot was a stone cutter. The couple later lived near Rockford, where Algot was a farmer. Algot and Anna are buried at Arlington Memorial cemetery in Rockford.

Reierson, then Haglund farmhouse, 2017.

---

2 Ancestry.com; nllha.org; *New London Times*, 8 June 1944; 8 March 1951; oral histories; Kandiyohi County Recorder.

Albert and Bertha married in Rockford, Illinois, on March 16, 1940. Bertha was living with her maternal grandparents, Vernor and Hulda Emerson, in Rockford. Vernor and Hulda would later live in Lake Andrew Township and are buried at First Lutheran Church of Norway Lake. Albert and Bertha's two oldest sons were born in Rockford. In about 1942, the family moved to St. Louis Park, Minnesota, lived there for 3 years, and then moved to Lake Andrew Township. The two older Haglund sons were soon enrolled as students at School District 25. Two more sons were born in Kandiyohi County. The four sons attended School District 25 and later New London High School, with other children of the neighborhood.

Albert was known for his music. He tuned pianos, played various keyboards and sang with a bass voice. In the 1960s Albert and neighbors sang in a trio and quartet. Other members of the trio were Orlynn Mankell and Donald Swenson. For the quartet, the trio added Russell F. Peterson, Orlynn's fellow 1941 confirmand at Lake Florida Mission Church.[3] The trio and quartet sang for neighbors, friends, at churches, and for special occasions. They primarily sang for services at Lake Florida Mission Church.

Albert and Bertha Haglund, c1948.
(image courtesy of Joyce Rupp)

The date of January 17 connected the Haglund and Mankell families. Orlynn and Bertha celebrated their common birthdate and so, during cold January days, the two families would visit and celebrate these birthdays. Albert died in Willmar on January 17, 2009, which was one more connection to the January 17 date. The Haglund family was active at Lake Florida Mission Church, where Albert taught Sunday School, and later at the Assemblies of God Church in Willmar and at Salem Covenant Church, northwest of Pennock, where Albert and Bertha are buried.

NORMAN/RAILSON FARM[4]

Death of Johanna Larson

Johanna (Norman) Larson died on January 24, 1947. During her later years, Johanna lived with her daughter Edith Railson at the Norman farm in Section 17. Prior to living with her daughter, Johanna had lived with her son Oscar at his Section 21 farm. It was at this farm where she and her husband William raised their four children, and mourned the early deaths of two. And it is where William died. However, in the 1930s, Oscar was renting this farm. So Johanna moved a mile west to the Norman farm where she was born and raised, and lived there until her death. During part of the 1930s, Oscar rented to Christian and Lena (Swenson) Korsmo. Three of the Korsmo children were born when at

---

3 Russell F. Peterson was the son of Carl and Tillie Peterson and not the Russell Peterson who owned Peterson Bus Service in New London. Carl and Tillie are buried at Lake Florida Mission Covenant Church cemetery. Russell later lived in Arizona.
4 *New London Times* 30 January 1947; ancestry.com; Kandiyohi County Recorder; plat maps. Information from a Korsmo descendant.

this Section 21 farm. By the end of the 1930s the Korsmo family was at a farm in Section 22, north of Lake Florida. In an interesting twist, Oscar was a lodger with the Korsmo family in 1940.

Johanna Larson's brief obituary was published in the *New London Times*:

> Funeral services were held on Tuesday afternoon from the Lake Florida church for Mrs. Johanna Larson, resident of this community for many years, who passed away last Friday, January 25, [sic January 24] at the Rice Hospital in Willmar at the age of 83.
>
> She had made her home for several years with her daughter Mrs. Edwin Railson of Lake Andrew Township. Surviving are her daughter, Mrs. Railson, and one son Oscar Larson of Sunburg.

MANKELL FARM[5]

1943

Cora and Herman's youngest three children were born in the 1940s: Douglas and Dale at the farm and Marlys born at Rice Hospital in Willmar. Douglas Marshall Mankell was born during a blizzard on November 6, 1943. Here is a story, written by Doug, recalling stories he heard about his birth during this winter storm:

> A bundle of humanity arrived in this world on November 6, 1943, weighing in at exactly 10 pounds and measuring twenty-one and one-half inches in length. The location of the birth was a farm house in Lake Andrew Township in Kandiyohi County in the State of Minnesota. According to the Certificate of Birth, the father's full name was Herman W. Mankell, who was 47 years old. The mother's full maiden name was Cornelia Christopherson, who was 40 years old. The baby's full name was Douglas Marshall Mankell. In response to the question about whether the baby was legitimate, the answer was "Yes." In response to the question about whether 1 percent silver nitrate was used to prevent infant blindness, the response was "Yes." It is also stated that "crown-heel length is best measured with baby suspended by ankles." The attending physician is listed as Hans Johnson, M.D. who certified that "I attended the birth of this child, who was born alive at 6:40 a.m. on the date above stated."
>
> The above description of my birth is obviously a rather clinical summary of what happened in that farmhouse on November 6, 1943. However, the above description does not include other information which I have been told regarding my birth. I have heard these stories from as far back as I can remember. As with all stories which are passed on from one generation to another, there is no way to guarantee their veracity. All I can do here is to share the stories which I have heard over the past decades about the circumstances surrounding my birth.
>
> First of all, I have been told that I was born in the midst of a raging snowstorm. It was not as bad as the Armistice Day snowstorm some days later in November of 1943. Nevertheless, it was a major snowstorm. My Dad used to describe the November 6th snowstorm in terms of feet. With each passing year, the snow got a little deeper—1 foot, one and

---

5   *Willmar Tribune* 14 September 1944; *New London Times* 14 October 1946, 25 July 1963; August 1976 15 Feb 1985; mankell.org; Mankell Family Collection; rootsweb.ancestry.com/~mnkandiy/Cemeteries.htm

a half feet, 2 feet, etc. I believe when he died, the depth of the snow was around 4 or 5 feet! Suffice it to say I was born in a major snowstorm.

I have also been told several stories about the doctor who delivered me, Dr. Hans Johnson. A relative of my Dad, his medical office was in the small town of Kerkhoven which is about 15 or 20 miles southwest of the farm on what is now U.S. Route 12. I have been told that Dr. Johnson's car got stuck in the snow about one-half mile from the farm. At that point, he either abandoned his car and walked to the farmhouse or took the skis from the top of his car and skied to the house.

Either option would have been a possibility.

After he had delivered that 10 pound baby, I have been told that Dr. Johnson stayed for breakfast with the family. Who prepared the breakfast? I am not positive, but I am sure it was not the men! After breakfast, one version of the story is that he returned to his car, got it "unstuck," and drove back to Kerkhoven. The other version is that he stayed in the farmhouse overnight and then headed back to Kerkhoven the next morning when the storm had subsided. I have no way of knowing which version is correct.

Another thing that can probably be said about my birth is that my arrival in the world may have surprised some people. My older sisters used to say that in those days, very little mention was made of a woman who was "expecting." The fact that a woman was pregnant was not openly shared, even with other family members. A new-born baby just surprisingly showed up! Was that the case with me? I don't know for sure. But it is possible that my birth in the midst of a raging November snowstorm may have surprised friends, neighbors, and even some of my siblings. I just showed up early one morning!

So that is the story of my birth in the middle of a snowstorm—and also in the middle of World War 2.

Doug graduated from Bethel College in St. Paul MN. He attended seminary at Fuller Theological Seminary and North Park Theological Seminary (Chicago, Illinois). He was ordained a pastor in the Covenant Church and served congregations in Illinois and Nebraska. Later he became a pastor of the Presbyterian Church (USA) and served congregations in St. Louis, Missouri, and Logansport, Indiana. On September 2, 1967, he married DeAnn Olson in Salina, Kansas. A nurse, DeAnn retired in 2013 as an inspector of nursing homes in the northwest area of Indiana. Retired and living in St. Louis, Doug and DeAnn have two daughters and five grandchildren.

1944

The Mankell family mourned the death of Cora's mother, Bastina Christopherson, who died on August 29, 1944. Bastina and August Christopherson and their family lived in Arctander Township, Section 26, about four miles from the Mankell farm.[6] Bastina and August were members of the Church of God congregation based in Willmar. The congregation had a worship site one mile north of the Christopherson farm at the former Nannestad Lutheran Church building. The cemetery for the Church of God was on land previously owned by the Christophersons, in Section 23, just across the road from the homestead. Bastina and August are buried in this small cemetery with about 40 other graves. Here are portions of her obituary:

---

6   August's parents were part of the 1873 blizzard story in the 1870s chapter.

> *Mrs. Bastine Hjelle Christopherson was born August 12, 1870 in Gudbrandsdalen, Norway. She was taken ill on August 22, last and passed away on August 29, thus attaining the age of 74 years and 17 days. She came to this country with her parents, from Norway, at the age of 17 years and settled in Kandiyohi County. In 1888 she was united in holy matrimony to August L. Christopherson, who preceded her in death in 1906.*
>
> *She was converted while a young woman and lived a true Christian life all these years. She as a faithful member of the Church of God and was a true believer in the Bible. Her prayer was that we shall meet in Heaven.*
>
> *Funeral services were held Saturday afternoon, September 2, at 2 o'clock from the Church of God in Willmar, with the Rev. Shields officiating. Several songs were sung. Burial was in the church cemetery in Arctander Township. One selection, "Sweet Bye and Bye" was sung at the grave by the church quartet. Pallbearers were the three sons, Otto, Julius and Eddie Christopherson, and the three sons-in-law, Herman Mankell, Elmer Myhre and Herman Landquist.*
>
> *Mr. and Mrs. Christopherson spent their years together on their farm in Arctander, and she continued living there after her husband's death until six years ago, when she moved to Willmar to spend the sunset of her life. Peace be to her memory.*

1945

Dale Herman Mankell (1945-1946) was born with health problems, including the inability to hold his head up. He lived only 15 months. His eight-year-old sister Mary Ann helped her mom Cora by watching over her little brother, carrying him around the house and farm. Dale is buried in the cemetery of the Lake Florida Mission Church, near generations of Mankell family. Here is Dale's obituary:

> *Funeral services for Dale Herman Mankell were held Wednesday afternoon, October 9, at the Lake Florida Mission Church, with the Rev. Theo. J. Paulson of Minneapolis officiating. A duet "In the Garden" was rendered by Mrs. Roy Edman and Mrs. Bennie Edman. The pallbearers were Wayne Railson, Kenneth Korsmo, James Carlson and Sherman Mankell. There were several beautiful floral tributes as well as memorial gifts.*
>
> *Little Dale was born July 5, 1945 and was baptized March 10 of this year. He died on October 8, after a lingering illness, at the age of one year and three months. He is survived by his parents, Mr. and Mrs. Herman W. Mankell, three brothers, Orlynn, Sherman and Douglas, and two sisters, Marjorie and Mary Ann. Also mourning his untimely death are his grandmother, uncles and aunts.*

1947

Marlys Elizabeth Mankell was born on June 7, 1947, and was the youngest of the siblings. She graduated from the University of Minnesota, enjoyed the outdoors, and, when young, played the trombone. In 1977, she married Gerald Schilz, a deputy sheriff of Hennepin County and later a realtor. Marlys died in 2001, at the age of 53, after a lengthy illness that left her increasingly immobile; Jerry died in 2002. Both are buried in Bloomington Cemetery, Bloomington, Minnesota. Marlys and Jerry were members of the Church of the Nativity of Mary in Bloomington. They had three children and four grandchildren.

Farm Laborers

Herman did not do a lot of the farming of the homestead because he sold insurance. He hired workers to do much of the labor. Some of the hired workers lived at the farm and stayed in the farmhouse. In the 1930s and 1940s, there were at least three hired laborers.

- Selmer Ellingson was the son of Elling and Martha Ellingson in Arctander Township (Section 34), southwest of the Christopherson homestead. The Ellingson family was part of the Church of God congregation, as were several members of the Christopherson family. Selmer's parents are buried at the Church of God cemetery next to the Christopherson homestead in Arctander Township. These families were neighbors and friends. Selmer started working for Herman in the mid-1930s and into the 1940s. He played the violin and preferred to work in the fields with horses, not tractors. Selmer later lived in Sunburg.

- Harold Kvamso was a hired hand after Selmer. Harold was the son of Martin and Ingeborg (Thorson) Kvamso, from Lake Andrew Township.

- Clarence Hatlestad worked at the farm in the late 1940s. He served in the army from November 1945 through December 1946 and was a Private in the Army's 538th Tank Maintenance Company. He arrived as a laborer at the Mankell farm after returning from the war. Before his enlistment Clarence worked for Alvin and Edna Halvorson; Edna was Herman's sister. Clarence was the son of Lars and Caroline Hatlestad who rented the Norman farm in the first decade of the 20th century. Born in 1918, Clarence did not live at the Norman farm. His mother Caroline died when Clarence was only a few days old; she died from pneumonia.

Herman Mankell sold insurance for more than 40 years. He represented Waseca Mutual and State Farm insurance companies. He also worked for the Lake Andrew & Arctander Insurance Company, for which he was a past president. During his four decades of insurance sales, Herman had "offices" in the farmhouse, with storage located under the staircase, and in the backseat of his car. For Waseca Mutual, Herman sold catastrophic crop insurance for wind and hail damage and homeowner policies. For State Farm, he primarily sold auto insurance. Many of his clients were neighbors; when he visited with them he often brought a record player and shared some of his favorite gospel tunes. When clients came to Herman's home he played his favorite records. In May 1971, Herman retired from the State Farm Insurance Agency. In August, 1976, he retired from Waseca Mutual Insurance Company having served the company since 1930.

In 1983, the *New London Times* printed an article about Herman. In this excerpt Herman talks about his insurance business:

> "I enjoyed it," Mankell said, "I met a lot of people, got to know almost everyone in the community."...He usually called on people when the weather was bad because then you could find them home. He carried a lot of material in his car, in fact he almost had an office in his car. "I would take notes, throw them in the back seat, come home and put them together," he said. One son verified this by adding, "He had so much stuff in the back seat you couldn't even sit there."

On his business card that Herman gave to his clients were "Seven Topics to Live By..."

1. Health enough, to make work a pleasure
2. Wealth enough, to support your needs
3. Strength enough, to confess your sins and forsake them
4. Patience enough, to see some good in your neighbor
5. Love enough, to move you to be useful and helpful to others
6. Faith enough, to make real the things of God
7. Hope enough, to remove all anxious fear concerning the future

When not farming or selling insurance, Herman was active in community service. He was on church and school boards and served as treasurer and secretary of the Lake Florida Mission Church Association. He was instrumental in bringing electricity to the farms in 1939. He served on the Lake Andrew Township Board for 25 years. In this civic responsibility, he served with his friends and neighbors: Earl Peterson, Otis Halvorson, Ellsworth Hatlestad. In 1971, Herman retired from the Lake Andrew Township Board of Supervisors.

MEMORIES AND FRIENDSHIPS[7]

Edith Railson's daughter Joyce Johnson wrote memories of her mom, her brothers, the farm, her friends and fun times with other families in the area—Korsmo, Mankell, Minor, and Dengerud. Joyce shared memories of going to the lake and of friendships with neighborhood girls, including Helen and Florence Korsmo, Mary Ann Mankell, and Phyllis Minor. Christian and Lena (Swenson) Korsmo and family lived in Section 22, where drivers turned to go south to Lake Florida.

> *Oh how I waited for summer so I could go swimming with the gang. There were Helen, Florence, Phyllis, Mary Ann and me. Florence told me just yesterday that the Korsmo's would watch to see when either the Railson or Mankell car drove up the Lake Florida road, then they would come to the lake to join us. Mom [Edith] and Cora [Mankell] would have to beg us to come out of the water as darkness fell. Oh, we never wanted this night to end. Then tomorrow night, there we were again.*
>
> Regarding Edith: *You taught me how to make delicious pie crust. You taught me how to sew on your New Home sewing machine. You taught me how to love animals—and to make sure to chase Mankell's grey tom cat home when he came over.*
>
> *Then there were Robert and Wayne's friends. Marvin Dengerud, the friend that Wayne would play tricks on and how Marvin would laugh! Then there were Orlynn and Sherman together with Robert and Wayne—their hunting, 4-H times, rural youth. Just life with Mary Ann and me full of teasing and lots of 'sisterly love'.*

---

[7] Norman Family Collection, Mankell Family Collection; mankell.org

Helen, Mary Ann and I were really jealous when Phyllis would bring homemade ice cream to country school and bury it in the snow until lunch time. We really wanted to taste but I don't think she shared it.

Then when Robert and Wayne were called to serve their country, I remember all the tears we shed waiting for them to come home again.

Similarly Mary Ann (Mankell) Petteway wrote an essay describing a summer day and a trip to Lake Florida in Lake Andrew Township. One wonders how many times the Korsmo or Railson girls joined the Mankell family at the lake on a summer afternoon or evening.

A Summer Afternoon

Every farm had one. It stood, parked under a cottonwood tree, ready to haul hay bales or straw or greasy farm equipment, looking like it came from a set used to film "The Grapes of Wrath." The color wasn't too bad; it still had its original finish of a dark forest green, but it was dented and scratched, the fenders were rusted, it had no windows, and one door was tied shut with a length of twine.

On a hot summer afternoon, my younger brother and sister and I would implore our mother to take us to the lake. After she had agreed, we would take a quick look around and discover that the only vehicle left for us was the truck. The truck! Oh no! We have to take the truck! We had to decide if it was worth the risk of being seen by somebody we knew or not to go to the lake at all. The lake always won.

We would make a lunch of strawberry Kool-Aid and thick cheese sandwiches on homemade dark bread, throw some inner tubes in the back of the truck, change into bathing suits, and pile into the cab. After a few kicks and sputters, the engine would roar into action. The floor shift would grind and screech and finally fall into place. Lurching and jerking, leaving behind clouds of black smoke, we would be off, Mom at the wheel.

I think our mom rather liked driving that old truck. She didn't seem to be embarrassed at all, laughing at us as we slunk into the seat and tried to disappear into the floorboards. She pushed her dress up to her knees, hands planted firmly on the steering wheel, and drove through the cloud of dust kicked up on the gravel road. Sometimes she would pick us up at school [District 25], *which was even worse, because then everyone would stand around and watch. I would sit at my desk as the clock edged towards the end of the day, dreading that I would hear the telltale sound of that truck rumbling down the gravel road.*

There are several lakes in the area from which we could choose, but Lake Florida was definitely the best. The water was clear, colder than some of the smaller lakes since it was fed by a natural spring, and there were several big leafy trees where our mom could rest in the shade. There were no lake homes and the only resort was quite a ways away so we didn't have to share our spot with strangers.

My dad never did learn how Lake Florida got its name. He was a man known for his story telling and I especially liked to hear his tales about the history of the area. Games Lake was named for the 'games' the Norwegian settlers played on May 17th, a day of celebration in their country and a custom they brought with them when they immigrated to this new land. Norway Lake and its subsidiaries, West Norway, Little Norway and East Norway, honor the immigration from Norway. "But Lake Florida," my dad would say, slapping his knee and laughing, "that one I don't know." He was born and raised on our farm as we all were, and his father before him. There was very little history of the area that he didn't know, but this strange name continued to perplex him.

The last mile to the lake is hilly and the truck jerked ahead with new energy after each successive downshift, carried out by Mom like a pro. Grinding and whining, we at last reached the crest of the final hill. Below was a panoramic view that Lake Superior or even what I imagined the ocean to look like could not rival. Sometimes I would close by eyes just before we reached the top, suddenly opening them on the other side. Then I could see the entire scene in one blink, the lake lying there like a giant blue gem edged in green.

Mom would pull into a shady spot and we would quickly scan for any familiar cars under the trees or familiar bodies in the water, hoping our friends had been as lucky as we were in convincing their mothers. We'd stumble out of the cab, red faced, brushing off the prickly straw and chaff which clung to our sticky bodies, inhaling the lake smell of water and fish and dampness. There were usually a few cows standing knee deep in the water, lazily swishing flies with their bushy tails. They would grudgingly move over to give us their space. The farmer whose farm adjoined the lake would amble down to smile and say hello. He was a tall lanky man, always wore bib overalls, and he didn't talk much. His wife would come down later on. She was tall and lanky also and wore an apron. Mom could usually persuade her to have some lunch with us.

The water was always cold. I would go in slowly, inch by inch, holding myself tightly with my arms to guard against splashes. This was better than plunging in; the shock of the cold would numb your body and your heart felt like it was going to stop beating.

The hours we spent in the lake zipped by. Mostly, we played with the inner tubes, perfecting dives from underneath or diving through the top, trying not to touch any of the edges. Finally, the sun would be sinking in the western horizon and we would emerge, wrinkled and shivering and teeth chattering, hoping to warm by the last rays. Cows were mooing in the distance, like a signal ending a day, as they got in line and leisurely ambled back to the barn from the pastures.

The truck was quieter on the way home, somehow. The engine purred instead of sounding like a tractor. Cooled by the water and grateful for the hot rays of the sun already disappearing, we were all quiet as we bounced and jostled home. Mom would park under the cottonwood, leaving the keys in the ignition, ready for its next venture into a summer afternoon.

DECEMBER 7, 1941[8]

On December 7, 1941, many families from the Township were preparing to witness and celebrate the confirmation of their 13-14 year-old children at Sunday services that morning. Twelve children from eight township families were confirmed in their Christian faith at the Lake Florida Mission Church. Four of the young people were from two families of the four farms:

- **Harvey and Jeannette Christenson**, children of Harvin and Sigrid Christenson
- **Marjorie and Orlynn Mankell**, children of Herman and Cora Mankell

---

8   Records of Lake Florida Mission Church; Mankell Family Collection; *Willmar Tribune* 12 Dec 1941; interview with Loretta (Gadney) Brandt.

**Back Row: Emil Dengerud Jr, Harvey Christenson, Russell F. Peterson, Pr. Theodore J Paulson, Orlynn Mankell, Dean Metcalf, David Danielson, Marvin Dengerud.
Front: Marjorie Mankell, Maxine Metcalf, Ruby Skoglund, Jeannette Christenson, Loretta Gadney.**

As part of the confirmation education process, these young people learned the commandments and studied Bible history. The youth met for six months in the homes where Pastor Paulson was staying during his scheduled rotation to the congregation. During the confirmation service, Pastor Paulson asked questions and the individual confirmands answered. In addition, the young people were on their knees and prayed for a lengthy amount of time.

After services were over, word soon spread throughout the U.S. and Lake Andrew Township about attacks at Pearl Harbor in the Hawaiian Islands. This is one of those dates in history when people remember what they were doing and where they were when they learned the news. When the Mankell family returned home for Sunday dinner to celebrate this special confirmation day for Orlynn and Marjorie, the family turned on the radio and learned of the attack. Since then, families connected to this religious milestone at the Lake Florida Mission Church remember these intertwined events—confirmands and their families could always instantly recall the date of their confirmation.

The country changed that day for both its military and civilian populations. While European countries and Asian countries had been involved in this war for several years before December 7, 1941, the attack on Pearl Harbor propelled a quiet giant into the fray. Lives and livelihoods in the township, the county, the state and the country changed for many years.

WORLD WAR II[9]

The United States entered the war after the December 7, 1941, bombing at Pearl Harbor. Women worried. Men answered the call or were drafted into service—2,263 men from Kandiyohi County. The civilian population responded to the war effort with bond drives, tin salvage drives, blood drives, rationing of food and gasoline; civic organizations aided the war effort. Production plants produced material for the war effort. No one from the township was in the honor roll of deaths—men who died during the war. However, one man who died in the war had a connection to the Brattlund family. Radioman, second class Donald A. Selvig served in the Navy in the Pacific arena. He died in a Japanese Prisoner of War camp in Osaka on March 28, 1943, and is buried in the Manila American Military Cemetery and Memorial in the Philippines. Born in 1920, Donald Selvig was the son of Albin and Julie Selvig, grandson of Caroline and Christian Selvig, and the great-grandson of Swedish immigrants Nils and Maria Brattlund.

One neighbor from Lake Andrew Township, Gerhard Tollefson, served in the U.S. Army from March 5, 1942, until November 14, 1945. Gerhard was a nephew of Lars and Caroline (Tollefson) Hatlestad, part of the four farms story in the first decade of the 20th century. Gerhard's daughter, Ann Tollefson, provides the following information about her father and his military service, much of it based on his letters and postmarks.

Gerhard Tollefson, CPL (Corporal)
3345th Quartermaster Truck Co.
Induction date: *March 5, 1942 Fort Snelling, Minnesota*
Truck Driver Heavy 931

Date of Arrival (Europe): *March 10, 1944*

Battles and Campaigns: *Normandy, Northern France, Ardennes, Rhineland, Central Europe*
Decorations and Citations:
    European-African-Middle Eastern Theater Service Ribbon,
    American Theater Service Ribbon,
    Good Conduct Medal 43

Date of Return to U.S.: *Nov. 6, 1945 (separation center was Camp McCoy, Wisconsin)*

---

9 *Centennial History of Kandiyohi County*, p. 100-104; *History of New London 1865-1990*, p. 119-122; ancestry.com; archives.gov; findagrave.com; Tollefson Family Collection

Gerhard had been working for Donald Combs in Lake Andrew Township prior to being drafted and inducted into the Army. His parents, Thomas and Anna, lived about a mile and a half south of Lake Andrew. Gerhard had begun dating his future wife Ingeborg Nelson who was living with the Combs family while teaching in the local country school in the township, [District 108 and at schools in other townships]. Ingeborg was born in Rock County, Minnesota.

After induction on March 5, 1942 at Fort Snelling, Gerhard rode by train to Fort Lewis, Washington to be trained for the 144th Infantry Co. 4. A postcard noted the towns that the train passed through on the way to Vancouver (March 10, 1942).

Gerhard was at Fort Lewis until early May 1942. He then was transferred to Santa Rosa, California until August 1942 and subsequently was in Petaluma, California until mid-October 1942. In late October and much of November, he was stationed first at Fort Cronkhite in Sausalito, California and then at Dillon Beach, California. From late November 1942 to mid-January 1943, Gerhard was stationed at San Francisco, California. While stationed in California Gerhard was hospitalized for hepatitis.[10]

Corporal Gerhard Tollefson.
(image courtesy of Ann Tollefson)

Gerhard was among troops transported to Camp Bell Haven, Miami, Florida by train in January 1943. Additional time was spent in Vero Beach and St. Augustine through the summer of 1943. During that time he was still listed as 144th Infantry.

At the end of August 1943, Gerhard was transferred to Fort Taylor, Key West, Florida and was now (in return addresses on letters) listed as Battery D for the 31st Coastal Artillery. He remained in Key West until early January 1944. By late January he was again at Camp Bell Haven and was now part of the 3345th Quartermaster Truck Company.

Gerhard's discharge paperwork indicates that he was in England as of March 10, 1944. His letters and his later recollections described a very rough voyage across the Atlantic. A letter from May 12, 1944 indicated that he was now located "on coast". Personal stories related that the day after D Day, cranes transferred trucks onto a pontoon bridge for entry into Normandy. His general location was "France" through the beginning of January 1945. Letters from February and early March 1945 are labeled as "Luxembourg". A March 16th letter states that he had just returned from a trip to Germany. He writes of the severe damage he saw in Germany—far worse than the damage that he had seen in France earlier in the war. Late in March his letters indicate that he was based in Germany. From May 22, 1945 to early September 1945, letters are written from Nuremberg, Germany.

---

10 An additional note from Ann: In his letters there is speculation that the hepatitis was due to one of the vaccinations that they were given after they were inducted. In researching this, it is true that there was some very bad judgment used in the production of yellow fever vaccine for the military. A decision was made to "stabilize" the vaccine but using pooled human serum that had been heated to 56 degrees Centigrade (which is hot enough to inactivate many viruses, but not hepatitis B). Retrospective studies suggested that several hundred thousand soldiers were infected with Hepatitis B when they were given the yellow fever vaccine. It was a time before Hepatitis B had really been identified and, obviously, vaccine development and production have changed tremendously since that time.

In late September and early October, he is at Camp Philadelphia. On October 9, 1945 he has returned to France.

But, as with many families, many people in the extended family served in WWII. Gerhard's uncle, Martin Sakariason of Lake Andrew Township, had completed his military service in about 1941 but was immediately called back into service after Pearl Harbor. He served in the Army Artillery in North Africa, Sicily, and Italy. Gerhard's future brother-in-law Walter Cogelow served in the Pacific, future brother-in-law Reuben Nelson served in Europe, future sister-in-law Anne Nelson served as an Army nurse in Paris. Gerhard had at least three cousins who served. George A. Boe, the brother of Orville Boe (Gerhard's brother-in-law), was among the Kandiyohi County soldiers killed in action in Europe. George died on January 8, 1945 at Alsace, France and is buried at the Epinal Cemetery near Lorraine, France.

After the war, Gerhard returned home to Lake Andrew Township and married Ingeborg Nelson in 1948. They had three children and by the mid-1960s owned a farm in Section 9. Gerhard (1920-1995) and Ingeborg (1919-1991) Tollefson are buried at First Lutheran Church of Norway Lake. Their graves are close to those of his parents Thomas and Anna (Sakariason) Tollefson, grandparents Thor and Gunvor (Amundsen) Tollefson, and great-grandparents Tollef and Kari (Larsdatter) Thorson.

NANNESTAD CHURCH BUILDING[11]

The Church of God congregation in Willmar purchased the Nannestad Lutheran Church building in 1912, but closed this congregation site after many years in Arctander Township. The old Nannestad church building, having served two different congregations, was torn down in 1942. The cemetery remains on the site and contains several graves of people from this four farms story: owners, their families, and one farm laborer.

Clarence H. M. O. Christenson (1907-1907)
Clara O. Christenson (1899-1955)
Hans Christenson (1841-1930)
John Syvert Christenson (1873-1955)
Karen (Stenseth) Christenson (1868-1904)
Lina Christenson (1842-1908)

Mina (Engen) Christenson (1881-1954)
Mathias O. Rustad (1866-1948)
Hilda (Hanson) Stenseth (1876-1902)
Maren Stenseth (1856-1919)
Nils Stenseth (1828-1882)
Nicolas N. Stenseth (1864-1902)

This cemetery has about 110 graves. Many of those buried are extended family members of Mina (Engen) Christenson and M. O. Rustad, including his father Lars O. Rustad, the first lay pastor of the congregation.

---

11 Christenson Family Collection; *Illustrated History of Kandiyohi County*, p 119; *Centennial History of Kandiyohi County*, p. 148; find-agrave.com; rootsweb.ancestry.com/~mnkandiy/Cemeteries.htm

CHAPTER 11:
1950-1959

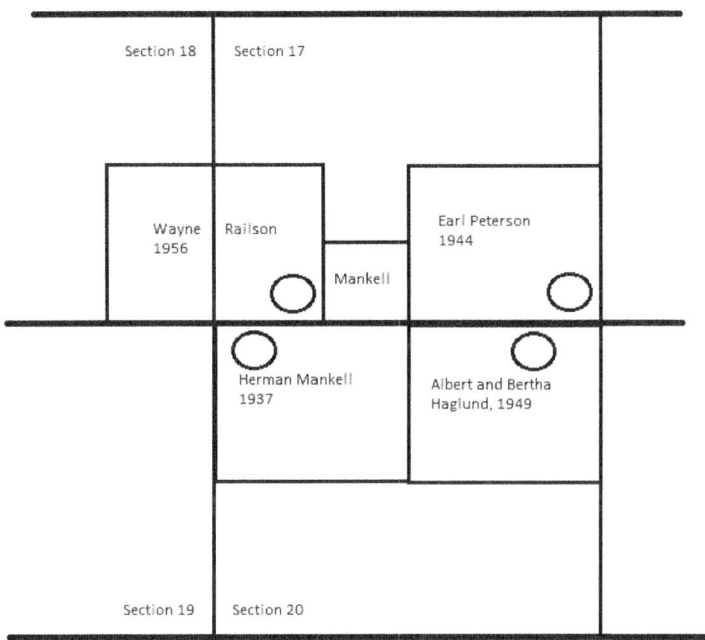

HIGHLIGHTS

- Community: beloved church closed
- Farm transitions: new owner of the Norman/Railson farm
- Life on a farm: faith, family and duty

The year 1955 was a sad year for many families in the area, including those connected to the four farms story. It was the year a local church closed—a church with roots to the Swedish immigrants. The same year brought the deaths of three people connected to one of the four farms. Transitions continued at one of the farms with a new owner. While the families experienced loss and change, there was also joy with friendships among the adults and the children at the farms. The 1950s saw the marriages of young adults from the farms and the births of children, bringing forth a new generation which helped to keep these farms relevant and active for more decades to follow.

STENSETH/CHRISTENSON/PETERSON FARM

Christenson family[1]

The decade began with a change of renters at J. S. Christenson's Solberg farm along the southeastern shores of Norway Lake.

1951

In 1951, after about 20 years of renting farms from J. S. Christenson, Gustav and Petra Swenson purchased a farm on the western edge of Dovre Township (Section 18), where they lived for many more decades. Their new farm had been the homestead of Swedish immigrant Jonas P. Bergman and then owned by his son Jonas August Berman. Jonas A. was the father of Lillian (Bergman) Carlson. Lillian grew up on the Dovre Township farm where her neighbor in Lake Andrew Township would later live. In Lake Andrew Township these Carlson and Swenson families were "across the road" neighbors in the 1930s—with both families renting from owners in this four farms story. Gustav and Petra's son, Donald Swenson, married Joyce Edman[2] in 1954 and they resided at the same Dovre Township farm, in a second house. Gustav and Petra are buried at the Spicer Cemetery. Donald died in 2017 and is buried near his parents' graves.

1952

In March of 1952, new renters arrived at Christenson's Solberg farm: Hubert and Verona (Skindelien) Thompson. Before their marriage Verona had been a teacher at District 16 on County Highway 40, about a mile to the southeast of the farm. She taught grades 1-8 during the 1947-1948 school year. Verona's Skindelien roots connect to Mina Christenson and to another renter from the 1920s, Elmer Skindelien (Verona's uncle), who rented the Christenson farm in Section 17.

Hubert was the son of Martin and Helga (Monson) Thompson and grew up in New London; Helga was an immigrant from Norway. A descendant of Norwegian immigrants who settled in Arctander Township (Sections 22 and 15), Verona was daughter of Sam and Myrtle (Foshager) Skindelien and grew up on their farm in Arctander (Section 14). After their 1949 marriage, Hubert and Verona briefly lived

---

1 *Willmar Tribune* 10 Jan 1955, August 1955, 15 September 1955; *Centennial History of Kandiyohi County*; Kandiyohi County Recorder; ancestry.com; interview with Verona Thompson, March 26, 2019.
2 Joyce is related to the Mankell family via another Swenson family. She is the daughter of Bennie and Eleanor (Swenson) Edman and granddaughter of Henry and Nellie Swenson who rented the Norman farm in an earlier decade. The Gustav Swenson and Henry Swenson families are not related.

near Atwater and then with her parents in Arctander Township. When they arrived at the Solberg farm they had one child. Two other children were born when the family rented from J. S. Christenson. Their youngest child was born after the family left this farm along Norway Lake. Hubert and Verona farmed about 120 acres at the Solberg farm and brought with them several milk cows, about 100 chickens, and 3 sows. Because the family had cattle, Christenson built a silo at this farm.

1955

Hubert and Verona rented from Christenson until 1955, when they purchased a farm near Murdock in Swift County. In later years, the Thompson family returned to Arctander Township to the farm where Verona had grown up. A veteran of WW II (TEC 5 U. S. Army), Hubert died in 2008 and is buried at the East Norway Lake Lutheran Church cemetery, where he and his family have been members for many decades.

In 1955, the Christenson family faced the deaths of three loved ones. The first to die was patriarch, musician, inventor, farmer, and local civic leader J. S. Christenson. Four of his pallbearers were part of the four farms story: Christian Korsmo, Herman Mankell, Gustav Swenson, and Oscar Larson.

The Passing of J. S. Christenson of Norway Lake Community

Funeral services for John Syvert Christenson, 81, Norway Lake resident, who died on January 6, at the Rice Hospital, were conducted from the East Norway Lake Lutheran church Sunday, January 9, at 2 p. m. Death was due to a heart condition and complications following an illness of several months.

John Syvert Christenson was born April 6, 1873, in Granite Falls to the late Paul and Olive Thori. He was fostered by Mr. and Mrs. Hans Christenson. Besides elementary school, he also graduated from Red Wing Seminary Academy. A life-long resident of the Norway Lake community except for three years residence at Red Wing, he was an active worker in the community. He served as town clerk for Lake Andrew Township for forty years, besides holding positions on the school board and school building committee. Mr. Christenson was a teacher in the public schools for several years, but of late had been a farmer. He was an active member of the Nannestad Hauges church and worked with the choir for many years.

In 1894, he was united in marriage to Carrie Dorothy Stenseth, deceased. After his wife's death, he later married Minnie Engen on May 7, 1905, who survives. Also surviving are one son, Rev. Harvin of Woodburn, Ore., and two daughters, Miss Clara at home and Mrs. C. R. (Hedvig) Knutson of Chula Vista, Calif. There are ten grandchildren and four great grandchildren and one brother, C. P. Thori of Almond, Wis., surviving. He was preceded in death by two sisters and a brother, namely; Mrs. Peter Christenson, Mrs. Bertha Knudsen and Martin Thori.

At the funeral service, performed by the Rev. Oliver Thompson, special music was furnished by the church choir and Mrs. Thomas Sands and Edwin Rykken, who sang a duet. Acting as pallbearers were Oscar Larson, Herman Mankell, Christian Korsmo, Gustav Swenson, Elmo Halvorson and Henry Henjum. Burial was in the Nannestad cemetery.

A total of $161. 50 was donated in memoriums to the following funds: St. Mark's church, Santal Mission in India, Six Lutheran World Action, WCAL, Rev, Alfred Knutson Station in Fargo, Ebenezer and Bethesda Homes, the organ fund, Sunday school of the church, Hauges [Nannestad] Cemetery, Helping Hand fund, and missions in general and Christian education.

Relatives present from a distance at the funeral were Mr. and Mrs. Leslie Stenseth of Minneapolis, Lena Christenson and Mabel Knudsen of St. Paul, besides friends and relatives from this area.

Six months after Christenson's death, his daughter Clara died in Woodburn, Oregon, where she lived near her brother, Harvin. She is buried in Nannestad Cemetery, next to her parents. Her obituary was in the *Willmar Tribune* (different spelling of her surname) and notes that she was a school teacher. Clara was a teacher in several of the rural schools: District 16 in Lake Andrew Township, District 13 in Colfax Township, District 69 in Arctander Township, and District 22 in Burbank Township where she was the final teacher before its 1944 closing. Several of her pallbearers had buried her father earlier in the year: Christian Korsmo, Oscar Larson, and Herman Mankell. Another man from the four farms story, Edwin Railson, was also a pallbearer.

Funeral Services Held for Clara Christensen, Norway Lake Resident

Funeral services for Miss Clara Christensen of Woodburn, Oregon, formerly of Norway Lake, were conducted Sunday, July 31, in the East Norway Lake church. Officiating clergymen were the Rev. Oliver Thompson and Pastor I. O. Melmon of Montevideo. Interment was the Nannestad cemetery near Norway Lake.

At the funeral, Pastor Thompson spoke on Romans 8:16-17, and Pastor Melmom spoke on the 23rd Psalm. Mrs. Thomas Sands sang "If I Gained the World but Lost the Savior" and "Just When I Need Him Jesus is Near." Organist was Mrs. Elmo Halverson. Pallbearers for Miss Christensen were Christian Korsmo, Oscar Larson, Herman Mankell, Edwin Railson, Oscar Erickson and Rudolph Knutson.

Miss Christensen died July 26 after being in a coma for about four days. She was 56 years, one month and 23 days old at the time of her death. Clara Otellia Christensen was born June 4, 1899, to John Syvert and Carrie Christensen at Norway Lake, Minn. She was baptized and nurtured by the Hauges congregations of the Spicer parish, and was confirmed at the Green Lake Lutheran Church by Pastor I. A. Johanson. She attended Sunday school in Lake Florida Mission Covenant church and parochial school as a student of Olaf Fosso.

Her schooling began in District 25, and she also attended Moorhead State teachers' college and Red Wing Seminary high school. After attending school at Red Wing, she taught school for 15 years. Part of her life was spent caring for her aged father and step-mother. Her mother died when Clara was five years old. When this home broke up last January by the death of her father, she went with her brother to Woodburn, Oregon, and made her home near him, where friends from Minnesota made her happy by their visits.

She is survived by her stepmother, Mrs. Mina Christensen, a half-sister, Mrs. Christian Knutson of Chula Vista, Calif; her brother, Pastor Harvin Christenson of Woodburn, Or-

egon; a sister-in-law, Mrs. Harvin Christensen, ten nieces and nephews and five grand nieces and nephews. A half brother, Clarence, preceded her in death. Out of town guests attended the funeral from Woodburn, Oregon; Minneapolis, St. Paul; Montevideo, Sacred Heart and the surrounding area.

Mina Christenson, widow of J. S. Christenson and step-mother of Clara, died on September 9, 1955, in Chula Vista, California, where she had lived with her daughter Hedvig, following John Syvert's death. Two women who attended the funeral were her friends from her years in Lake Andrew Township. Minnie (Hedin) Selvig was the daughter-in-law of C. C. and Caroline (Brattlund) Selvig. Clara (Swenson) Berg was born in Arctander Township, the daughter of Gunder and Gemine Swenson, and the sister of three people who are part of the four farms story: Swen Swenson who was the Jericho blacksmith, Henry Swenson who rented the Norman farm, and Minnie (Swenson) Mankell.

Funeral Services Conducted for Mrs. J. S. Christenson

Funeral rites for Mrs. J. S. Christenson, 84, formerly Norway Lake resident, were held Wednesday, September 14, at 2 p. m. form the East Norway Lake church. The Rev. Oliver Thompson, pastor, officiated. Burial was in the Nannestad cemetery.

Mrs. Mina Christenson, housewife, died September 9 and the home of her daughter, Mrs. C. R. Knutson in Chula Vista, Calif. , where she had been living since February 1. Mrs. Christenson's death was caused by a cerebral hemorrhage due to arteriosclerosis.

She was born November 26, 1870, near Norway Lake to the late Martin and Helene Engen. On May 9, 1905 [sic May 7] she was united in marriage to J. S. Christenson, who died January 6. The Christensons made their home on a farm in the Norway Lake community. Mrs. Christenson was a member of the East Norway Lake church where she served as church organist for a number of years.

Surviving are a daughter, Mrs. Knutson (Hedvig) of 765 DeMar Avenue, Chula Vista, and a son, the Rev. H. N. Christenson, 286 East Lincoln, Woodburn, Ore. Also surviving are ten grandchildren, 5 great grandchildren and a brother, Andrew Engen of New London. Mrs. Christenson's death was the third one in the Christenson family in the last eight months for her husband died January 6 and a daughter, Clara, died July 26, of this year. Also preceding her in death were two brothers, Hans Christian and Michael, a sister Mrs. Sam Peterson, and an infant son, Clarence.

Acting as pallbearers were Melvin and Henry Engen, Carrol Peterson, Henry Peterson, Rudolph and Alfred Knutson. Special music was furnished by Mrs. Thomas Sands. Funeral services were also conducted at Chula Vista, Saturday, September 10, at 11 a. m. with the Rev. H. N. Christenson officiating.

Attending from a distance were Mr. and Mrs. C. R. Knutson of Chula Vista, Calif; the Rev. H. N. Christenson of Woodburn, Oregon; Sam Peterson and daughter, Nella of Robbinsdale; Mr. and Mrs. Hans Jorgenson, Mrs. Thora Olson, and Mr. Lund of Montevideo, Mrs. Clara Berg of San Clemente, Calif. And Mrs. Minnie Selvig of Minneapolis.

Peterson Family[3]

Earl and Eldora Peterson, owners of the Stenseth/Christenson homestead, farmed their 160 acres for several decades and this is where they raised their five children, with their three youngest children born in 1952, 1958, and 1961. It was during the 1950s that their oldest daughter Nancy became good friends with Marlys Mankell who lived one mile to the west. These girls attended school together in the one-room schoolhouse, though in different grades. Here are some of Nancy (Peterson) Salmi's memories of this decades' long friendship.

> *I think my first memory of Marlys is when we were 3 and 4 years old and our mothers would spend the afternoon visiting in one of our homes while we played with our dolls and doll dishes. There is a photo at home on the farm in which we are playing with our dolls. During the winter, we would go skating on our big slough. Marlys was a wonderful skater—I just wobbled along! In the summer, we rode our bikes everywhere, often riding west of the Mankell farm to Lake Mary. Cora Mankell and my mother, Eldora, would take us to Lake Florida to go swimming. There wasn't a public beach, but we would walk through tall grass to get to a nice sandy area where we could swim. We loved our birthday parties, which always included friends from District 25, and I remember the layered cherry birthday cake with white or pink icing that Cora Mankell always served at Marlys' parties. As we got older, we both became avid readers of the books in the District 25 library and the Willmar bookmobile that would stop at District 25 every two weeks. We had many wonderful conversations about our favorites.*

In the 1990s, Marlys (Mankell) Schilz wrote about one of their adventures which occurred in 1958, when she and Nancy were 11 and 12 years old. Part of this story, called "A Rock," occurred at School District 25. The next chapter will have more recollections of this country school from past students.

> *Some people say that they climb a mountain because it is there. I have a story that needs to be told simply because it happened. It was a hot, summer day. . . sultry, my mother would have called it. Sultry is somewhere between sticky and muggy. We were talking about starting a club, my friend, Nancy and I.*
>
> *We did not have a purpose for our club or name yet, but we did know that there would be "No Boys Allowed". Not that we knew of any boys clamoring to join our club. Not that we knew of any boys period. But. . . back to the story. We drove our bikes down to the end of the driveway into the hot sun, emerging out of the canopy of cool cottonwood shade trees. We were going no place. We found ourselves in our neighbor's pasture. The sign said, "NO TRESPASSING" but we knew that didn't mean us. We weren't strangers. We opened the gate and closed it dutifully behind us, something farm kids know instinctively. We walked along the river bed, hopping on the stones trying to keep our tennis shoes dry. It wasn't too hard. The water was hardly at flood stage.*
>
> *We both spied it, simultaneously. "It" was a rock, about the size of a cantaloupe. Light pink in color, it was ubiquitous to the area. Sitting alone, it looked like it had been kicked out of one rock group and was looking for a new group. . . perhaps something a little more new age. We brought the rock to my house. After cleaning it up, we could see more*

---

3 *Willmar Central Tribune*, 12 March, 2002, 15 Oct 2007; hafh.org; "Townships are oldest form of government in Minnesota", *Farm Horizons*, April 2014.

clearly the strange symbols or hieroglyphics. We wondered what it was. It is dangerous for two 11 year-olds to wonder on a quiet afternoon. We talked of spaceships and aliens and UFOs. We decided that it was connected to the Kensington rune stone. We got on the internet. Ooops, I'm ahead of myself. We got out the World Book Encyclopedia and got some information. We mailed a letter to the Minnesota Historical Society describing what we found and our theory. We also drew a picture of the rock. At no time did my mother ask "What's that rock doing under your bed?" Probably she clunked it with the dust mop every week.

The summer went on, the county fair came and went, the state fair came and went, school started and stayed. One afternoon a knock came to the school house door and I could hear two male voices along with my teacher. My stomach fell to my feet when I heard Nancy and my name mentioned. I was sitting towards the back of the room and couldn't resist peeking around the corner. There were two "suits". They looked like the FBI or undercover agents. Someone should tell those guys that if they want to go incognito in a farm community, they shouldn't wear suits. I did a quick review of my recent criminal history. Not too bad. The details are a little fuzzy from here on out. I think it's called "selective forgetting". We got to Nancy's house somehow. Maybe we took a ride in a state car. After all, the teacher couldn't leave a classroom full of kids. At their first look at the rock, I watched their faces fall like warm wax. Were those tears I saw in one man's eyes? But somehow the fact is that two administrators from the Minnesota Historical Society drove over 200 miles [round trip] to see a very unusual rock. A very unusual rock that had too many run-ins with farm machinery. A very normal rock that had two girls with creative imaginations on a roll, or so they thought.

Earl Peterson on the Township Board

Following in the footsteps of his father Emil, Earl Peterson served for 30 years on the Lake Andrew Township Board. Residents of the township voted to elect three Township Board Supervisor positions to staggered three-year terms. Earl served with his neighbors and friends, including Herman Mankell, and Ellsworth Hatlestad, a nephew of Lars Hatlestad who rented the Norman farm decades earlier. On election day in March 2002, Earl was featured in an article in the *West Central Tribune* which highlighted his civic service to Lake Andrew Township, the importance of direct voting, and township volunteerism. He served as a Township Supervisor, with primary responsibility for road maintenance; other positions included Township Treasurer and Township Clerk. Here are excerpts:

At 85, Earl Peterson is one of the oldest local elected officials currently in office. It's a distinction he'll be giving up today.

After 30 years of service, the chairman and senior member of the Lake Andrew Township Board will be forfeiting his seat and will not be seeking another term during today's election. Three others have filed to take his place...

"I've enjoyed the years I've served and the ones that kept electing me all the time," said Peterson with his trademark Scandinavian brogue and blue eyes that literally twinkle under white eye brows. But his health isn't as good as it used to be and, besides, he said, there are young, active people in the community that can do a good job.

> It's a trend that's happening statewide, said Jean Woorster, Administrative assistant for the Minnesota Association of Townships. [There are about 1,790 townships in Minnesota] Younger residents, especially those living in growing townships, are taking a keen interest in township government and filing for office as experienced leaders retire.
>
> "When people learn about the value of town government and the honor and power of participating in a grassroots government," participation increases, said Woorster. In some townships, however, it's difficult to find anyone to run for office. It's not uncommon for township officials to serve for decades. Woorster said in some cases there have been three generations of families serving on town boards over the years. "Their dedication is just unbelievable," she said, "and for the most part it's all volunteerism."
>
> Peterson, whose father [Emil Peterson] was on the Lake Andrew Township Board for about 40 years, was elected to take the place of another longtime officer who'd retired. While Peterson's experience is vast, he said he calls upon the expertise of his colleague, Lake Andrew Township Clerk Ellsworth Hatlestad, who is just completing his 50th year in office.
>
> Peterson said he's going to miss the close interaction with residents that's required of a township supervisor. "There's a lot of good people out there," he said. "There's also just a lot more people—period."
>
> When he was first elected as a supervisor in 1972, all the roads were gravel, tractors were the primary vehicles and cows were in pastures on the lakes. There were just 200 registered voters. Today, just about every road in the township is tarred, the roads are filled with people driving cars to work in town and there are houses on the lakes. There are currently 700 registered voters.
>
> "It's been an interesting 30 years. There's been some big changes." Said Peterson, who's predicting a good voter turnout at their election..."It's really a privilege, and it's critical for people to come out and vote and attend their annual township meetings," said Woorster. It's the only form of government where the citizens actually approve the budget and provide direction for the board regarding services and taxes, she said. "People are closer to the town board than any other form of government," said Peterson. He bristles at the mention of eliminating township government—something that gets brought up occasionally in the Legislature. "I hope they don't do away with it. If you lose township government you've lost the grassroots."

One task of the Lake Andrew Township clerk and supervisors, including Earl, was to help farmers keep the pocket gopher population under control. Gophers wreaked havoc in the farm fields because of their tunnels and appetite for plant roots. Periodically gophers needed to clear their tunnels, bringing black dirt to the surface. Local farm kids found these tell-tale clues, trapped and killed these rodents, and brought the right hind claw to the township officials as proof of each dead gopher, for which the township paid money. Marlys and Douglas Mankell were two of the local farm kids who put change in their pockets from this financial opportunity. Marlys wrote:

> As a child I would trap pocket gophers with my brother Douglas. The traps and later, hopefully dead gophers, bounced along in the wire bicycle baskets that moments earlier held our lunch buckets. We also carried a metal rod and wood boards about the size of shingles.

Mounds of dirt left by pocket gophers were easily spotted in fields and ditches. We looked for the blackest, freshest piles of dirt we could find. The rod was used to poke around in the dirt to find the hole or "door" that led to the underground network of tunnels. This was the reason we were trapping the gophers in the first place. The township board would pay 25 cents for each dead rodent for payment of the right hind claw neatly chopped off and stored in a jar.

Using our hands as paws, we dug out the remaining dirt from the hole. We carefully placed the trap on the floor of the hole, sprinkling a little dirt on top for camouflage. We placed the board over the hole and meticulously covered the board with dirt. If a small glint of light got in the gopher would plug the hole and trap. The line of traps had to be checked daily.

There were 5 trap scenarios.
1. *The trap may be untouched.*
2. *The gopher hole would be entirely plugged. I always felt sorry for the gopher working all night carrying all that dirt in his pockets.*
3. *The trap contained one dead gopher.*
4. *The trap contained one live gopher, which required the use of the metal rod.*
5. *The metal trap had disappeared.*

Deaths of Earl and Eldora Peterson

Earl died on October 11, 2007. With Eldora at a nursing home in Willmar, his death brought an end to the Peterson family living on the farm, though the farm remains in the family.

Earl Victor Peterson, 90, of New London died Thursday evening at Rice Memorial Hospital in Willmar. The service will be 2 p. m. Tuesday at First Lutheran Church of Norway Lake in rural New London. Burial will be in the church cemetery. Visitation will be from 5 to 8 p. m. today at the Johnson Funeral Home in New London and one hour before the service at the church.

He was born Oct. 13, 1916, on the family farm in Lake Andrew Township to Emil and Anna Peterson. He grew up on the family farm and attended District 108 School. He married Eldora Anderson on June 9, 1945, at Tripolis Lutheran Church near Kandiyohi. They lived for 62 years on the farm in Lake Andrew Township. He farmed for over 30 years. In 1975, he began working as a custodian for the Willmar Public Schools, retiring in 2002. He began working at the Shores of St. Andrew Bible Camp near New London in the early 1970s, continuing until his death.

He was a member of the Lake Andrew Township Board for 30 years and served for several years as chairman. He was a member of Lebanon Lutheran Church where he served on the church council and was an usher. He later became a member of First Lutheran Church of Norway Lake and served on various committees.

He is survived by his wife; [four] daughters... and son; six grandchildren; six great-grandchildren; and sisters: Mercedes Peterson and Fern Ristow, both of Willmar. He was preceded in death by his twin brother and three sisters.

Eldora died four years after Earl.

> *Eldora E. Peterson, 92 of New London died on Wednesday, December 28, 2011, at Bethesda Heritage Center in Willmar. A funeral service will be held at 11:00 am on Tuesday, January 3, 2012, at First Lutheran Church of Norway Lake. Burial will be in the church cemetery...*
>
> *Eldora Euane Peterson was born on May 28, 1919 on the family farm near Kandiyohi, the daughter of Harry & Hilma (Noid) Anderson. She lived on the family farm until the mid 1930's when her family moved to Willmar. She was baptized and confirmed at Tripolis Lutheran Church. She attended grade school in Kandiyohi, graduated from Willmar High School, and attended Business College in Minneapolis. She worked at Horman-Berquist Hardware until her marriage to Earl V. Peterson on June 9, 1945 at Tripolis Lutheran Church. They lived on their farm in Lake Andrew Township for 62 years. Eldora was a homemaker, a cook at Walnut Chalet in New London, and was employed by Green Lake Lutheran Ministries at the Shores of St. Andrew Bible Camp. She served as president of the New London PTA, and was active at Lebanon Lutheran Church in New London and First Lutheran Church of Norway Lake. Eldora enjoyed crocheting, embroidery, giving readings at special occasions, gardening, reading, and cooking and baking for family and friends.*
>
> *She moved to Bethesda Heritage Center in March 2007. Eldora died on Wednesday, December 28, 2011 at Bethesda Heritage at the age of 92. She is survived by her daughters... and son...; and sisters-in-law, Joan Anderson, Fern Ristow, and Mercedes Peterson. She was preceded in death by her husband, her parents, and her brother, Harry E. Anderson; and two sons-in-law, Jon Brandt and Robert Salmi.*

The family's large white farmhouse, originally built by the Stenseth family, remains on the farm and is visible to drivers, bikers, and walkers at "Peterson's Corner"— the intersection of the gravel road and County Highway 5.

Peterson farmhouse, c2018.

BRATTLUND/REIERSON/HAGLUND FARM[4]

Martin & Anna Reierson
Martin and Anna Reierson left Lake Andrew Township in the 1920s, yet owned property in Section 20 until the late 1940s, thus maintaining their connection with area families for many decades. Anna died on February 22, 1951; Martin in 1966. Here are their obituaries.

---

4 *New London Times*, 8 March 1951, 12 September 1984, p 16; hafh.org; *Willmar Tribune* 27 May 1966, 21 January 2009;

Anna Bertine Reierson was born May 25, 1876 and was baptized by Rev. Estrem and later confirmed by Rev. Hegge. On May 30, 1894 [sic May 31] she was united in marriage to Martin Reierson. They resided on a farm in Lake Andrew Township until March of 1923, when they moved into New London, where they made their home until the present time.

On February 22, 1950, Mrs. Reierson was seriously injured in a car accident, from which she never recovered. She passed away to be with the Lord, exactly one year later on the day of February 22nd, 1951. Funeral services were conducted by Rev. C. T. Olson at the Trinity Lutheran Church of New London. Mrs. Olson sang "Take me as I am" at the chapel, accompanied by Mrs. Soren Hille. Rev. and Mrs. Dahle of Spicer rendered two solos, "Han skal opne Perle Porten" and "Beyond the Sunset".

Anna Reierson, c1942.

The pallbearers were: Alfred Arneson, Alfred Finstad, Theordore Syverson, Emil Olson, Andrew Andreen, and P. L. Peterson. She is survived by her husband, one sister, Mrs. Marie Thomton; two brothers, Nels of Spicer and Engel of Willmar. Besides a number of nieces and nephews.

Those attending the funeral from a distance were: Mrw. A. W. Rasmussen (Stella Berry) from Chicago, Orton Thomton of Bemidji, Mrs. Wally Metze, Clarice Thomton, Mrs. Josie Melhus and Eddie Gustafson of Minneapolis, Mr. and Mrs. Robert Berry, Mrs. And Mrs. Maurice Berry and Mr. and Mrs. Burton Berry of Isle Minn., Mr. and Mrs. Norman Thomton of Montevideo, Mr. and Mrs. Herman Anderson of Dawson, Rev. and Mrs. A. Johnson of Clarkfield and also a number from Willmar.

She will be sadly missed by her husband, her relatives, her niece Stella, whom she tenderly cared for and a host of friends. Sleep dear Annie, sleep. Take thy well-earned rest. Lay thy aching head upon the Savior's breast. Cradle there thyself, in the Savior's love. He will bear thee safe, to thy home above. S. R.

Martin Reierson died on April 22, 1966. Here is his brief obituary published in the *Willmar Tribune*:

Martin Reierson, c1946.
(images courtesy of the Burton Berry family)

Burial rites for Martin Rierson, [sic] a long-time resident of New London, were conducted April 26 at the Trinity Lutheran Church in New London with the Rev. B. R. Quanbeck officiating. Mr. Rierson, 94, died April 22 at New London.

Mr. Rierson was born November 10, 1871 [sic 1870] in Lake Andrew Township. He was married to Annie Alvig on May 31, 1894. Preceded in death by his wife, four sisters and one brother, he is survived by one sister, Mrs. Josie Kjos of Willison, North Dakota and one brother, Gilbert, of New London.

Albert & Bertha Haglund

Bertha Haglund died on September 5, 1984. Here is a portion of Bertha's obituary, published in the *New London Times*:

> Bertha C. Haglund, 63, of rural New London, died Wednesday morning at her Lake Andrew Township home following an extended illness. Funeral services were held Saturday at the Salem Covenant Church of rural Pennock with the Rev. David Hannig officiating. Interment was in the church cemetery. The Harvey Anderson Funeral Home of Willmar was in charge of the arrangements...She was preceded in death by her father and one brother.

Albert Haglund died on January 17, 2009. His obituary highlights his musical talents.

> Albert Haglund, 90, of Willmar, formerly of Rochester and New London, died Saturday at Rice Memorial Hospital in Willmar. The service will be at 10:30 am Friday at Salem Covenant Church in rural Pennock. Burial will be in the church cemetery...

> He was born April 26, 1918, in Rockford, Ill., to Algot and Anna (Murat) Haglund. He grew up in Rockford where he attended school and also went to college to study music. He married Bertha Thorson on March 16, 1940, in Rockford. They moved to Minneapolis in 1943 and he worked at a glider factory during World War II. They moved to a farm in Lake Andrew Township west of New London in 1945 and he farmed and taught piano. He was the organist at the Willmar Assemblies of God for more than 20 years and later at Salem Covenant Church for several years. He worked for 25 years at the Willmar Regional Treatment Center. He and his wife performed [and] sang at various functions, and he played piano, accordion, and the Swedish Harp. After his wife died in 1984, he continued to live in Willmar until moving in 1989 to Rochester.

> He married Rose Yost in 1989. They later divorced. He returned to Willmar in 2008 when he entered the Willmar Commons nursing home. He was a member of Salem Covenant Church in rural Pennock.

NORMAN/RAILSON FARM[5]

Edwin & Edith Railson

The two sons of Edwin and Edith Railson, Robert and Wayne, served in the U. S. Army during the early 1950s and served during the Korean War. One of Robert's overseas duties was as a driver for the officers. Robert's oldest child was born when Robert was in Korea. At the age of two, the son met his father. With both brothers serving in the U. S. Army in the early 1950s, Joyce (Railson) Johnson shared her worries that many families experienced when loved ones served during war time.

> When Robert and Wayne were called to serve their county, I remember all the tears we shed waiting for them to come home.

---

5 Norman Family Collection; *Willmar Tribune* 28 January 1969; Railson Family Collection

CH 11: 1950-1959

Edwin and Edith Railson farmed until 1956; their son Wayne then became the owner. Wayne farmed until the last years before his 2015 death. Wayne had Belgian horses on his farm.

Edwin died on November 11, 1968, with his obituary published in 1969. Some of his pallbearers and the vocalist connect to the four farms story—as neighbors, former neighbors, or schoolmates.

> *Funeral services for Edwin H. Railson were conducted November 20, 1968, at 1:30 pm at the First Lutheran Church of Norway Lake with Pastor Ronald M. Jensen officiating. Mr. Railson died very unexpectedly November 17 at his home in Lake Andrew Township as the result of a heart attack. He was 71 years of age.*
>
> *Organist for the service was Mrs. Russell Hande. She also accompanied Mrs. Harold Strand as she sang "What a Friend We Have in Jesus" and "When I Survey the Wondrous Cross." "O Blessed Son, Whose Splendor" was sung by the congregation.*
>
> *Honorary pallbearers were David Danielson, Marvin Dengerud, Hugh Geer, Lawrence Johnson, Herman Mankell and George Rhyner. Serving as active pallbearers were Harlan Aasen, Virgil Clark, Ronald Hubin, Kenneth Korsmo, Orlynn Mankell and Kenneth Minor, with interment at the First Lutheran Church Cemetery.*
>
> *Edwin Railson was born March 18, 1897 in Lake Andrew Township to Olaf and Nellie Railson. He was a lifelong resident of Lake Andrew Township, Kandiyohi County, having farmed there all his life.*
>
> *He was united in marriage to Edith Larson on April 8, 1925. She survives together with two sons and one daughter, namely, Robert and Wayne of Lake Andrew and Mrs. Lloyd V. Johnson (Joyce) of Willmar... He was preceded in death by his parents.*

During her later years, Edith Railson shared some of her favorite memories about her many years on the farm and in Willmar. Here are some excerpts, written by other family members.

> On their honeymoon Edwin and Edith *"took a train to Crosby North Dakota to visit Edith's cousin Blanche who was employed as dental technician there. Then they surprised another of Edith's cousins, Lydia Dahlstrom and her husband Sig Otheim, also living in Crosby."*
>
> On Sundays *"the Railsons seldom knew in advance that [relatives] were coming but somehow that didn't matter in those 1930s! Edith was always ready with a full dinner at noon serving fried chicken, or pot roast, or meat loaf with all the extras of vegetables and salads. For dessert there was always a pie or two, either apple or pumpkin with whipped cream."*
>
> When Corrine Johnson *"would visit with Edith and continue the tradition of remembering her on her birthday...[they would] talk about family history. This was always an uplifting time for both of them because Edith had a dry sense of humor and could bring out laughter even in her nineties."*
>
> *"Some years after her husband's death, Edith moved to an apartment in Willmar. She maintained her life there for almost twenty years...She continued to cook noon meals for her son, Wayne, when he had noon break and would come to check on her."*

> *"In the last several years of her life, Edith had difficulty recognizing her friends and sometimes her family members."*

Edith Railson died on May 15, 1996, almost 30 years after her husband. Edith and Edwin are buried at the cemetery of First Lutheran Church of Norway Lake. Here is an excerpt from her obituary.

> *Edith Wilhelmina Railson was born on October 9, 1899, in Lake Andrew Township, Kandiyohi County, Minnesota, the daughter of Johanna (Norman) and Wilhelm Larson. She grew up in the Norway Lake community, was baptized and confirmed at the Lake Florida Mission Church in Swedish, and attended rural schools in the Norway Lake area. Edith then attended seamstress school in Willmar and then returned to the family farm. On April 8, 1925, she was married to Edwin Railson in Willmar. They made their home on a farm in Lake Andrew Township, where they lived and farmed until 1956. Edith moved to Willmar in 1975 and has resided at the Bethesda Homes since 1994. She was an active member of the women's organizations in her church and also 4-H. Edith died last Wednesday morning at the Bethesda Pleasant View Nursing Home. She had attained the age of 96 years, 7 months and 6 days.*

Wayne Railson

Wayne married twice, first in 1972 and then in 1980. With the second marriage, Wayne became a step-father to five children. He died on August 1, 2015 just two months after his sister Joyce. Here is a portion of his obituary in *Willmar Tribune* where another nickname is provided:

> *"Wayne" Richard Railson, 83, of Willmar formerly of New London, died on Saturday, August 1, 2015 at Rice Care Center in Willmar. His funeral will be 10:30am Thursday at First Lutheran Church of Norway Lake in rural New London. Burial will be in the church cemetery...*
>
> *Richard "Wayne" Orlando Railson was born on May 8, 1932, the son of Edwin and Edith (Larson) Railson. He grew up in Lake Andrew Township where he attended country school. He farmed with his parents and brother, until entering the United States Army in September of 1954. Wayne received an Honorable Discharge in June of 1956. He returned to rural New London and continued farming with his family. Wayne was united in marriage to Ione on February 9, 1980 at First Lutheran Church of Norway Lake. He welcomed her children into his family. The couple farmed on the family homestead and Wayne began working for Perkin's Lumber in Willmar doing deliveries, where he was known to all as "Lars."*
>
> *Wayne was a lifelong member of First Lutheran Church of Norway Lake where he was baptized on May 29, 1932 and later confirmed his faith. He served as a member of church council and was an usher. He was also a member of the New London American Legion Post 537. Wayne enjoyed farming and his job at Perkin's Lumber. He was a devoted husband and family man always very proud of all of his family especially his grandchildren.*

Wayne Railson, c1990.

MANKELL FARM[6]

Orlynn & Vivian Mankell

From 1952-1954, Herman and Cora's eldest son Orlynn served in the U. S. Army, with training at Fort Riley Kansas; he was stationed in Korea after the war's 1953 resolution. A corporal, he worked with communications, including for special events. The one story he shared with family about his time in Korea was when he met, and spoke to Marilyn Monroe, a movie star who had come to Korea to entertain the troops.

Corporal Orlynn Mankell, c1954.
(image courtesy of the Mankell Family)

On November 19, 1954, the Mankell family, with their neighbors and friends, celebrated a wedding when Orlynn married Vivian Jordin. The ceremony was at Zion Irving Lutheran Church in Irving Township, the home church of Vivian, her parents, and her Norwegian ancestors. Vivian's parents were Walter and Inga (Johnson) Jordin, from Irving Township, east of New London and north of Atwater, Minnesota. Walter was the son of Swedish immigrants who first settled in Meeker County, Minnesota, and later farmed in Kandiyohi County and were members of Lebanon Lutheran Church in New London. Inga was the daughter of Norwegian immigrants who lived in Irving Township, east of New London. Vivian and Orlynn met through mutual friends: Donald Swenson and his wife, Joyce Edman. Both had a connection to the four farms. Donald had been a classmate of Orlynn's at District 25 when his father Gustav rented the Christenson farm in the 1940s. Joyce was Orlynn's second cousin. Her mother Eleanor (Swenson) Edman had lived at the Norman farm in the 1920s when her parents Henry and Nellie Swenson were the renters. The Swenson family also attended the Lake Florida Mission Church with the Mankells.

Soon after their marriage, Orlynn started construction on their new house on the Mankell homestead. This small house was to the west of the white farmhouse. While the house was being built, he and Vivian first lived at a cottage at the Larimer Resort on the south shore of Norway Lake. They later stayed in the farmhouse with Herman and Cora. In 1955, Orlynn and Vivian welcomed their first child and on their first wedding anniversary the new family moved into their home. Two more children were born—in 1958 and 1961. Another generation was on the Mankell homestead. New friendships formed "on the mile" when Vivian Mankell and Eldora Peterson became friends and their daughters, Carolyn and Lorna, became friends.

Vivian Jordin and Orlynn Mankell, 1951.
(image courtesy of the Mankell Family)

---

6   *Niederasphe to Norway Lake*; Mankell Family Collection; *Free Press Times* 10 January 1994; *Kandiyohi County Times* 4 October 1999; *New London Times* (later the Free Press Times, Kandiyohi County Time) 3 September 1959, 25 July 1963, 14 February 1985;

In this decade and over the next decades, the Mankell family mourned the deaths of five people who owned and lived at the farm: Minnie in 1959, Cora in 1963, Herman in 1985, Vivian in 1994, and Orlynn in 1999.

Minnie Mankell (1875-1959)

Minnie (Swenson) Mankell died in 1959. At the time, she was residing at the New London Rest Home. Minnie's pall bearers included grandsons, nephews and neighbors.

> Mrs. Minnie Mankell passed away on Aug. 31, 1959 at the age of 84 years after a lingering illness. She lived in this community all her life and was a member of the Lake Florida Mission Church. Funeral services were conducted by the Rev. Jerry Johnson at the Covenant church in New London. Two songs were sung by Reynold Nelson, accompanied by Mrs. Rudy Lindquist.
>
> Pallbearers were Orlynn Mankell, Sherman Mankell, Roy Swenson, LeRoy Swenson, Earl Peterson and Martin Sakariason. Interment was made at the Lake Florida cemetery.
>
> She was born June 12, 1875 and was the eldest daughter of the late Gunder and Gemine Swenson of Arctander Township Three sisters and three brothers survive her namely Mrs. Clara Berg and Mrs. Axel Quale of California, Mrs. Helen Lamphere of South Dakota, George and Gerhard Swenson of Spicer and Melvin Swenson of Minneapolis.
>
> In 1895 she was united in marriage to the late Oscar Mankell. Her three surviving children are Herman and Mrs. Edna Halvorson of New London, and Mrs. (Alice) George Alvig of Spicer. Eight grandchildren and two great grandchildren survive her. She lived on the Mankell farm before moving to Willmar in 1929. Her later years were spent with her daughter, Mrs. Edna Halvorson and at the New London Rest Home where she passed away.

Minnie Swenson, c1940.
(image courtesy of the Mankell Family)

Cora Mankell (1903-1963)

On May 18, 1963, Cora Mankell died while tending her vegetable garden. Her obituary was published in the *New London Times*. Her pallbearers included men from the four farms story: Earl Peterson, Robert Railson, and Donald Swenson.

> Funeral services of Mrs. Herman Mankell were held on May 22, 1963, at the New London Covenant Church with Pastor Vernon A. Luiten officiating. Special music was furnished by Kermit Hjelle who sang "Safe in the Arms of Jesus" and "The Old Rugged Cross". The organist was Mrs. Russell Hande. Reverend Nath. Franklin spoke briefly. Pallbearers were Alloys Christopherson, Marvin Hjelle, Arling Myhre, Earl Peterson, Robert Railson and Donald Swenson. Interment was at the Lake Florida cemetery.

Cornelia Bernice Christopherson was born July 12, 1903, in Arctander Township, the youngest child of August and Bastine Christopherson. She received her elementary education in School Dist. 56. She attended high school in St. Cloud, Minnesota, and the State Teachers' College of that city. She taught in several rural districts in this area. On October 30, 1926, at the Lake Florida Covenant Church, she was united in marriage to Herman W. Mankell. Pastor John Anderson performed the ceremony. She lived the remainder of her life at their home in Lake Andrew Township. On the morning of May 18, 1963, she was stricken suddenly at her home and passed away shortly following.

Cora Mankell, 1954.

Those who survive her passing are her husband, Herman and the following children: Orlynn, of rural New London; Marjorie, (Mrs. Bill Larimer) of Long Lake, Minnesota; Sherman, at home; Mary Ann, (Mrs. James Petteway) of San Diego, California; Douglas, of St. Paul; and Marlys, at home. She is survived by the following brothers and sisters: Anphia (Mrs. Elmer Myhre) of Willmar; Otto, of Pennock; Mrs. Millie Bergan, of Minneapolis; Mrs. Ellen Landquist, of Minneapolis, and Edward, of Syracuse, New York. She is also survived by four grandchildren, numerous nieces, nephews, cousins and other relatives, and by a legion of friends. She was preceded in death by a son, Dale, in October, 1946. Those in attendance were from New London, Willmar, Pennock, Spicer, Murdock, Renville, Belgrade, Kerkhoven, Sunburg, Minneapolis, St. Paul, Newfolden, Stephen, San Diego, California, and Syracuse, New York. They shall remember a Christian woman.

In 1991, Cora's daughter Marlys wrote about her memories of the day that her mother died. This essay reflects on being a 15-year-old girl, the family's vegetable garden, the shock and pain of that day and days that followed, the need for family and neighbors—the Peterson family.

It was May 18, 1963. I got up around 9:00 on a cold, windy Saturday. I dressed and came downstairs and had a homemade donut. It was a little hard but was good anyway with warm coffee. I was learning to drink coffee. I was 15 years old. Mom wanted to plant the garden around May 15. We left about 10:00. I went in the old pick-up (I drove) to a corner of a field about ¼ mile away. Mom was disgusted that my brother was getting a late start planting corn.

The wind was cold as I crouched along a row planting carrots. To make starting easier Mom had mixed the tiny carrot seeds with some dirt in a coffee can. Probably something she'd read about in the Farm Journal*. It worked. I had a question. I don't recall what it was. I looked up saying "Mom". It was then that I noticed she'd gone to sit in the truck.*

The passenger door was open and I could see she was slumped back. I ran over to the truck. She could not answer and I could see a glazed look in her eyes. A gurgling noise was coming from her open mouth. Later I found out that was called the "death rattle". I pushed her into the truck so that I could close the door. I was about to drive home when I saw my brother (Orlynn) driving to the field on the tractor with the corn planter. I ran to him.

"Something's happened to mom." He rushed to her. He looked at her and told me to run home and call the ambulance. At first, I thought maybe she had fainted, though I know she had not. I ran home and told Vivian, who called the ambulance. She took me to the back bedroom.

Later she came and told me that Mom was gone. I cried. Dad came home. Sherman came home from the field. The minister came. He hugged me. I hadn't been hugged till then. Vivian and I drove up to Christophersons. Otto, Vivian and I were sitting at the kitchen table. Ella walked into the room.

Laughingly, she said, "My gracious, what is the matter then?" "Cora is dead." Otto said. Ella cried and asked if Douglas had the news yet. Otto called his brother Edward. Vivian offered to pay for the calls. We drove over to the Petersons and I was there for the afternoon. My sister Marjorie came home. We cleaned the house. Bette, Sherman's girlfriend, came and stayed the evening.

The next day, Sunday, we went to the airport to pick up my sister Mary Ann. I remember her perfume as we hugged. We stopped at a restaurant. My sister said that I was a "trooper". We arrived home. My two sisters and I hugged on the porch. People were over drinking coffee and eating. Monday we cleaned house. People brought over hot dishes and cakes. Monday night we went to the funeral home.

Mom was wearing a blue print dress. My eyes immediately went to her bright red polished fingernails. Mom never wore nail polish. It bothered everyone and it was later removed. The funeral director had said that her nails were dirty from gardening. It was a difficult time. My dad said, "I wish we could have talked." The funeral was Tuesday afternoon. I saw a few school friends. I felt that everyone was looking at me. We went to the cemetery (at Lake Florida Mission Church) and then home for "lunch". People were nice but I also wanted to leave. I liked the attention though in an odd sort of way. It wasn't long before the attention wore off. I was alone. I went back to school.

The following weeks were the hardest. Sometimes I would go to the "garden" where she died. I wanted to see what she saw during her last minutes on earth. I wanted to walk on the ground where she last walked. Sometimes I went to the cemetery. I put cut flowers on her grave. Sometimes I drove to Christophersons. Ella was so nice. She gave me lunch.

I write these things not to dwell on them. I write these things because I do not want to forget the most significant life-changing event in my life.

Herman Mankell (1896-1985)

Herman Mankell died more than two decades after Cora, on February 11, 1985. His pallbearers were four grandsons, a nephew, and a neighbor.

Funeral services for Herman W. Mankell were conducted February 15, 1985 at the Evangelical Covenant Church in New London, with the Rev. Tim Anderson officiating. Special music was provided by Wellington Nelson and Herbert Kallevig, vocalists, and Saralyn Olson, organist. Pallbearers were: Kurt Mankell, Grady Larimer, Kayne Larimer, Jason Petteway, all grandsons of the deceased, Al Christopherson and Wayne Railson. Interment was in the Lake Florida Covenant Church Cemetery, rural Spicer.

Herman Mankell, c1980.

> *Herman Mankell was born May 14, 1896, in Lake Andrew Township to Oscar and Minnie (Swenson) Mankell. He attended rural District 25 School and graduated from New London High School. On October 30, 1926, he married Cornelia Christopherson. He farmed on the home farm in Lake Andrew Township all his life, and was also involved in the insurance business for over 40 years with State Farm Insurance, Waseca Mutual and the Lake Andrew Arctander Insurance Co., of which he was a past president. He also served on church and school boards and the Lake Andrew Town Board, and was active in the 1930s in securing REA for Kandiyohi County. He was also noted for his interest in the history of the community.*
>
> *Mankell died February 11, 1985 at the Glen Oaks Nursing Home in New London at the age of 88 years. He is survived by six children, Orlynn of New London, Marjorie (Mrs. Bill) Larimer of Rochester, Sherman of New London, Mary Ann Petteway of San Diego, Calif., Douglas of St. Louis, Mo., and Marlys (Mrs. Jerry) Schilz of Bloomington; 15 grandchildren and one great-grandchild.*
>
> *Also surviving are two sisters, Edna Halvorson of New London and Alice (Mrs. George) Alvig of La Mesa, Calif. He was preceded in death by his wife and one son, Dale Herman.*

Herman was remembered by a former neighbor, Harvey Christenson, who was the son of Harvin Christenson. Harvey wrote a letter to his former District 25 classmate, Orlynn, and testified to the friendship between their fathers, Herman and Harvin, and also between their families. Harvey reminisced about Herman and provided a glimpse to one activity Herman and Cora's children did in the fields—as did other farm children. They removed problematic weeds from the planted fields.

> *I remember when your dad (Herman) paid you kids to pick mustard plants from grain fields. 1 cent a plant, I believe. We have good memories of your dad, Herman—one of the kindest men around and a good friend of our Dad. He sold me my first car insurance on my Ford.*

Vivian Mankell (1931-1994)

Vivian Mankell died on January 6, 1994, at Rice Hospital's hospice care unit, after two years of treatments and two surgeries due to cancer. Here is a portion of her obituary, published in the *Free Press Times*.

> *Vivian J. Mankell, 62 of New London, died Thursday, January 6, 1994 at Rice Memorial Hospital in Willmar after a lengthy illness. Funeral services are scheduled for Tuesday, January 11, 1994 at the First Lutheran Church of Norway Lake in rural New London with the Revs. Joyce and Irving Sandberg officiating. Interment will be in the church cemetery.*

Vivian Mankell, 1991.

Vivian Mankell was born June 17, 1931 in Irving Township to Walter and Inga (Johnson) Jordin. She grew up and attended the Atwater Public Schools.

On Nov. 19, 1954 she married Orlynn Mankell and they made their home on the Mankell family farm in Lake Andrew Township. For several years she was employed by The Big

Store in New London. She was an active member of the First Lutheran Church, participating in the choir and the women of the ELCA...She was preceded in death by her parents, and her brother, Noel Jordin.

Orlynn Mankell (1928-1999)

On September 24, 1999, Orlynn Mankell died from injuries sustained the previous day in a one-car accident on Highway 23, south of Spicer. In his capacity as president of the Lake Florida Mission Covenant Cemetery Association, his final task before his death was to arrange for a burial at the Lake Florida Church cemetery.[7]

His death in 1999 brought an end to five generations of the Mankell family living on the Mankell homestead. A portion of the homestead remains in the Mankell family. Orlynn's obituary was published in the *Kandiyohi County Times*. The pallbearers included three men from the four farms story: Earl Peterson, Wayne Railson, and Donald Swenson.

Orlynn Mankell, c1990.

Funeral services of Orlynn A. Mankell, 71, of New London, were held Tuesday, Sept. 28 at 2 p. m. at the First Lutheran Church of Norway Lake, rural New London, with Rev. Joel Njus officiating. Interment was in the church cemetery.

Mr. Mankell died Saturday, Sept 25, 1999, [sic—Friday, Sept 24] at the Hennepin County Medical Center in Minneapolis. Orlynn Augustus Mankell was born January 17, 1928 on his family's farm in Lake Andrew Township, near New London. He was the son of Herman and Cornelia (Christopherson) Mankell. Orlynn was baptized and confirmed at the Lake Florida Mission Covenant Church, near New London. He grew up on the family farm, attended country school at District 25, and graduated from the New London High School in 1946. From 1952-1954 he served his country in the U. S. Army during the Korean War. On November 19, 1954 Orlynn was married to Vivian Jordin at the Zion Lutheran Church near Hawick. Following their marriage they farmed in Lake Andrew Township. Vivian died in January of 1994.

Mr. Mankell was a member of the First Lutheran Church of Norway Lake where he was an active member, having served in many positions. He was once employed at the ASCS office, served on the Pioneer Library Board and was a past president of the Lake Andrew Arctander Insurance Company. He was the current President of the Lake Florida Mission Covenant Cemetery Association.

He was an avid reader of history, especially World War II history. He was a noted historian, and helped write the history book for the First Lutheran Church of Norway Lake. He enjoyed helping build the log church for the Norway Lake Historical Society, and he enjoyed his Norwegian language course, taught by Pastor Njus...He was preceded in death by his parents, wife, and brother, Dale.

---

7 Orlynn was preparing the gravesite for Madelyn Swenson, mentioned in Chapter 7 as the future wife of Henry (Lolly) Swenson, Jr., who lived on the Norman farm as a child in the 1920s.

Orlynn and Vivian Mankell are buried in the cemetery at First Lutheran Church of Norway Lake. The church choir, in which Orlynn and Vivian were members for decades, sang at their funeral services. Music included "I Have a Future All Sublime" a Swedish hymn composed by Nils Frykman (1883), a Swedish immigrant and a former pastor of the Lake Florida Mission Church.

The Farm House
In October 1991, the Mankell family sold the white Victorian-style farm house. After serving five generations of the Mankell family, the house was moved two miles south to the north shore of Crook Lake.

Mankell Farm House, c1930.
(image courtesy of the Mankell Family)

LAKE FLORIDA MISSION CHURCH[8]

The 1870s witnessed the beginnings of the Lake Florida Mission Church; the 1950s, the congregation's closing. As described in the earlier chapters, families of three of the four farms worshipped in their native Swedish language (and later English) at this small congregation. By 1955, one family of these three maintained membership—the Mankell family. The Stenseth/Christenson/Peterson farm had roots in the Lutheran tradition. The Stenseth and Christenson families attended Nannestad Lutheran and later East Norway Lake Lutheran in Arctander Township. The Peterson family who arrived in the mid-1940s worshipped at Lebanon Lutheran Church in New London. In the early 1970s, the family transferred membership to First Lutheran Church of Norway Lake. The initial settlers at the Brattlund/Reierson/Haglund farm were founders of Lake Florida Mission Church, but when the Brattlund family moved to Willmar, their affiliation changed to another Swedish-speaking church, First Covenant in Willmar, though the two immigrants are buried at the Lake Florida Mission Church cemetery. Martin and Anna Reierson were connected to East Norway Lake Lutheran Church and later Trinity Lutheran Church in New London. The Haglund family was affiliated with Assemblies of God in Willmar and Salem Covenant Church northwest of Pennock.

The first settlers of the Norman farm were members of this Lake Florida congregation. Two generations later Edith and Edwin Railson were members of First Lutheran Church of Norway Lake, though Edith's brother Oscar L. Larson would be buried at Lake Florida Mission Church in 1974, near their parents. The first settlers of the Mankell farm, H. W. and Elizabeth, were two of the earliest members of Lake Florida Church. Their son Oscar and his family, followed by their grandson Herman and his family maintained their affiliation with the Lake Florida Mission Church. Herman and Cora and their

---

8 Findagrave.com; Mankell Family Collection; mankell.org; Ancestry. com; *Keeping the Faith*; *Willmar Tribune* 10 August 1945; Lake Florida Church collection; *Illustrated History of Kandiyohi County*;. *Willmar Daily Tribune*, 1929; *A Century of Christian Service Through the Ministry of First Covenant Church, Willmar Minnesota…since 1883*.

unmarried children were members of Lake Florida at its closing. They then worshipped at the New London Covenant Church. The family maintained their emotional connection with their former church in Lake Andrew Township with the family burials in the church cemetery: Minnie Mankell in 1959; Cora Mankell in 1963; Herman Mankell in 1985. After their 1954 marriage, Orlynn and Vivian Mankell worshipped for a few years at her home congregation: Zion Irving Lutheran Church, east of New London. In the late 1950s, they transferred their membership to First Lutheran Church of Norway Lake.

"This is the day the Lord has made. Let us rejoice and be glad in it." Psalm 118:24
For many years, until his death in 1999, Orlynn Mankell opened the former congregation's annual homecoming services with this scripture verse. Held on the first Sunday of August, former members, descendants of former members, and neighbors come together to worship and keep memories alive of this church, located ½ mile east of the Lake Andrew Town Hall (and District 25 school in past years) on County Road 29.

The final pastor of the congregation was Rev. Theodore J. Paulson who served two calls: 1916-1920, 1937-1955. In 1945, Rev. Paulson wrote for the local newspaper, describing the congregation's milestones, pastors, and its members (with some sentiment) who celebrated 70 years of ministry to the Swedish community.[9] Here are some excerpts.

> *From what can be known of old records of Swedish emigrants and Scandinavians in general who came to* [the township] *before the year 1868, we find that some of them who cared for their spiritual welfare began to come together for religious services and prayer meetings as early as 1868. They were poor but God-fearing and hungry for the word of God.*
>
> *One of the leading members among the emigrants was A. P. Skoglund, who with his wife were active to promote religious gatherings...*
>
> *A church was organized around 1870 which in 1874 united with the Lutheran Augustana Synod of the USA and accepted its Constitution. From this date we count the Seventy years anniversary. We are some months behind time with our celebration because we wanted to have our festival in the midsummer when the peonies and roses are in blossom...*
>
> *The first members of this church were according to the old records, N. Brattlund, P. Warholm, Lars Hedin, A. Hedin, H. Hakanson, B. N. Bloom, John Nord, J. A. Skoglund, Sr, A. P Skoglund, O. Johnson, L. Rodlund and N. Larson. Twelve honest God-fearing men together with their wives and children. It may be of interest to know that the first chairman of the church was N. Brattlund...*
>
> *When the Mission church at Lake Florida began its career in 1879 it is stated that it had in the treasury—now listen!—94 cents. It began with a clean record free of debt...*
>
> *A new period, perhaps the most fruitful, began when another Salem Mission church pastor, Rev. Nels Frykman, was called to ministry to the Lake Florida Mission church. He began his ministry here in 1891 and continued for seventeen years, or until the end*

---

9   Paulson's 1945 article celebrated 70 years from its 1874 affiliation with the Augustana Lutheran Synod, though the church officially began in 1870.

Rev. Theodore J. Paulson.
(*A Century of Christian Service Through the Ministry of First Covenant Church, Willmar Minnesota...since 1883*)

of 1907. Rev. Nel Frykman was not only a good preacher, but also a deep thinker, almost a philosopher. Yet he was "par excellence" a poet and a singer. Add to that his saintly life, his God given humor and friendly disposition. It must have been a jubilee every time he came here on a visit. Several of his songs have been translated into the English. In the morning of March 30, 1911, this sweet singer in Israel went home to sing in the heavenly choir. The pleasant memory of him will never die....

In 1908 Rev. A. W. Franklin, also a Salem church pastor, began his ministry here. He was a practical preacher and also a literary man. His periodical, "Dufvan" was read in many homes...

I have been pastor of this church from the fall of 1916 to August 20, 1920, when I was also pastor of the Litchfield and New London Mission churches, and often preached at Colfax and Irving, a large pastorate and much traveling on muddy roads in the fall and spring and in snowdrifts in the winter months. But it was all joy and pleasure to serve and contented people...

At present the church consists of 33 members. Everyone is willing to serve. There is perfect harmony between the members and their pastor. Although small, this church is loyal to God and his word, and have not denied the blessed name of Jesus Christ. More than 125 members have since its beginning belonged to this church. Most of them have gone home to the church Triumphant and their earthly remains rest in the cemetery beside the church. When we walk among their graves may we remember that we step upon holy ground. Their prayers for us are upon the altar before the throne. Our hope is that we shall meet them with joy at the glorious Day of the Lord. Some members have moved away from here to join other churches.

My friends! I hope that you will not misunderstand me if I express the thanks and appreciation to certain members of this church, especially to our old, venerable chairman, Mr. John A. Skoglund for what he has been to this church. He has served as janitor, secretary, chairman and everything except preacher. May the sunshine of heaven lighten his path as he walks on his pilgrim way. Another one is Mrs. Walter Skoglund, who for several years, Sunday after Sunday, sacrificed time and comfort to superintend and teach the children in the Sunday school. Her reward shall be great in heaven. There is an old member of this church, Mr. Herman Larson [brother-in-law to Johanna Norman Larson], whose earthly remains are resting in a grave beside this church. He was a faithful janitor for many years. More than one cold Sunday morning he walked up here to keep the church warm. God bless his memory and his family!

Another one we must not forget is Mrs. Willie Larson [Johanna Norman]. She cannot be with us to celebrate because she is tied to a sickbed and has been so for many years. We all sympathize with her, and our prayers go up to God for her that he may strengthen her faith and comfort her heart.

> *Here I must close my incomplete history. Permit me, dear friends, to thank you all for your loyalty and for your kindness to me. You have been willing to make some improvements both inside and outside the church during the last years. My earnest desire for you is that you all may stand before the throne of the Lord at last without spot and blemish. Then my work among you has not been in vain.*

Rev. Douglas Mankell, son of Herman and Cora, remembers Rev. Paulson:

> *He lived in Minneapolis and traveled by train to Willmar on Friday evening. A member of the Lake Florida congregation picked him up and then the pastor stayed with the family for the weekend. On Sunday evening or Monday, Paulson's host family took him to Willmar to get on the train for his return to Minneapolis. I recall many times he stayed with us on the farm. Marlys moved into her sisters' bedroom so that Rev. Paulson could sleep in her room. I recall him being old, in his late 70s or early 80s and he always wore a black suit, white shirt, and tie when he stayed with us for the weekend. He was always a part-time pastor during the years I remember him. For funerals he may have spent extra time in the Lake Florida community. I cannot think of the Lake Florida church without thinking of Rev. Paulson.*

In 1950, the church became part of the Evangelical Covenant Church of America, and officially known as the "Mission Covenant Church of Lake Florida." The trustees for this renewed church were Walter Skoglund, Herman Mankell, Oscar Erickson, Reynold Larson, Walter Carlson, Nellie Swenson and Victor Danielson.

The congregation dissolved in 1955 due to a small number of members; most of the people then joined the New London Covenant Church or the Salem Covenant Church near Pennock. A perpetual care fund began in 1961, following a fund-raising event which surpassed its goal of $4,000. The committee members were Anna Danielson, Victor Danielson, Oscar Erickson, Herman Mankell, Walter Skoglund, and Frances St. Mane. The perpetual care fund pays for the ongoing upkeep of the church and cemetery and is governed by the Church Association. Former members and their families continue to care for the church building and the cemetery grounds more than 60 years after its closing.

Here is a list of people buried at the cemetery who are a part of this four farms story and part of this congregation's history. These names include farm owners, their descendants, and farm renters.

Brattlund, Maria (1817-1905)
Brattlund, Nils (1819-1900)
Dahlstrom, Clara (Norman, 1856-1894)
Haglund, Wesley (1942-2015)
Larson, William (1857-1911)
Larson, Johanna (Norman, 1863-1947)
Larson, Lillie (1896-1910)
Larson, Oscar 1893-1974)
Larson, Victor (1897-1909)
Mankell, Cora (Christopherson, 1903-1963)

Mankell, Dale (1945-1946)
Mankell, Elizabeth (1832-1914)
Mankell, Herman Wilhelm (H. W., 1835-1889)
Mankell, Herman (1896-1985)
Mankell, Minnie (Swenson, 1875-1959)
Mankell, Oscar (1868-1936)
Mankell, Otto (1872-1939)
Norman, Gustaf A (1867-1893)
Norman, Johannes (1827-1884)
Norman, Maria (1823-1906)

Swenson, Henry G (1877-1948)
Swenson, Henry (Lolly) Jr. (1925-1995)
Swenson, Madelyn (Thostenson, 1935-1999)

Swenson, Nellie (Larson, 1884-1974)
Swenson, Wallace (1909-1984)

Those who worshipped and those baptized, confirmed, or married at this congregation have fond memories of this place. Former members have shared their memories and thoughts of this congregation.

Marjorie (Mankell) Larimer, c2005

We did not meet there in the winter because it only had a wood burning stove. I still remember having very cold feet! We met in homes during these colder months. The pastor (from Minneapolis) stayed in area homes when he came. We would meet him at the train station in Willmar, when it was our turn to have him for the weekend. I remember very well the singing there. I am sure the old hymns 'floated down' as far as the Larson farm [across County Road 29]! I can still hear them sing 'The Old Rugged Cross'—sometimes accompanied by the piano and organ!

Marlys (Mankell) Schilz, c2000

The gravel crunched under the balloon bicycle tires as I rode down the country road. I could feel the hot sun baking my back, the taste of dust and grit when an occasional car drove by. I turned into the driveway and saw my destination at the end—a small white country church nestled in a grove of trees with the traditional cemetery alongside. The long driveway stretched ahead like train tracks, two narrow paths with grass overgrown in the middle and along the sides. I stayed in the right lane, out of the way of oncoming traffic, I suppose.

I could feel the weeds stinging my ankles and tried to pedal with one leg. Preoccupied with this dilemma I barely noticed the strains of music. As I got closer to the church, the organ music was there all right. It was LOUDER. I looked for a car—none. Bicycle?—none. The single entrance/exit was closed. I walked around the cemetery for a while which was not exactly comforting. I recalled what my mother would say, "It's the live ones you have to be afraid of." I walked up the front steps to the church door. I hesitated as I placed by hand on the door handle. Suppose the forlorn ghosts were practicing their music lessons. Suppose I would see the organ keys play by themselves. I swore off late night horror movies.

Finally I gathered enough courage and opened the door. As my eyes adjusted to the darkness, I could hear a familiar voice. "What are you doing here?" I asked the same question. My friend from childhood answered, "Sometimes I walk over here and play this old pump organ. My grandmother was the organist here for many years." We chatted, but just for a bit. We each came seeking solitude, and each wanted to preserve it.

Loretta (Gadney) Brandt, 2019

The first pastor I remember was Chester Dahlberg. He was young and full of spirit. We had Sunday School each Sunday with about four divisions as to age. One year we had Bible School for the community held at District 25. That was a great time with singing, learning Bible verses and crafts. The older children met in the basement and that is where we had our final program with supper and showing off what we had done.

Our Christmas programs were exciting with a tree lighted by wax candles, candles held in sconces on the walls, and windows darkened as the program was always in the afternoon. We sang songs and gave recitations and ended up with a bag of candy and an apple.

In the 1940s we had a group called the Leaguers, who sang in church and the night meetings on Sundays. Rev. Paulson would come from the Twin Cities to stay at one of the church members' homes and that is where we had our Sunday night meetings followed by a big lunch. We also went to other church gatherings in the area, listening to the pastors, singing and playing games outside. The piano at the church was a used one from Willmar that was brought there by Harriet Gadney in someone's pick-up truck. The big boys were there to help get it up on the stage and is still in good sound. The old organ has been repaired and working well. I enjoy playing the old songs on it.

Since the church disbanded in 1955, we have held services once a year with a speaker, potluck lunch and some great singing. I hope that it can continue for the next 150 years.

Orlynn Mankell, 1998

What has to remain as a classic of the old traditional "little white church" is the historic Lake Florida Mission Church of rural Spicer, Minnesota, where it has been standing now for well over a century. While many of these old churches stand today as prominent landmarks, the one at Lake Florida is secluded away at the end of a long driveway. From the highway you have to look twice to notice it.

Swedish immigrants built the church in 1873. They referred to themselves as the Mission Friends and were in disagreement with Sweden's State Church. The Lake Florida church has never achieved any real landmark status but certain facts about it do probably stand out.

These old Mission Friends never liked things too elaborate or showy and it is certainly reflected in their place of worship with its plain, pristine, and yet appealing design. Secondly, throughout its long history it has never been beset by fire, lightning strikes or damaging windstorms.

The interior is all wood boarded and has never known anything like drywall, plaster, paneling or composition tile. The building has always received excellent care and with nothing added to the walls or ceiling, no restoration has ever been needed. The siding on the main section is just the way the builders put it up in 1873 and held in place with the old square nail.

The church can also be considered as an example of 1870s Americana. The sixteen pews are also original and are generally believed to go back to Civil War times. Even the door locks and hinges have that old look about them.

If you could have visited the old Lake Florida Mission a hundred years ago, you would have met men like Gustaf, Anders, Frans, Jonas, and Vilhelm; and a few of the wives: Elize, Terese, Kajsa, Britta, and Lisabet. Most of the members came from Varmland Province, Sweden.

In 1910 the entry was added. The pastor of the time makes note of it, "The elderly church is putting on its festival garments." To some at least the church was even then getting a little old. A steeple was also added which can be described as being modest and unassuming and which sort of describes the Friends themselves. The three distinctive round windows were put in and were described as being Old Swedish. The Lake Florida Church has always been sort of a timeless place—and where the newest sections are 88 years old!

The church is much photographed. A photo from the front in 1910 and today would be identical except for the light fixture above the door with its own distinctive shadow.

Visitors visit the church during the summer months. The guest book shows visitors from every state, and includes a few from foreign countries. Now and then visitors make notations after their names. "A beautiful experience" writes one. "A real treasure" says another. Regular services are no longer held, but a homecoming service is held every summer for the descendants of the church.

The church building is sequestered away at the end of a long driveway, with a background of huge ash and cottonwood trees, which line the churchyard. You are away from traffic noise and some days the only sound is the rustle of an afternoon breeze high in the cottonwoods. In this tranquil and immaculate setting stands this church.

The church of Lake Florida played an important role in the lives of its founders. It seemed to be on the mind of the church secretary when he make a brief notation in the old records well over a century ago. "May the Lord water his church at Florida so that it might become more fragrant and blossom like a lily in Zaron."

The historic, old, Lake Florida Mission Church stands today, quiet and serene, just the way it has for the last 125 years—and never with any real fanfare. Chances are it is good for a hundred years more.

Lake Florida Mission Church, 2005.
(image courtesy of the Mankell Family)

FAITH, FAMILY, AND DUTY

Church Activities

The men and women in these stories of the four farms were people of faith, and over the decades these generations of the faithful worshipped at different local churches. Women of faith—no matter the decade, the language, or the size of the congregation—cared for the altar so that the pastor would have what he needed for a Sunday worship service. For many years, Vivian Mankell served on the Altar Guild at First Lutheran Church of Norway Lake. Here is Vivian's checklist of things she needed to do, especially for communion and special events like baptisms:

- ✓ Take care of flowers
- ✓ Be sure to water flowers
- ✓ Put offering plates on altar
- ✓ Check altar candles—let not get too short
- ✓ Candles are in the cupboard in the sacristy
- ✓ Use rag or gloves when handling candle holders or brass vases
- ✓ Baptism towels in cupboard
- ✓ Put baptism towel on fount
- ✓ Make sure fount is out of the way on communion Sunday
- ✓ Fill wine glasses and wafer tray for communion
- ✓ Put small table behind altar and put wafers on it
- ✓ Put common cup on altar
- ✓ Put communion cards in pew holders
- ✓ Wash communion glasses

Women of the congregations highlighted in this story gathered in members' homes for "Ladies' Aid" often subdivided into smaller groups called "Circles".[10] These gatherings provided the women an opportunity for Christian fellowship, Bible study, and local service and church projects. Each host provided lunch. Those hosts in the four farms families included the following women:

- Anna Reierson, East Norway Lake Lutheran Church
- Minnie Mankell, Lake Florida Mission Church
- Cora Mankell, Lake Florida Mission Church
- Johanna Larson, Lake Florida Mission Church
- Karen Stenseth, Nannestad Lutheran Church

---

10 *To God Be the Glory*, p. 21-24; *Keeping the Faith*, p. 116-117. *Willmar Tribune* 20 May 1908, 10 Nov 1909, 10 June 1914, 10 May 1918, 27 September 1916, 11 September 1918, 15 June 1921; *Niederasphe to Norway Lake*

- Mina Christenson, Nannestad Lutheran Church and later East Norway Lake Lutheran Church
- Vivian Mankell, First Lutheran Church of Norway Lake
- Eldora Peterson, Lebanon Lutheran Church and later First Lutheran Church of Norway Lake

Vivian Mankell's daughter, Susan Muellner, reflects on her memories of Vivian preparing for this annual event at their house.

> *She was never too busy for church. A big annual event for Mom was hosting circle. The house was cleaned from top to bottom for this occasion. We kids loved it—such good things to eat and lots of leftovers: ham salad buns, lemon/macaroni ring salad, dessert, nuts and mints, and coffee. And the table always looked so nice.*

Eldora Peterson's daughter, Nancy Salmi, also remembers the cleaning and cooking her mother did when preparing for church women coming to the house.

> *The house was cleaned from top to bottom. Lebanon ladies served two items: sandwiches and dessert. And, of course, coffee. Mom would make her wonderful buns for the sandwiches and one of her favorite desserts or would try a new recipe.*

Farm Life

The men of the four farms in these stories worked hard as they followed a planting and harvesting season and/or the daily routine of having milk cows. These chores, often with help from wives and children, included the following:

- Milk and feed the cows at dawn and at dusk
- Arrange for cream and/or milk to go on trucks to the local creamery, primarily New London
- Feed other livestock such as chickens, pigs, sheep, goats, and horses
- Pick eggs
- Kill and clean a chicken for supper
- Repair tractors and machinery in preparation for, and during, planting and harvesting
- Plow and drag the fields to prepare for planting
- Plant corn, soybeans, and/or grains such as wheat and oats
- Cultivate and spray the fields to reduce the weeds
- Cut alfalfa periodically to feed the animals
- Harvest the grains in the summer and the corn and soybeans in the fall
- Bale the straw which remained after grain harvest and fill the barn's hay loft with the bales
- Truck the harvest to the local elevators in New London or Spicer
- Muck out the barns

- Join with neighbors to fill silos with corn silage—food for the cattle during the winter months
- Remove snow from the driveways and pathways during the winter
- Enjoy coffee at local restaurants and visit with the neighbors

While the men primarily worked outside the house, the women's activities primarily revolved around the household and children:

- Clean the house
- Wash clothes
- Prepare meals
- Bake
- Sew and mend clothes
- Care for the children
- Raise the chickens from brooder house to hen house; clean eggs
- Clean the milk/cream separator
- Plant and tend the vegetable gardens
- Can or store produce from the garden
- Plant and care for flower gardens
- Volunteer for the local school or 4-H club
- Enjoy coffee with neighbors

In 1991, Marlys Mankell Schilz wrote this recollection about her mom Cora and the importance of aprons for her many farm and household duties. What was true for Cora was true for most farm women highlighted in this book:

> *When I am working around the kitchen and spill something on myself I think, "Why don't I wear an apron like my mother did?" Even when I'm getting ready to go out, I put on my good clothes last if I need to do something in the kitchen before I leave. My mother would have just taken off her apron. Much easier.*
>
> *An apron however had several functions. First of all, it was a portable ready-made towel. Sweat, tears, it could also be a dust cloth. Used for carrying eggs, and flower bulbs, potatoes from the cellar. Fancy aprons—useless. They are for decoration. She wore them also however when the church circle came around. There were company aprons and everyday aprons. Always had pockets—handkerchiefs—and if chilly, she wrapped the apron around elbows.*
>
> *Apron was a symbol—taking it off was a symbol of work being done. Maybe then we could go swimming; mostly she sat on the step watching her kids play ball in the back yard.*

CHAPTER 12:
1960-1964

School and Town Hall in 2012, before it moved to the Peterson farm.

This story of the four farms ends with the closing of School District 25,
the school attended by generations of children.

SCHOOL DISTRICT 25[1]

In 1959 and early 1960, local residents of the county voted on the proposal to consolidate the rural schools with the New London and Spicer schools. The rural school districts chosen for consolidation had been sending their junior and high school age students to the New London High School for many decades, with the country schools primarily serving grades 1-6 or 1-8. Some schools had kindergarten, but not always District 25. By this time, District 25 had a new identifier: District 770. Families across the county's northern townships voted on the issue of consolidating into the New London-Spicer school district. The first vote, held on August 14, 1959, failed. Here is the summary from the *New London Times*:

School Consolidation Proposal Turned Down in This Area

Nineteen rural school districts in the New London high school area turned down a proposal for consolidation with the New London Independent School district No. 345 in an election held Friday evening, August 14th.

The total vote at the three polling places was 286 in favor and 326 against consolidation. H. O. Torgerson, superintendent of the New London school, states that New London school authorities are of the opinion that the "yes" vote did not come out to vote in [the] election. He further states that there is a possibility that there will be another school consolidation election later this fall.

School enrollment at the New London school last year at about 575, has more than doubled in the past dozen years. This has been brought about by the increased population in the district, the addition of the Spicer students in the high school, and that some rural schools are sending 7th and 8th grade students to the New London school.

Pressure continued on the families in these rural school districts to change their votes. The families and school leadership prepared for another vote in February 1960. An advertisement in favor of consolidation was published in the *New London Times*, with these eight principle reasons (Item #3 used language common in the 1960s) promoted by the Citizens Committee for Education. This list had no mention of building a new high school, which was part of the consolidation plan, though this may be understood in the first item on the list.

1. School in New London is over-crowded.
2. Broader curriculum can be offered.
3. More services, such as Kindergarten, special class for retarded can be offered.
4. Will provide for athletic events, nearer the school building.
5. Will provide for improved transportation services by reducing time and distance on bus route.
6. Help attract superior teachers.
7. State Department of Education frowns on our classes and lack of room.
8. Provide more opportunities for adult education.

---

1 Mankell.org; *History of New London, 1865-1990*, p 33-34; memories of former District 25 students. *History of New London, 1865-1965* p. 33-41; *History of Spicer on Green Lake*, p 106; *New London Times* 20 August 1959, 18 Feb 1960.

On February 17, 1960, the referendum passed; the vote was 541 in favor, with 323 against. With the addition of hundreds of new pupils from the country schools to the town schools which had overcrowded classrooms before the consolidation, the school district built a new Junior-Senior High School. When the new building opened in the fall of 1963, the one-room rural schools closed, including District 25 (aka 770). The consolidation meant that children in Lake Andrew Township would no longer walk or bike to school. Nor would their parents drive them the short distances to the school. School buses, which had been transporting the junior and senior high school students to New London, now added the younger students to the routes. These buses drove on the county highways and township roads, bringing students from their homes to New London and back again.

School merger headline, February 11, 1960, *New London Times*.

MEMORIES

Generations of farm families attended District 25 during its 95 year history. Teachers of District 25 educated the children who lived within approximately a two mile radius of the school. Several people who had attended this country school have provided their favorite stories and memories of their school years (spanning 1930s to 1963). Many of them were from the four farms families and others were classmates and neighbors. Two students (Joyce Johnson and Marlys Schilz) died several years ago; their memories are from earlier projects. Other former students have provided stories for this book and have permitted their names to be included. Each person in this list also had other family members attend this school, including siblings, parents, aunts, uncles, grandparents, great-grandparents. These contributors (with direct lineage at the same school) are the following:

- **Sandy (Railson) Anderson**: father Robert Railson, grandmother Edith Larson, grandfather Edwin Railson
- **Loretta (Gadney) Brandt**: mother Esther Larson
- **Patricia (Clark) Broberg**: father Virgil Clark
- **Mary (Peterson) Jeseritz**: grandfather Emil Peterson
- **Joyce (Railson) Johnson**: mother Edith Larson, father Edwin Railson
- **Florence (Clark) Kriens**: brother Virgil Clark and sister Alice Clark
- **Rev. Douglas Mankell**: father Herman Mankell, grandfather Oscar Mankell

- **Susan (Mankell) Muellner**: father Orlynn Mankell, grandfather Herman Mankell, great-grandfather Oscar Mankell
- **Steve Nelson**: father Reynold Nelson, grandfather Knute H. Larson
- **Nancy (Peterson) Salmi**: grandfather Emil Peterson.
- **Marlys (Mankell) Schilz**: father Herman Mankell, grandfather Oscar Mankell

Here are their stories arranged by various categories. That some memories repeat from student to student shows the impact and legacy that the school and its people—teachers and classmates—impressed on these students many decades ago.

General Reflections

Douglas Mankell
I have many wonderful memories of District 25, the one-room school house which I attended for eight years. For seven of those years, I had the same teacher—Mrs. Alphie Gustrud from New London. For all eight years, I had the same four people in my class: Roger, Gail, John, and myself. District 25 was a place of learning, fun, and building relationships with other children who were as young as five and as old as twelve.

My memories of District 25 are very positive! It was where my official educational journey began and where friendships were formed which continued for many years. That school will always occupy a special place in my heart.

Sandy (Railson) Anderson
We participated in the classroom together, ate together, had recess together, the works, how did those teachers do that without a break all day and no other adult around to assist?! Of course we can't forget about the Christmas and other holiday programs, who would have been in charge if not for the good ole' multitasking teacher??! Among her daily duties, of course, included being solely responsible for any ill children, putting another log on the fire and so on. Even though we had to deal with 'other than ideal situations' actually, I think BECAUSE of that fact, we all learned to get along, stand up for ourselves, and have a realistic view of our world. I am really very thankful for the entire experience, those were the days.

Mary (Peterson) Jeseritz
Dist. 25 was a special school. We were so fortunate to have a library, a basement and a kitchen. The best memory from the school is the friendship we had with all the families who had children in the school. We were one big family!!

Transportation

Douglas Mankell
I traveled the two miles to school in the morning and home in the afternoon in various ways. Depending upon weather conditions and parents' schedules, I rode my bike, walked, or rode in a car to school. I did my share of each of those.

Florence (Clark) Kriens
I lived on a farm on the west side of Lake Florida. I walked to school 3 ½ miles, I would stop and get David Danielson [Section 27] & Korsmo siblings [Section 22], and along the way the Dengerud boys [Section 28] who were about ½ mile from the school. When my sister, Alice, and David's sister, Arlene, went to high school, our school bus driver told David and me that we could ride to District 25.

Sandy (Railson) Anderson
I mostly remember walking the mile or so to and from school, I'm sure we rode bikes some, which made for more "bonding time".

Mary (Peterson) Jeseritz
When the weather was nice we would walk or ride bike to school. In the winter we would carpool with Mankells. My Dad and Herman Mankell would take turns driving us to school. I remember the school day starting at 9 and dismissing at 3.

Pat (Clark) Broberg
Most of the kids lived within a few miles, and many walked. I know we had a car back then, but I do remember walking home with the neighbor kids, skipping, or throwing rocks, bouncing balls, and visiting the whole way home. Sometime one parent came and took many families and dropped them off at their driveways.

Susan (Mankell) Muellner
The commute to school was short—one mile east on the gravel road to Peterson's corner and one mile south on the tar County Road 5 (Little Crow Trail) to the school at the corner of County Road 5 and County Road 29. We car pooled with the Petersons. Our farm was on the northwest corner of the school district. The school building also served as the Lake Andrew Township Town Hall, the heart of the community and a milestone to travelers when giving directions from/to Willmar, New London, Spicer, or resorts on Lake Florida or Norway Lake further north.

Students came from all four directions during the years I attended:
   Families from the east: Nelson
   Families from the south: Dengerud
   Families from the west: two Danielson families, Arends, Aasen and Clark
   Families from the north: Hjelle, Railson, Peterson, Mankell

School Building

Steve Nelson
The school itself was configured of a main class room, a library off to the west side of the class room and coat racks and bathrooms also on the west side of the class room. Girls to the north the boys to the south. The library had numerous books applicable to the age of the reader. A large front porch, which no one used was also on the west side of the main building. I never saw anyone on the porch as it was rumored to be unsafe and we'd fall directly through it to the dirt below. Above the porch was a large bell tower with a large bell that could be rung from the girls coat room. In my 6 years there I never heard the bell ring once.

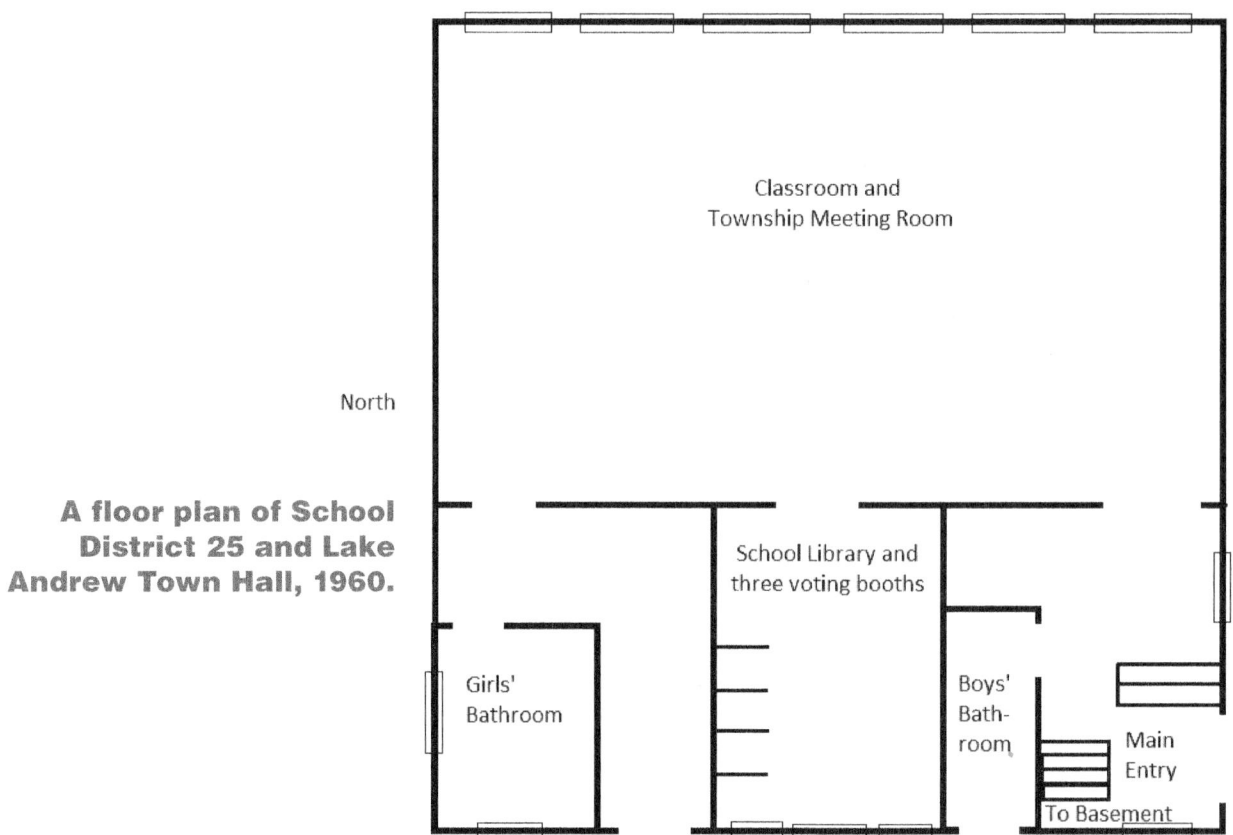

A floor plan of School District 25 and Lake Andrew Town Hall, 1960.

Susan (Mankell) Muellner

Our school building was a bit more elaborate than some neighboring schools. We had a full basement, with a furnace, kitchen and gathering room, which was the scene of kickball games at recess if the weather was particularly bad. District 25 was a "one-room" school, with blackboards at the front and back, tall ceilings, individual desks with tops that opened up to hold our supplies inside (mine was usually messy) and "huge" maps that rolled up and down like window shades. Doors had transoms at the top. There was a library and "cloak rooms" for boys and girls and…..indoor bathrooms!! (Note: I learned my first four-letter word from one of the "rough kids" in the cloak room, not understanding its meaning though…)

Pat (Clark) Broberg

We had a small room off of the main room which was our library and we had a girl's bathroom and cloak room for our coats. The main entrance had the boy's bathroom and hooks for their coats, and steps leading down to the basement. We did have a water fountain. We did have a furnace.

Teachers & the Classroom

Loretta (Gadney) Brandt

My first teacher was Viola Newstrom. She was a good teacher, very pretty and I liked her. Other teachers were Harriet Reese, Florence Jendro, Frances Klein, Mrs. Rodney Shelman, Lillie Jensen and Ida Amundson. In order for us to pass from grade 7 to 8 we needed to take a MN State Test and then the same to pass from 8th to 9th grade. Teacher Elvera Skavdahl[2] drove a small blue coupe named "Betsy."

Steve Nelson

Mrs. Alphie Gustrud was our teacher. She was rather remarkable considering she had to prepare lesson plans for 8 grades, but she was an experienced teacher having taught my father 40 years earlier. She drove a 1966 Oldsmobile which she always parked on the north side of the school building probably to avoid broken wind shields from errant throws from the softball games played in the school yard every spring day recess.

Mrs. Gustrud was a strict disciplinarian so if anything happened that she viewed as wrong, it was punishable by humiliation in front of the whole school. I even remember several times when she couldn't find the culprit she would bring out the school bible and go down every aisle making us put our right hand on the bible and deny being the guilty person. Needless to say things ran smoothly. The only time I got a lecture from her was the time someone brought some bakery sweet rolls to school. I don't remember who. Now us farm kids may have tasted a glazed doughnut but I don't remember when or where it could have been. Anyway, when my turn came to pick a doughnut there were two left, one being about an eighth inch larger than the other. I thought about my choice but being tempted I took the larger of the two. Bad decision! I was admonished in front of whole school. I never forgot it but I learned a lesson in sharing that day that is deep within my soul.

All in all these 6 years set the foundation for the rest of my life. I learned to read, arithmetic, and proper English punctuation. But all the life lessons were probably the biggest reason who I am today. I owe a lot to Mrs. Gustrud.

Nancy (Peterson) Salmi

I loved Mrs. Gustrud and District 25. To me they are inseparable. Mrs. Gustrud was beautiful, elegant, intelligent, and a fabulous teacher. Some of my favorite memories of Mrs. Gustrud is her reading to us for 15-20 minutes after lunch, standing at the front of the room and slowly moving to stand

Mrs. Alphia Gustrud, the longest serving teacher at District 25: 1917-1920, 1951-1960. In this 1958 photo she was in costume to celebrate the State of Minnesota's 100th birthday.

---

2 Elvera Skavdahl married Fred Harris from Irving Township. Fred owned the New London Variety Store until his death in 1970. Mrs. Harris was this author's 4th grade teacher at the New London Elementary School.

in front of each row before she finished. When she finished reading the Bobbsey Twins or Five Little Peppers, she would gift the book to one of her students. Thursday afternoons, we would have spelldowns. She divided us into 2 groups according to upper and lower grades. There was a lot of fun competition to win your group's spelldown. Once, I had to sit down right away because I spelled "baby" with 2 "b"s. I never misspelled the word again. Mrs. Gustrud encouraged us to help and learn from each other. For several years, Glenn and I were the only 2 students in our class. Glenn was a math whiz and I loved reading and history so we were allowed work together, actually tutoring one another in the upper grades. At Easter, every student made their own Easter hat out of a white paper plate and crepe paper, also decorating the hat with crayons. It is incredible, now, to look at the photos taken by Mrs. Gustrud of all students, boys and girls from 1st to 8th grade, lined up wearing their hats. I can't remember one boy objecting to the project. Once a year we had "doll day". Every girl would bring their doll to school and Mrs. Gustrud would take a group photo. Mrs. Gustrud always had the classroom beautifully decorated. Every morning would begin with Mrs. Gustrud playing the piano while we sang. What a wonderful way to grow up!

Douglas Mankell

We listened to Mrs. Gustrud read a chapter from one of the Bobbsey Twins books every day after noon recess. After seven years of listening, I became well-acquainted with those books!

I ran after a rebellious student who ran away from school one day. Mrs. Gustrud requested that I catch the rebellious fourth grader and return him to school. After a long run through a nearby soybean field, I finally caught the runaway scholar and returned him to school. To the best of my knowledge, he never ran away from school again!

Steve Nelson

Stress could be part of our lives even at that young an age. Every one of us had to do a talent performance in front of the class. I played a couple of simple and short piano pieces. Reading the jokes out of the latest Readers Digest was common. Westerns were the rage on TV so gun fights and card games which ended badly where depicted by the older boys. But spelldowns were the worst. The students would get in a long line—oldest to youngest. Mrs. Gustrud would start with the youngest and progress upward giving each of us a word to spell. If we got it wrong we had to sit down. I did okay but I remember getting the word "reindeer" and of course spelling it with an 'a' instead of the 'e'. Down I went. These spell downs got very competitive near the end as the same 3-4 kids were left standing as the words got tougher. We had spelldowns once a week.

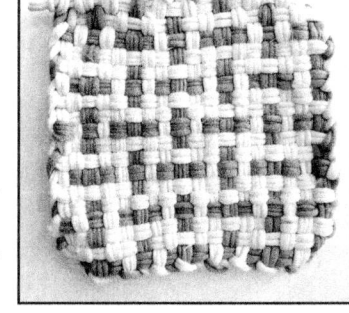

Example of a woven potholder. This was made by the author in the late 1960s.

I'll always remember the importance Mrs. Gustrud put on penmanship. The classes older than me had charts which showed proper cursive. I didn't get that so my cursive is nonexistent while my older sister could write manuscripts. We also had crafts which were accomplished in various degrees by the more/less talented. I remember making pot holders out of yarn strands which were looped to the end of a metal loom which was about 4 inches x 4 inches square. Once all the hooks on two opposite sides were connected with yarn we then had a wooden needle to connect the opposite

Susan Muellner's craft project from District 25, c1963.

ends by interweaving these strands between the other lines so the pattern ran perpendicular to each other. We than weaved the ends together to complete our pot holder. I must have made a dozen of these. Right to left first, top to bottom secondly. Multiple colors. We made valentines and Christmas cards to take home.

She was adamant that we were patriotic. Every day two assigned students would raise the flag out on the west side of the building. Just before we were dismissed the same persons would take down the flag and fold it into the familiar triangular shape. I still can fold our flag properly. After the morning flag raising, we all said "I pledge allegiance to the flag..." Then our day would start. My early years were committed to learning reading, writing, and arithmetic. In the 4th grade we had a whole session on Minnesota history. A pertinent word in the lesson was chosen to be used in a common sentence. We had been studying the early French explorers and about the many hardships they experienced. So the chosen word was hardships. One of my classmates was picked to use that word in a sentence. He proudly exclaimed "here come the hard ships." Must have been the opposite of soft ships. Everyone was laughing so hard we almost got reprimanded for making fun of someone.

Mary (Peterson) Jeseritz

The teacher would ring the hand bell to signal the beginning of school. There was no kindergarten so grades 1-8 attended. Eventually grades 7-8 went to New London. We would sit by grades in rows with younger students always by the windows.

I had 3 teachers while attending Dist. 25. Mrs. Gustrud was the 1st. She was a wonderful teacher. I remember her reading Bobbsey Twin books to us. When she would finish a book, she would give it to a student to keep. Eventually every student in the school received a book. Mrs. Richardson was the next teacher after Mrs. Gustrud retired. She was there only a short time. The last teacher to teach at Dist. 25 was Mrs. Birkland. She, too, was a wonderful teacher. Only grades 1-6 attended at that time.

Susan (Mankell) Muellner

After the pledge of allegiance, our day began. About fifteen students attended during the years I was there. I was in a class of four: Sandy Railson, Pam Nelson, Keith Aasen and me. Our teacher, Mrs. Birkland, conducted our classes at the little table at front of the schoolroom. The "upper grades" sat at a larger table in the back of the room for their lessons. We did our assigned work at our desks when other classes were having their lessons at their table. And yes, we did study the Dick and Jane books, as in "See Spot run." I remember a lot of reading, phonics and math. However, a good part of my education took place when I listened in on what the upper grades were learning at their sessions at the big table, in particular when they studied math. I also recall a special "Social Studies lesson" in February 1962. Mrs. Birkland allowed us to sit in her car to listen to announcers on the car radio describe John Glenn's historic orbit of the earth in Friendship 7. At the time, this 6-year-old did not understand its full significance, but this has turned into a special memory for me.

Sandy (Railson) Anderson

Attending Dist. 25 during my 1st and 2nd grade years brings back so many memories. How things have changed! My grade level was a handful of students, who, as the rest of the classes attended to by a single adult, were expected to quietly work on our school work as the teacher met with each of the other classes. As I remember it, the majority of the time, that is exactly what we did. Who would dare step out of line when the whole neighborhood, parents, and relatives would most certainly know by the end of the day if you did?? Maybe that is why a particular incident stands out to me, guess it was humiliating at the time. I remember like it was yesterday, being caught by the teacher playing a little game quietly with friends (though it did involve some fairly large hand, arm, and leg movements)! Guess there wasn't much forethought going on, as we must have been thinking the teacher wouldn't notice as long as we were quietly making a display of ourselves during study time! I remember both Mrs. Gustrud and Mrs. Birkland, not sure entirely which teacher was there at that particular time, but she gently discouraged our game and that was about it, still humiliating. After subbing for the last number of years in the schools, I have no doubt that some of the old fashioned intimidation is badly needed.

District 25, renovated in 2013.

Pat (Clark) Broberg

We had an old upright piano along with our American flag; we always said our Pledge of Allegiance each morning. We sang songs as a group. Our morning would begin with our lessons, either at our desk or we went to the back and sat at a small table when we had like group time in learning. When we had library time, we could go choose a book and go and sit at our desk to read. We had a large collection of books on the shelves. We also had a bookmobile that came around; this was so fun to go and choose a book to bring home until they came again.

Classmates & Friendships

Douglas Mankell

I was frustrated by an unnamed classmate who occupied the desk immediately in front of me when I was in the second or third grade. From time to time, this girl had the nasty habit of turning around in her desk, sticking her finger in the jar of white paste on my desk, and then eating the paste! It was totally disgusting! She eventually lost her taste for my paste and we were friends once again.

Susan (Mankell) Muellner

The town hall building was also the scene for school board meetings, township meetings and 4-H. Again, it was the heart of the community. Going to school did not really involve *meeting new kids—everyone knew everyone already—and that meant good and bad (as parents of little kids knew all about the rough crowd of some of the older kids). Kids knew each other, parents knew each other, grandparents knew each other, and great grandparents knew each other in years past too. Some of the kids I went to school with were also in my Sunday School class. In fact, Sandy Railson, Pam Nelson and I were in the same Sunday School class (starting at age 3), the same country school class and the same town school class.*

Lunch

Loretta (Gadney) Brandt
Our lunch time was usually eating out of a tin pail or lunch box filled with a sandwich, apple and some sweet treat. Winter time we could bring food in a container that could be set in a pan of hot water on top of the wood burning stove. I was scared many times by the big boys being mean to the teacher. One incident, during our lunch time, the student had the teacher up in front of the open door of the furnace and [the teacher's] dress got burned from the sparks. The parents were called and their son was dismissed from school.

Florence (Clark) Kriens
For our lunch we had a flat top stove top & it was square. So we children could bring a container to warm up in a metal dish pan at noon.

Pat (Clark) Broberg
In the basement there was a small kitchen. Many times they served from the window, and we set up chairs and tables for a lunch room. Still remember getting milk in the small glass bottles with the tinfoil caps, we especially loved the chocolate milk.

Mrs. Gustrud and her class, 1958.

Douglas Mankell
I put my small bottle of milk in a snowbank when I arrived at school to keep it cold. The school had no refrigerator so I had milk only when snow was on the ground.

I carved my initials on the raw potato in my lunch bucket and upon arriving at school, putting it in the roaster oven for lunch at noon. My classmates did the same thing so we knew which potato out of 25 belonged to whom.

Steve Nelson
About twice a year Mrs. Gustrud would bring an electric potato cooker to school. We all were instructed to bring a baking potato from home for noon lunch. Well, as with all the best laid plans, the cooker didn't function properly so we missed noon lunch and had potatoes at 3:00 in the afternoon.

Mary (Peterson) Jeseritz
Students would bring their lunch to eat each day, but sometimes we would make lunch together in the kitchen in the basement. I remember having soup and sometimes baked potatoes. Those days were really special. Also, milk would be delivered to school. I don't remember what year that started, but we would be able to have chocolate milk one time a week. We thought that was wonderful!

Joyce (Railson) Johnson
Helen, Mary Ann, and I were really jealous when Phyllis would bring homemade ice cream to country school and bury it in the snow until lunch time. We really wanted to taste but I don't think she shared it.

Recess Games

Loretta (Gadney) Brandt
Games played were softball, dodge ball, sheep run sheep, and going down the big slide. In the winter we did music ring games in the basement like "Three old maids went skating on the ice" or "Three in a boat and it won't go around." We went sliding and skating in a pond east of the school.

Steve Nelson
Recess, as we called it, was a 15 minute break in the morning and one in the afternoon and an hour for eating lunch and all school softball games in the spring and fall. Those softball games were very competitive. We chose sides by throwing a bat and whoever got the last 3 fingers before the knob got to choose first. There were usually 12-13 kids on each side. Of course if one of the smaller girls would come to bat the opposing infield would be playing within 10 feet of the batter. If she hit the ball she'd be tagged out even before she got out of the batter's box. One time one of the older girls was playing outfield and was getting ready to catch a fly ball. Her glove was up but the ball sailed over her glove and hit her right between the eyes. Broke her glasses right in two. Outside of shock she wasn't hurt. In the winter we played "Red Rover" and "Pump, Pump Pullaway" in the basement.

Florence (Clark) Kriens
We played games like "Pump, Pump, Pullaway," but I can't remember to this day how to play it.

Douglas Mankell

We spent part of noon recess in nice weather on the school lawn pouring water down the holes of striped gophers and then hitting them with baseball bats when they came up for air. The gophers were fast and erratic in their movements so rarely did we kill any of them, although we did our best to send them to their gopher graveyard!

We spent part of noon recess catching and then paddling on the posterior any classmate who had a birthday that day. After the birthday boy or girl was pinned face down on the ground, the other classmates lined up to administer the paddling. The words spoken by each paddler were these (i.e. if the classmate on the ground was nine years old): "1-2-3-4-5-6-7-8-9. A pinch to grow an inch and a knock to grow a block." Those final words included a pinch on the posterior followed by a punch on the posterior. Everyone seemed to enjoy this somewhat barbaric way of celebrating birthdays. We usually did not have non-participants on either the giving or receiving end! We also had no adult supervision during noon recess. Mrs. Gustrud stayed in the school building during recess, eating her lunch in relative peace and quiet. For this reason, those of us on the playground developed our own ways of having fun, some of which would probably be deemed inappropriate by today's standards.

We played games in the snow during noon recess in the winter time. We enjoyed playing Fox and Geese, making snow angels, and jumping off the high bank east of the school into the deep snow on the bottom. In warmer weather, we played on the playground equipment and also played softball and soccer/kickball.

Mary (Peterson) Jeseritz

Recess was at least an hour long as that was when the teacher had time to prepare. There was never any supervision on the playground which is unheard of today. We would play on the playground equipment which included swings, a slide, teeter totter, and a merry-go-round. The games we would play were Red Rover, Red Rover, soccer, dodgeball, and softball. We would have some of the best softball games. In the spring, Dist. 16 would come and play against us! In the winter we would often play King of the Hill. When it was too cold to play outside, we were fortunate to have a basement to play in. Often, we would play dodge ball and gray duck.

Susan (Mankell) Muellner

Recess was usually a highlight of the day. Sometimes we played on the playground equipment and on other days, activities were more organized. I was always the last to be chosen for softball teams, so those days were agonizing for me since the older boys also made fun of my softball abilities. We also played "kick the can". Basically, the person who was "it" hid their face as the rest of us ran to hide. Then we tried to run in and kick the can while "it" tried to tag us out before we could do that. And I think we did actually use a real, battered, bent-up tin can.

Pat (Clark) Broberg

When recess came we had races, tag, or a ballgame or free time. We had a nice big area, with swings, slide, and even a tree to climb. Or we could sit out front on the steps.

District 25 door with transom window.

Bathrooms

Steve Nelson
We did have indoor bathrooms but no flushable toilets. The boys' bathroom toilet went straight into a holding tank which was directly beneath the seat. The first time I saw the bottom below the toilet I nearly vomited. It was the grossest thing I'd ever seen, even though I regularly cleaned calf pens at home. There was a window high above the toilet that let just enough light to see clearly. Remember I'm 6 years old. Once I got past the initial shock I developed a fear of falling in. I remember standing back at least two steps and trying really hard to pee far enough to get it into the toilet. That sight drove my bathroom caution and water intake for the next two years until a drain field was installed along with flush toilets.

Douglas Mankell
We used the somewhat primitive bathrooms inside the school building. Outhouses were also available but they were rarely used because they were even more primitive.

Special Events

Loretta (Gadney) Brandt
The fun things I remember were our programs given up on a stage built by the big boys. There were curtains to close and open between acts. One act I did was singing "On the Good Ship Lollipop" complete with an airplane, leather cap and suit. Another act, I sang "An Apple for the Teacher" with [classmate] Orlynn Mankell as the teacher. There were recitations readings and other stories acted out. My sister Doris and Joyce Reese did a tap dance number. Miss Newstrom's sister would come and fix all the girl's hair and helped the boys to look good, too.

Steve Nelson
We also had an extensive Christmas pageant. Some of the fathers set up a 12 inch high wooden stage with a green curtain that could be withdrawn or closed depending on the situation. It encompassed the whole north end of the classroom. All the students would sing Christmas carols—both secular and religious. A rendition of the manger scene was done including costumes and the biblical scripts. We had practice every day for two weeks prior to the performance.

Douglas Mankell
We were transported one afternoon in several District 25 parents' cars to District 56 in Arctander Township to play a game of softball against that school. My cousin, Al Christopherson, was on the opposing team. I forgot who won the game, but it was a pleasant break from the normal school schedule.
We went on a field trip one year to the General Mills headquarters in Minneapolis and end-of-the-school-year trip another year to an Indian reservation on Mille Lacs Lake in northern Minnesota.

We performed in a Christmas program every year for our parents and other relatives. The stage on which we performed our programs consisted of several long planks of wood placed on top of several sawhorses with a large green curtain in the front which could be opened or closed. It was not a fancy arrangement but it worked.

Mary (Peterson) Jeseritz

Some of the best memories I have of Dist. 25 were the Christmas programs. The month of Dec. would be spent learning and practicing for the program. One day we would come to school and the dads had put up the stage and hung the curtain for the program. The night of the program the school would be packed with families. I thought it was a magical night. My favorite program that I remember was when we presented the Lawrence Welk Show. I remember being one of the Lennon Sisters. We sang "Silver Bells."

Valentine's Day was also a special day. Everyone would decorate a headband with hearts and wear that day. Also, we decorated bags which held the valentine cards people had brought.

Nancy Peterson and Marlys Mankell.

Celebrating Valentine's Day, February 1959.
(image courtesy of the Mankell Family)

Susan (Mankell) Muellner

Since the school building also served as city hall, the building was transformed on election day! Lake Andrew township citizens cast their ballots in the election headquarters in the basement. My grandfather would spend the entire day at school in his official township capacity. It was exciting for us kids to see parents, grandparents and neighbors "at school" that day. Since Lake Andrew Township covered a few school districts, parents from other school districts also came to "our school" that day.

School and church were centers of the community. Just as in church, a highlight of the school year was the District 25 Christmas program. The place was packed on a weekday evening with parents, grandparents, aunts and uncles and younger and older siblings. It could be so cold outside but warm and stuffy inside. It was so exciting to await the opening of the "curtain", a heavy linen-type material strung across the front of the school room on a wire. In first grade, the theme was "Christmas Around the World". I played Swedish Lucia, but the candles on my head were not lit. I also recall a skit when I wore a headpiece with some reindeer antlers. The second grade theme was Christmas on television, specifically "The Lawrence Welk Show" and "Sing Along With Mitch". I sang "Silver Bells" as one of the Lennon sisters (and I think I actually sang alto.) If I recall, Teddy Dengerud was Mitch Miller, demonstrating Miller's signature bent elbows going up and down as he directed his male "chorus." The enthusiastic applause at the end of the program was followed with cookies, coffee and Kool-aid served in the basement.

Pat (Clark) Broberg

I remember going to the school [in Dovre Township] *south on Country Road 5, maybe once or twice for a ballgame against the kids that attended that school and having a picnic with them. Our teacher Mrs. Birkland lived close to this area.*
We did have Christmas programs that were presented on a small stage, with curtains to pull between acts. We always a Christmas tree to decorate, and parents usually brought snacks to share when it was done. It was always standing room only, it seemed.

Consolidation & Closing

Steve Nelson

I only spent 6 years there due to the consolidation vote into the New London school district. My older siblings spent 8 years in this building. My mother, Charlotte, was on the local #25 school board and was deeply opposed to the consolidation. H.O. Torgerson was superintendent of the "town school" and felt a new Jr.-Sr. high school had to be built. The Spicer school was a part of the Willmar district at that time and they also became part of the merger plan. Mr. Torgerson realized that to build a new school more tax payers would have to be involved so the target became all the country schools and Spicer. The vote passed closing all these rural schools although it didn't pass in our district. I started 7th and 8th grades getting on the bus and spending those two years at Old Grey before the new school was completed. The District 25 school board had just purchased new desks so there was animosity toward the N.L. school for just confiscating them. The larger desks were taken but some of the smaller desks were given to local families.

Pat (Clark) Broberg

All this came to an end one day when we were told we had to go to town school, and it was going to be so much fun. I still remember going that first year hating the bus ride, and not knowing if we would have new friends. We did eventually get acquainted, and life went on.

The school was still open for 4-H meetings, (Little Crow 4-H club) and with voting for elections.

We did have an all-school reunion, though I do not remember the year, but do remember my Dad's brothers and sisters coming back and attending this as well. Lots of people attended and had a large potluck picnic and ballgame.

After the school closed I still remember a lot of the families getting together to visit. Back then it was fun to go for a ride and just stop in at someone home to visit talk about the crops, cattle, and families. The wife always had to be ready at moment notice to put out some goodies for a quick lunch.
I remember when they put the cornerstone in with information. I believe families put memories in a container to be opened years later. I do not remember if they ever did open this at another all school reunion. It was located in the northwest corner of the building; I believe the years were engraved in the concrete.

I was very fortunate to have gone to a country school, to know my neighbors, connect with their families, and have a good education.

Susan (Mankell) Muellner

In 1959, New London and Spicer consolidated into the New London-Spicer school district. Country schools were fully consolidated into the town school buildings once construction of the new junior-senior high school in New London was completed by the fall of 1963. Between 1959 and 1963, some country school districts consolidated into town sooner than others, and older grades (6-8, I believe) transitioned to "town school" before lower grades. Grades 1-4 remained in District 25 through May 1963 when the school closed. I attended the rural one-room school from September 1961 through May 1963 for my first and second grade years.

> Since I left after second grade, I was only a "little kid" in my years at District 25— I never reaped the rewards of being a big kid there.
>
> In the fall of 1963, I took the bus to New London (complete with some of the very same rough kids and good kids) to begin third grade at "Old Gray". However, a significant downside of going to town school was that girls were now required to wear dresses! On the bright side, though, Mrs. Birkland was also my third grade teacher! So I had a familiar face for this next step, the first of several on my way to graduation from New London-Spicer High School in 1973.

Marlys (Mankell) Schilz reflected on the closing of the school, the spring of 1963. She wrote this short essay in the late 1990s. "The Last Day of School"[3] ends with her reflections on her impending death.

> It was the last day of school, not just the end of the school year but the end of the school. It was called consolidation. The following school year, our small, country district was joining with the town school. My mother didn't like this progressive plan. She was proud of our small school and its products. She knew it was the end of an era.
>
> Recently, I read about a "new" learning method where there was a mix of older and younger kids in the same class at different levels. The kids met in small groups with the older ones helping the younger kids. It did not sound new to me.
>
> I've been thinking about that final day. I walked home alone. At least I thought I was alone. Every few feet I would turn around and walk backwards, my lunchbox bouncing on my knees. I looked at the school as if taking a final picture. I was glad to be leaving or so I thought. Finally, one time I looked and in one fragile moment, it was gone. In just one step I went from reality to the unknown. My mind was playing a movie of bits and pieces of all the years. I remember the time that an angry first-grader took off walking home cross-country. My brother in eighth grade was sent to retrieve him. I can still see my friend running across the ball field, her index finger shaped like a letter L pointed in the wrong direction. Then there were days of hot lunch where our teacher would bring a roaster. We each had brought a potato with our initials carved on the skin, along with butter and salt. I have never tasted a potato that good. Also, I recall the excitement of Christmas programs on the make-shift stage.
>
> What do potatoes, softballs, and Christmas programs have in common? "These are the things that bounded me" said Edna St. Vincent Millay. I have been bound by this earth too. I have made a proverbial "leap of Faith" over assets, academics, accounts, affections, accomplishments and acquisitions. I landed on a belief system and statement of faith. I am told that I'm going home. I don't know about this unknown home. It is a "house of many mansions" which sounds more like an architectural nightmare than a home.
> "It is appointed unto man to die." We all must go through the doors of death to get to the heavenly place. Like a new school. Someday soon it will be my last day of school. I have to cross this thresh-hold to go to a new school. What will it be like? Will I look back? The mystery will be solved. I believe God's promises. God is not a mystery. God is love. GOD IS.

---

3   By the fall of 1962 Marlys was attending high school in New London so this essay seems to combine her last day as an 8th grader at District 25 with the consolidation and the last school day of District 25.

Lake Andrew Town Hall board: left to right: Herman Mankell, Otis Thorson, Otis Halvorson, Ellsworth Hatlestad.

The story of District 25 as an active place for children to receive an education ended in 1963. However the story of the building doesn't end. It remained at its location in the northwest corner of Section 28 for almost another 50 years, serving as the Town Hall and voting location for the Lake Andrew Township residents. It was also the location for the monthly meetings of the Little Crow 4-H Club and for family reunions. Former students would come to the Mankell farm for a key and then bring their children to the school to walk through the building and share stories. In 2011, the Township Board decided that the township needed a newer structure to serve as the Town Hall. Many people in the community were saddened to see the end of a building which was a local landmark and had served the community for 100 years. One family, the Petersons from the four farms story, decided to save the building. Following the deaths of Earl and Eldora, their children honored their parents' wishes and purchased the building from the township. While Earl attended School District 108, his older sisters and father Emil attended District 25; Earl and Eldora's three oldest children had also received their elementary education at this country school. Earl had spent many years serving as a Township Supervisor holding regular meetings in the building. This family had an emotional connection to the building and soon brought another legacy to the four farms story.

On July 17, 2012, the Peterson family moved the one-hundred-year-old building with its recognizable bell tower one mile north to the Earl and Eldora Peterson farm (the Stenseth/Christenson/Peterson farm of the four farms story). The township then built a new facility at the Section 28 location to be the Lake Andrew Town Hall. The children of Earl and Eldora placed the school house near Highway 5, renovated the building, and saved memorabilia, keeping the story of District 25 alive for generations to come.

School Building at the Peterson farm, Highway 5.

Riding the School Bus

I did not attend District 25, because it closed one year before my first year of school. Beginning with the 1963-1964 academic year, I attended the New London grade school, called "Old Gray". It was my first school year and it was the first year for one other five-year-old girl from the four farms and my friend, Lorna Peterson.

During this first year, and all my years attending the New London-Spicer schools, I took the school bus. At the end of the school day it brought me, my siblings, and our neighbors to our homes. Driving south on County Highway 5, the bus stopped first at the corner of the gravel road ("Peterson's Corner") to drop off the Peterson children.[4] We Mankell children often chose to get off the bus and walk one mile west to our farm. We arrived home more than 15 minutes before the school bus, coming from the west, finished its circuitous route and drove by the Mankell farm with no kids to disembark that day. As we walked home on the gravel road, for that one mile, we passed by the farm houses, flowers, barns, animals, crops, and the black dirt fields of the four farms.

---

[4] See Appendix 2 for a diagram of the bus route in the 1960s.

APPENDIX 1
1939 MAP WITH NEW REA LINES

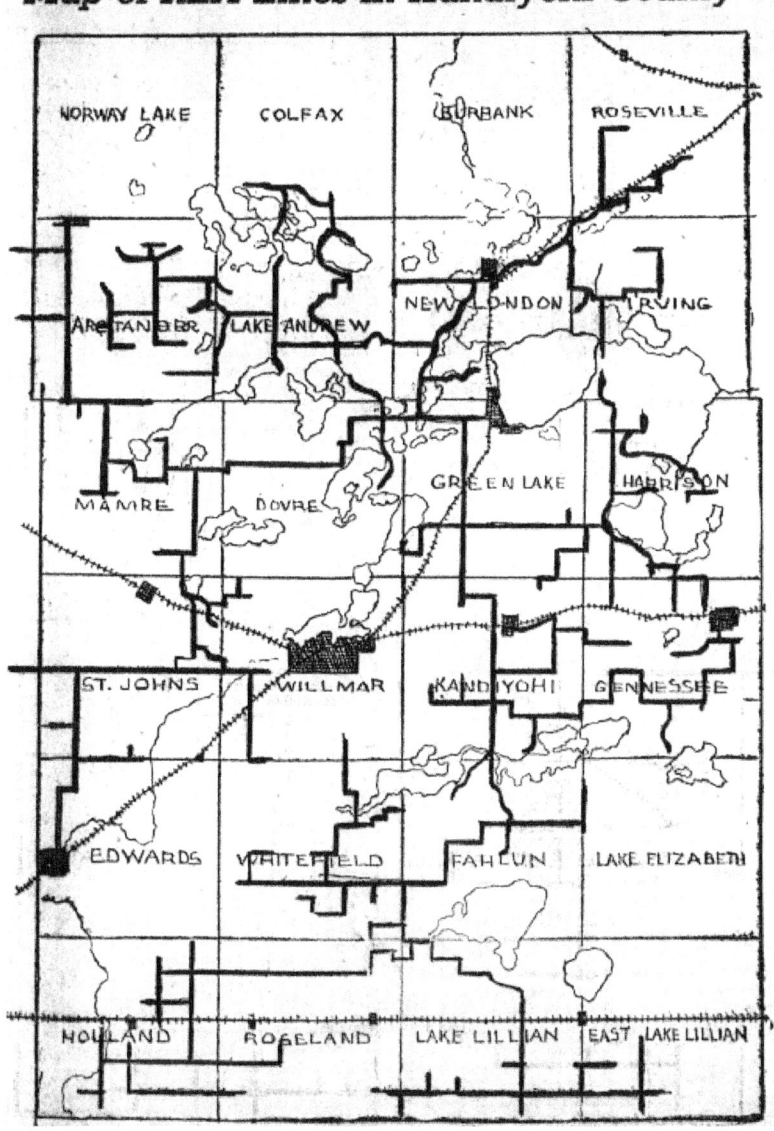

Willmar Daily Tribune, November 10, 1939. (reprinted with permission)

APPENDIX 2
SCHOOL BUS ROUTE

The map below indicates the approximate school bus route of the late 1960s. Coming from New London (off the map 7 miles to the east) the bus turned south on Highway 5 (upper right corner), stopped at Peterson's Corner ("P"), and drove south to Crook Lake, passing the former country school ("#25"). It turned around and drove north to the intersection of highways 5 and 29. It then drove west one mile and turned south, then west, back to County highway 29 and into Arctander Township. After a few more stops the bus turned north for 2 miles, then east, and drove through Jericho (aka "Norway Lake"), passing the four farms on its return to New London.

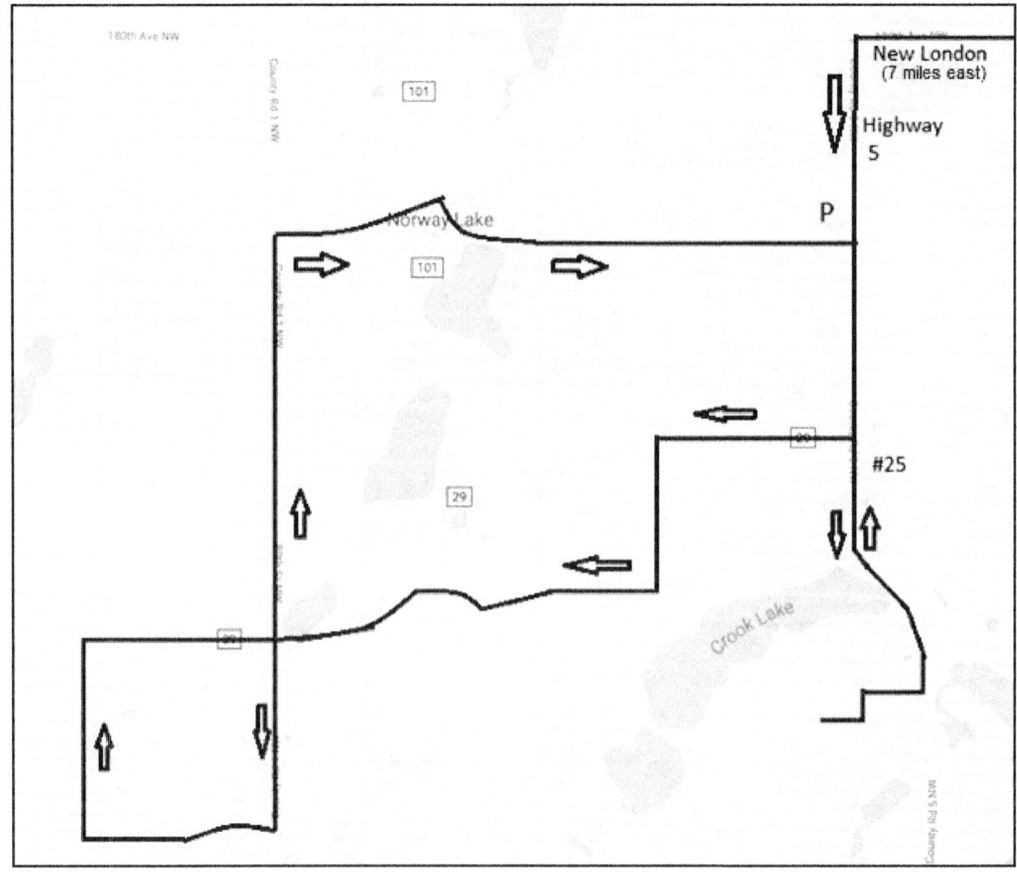

APPENDIX 3
FARM OWNERS & RENTERS

Original owner	Mankell HOMESTEAD	Norman FARM	Brattlund HOMESTEAD	Stenseth HOMESTEAD
1860's (1864+)	Arrival: **1864** Herman W. Mankell, owner	Arrival: **1869** Johannes Norman, owner *Land not obtained via Homestead Act*	Arrival: **1868** Nils Brattlund, owner	
1870's	Homestead final: **1872**		Homestead final: **1875**	Arrival: **1870** Nils Stenseth, owner
1880's	Family not on farm 1880-1885 **1882-1884**: *Rent to Selvig* **1884-1888**: *Acreage rented to Per Hoej* **1889**: to widow Elizabeth	**1884**: to widow Marie		Homestead final: **1882** **1882**: to widow Karen
1890's	**1896**: Oscar purchases family shares		**1896**: Sophia (Brattlund) Rice, owner **1897**: Sold to Martin Reierson	**1899**: Sold to J. S. Christenson (married Stenseth daughter)

APPENDIX 3

Original owner	Mankell HOMESTEAD	Norman FARM	Brattlund HOMESTEAD	Stenseth HOMESTEAD
1900's		**1900-1901**: *Rent to Fred Amundson* **1904-1910**: *Rent to Lars Hatlestad* **1906**: Marie's descendants, co-owners **1909**: William Larson, owner		
1910's		**1910-1926**: *Rent to Henry Swenson*		
1920's	Operated by son Herman	**1921**: Edith Larson, owner (daughter) **1910-1926**: *Rent to Henry Swenson* **1926**: Edith and Edwin Railson arrive at farm.	**1922-1928**: *Rent to Gordon Johnson* **1928-1938**: *Rent to Walter Carlson*	**1922-23**: *Rent to Elmer Skindelien*
1930's	**1936**: to Widow Minnie	**1930**: Edwin Railson, co-owner with Edith	**1928-1938**: *Rent to Walter Carlson*	**1930-1939**: *Rent to Gustav Swenson*
1940's	**1942**: Ownership to Herman		**1940-45**: *Rent to Harold Strand* **1945**: *Rent to Albert Haglund* **1949**: Sold to Haglund	Harvin Christensen family returned to farm **1944**: Sold to Earl Peterson
1950's		**1956**: Wayne Railson, owner		

BIBLIOGRAPHY

Allen, James T. *Digest of United States Patents of Air, Caloric, Gas, and Oil.* Washington, D. C.: The Columbia Planograph Company, c1906

Ancestry.com (military, census, immigration, birth, marriage, and death records; family trees, city directories, records of the Evangelical Lutheran Church in America, records of the Swedish Covenant Church, Minnesota Wills and Probate records 1801-1925).

Anniversary Album, 1859-1944: Lebanon Lutheran Church. New London, MN, 1944.

Arkivverket Digitalarkivet (Norwegian Census and Parish records). arkivverket.no/arkivverket/Digitalarkivet

Armenian-Genocide.org

Barry, John F. *The Great Influenza: The Epic Story of the Deadliest Plague in History.* New York City, NY: Penguin Group, 2004.

Berry Family Collection. Materials from the Burton Berry family.

Boyd, Gregory A. *Family Maps of Kandiyohi County, Minnesota, with Homesteads, Roads, Waterways, Towns, Cemeteries, Railroads and More.* Norman OK, Arphax Publishing Co. 2010.

Brandt Family Collection. Materials from and interview with Loretta Brandt, March 2019.

Canada Census, 1911, 1916, 1921.

(www.bac-lac.gc.ca/eng/census/Pages/census.aspx)

The Centennial History of Kandiyohi County, 1870-1970. Kandiyohi County Historical Society, 1970

A Century of Christian Service Through the Ministry of First Covenant Church, Willmar Minnesota…since 1883.

BIBLIOGRAPHY

Christenson Family Collection. Includes a "scroll" of Harvin Christenson which notates milestones in the Stenseth and Christenson families; diagram of Christenson farm. Interviews with Grace Christenson. Material from Lloyd Ashland and Grace Christenson Ashland Burr.

Connor, J. D. editor. *National Register of Belgian Draft Horses.* American Association of Importers and Breeders of Belgian Draft Horses, 1912.

Curtiss-Wedge, Franklyn, compiler. *The History of Renville County, Minnesota.* Volume 2. Chicago, H.C. Cooper, Jr, 1916.

Executive Committee Papers, 1933. Minnesota Historical Society, St. Paul, Minnesota.

Familysearch.org (census, birth, death, marriage records, parish records in Norway).

Farm Horizons, April 2014, "Townships are oldest form of government in Minnesota". Dassel-Cokato, MN: *Herald-Journal.* http://www.herald-journal.com/farmhorizons/

Findagrave.com

"From Churns to Butter Factories" *Annals of Iowa*, Winter 1989.

Gjerde, S.S. & P. Ljostveit. *The Hauge Movement in America.* Hauge Inner Mission Federation, 1941. http://www.haugeinnermission.com/site/cpage.asp?cpage_id=180001633&sec_id=180000138.

Governor John S. Pillsbury Papers. Minnesota Historical Society, St. Paul, Minnesota.

Harvey Anderson Funeral Home: hafh.org.

Hauge Family Collection. Conversations with Myron Hauge, Fall 2018.

Henjum Family Collection. Material from Marlin Henjum.

The History of New London, Minnesota, 1865-1965.

The History of New London, Minnesota, 1865-1990. New London History Book Committee, 1990.

History of Spicer on Green Lake. Compiled by the Spicer History Editorial Committee, c1991

The Illustrated History of Kandiyohi County. Alternate title: *Illustrated History and Descriptive and Biographical Review of Kandiyohi County, Minnesota.* Published by Victor E. Lawson and Emil J. Nelson, 1905. Digitized version from Minnesota Reflections, Minnesota Historical Society. (http://reflections.mndigital.org/cdm/ref/collection/p15160coll5/id/944)

BIBLIOGRAPHY

Kandiyohi County Historical Society, Willmar, Minnesota. Images are published with permission. Collections include

- church histories
- enrollment records of rural school districts (on microfilm)
- *Kandi Express* newsletter
- newspapers (on microfilm)
- photographs
- plat maps
- Ruth Sorenson collection (baseball)

Kandiyohi County Recorder's Office. Willmar, Minnesota. Includes property records and death records.

Keeping the Faith…Sharing the Faith: 1862-1992, First Lutheran Church of Norway Lake. First Lutheran Anniversary Committee, 2002.

Keillor, Steven J. *Cooperative Commonwealth: Co-ops in Rural Minnesota, 1859-1939.* St. Paul MN: Minnesota Historical Society Press, 2000.

Lake Florida Mission Church Records. (One membership register, c1914, is available on ancestry.com)

Leite Family Collection. Material from Dan Leite.

Levin, Barb, compiler. *Old Norway Lake Reminiscences, Stories by Gabriel Stene, The Pioneer Kid.* Willmar, MN: Lakeside Press, 2018.

Lilly, Mark. "Rural Baseball and The Community: West Central Minnesota and the Corn Belt League." A Major Paper submitted to the Faculty of the History Department, University of Minnesota, 1993.

Mankell Family Collection. Includes photographs, art, published articles, essays, genealogy files, church histories, oral histories, family bibles, music, maps. Collected by Herman Mankell, Orlynn Mankell, Carolyn Sowinski, Kurt Mankell, and extended family.

Mankell.org (website of the author)

Minneapolis Tribune.

Minnesota Association of Fire Mutual Insurance Companies. Correspondence with Vice President Dan Rupp.

Minnesota. *Twelfth Biennial Report of State Dairy and Food Commissioner,* 1907

Minnesota Department of Transportation, 1927 and 1940 maps. Available at Map Room of Library of Congress.

Minnesota Official Marriage System. (moms.mn.gov)

Mnopedia.gov

National Archives and Records Administration (NARA), Washington, DC.

———Record Group 15: Records of the Veterans Administration (Civil War Widow Pension Files).

———Record Group 49: Bureau of Land Management, General Land Office Records (indexed at glorecords.blm.gov).

New London Times. (1886-1970; Later *Free Press Times, Kandiyohi County Times, Lakes Area Review*) New London, Minnesota

Norman Family Collection. Includes "The Descendants of Johannes Andreasson Nerman 1827-1884 and Maria Johansdotter 1923-1906". Material from Christy Hicks.

Norway Census, 1801 and 1865. http://digitalarkivet.arkivverket.no/

Norway church records. https://media.digitalarkivet.no/

Norwayheritage.com

Passenger Lists and Immigration Records; indexes via ancestry.com and familysearch.org

Pejsa, Jane Hauser. *Hulda and Hans Melgaard, The One Hundredth Wedding Anniversary Book.* 1993.

Peterson Family Collection. Material from Lorna Peterson, Mary Jeseritz, and Nancy Salmi.

Peterson, Cynthia L, *Little Dairy on the Prairie: From Butter-makin' Women to High-teck Agriculture.* Office of the State Archaeologist, University of Iowa, 2005.

Pine River Journal

Plat Book of Kandiyohi County, 1886, Map and Index. Reprinted and available at Kandiyohi County Historical Society, Willmar, MN.

BIBLIOGRAPHY

Plat books of Kandiyohi County. Years: 1886, 1900, 1932, 1942, 1945, 1950, 1954, 1956, 1961, 1957, 1972, 1977, 2001. Several are available at Kandiyohi County Historical Society

Plat maps: Digitized Plat Maps and Atlases, John R. Borchert Map Library, University of Minnesota Libraries. (https://www.lib.umn.edu/borchert/digitized-plat-maps-and-atlases)

Railson Family Collection. Material from Sandy (Railson) Anderson.

rootsweb.ancestry.com/~mnkandiy/Cemeteries.htm

Rowley, Bill, *Major Drought Years*. New York: AP Newsfeaters, 1953. Map available at Library of Congress.

Rønning, N. N. Bethesda Children's Home, Fiftieth Anniversary, 1896-1946. Beresford, SD: Board of Directors, 1946.

St. Paul Daily Globe (St. Paul, MN). Minnesota Digital Newspaper Hub of the Minnesota Historical Society. newspapers.mnhs.org/jsp/browse.jsp

Skoglund Family Collection. kevinskoglund.com

Sotendahl, Mons og N. J. Njus. *Festskrift, En Fremstilling af det Kirkelige Arbeide Norway Lake fra 1862-1916*. (Translated version by Debbie Boe, available at Minnesota Historical Society Library)

Sowinski, Carolyn. *Niederasphe to Norway Lake: Mankell Family, Minnesota, and Immigration*. 2015. (available from the author)

———. *Almost Saved, But Lost: The January 1873 Blizzard in Kandiyohi County*. North Charleston SC: CreateSpace Independent Publishing Platform, 2017. (available at amazon.com and Kandiyohi County Historical Society)

Stateparks.com/sibley.html

Swedish Church Records. (http://www.riksarkivet.se)

To God Be the Glory, East Norway Lake Lutheran Church, 1875-1975, Centennial Committee, 1975.

Tollefson Family Collection. Material from Ann Tollefson, March 2019.

United States Department of Agriculture. "Crop Production Historical Track Records". April 2016. https://www.usda.gov/nass/PUBS/TODAYRPT/croptr16.pdf

United States Patent and Trademark Office

- Christensen, J. S. (1908) (Patent No. 897,271)
  https://pdfpiw.uspto.gov/.piw?PageNum=0&docid=00897271&IDKey=1FDF16D-0CA6D&HomeUrl=http%3A%2F%2Fpatft.uspto.gov%2Fnetacgi%2Fnph-Parser%3FSect1%3DPTO1%2526Sect2%3DHITOFF%2526d%3DPALL%2526p%3D1%2526u%3D%25252Fnetahtml%25252FPTO%25252Fsrchnum.htm%2526r%3D1%2526f%3DG%2526l%3D50%2526s1%3D0897271.PN.%2526OS%3DPN%2F0897271%2526RS%3DPN%2F0897271

- Christensen, J. S. (1909) (Patent No. 922,457)
  https://patents.google.com/patent/US922457A/en
  https://pdfpiw.uspto.gov/.piw?PageNum=0&docid=00922457&IDKey=A18E2B192875%0D%0A&HomeUrl=http%3A%2F%2Fpatft.uspto.gov%2Fnetacgi%2Fnph-Parser%3FSect1%3DPTO1%2526Sect2%3DHITOFF%2526d%3DPALL%2526p%3D1%2526u%3D%25252Fnetahtml%25252FPTO%25252Fsrchnum.htm%2526r%3D1%2526f%3DG%2526l%3D50%2526s1%3D0922457.PN.%2526OS%3DPN%2F0922457%2526RS%3DPN%2F0922457

- Halvorson, L. (1898) (Patent No. 600,147)
  https://pdfpiw.uspto.gov/.piw?PageNum=0&docid=00600147&IDKey=485B1F0066F3%0D%0A&HomeUrl=http%3A%2F%2Fpatft.uspto.gov%2Fnetahtml%2FPTO%2Fpatimg.htm

Urdahl, Dean. *Uprising, a Novel*. St. Cloud, MN: North Star Press, 2007

Warren Sheaf. Warren, MN.

Wikipedia.com

"Willmar Seminary Papers" at Norwegian American Historical Association, Northfield, MN.

Willmar Tribune, 1895-1931; *Willmar Weekly Tribune*, 1931-1950; *West Central Minnesota Daily Tribune*, 1950-1959; *West Central Daily Tribune*, 1959-1980; *West Central Tribune*, 1980-present. *West Central Tribune and Forum Communications Company*, Willmar MN. Issues from 1895-1922 are available online from the Library of Congress: https://chroniclingamerica.loc.gov/. Images are published with permission.

INDEX

This index includes the names of people who are part of the **Four Farms** story. If a person is mentioned once—in an obituary, list, or wedding, then generally he or she is not included. Children born after parents moved away from the four farms are not indexed unless they later become part of the four farms story.

Married women are indexed by married surname with her maiden name in parentheses.

AASEN, Ole 176

ALVIG
Alice (Mankell) 98, 126, 195
Birdie Sophia 121
George 98, 121
Nels and Bella (Reierson)..98, 121

AMERICAN RED CROSS
................................167-168

AMUNDSON
Frederick and Gunda (Hagen) ....
.... 129, 134, 121-122

ANDERSON
Sandy (Railson) 256-269

ARCTANDER & LAKE ANDREW MUTUAL FIRE INSURANCE COMPANY
.... 78-80, 215

AUGSBURG SEMINARY...50

AUTOMOBILES..131-133, 163

BETHESDA CHILDREN'S HOME (South Dakota) 112

BIRKEMEYER, Joe.......... 165

BLIZZARDS
1872.................................57-59
1873.................................60-62

BORGEN
Sven Gunderson and Margit ....
....22-23

BRANDT, Loretta (Gadney).....
....256-269

BRATTLUND
Carl............................. 26

Kristina............................ 26-27
Johanna............................ 26
Lovisa................................ 26
Maria Cajsa...................... 26
Marie 20, 25, 73, 87, 119
Nils 20, 25, 29, 39, 41, 56, 58, 62, 73, 87, 99, 119, 187
Nils Johan Nilsson................. 25
Olof 26-27

BROBERG
Patricia (Clark).............. 256-269

CARLSON
Walter and Lillian (Bergman)......
.... 177-178, 192-193
Wendell 192-193, 199

CAMP GRANT, Rock Island, Illinois............. 168-169

INDEX

CHIPPEWA INDIANS 14

CHRISTENSON
Children of Harvin and Sigrid..208
Carrie (Stenseth) ....
...35, 38, 84-87, 105, 112-114, 222
Clara 87, 226-227
Clarence 87, 114-115
Grace 199
Hans 65, 69, 79, 139, 190, 222
Harold 199
Harvey 218, 241
Harvin 87, 116, 125, 138-140, 151, 176-177, 190-192, 199, 208-209
Helen 199
Jeannette 199, 218
John Syvert (born Thori) ....
.... 35, 65, 69, 84-87, 105, 112-115, 125, 128, 131-134, 138-141, 154-158, 165-168, 176-177, 190-192, 222, 225-226
Lena 115, 222
Martin 119
Mina (Engen) 87, 105, 114-116, 138-141, 190-192, 222, 227
Sigrid (Larson) 176-177

CHRISTOPHERSON
Anna (Tangen) 181-182
August 127, 181-183
Bastina (Hjelle) 181-183, 213-214
Lars 50-51, 60-61, 181-182

CHURCHES
Bethany (Betani) Lutheran of Long Lake 191
Church of God 51, 213

East Norway Lake Lutheran ....
.... 17, 44, 88, 96, 107, 115, 112, 122, 139, 177
First Lutheran Church of Norway Lake 17, 90, 122, 124, 191, 195, 222, 243
Green Lake Lutheran 19, 90
Lake Florida Mission ....
.... 17, 54-55, 98, 186-187, 201, 218-219, 243-249
Lake Florida Swedish Lutheran ..
.... 51-55
Lebanon Lutheran 177, 191
Monson Lake 92
Nannestad Lutheran ....
.... 17, 18, 46-51, 98, 100, 111-112, 115, 138, 222
Salem Covenant 211
St. Paul's Lutheran (Minneapolis) 85, 112
Tripolis Lutheran 26, 42, 209
Vikor (Solomon Lake) Lutheran .
.... 88, 121
Zion-Irving Lutheran 237

CLARK
Alfred and Martha 21-22

CORN BELT LEAGUE
.... 201-203

COVELL, Burton S. 86, 106

CREAMERIES 102-104
List of creameries, footnote. 102

CROP LOSSES 67

DAHL, Ole 30

DAHLSTROM
Anna (Anderson Ostlund) 91
Clara Mathilda (Norman) ....
.... 28, 89-91
Peter 89-91
Children of Clara and Peter .. 91
Children of Anna and Peter .. 91

DANIELSON
Andrew and Sophie (Quam) ... 96
Carl J. 204

DAKOTA INDIANS 14

DAKOTA WAR OF 1862 14

DOVRE TOWNSHIP ....
.... 70, 164, 177-178, 193

DROUGHT 193, 200-203

EBERHART
Gov. Adolph O. 158

ELECTRICITY 203-205

ELLINGSON, Selmer 215

ENGEN
Casper 171
Christopher and Ragnhild (Svensdotter) 22, 79
Martin and Helene 114

ERIKSON, Erik 30

INDEX

ESPELIEN
Hilda (Haramoen) 171-172

ERIXON
Esther (Mankell) ....
.... 24, 42, 98-101, 106, 153
Gustave 24, 100-101

EVENSON, Martin 92

FARM LIFE 251-252

FARME, Selma Regina 117

FILLMORE COUNTY ....
.... 38, 46-47, 50

FJELSTAD, Rev. R. K. ... 86, 107

FREDERICKSON, W. D. ... 159

FRYKMAN, Rev. Nels ... 54-55

GOPHERS 230-231

GORDHAMER
Andrew 43
Axel 139
Eddie 139
Halgrim and Marie 43
Jenny (Mankell) 24, 31, 43-44

GRASSHOPPERS 62-70

GUSTRUD, Alphia 256-269

HAGADORN
Colonel Charles 169

HAGLUND
Albert and Bertha (Thorson) ......
.... 210-211, 234
Algot and Anna (Murath) 210

HALSTENSON, J. 77

HALVORSON
Alvin 98, 138, 195
Edna (Mankell) .. 98, 150, 182, 195
Elmo 138, 195
Hans and Margit 117
Johannes and Olena 22
Rev. Johannes 48-50
Lars 131-132
Otis 254

HANDE, Halvor 60

HANSON
George C. 111
George Sr. and Jonette Rebecca
.... 112

HATLESTAD
Caroline (Tollefson) ... 122-124, 170
Clarence 215
Ellsworth 229-230, 254
Lars 122-124, 128, 201
Nellie 170
Severin and Pernille 122-123

HAUGE, Hans Nielsen 47

HAUGE SYNOD 47

HAYWOOD TRIAL ....
.... 97 (and footnote)

HEDIN, Lars 30

HIGHSTROM, Adolph 191

HIGHWAY 5 .... 17, 163-165

HOEJ, Per 77

HOLTER
Hans 50, 139
Rev. Karl C. 49-51

HOMESTEAD ACT of 1862 ..
.... 14, 20

HUDSON, C. W. 68

INFLUENZA PANDEMIC
of 1918 168-172

IVERSON
Johannes .... 32 (footnote)

JERICHO ....
...... 18, 43, 103-104, 127-129, 203

JEZERITZ
Mary (Peterson) 256-269

JOHNSON
John Gunder and Ellen
(Monson) 177
Hans and Margit 98, 117, 195

Dr. Hans 212-213
Joyce (Railson) 194, 216, 264
Lars Johan (L.J.) and Katherine (aka Larson) 90

JORDIN, Walter and Inga . 237

KALLEVIG, Ole 117

KANDIYOHI COUNTY ELECTRIC POWER ASSOCIATION 205

KNUTSON
Agnes (Larson) 171
Hedvig (Christenson) and Christian 87, 114, 116

KUBBEROLLAR 185

KOREAN WAR 237

KORSMO
Christian and Lena (Swenson) 138-139, 199, 211

KRIENS
Florence (Clark) 256-269

KVAMSO
Harold 215
Thomas 139

LADIES' AID 250-251

LAKE ANDREW & DOVRE HORSE COMPANY .. 162-163

LAKE ANDREW & DOVRE TELEPHONE COMPANY 129-130

LAKE ANDREW TOWNSHIP BOARD AND TOWN HALL 17, 55-56, 70, 134-135, 229-230, 270

LAKES
Green Lake 14
Lake Andrew ... 14, 17-18, 23, 106
Lake Florida 17-18, 216-218
Lake Mary 15, 22
Norway Lake 14, 17-18, 23-24, 201-203

LAKEWOOD CEMETERY (Minneapolis) 42, 44, 46, 51, 94, 112, 195

LANDQUIST
Amanda (Mankell) and Julius 24, 31, 76-77
Herman 198

LARIMER, Marjorie (Mankell) 183, 199, 218, 247

LARSON
Alfrida (Stenberg) 89
Augusta 90
Helena 178-179
Herman 89, 134
Johanna (Norman) 29, 31, 89-93, 117, 124-125, 147-149, 211-212
Lars H. (L.H.) 129-130
Lillie 90, 147-149
Oscar L. 90

Victor 90, 125-126
William 73-80, 89-90, 93, 123-125, 128, 138, 147-149

LINDBERGH, Charles A. . 156

LITTLE CROW, Chief 15

LITTLE CROW TRAIL ... 15

LUNGSTROM, John 52, 79

LUNDIN, Mabel 133

MAMRE TOWNSHIP 70, 85, 111

MANKELL
Bette (Mattson) 196
Cora (Christopherson) ... 181-183, 194-199, 212-216, 238-240, 252
Dale Herman 214
Rev. Douglas 212-213, 230, 246, 256-269
Elizabeth (Olsdotter) 20-24, 40, 42, 75-78, 93, 152-153, 187
Herman 98, 139, 150, 154-157, 165-166, 180-183, 194-199, 212-216, 204, 229-230, 240-241
Herman Wilhelm (H.W.) 15, 20-24, 29, 31, 39-40, 56, 58, 69, 74-78, 80, 96-100, 105, 107, 126-127, 187
Minnie (Swenson) 96-100, 106-107, 126-127, 149-151, 180-183, 196-197, 238
Orlynn 80, 183, 199, 218, 237, 241-242, 248

INDEX

Oscar 24, 42, 80, 96-100, 106-107, 126-128, 134-135, 138, 149-151, 162, 165, 173, 180-183, 196-197
Otto 24, 80, 198-199
Sherman 196, 203
Vivian (Jordin) 237, 241-242

MARKHUS, Rev. L. J. 64

MELOM, Rev. Idan 48

MINOR, Phyllis 216

MELGAARD
Hans 93-94
Hulda (Mankell) .. 24, 93-94, 195

MINNESOTA STATE FAIR
.... 116, 131

MONONGALIA COUNTY ..
.... 14-16, 55

MOSES, Rev. J. C. 24

MUELLNER
Susan (Mankell) 256-269

MUTIAL INSURANCE COMPANIES 78-79

NEAR EAST RELIEF FUND 172-173

NELSON
John 163
Steven 256-269

NEW LONDON-SPICER SCHOOL DISTRICT ....
.... 254-255, 270

NJUS, Rev. Joel 63-65

NON-PARTISAN LEAGUE .
.... 154-157

NORMAN
Gustav Albert 28, 75, 80, 88, 90
Johannes 20, 27-30, 39-41, 56, 58, 74-75, 79, 187
John Andrew and Christine (Sampson) 20, 89, 92
Marie 20, 27-30, 39-41, 56, 58, 74-75, 79, 93, 99, 121, 124-125, 187

NORWAY
Buskerud 92, 98
Gudbrandsdalen 48
Hordaland 88, 121
Møre og Romsdal 122
Nannestad Parish, Akershus ....
.... 18, 38, 50
Oppland 98
Stavanger 190

NORWAY LAKE LUTHERAN HISTORICAL ASSOCIATION 210

NORWAY LAKE TOWNSHIP 16, 18, 70

NORWAY LAKE BAND ....
.... 106-107, 147, 165-166

NORWAY LAKE CHOIR ....
.... 105-107, 147

NORWAY LAKE CREAMERY ASSOCIATION
.... 43, 102-104, 128

NORWAY LAKE LAKERS
Baseball Team 80-82, 201-203

NORWAY LAKE SETTLEMENT ... 14, 24, 53, 210

NORWEGIAN BOARDING SCHOOL (at First Lutheran Church) 122-123

OLSON
Johanna (Brattlund) and John .....
.... 26-27, 42

OPPEDAHL, Rev. T. J. .. 47, 51

OSMUNDSON
Thomas and Bergit (Svensdotter)
.... 22, 65
Sam 132

PATENTS 116-117

PAULSON
Rev. Theodore 244-246

PEARL HARBOR 218-219

PEJSA, Jane (Hauser) 94

PEOPLE'S PARTY ... 134-135

PETERSON
Earl 209, 228-232, 270
Eldora (Anderson) ....
.....................209, 228-232, 270
Emil................................134
Russell F. 211, 219

PETTEWAY, Mary Ann
(Mankell) 197-198, 217-18

PILLSBURY
Governor John 67-68

PRAIRIE WET MUTUAL INSURANCE COMPANY 80

PRE-EMPTION ACT of 1841
.... 14

PUBLIC LAND SURVEY SYSTEM 16

QUAM
Anna (Mankell) ....
..................24, 31, 45-46, 77, 152
Anna (Thompson)....................45
Johannes 77
John 24, 77, 106
Nels ....
...242, 45-46, 77, 79-80, 117, 120
Sophia (Mankell)........................
.... 24, 42, 77, 95-96

QUAM & MANKELL STORE 198

RAILSON
Edith (Larson) ....
.... 909, 124, 178-180, 235-236

Edwin...90, 133, 178-180, 235-236
Even 65, 107, 210
Oluf B. (O. B.) 134, 165
Robert 193, 199
Wayne 194, 199

RAINES, Dr. J. M. 171

RAMSIN, Anders J 74

RASMUSSEN, Stella (Berry) and Andrew 141-143

RED WING SEMINARY ....
....140, 176

REIERSON
Anna (Alvig) ....
...... 87-88, 121, 141-143, 232-233
Bjorn and Sigrid (Oldsdatter) ......
.... 35, 56, 69, 88, 142, 177
Ole and Britha (Fladebo) 88
Martin......35, 87-88, 114-115, 121, 128, 141-143, 165, 177-178, 232-233

REIGSTAD, Willard..........203

RICE
Albert E. 44-45, 59
Cushman.......27, 45, 62, 143-144
Sophia (Brattlund) 26-27, 31, 34-35, 44-45, 87, 132, 143-146

RICE COUNTY..............20-21

ROOSEVELT, Pres. Franklin D..............................203

RURAL ELECTRIFICATION ADMINISRATION (REA)........
....................................203-205

RUSTAD
Rev. Lars O. and Mari ...47-49, 82
Matthias....................................82
Ole 82, 100

ST. CLOUD LAND OFFICE
.... 20-21, 27, 38-41

ST. PAUL AND PACIFIC RAILRAOD........ 23, 27, 40, 75

SALMI, Nancy (Peterson)..........
.... 228-229, 256-269

SCHILZ, Marlys (Mankell) ....
.... 214, 230-231, 247, 269

SCHOOL DISTRICTS
16.....................30, 35, 44, 85, 158
List of Teachers 35
25 ....30-34, 85-86, 132-133, 157-161, 183-185, 199
List of Teachers 34, 158, 160
69 85-87
104 133
108 160
Consolidation.................254-255

SCHULZ, C. G...................158

SELVIG
Bernt and Hanna (Christenson)..
....73

Caroline (Brattlund) ....
............26-27, 31, 73-74, 119, 146
Christian 73-74
Donald 220

SHIELDS, Mike ... 118, 134, 165

SIBLEY STATE PARK............
........................106 (in footnote)

SKOGLUND
Anders P 79
John A 44, 79
Peter 79, 130

SLATTUM
Ole 34, 49, 69, 79, 124

SOLBERG
Christian and Maria.............138

SOTENDAHL, Rev. Mors....117

STENE
Gabriel........31-34, 43, 57, 61, 65, 82, 117, 130-132, 173, 183-185
Iver Gulveson 30, 38, 50
Wilda (Quam) 82

STENSETH
Hilda (Hanson).......................
........................38, 85, 110-111, 222
Jeanette 112
Karen (Larsdatter) 20, 38-39, 46-47, 61-62, 117-118, 222
Leslie 112
Lina 38

Maren....................38, 140, 222
Nicholas...38, 72, 85, 110-111, 222
Nils 20, 38-39, 46-47, 55, 60-62, 72, 222
Sorine..38

STOCKHOLM TOWNSHIP.
....55

STRAND
Harold and Valborg (Knudson)..
....210

STYLES, Ida M. 120

SWEDBERG, Bolla Matilda (Larson) and Charles 89

SWEDEN
Göteborg och Bohus 20
Gothenburg.............................20
Skaraborg (later Västra Götaland County) 28, 74
Kronoberg County................ 177
Stockholm 29
Värmland County........25-27, 89

SWENSON
Donald 190-191, 199
Gunder and Gemine (Negaard).
.... 22, 58, 60, 69
Gustav and Petra (Stulen)............
.... 190-191, 224
Henry and Nellie (Larson) 93, 124, 128, 146-147, 165, 178-179
Swen 106, 127-129

SYVERSON
Amund 30-31, 33, 56
Carl A........................79, 131-132

THOMPSON, Hubert and Verona (Skindelien).......224-245

THORI, Paul 65, 84

THORSON
Cornell and Beda (Emerson) ......
.... 138, 210
Otis..254
Reier 79

TOLLEFSON
Gerhard and Ingeborg (Nelson)
.... 220-222

WALBY, Martin 125

WILLMAR... 43-44, 74-76, 131, 143-146, 154-155, 163, 168, 179

WILLMAR SEMINARY..75-76

WITTICH, Matilda...... 24, 154

WORLD WAR I.......... 166-168
WORLD WAR II....... 220-222

YOUNG
John 24, 76-77
Mary (Mankell)...... 24, 31, 76-77

YOUNGQUIST, Rev. C. M. ..54

ABOUT THE AUTHOR

The daughter of Orlynn and Vivian Mankell, Carolyn grew up in Lake Andrew Township and was a member of First Lutheran Church of Norway Lake. A graduate of New London-Spicer School District, she received her BA in History from St. Olaf College, Northfield MN and an MA in American History and an MA in Library Science from the University of Wisconsin—Madison. She has worked or volunteered at several archives and historical societies. She currently lives in Germantown MD, provides genealogical research for clients, and works for the Metropolitan Washington D.C. Synod (ELCA). In her spare time she sings with the Choral Arts Society of Washington. Carolyn maintains a website devoted to her family genealogy (mankell.org) and has been involved with four other publications:

- *Parish History Collection: a Directory of Works at the University of Notre Dame*, compiler
- *St. Thomas Lutheran Church, Bloomington, Indiana: Reflect, Rejoice, Renew*, compiler
- *Niederasphe to Norway Lake: Mankell Family, Minnesota and Immigration*, author
- *Almost Saved, But Lost: the January 1873 Blizzard in Kandiyohi County, Minnesota*, author

Printed in Dunstable, United Kingdom